THE PRESIDENTIAL BRANCH

From Washington to Clinton

SECOND EDITION

John Hart
The Australian National University

Chatham House Publishers, Inc.
Chatham, New Jersey

THE PRESIDENTIAL BRANCH
From Washington to Clinton
SECOND EDITION

Chatham House Publishers, Inc.
Box One, Chatham, New Jersey 07928

Publisher: Edward Artinian
Editor: Christopher J. Kelaher
Production supervisor: Katharine Miller
Cover design: Antler & Baldwin Design Group, Inc.
Composition: Bang, Motley, Olufsen
Printing and binding: Quebecor Printing Fairfield

LIBRARY OF CONGRESS CATALOGING-IN-PUBLICATION DATA

Hart, John 1946–
    The Presidential branch : from Washington to Clinton / John Hart.
    — 2nd ed.
      p.   cm.
    Includes bibliographical references and index.
    ISBN 1-56643-010-0
      1. Presidents—United States—Staff—History.   I. Title.
JK518.H36   1995
320.473—dc20

94-29016
CIP

Manufactured in the United States of America
10 9 8 7 6 5 4 3 2 1

CONTENTS

PREFACE TO THE
SECOND EDITION

In September 1993 the Clinton administration launched its National Performance Review report, the result of an intensive six-month study under Vice President Al Gore aimed at redesigning, reinventing, and reinvigorating the entire national government. No department or agency escaped the reach of the "reinventing government" team, a team dedicated to cutting red tape, reducing costs, and making the federal government perform more efficiently. But the agency at the center of government, the Executive Office of the President, received only cursory attention from the National Performance Review. The reason given by Vice President Gore was that the presidential staff is "regularly reinvented with each change of administration," the implication being that incoming presidents automatically refashion the character and nature of the way the White House operates by virtue of the new staff appointments they make.

In many respects, incoming presidents do "reinvent" the White House, though not necessarily in the sense that the Clinton administration has used the notion of "reinventing government." More often than not, presidents-elect give surprisingly little attention to the nature and organization of the presidential staff before they assume office, and there is a lot of evidence in the history of post-Brownlow presidential staffs that presidents and their staffs have had an almost unlimited capacity to make the same mistakes that their predecessors made. But the "reinvention" of the presidential staff that does take place with each new administration brings to the White House new personalities, new styles of operation, new decision-making structures, different priorities, and different images of presidential leadership. While such changes may not amount to a complete transformation of the institutional basis of the Executive Office of the President, they are nonetheless important and often have a significant bearing on the performance of a particular president. From the political scientist's perspective, then, Vice President Gore's assertion that the White House regularly reinvents itself with each new president serves as a convenient reminder that books about the presidential staff may also need some "reinventing" from time to time.

The first edition of *The Presidential Branch* was written halfway through President Reagan's tenure and appeared in print shortly after the

Iran-*contra* episode was first revealed to the public. Almost a decade has since passed. Iran-*contra* has run its course and two further presidents have occupied the Oval Office. This new edition updates the original text by considering the impact of Iran-*contra* on the presidential branch and by describing the salient changes in presidential staffing during the Bush administration and the first year of the Clinton presidency. Evidence is now emerging to show that George Bush presided over a very unhappy presidential staff, wracked by ambition, petty jealousies, internal feuding, disloyalty, discord, and ineffectiveness. There may be no way of quantifying the damage that the Bush staff brought upon itself, or the contribution that it made to the president's electoral defeat in 1992, but the political scientist can say with some certainty that the Bush experience stands in stark contrast to the kind of White House that Louis Brownlow hoped would emerge from his efforts to fashion a new staff for the modern presidency more than fifty years ago.

President Clinton, too, encountered staffing problems in the early months of his administration. The "Travelgate" scandal, the suicide of a senior White House aide, poor staff work particularly on presidential appointments, and the abrasiveness and arrogance of some of his younger, inexperienced staff became major embarrassments for the new president. But, to his credit, the president moved extraordinarily quickly to correct the problems inside the White House, and by the end of his first year in office, some of those embarrassments had been consigned to distant memory. President Clinton also initiated some interesting changes to the presidential staff system, and although it is too early to assess, for example, his experiment in economic policy coordination (the National Economic Council) or his attempt to reduce the size of the White House staff by 25 percent, those initiatives can usefully be described and explained in the light of past experience.

I have also taken the opportunity in this new edition to correct a few minor errors that appeared in the original version, to update the statistical data in the tables where necessary, and to add some new material. For example, I ought to have given more coverage in the first edition of this book to the role and function of the Office of U.S. Trade Representative and not treat it just as a part of the economic policy apparatus. That has been corrected in this version by an additional section on trade policy making in chapter 3.

The central argument of this book, however, has not been reinvented. In fact, the major institutional trends and developments in the history of the presidential branch described in the first edition have not only remained unchanged since the mid-1980s but have been reinforced by the Iran-*contra* episode and the experience of the Bush and Clinton presidencies. The centralization of decision-making responsibility in the hands of White House staffers continues unabated; the misuse and abuse of staff power is fast becoming the norm rather than an exception; the size of the presidential staff expanded further under George Bush; and the position of Cabinet members in the decision-making process appears just as tenuous now as it was during the days of the Nixon presidency. Neither has Congress shown much sign of retreating from its traditional hands-off attitude to the presidential staff. The notion of comity, which has long protected the presidential staff from the usual exercise of congressional oversight, survived a twelve-year period of divided government when one might have expected the Democratic majority in Congress to challenge the behavior and power of a Republican presidential staff in the White House. Comity was indeed tested during those years, but it was not successfully challenged, and the presidential branch is still almost immune from effective congressional scrutiny. Finally, one also has to concede that the efforts of reformers to persuade presidents to change the way the presidential staff functions continue for the most part to be ignored. With the one exception of President Clinton's initiative in establishing a National Economic Council, the reform agenda of the post-Watergate period still falls on deaf ears.

In revising and updating *The Presidential Branch,* I have received helpful and constructive comments from many sources, and although I have not incorporated every suggested revision, I am very grateful to those who have given their time to talk about the book with me or to listen while I aired what might have seemed to be rambling and unformed ideas about the latest developments in presidential staffing. In this regard I would especially like to thank Colin Campbell, Louis Fisher, James Lengle, Mark Peterson, James Pfiffner, Gerald Pomper, Beryl Radin, and the late Aaron Wildavsky for their input into this new edition. Some of those mentioned might not recognize their contribution to this book, but in at least two instances they persuaded me that something I intended to write ought not be written. Hence their input does not appear in print, and for that I am particularly indebted.

The research for this book was begun in Canberra and completed during a period of sabbatical leave in Washington, D.C. A number of people in Washington were more than helpful in directing me to valuable sources of information that I have utilized in this new edition. For their time and assistance, which they gave so willingly, I am deeply grateful to Rogelio Garcia of the Congressional Research Service, Ron Geisler, Executive Clerk at the White House, and Mary Weaver, who at the time was on the staff of the House of Representatives Post Office and Civil Service Committee. I also wish to thank Rosemary Dickson, librarian at the U.S. Information Service in Canberra, who went out of her way to locate material for me while I was working on this revision in Canberra and helped make the task of writing a book on U.S. politics in Australia much easier than it otherwise might have been. As always, I am grateful to the Australian National University for its generous study-leave arrangements, which enabled me to be in Washington during the first year of the Clinton administration and observe the changes in the White House at close range. I would also like to thank James Thurber and the Center for Congressional and Presidential Studies at the American

University for inviting me to be a visiting research fellow during that year and providing access to library facilities while I was away from my own university.

The first edition of this book went out of print earlier than one might reasonably have anticipated, mainly due to the fact that its publisher went out of business unexpectedly. I am therefore deeply indebted to Ed Artinian of Chatham House, who gave me an equally unexpected opportunity to update the text and make it available to readers again. His enthusiasm was infectious, and it has been a pleasure working with him.

The Presidential Branch had its origin in discussions I had with Nelson Polsby over a decade ago, and without his help and encouragement would probably never have been written, at least not by me. I owe him an immense debt of gratitude and value his continued advice, assistance, and friendship. As the title of this book is now being used by other writers beside myself as a way of describing the institution of the Executive Office of the President, I ought to make clear that the term "the presidential branch" originated with Nelson Polsby. I simply borrowed it with his permission.

Finally, I thank my wife, Beverly, for her contribution to this book. She not only commented on what I wrote and made many suggestions for stylistic improvement, but she also made it possible for me to spend an extended period of time in Washington living in some comfort and without the usual disruptions to family life that sabbatical leave can sometimes entail.

I would like to emphasize that no individuals mentioned above are responsible for the opinions expressed in this book, or for any errors or omissions. That responsibility is mine alone.

1. THE PRESIDENTIAL BRANCH: AN INTRODUCTION

Whatever else might explain Bill Clinton's victory in the 1992 presidential election, we can be fairly certain that it had little to do with his campaign promise to reduce the size of the White House staff by 25 percent. Governor Clinton's commitment to cut the number of presidential aides was never an issue in the election campaign, and consequently it attracted hardly any attention in the media. Neither was it a particularly controversial commitment, partly because President Bush and Ross Perot had promised even larger reductions, and partly because, in the post-Watergate age, pledging to cut the size of the White House staff has become almost a ritual for all presidential candidates.

The events of Watergate in the early 1970s focused massive political, journalistic, and academic attention on the role of the presidential staff in the American system of government. Just as that attention was beginning to wane in the 1980s, the Iran-*contra* episode reminded us again of the inherent power possessed by those chosen to work in the White House alongside the president. As a former presidential staffer noted, "the Watergate and Iran-*contra* scandals have strengthened the popular inclination to paint the staff deep purple if not black, to view the place as crawling with scoundrels and miscreants."[1]

In addition to the major scandals, that image has been reinforced by the controversial behavior of senior White House staffers during the post-Watergate years. From Hamilton Jordan to Donald Regan to John Sununu and Richard Darman, there seems to have been no limit to the capacity of those working in the White House to evoke criticism and reproach, usually about their excessive arrogance and power. Whenever presidential aides hit the headlines in this way, serious questions are raised about the power of presidential staffers and their insulation from accountability inside the White House. Their haughty behavior has left such an indelible mark on the presidency that aspiring presidential candidates now use the election campaign to assure voters that things will be different when they take over the reigns of power. Predictably, that expectation is accompanied by promises to reform the presidential staff system, which almost always translates into cutting the size of the White House staff, and those who are elected invariably begin their administration with all good intentions of doing so.

In the campaign it matters not that reducing the number of White House staff may have little effect on the behavior of those who work at the center of power in American government. The pledge to "downsize" sends a symbolic message that the presidential candidate is sensitive to concerns about the abuse of power and privilege in the White House and is not going to let what happened in the previous administration happen in the next. That seems to be all that needs to be said in presidential election campaigns about the complex problems of presidential staffing. In any event, campaign promises to reduce the size of the White House staff rarely, if ever, capture the attention of voters and cannot compete with such issues as the state of the economy, unemployment, the budget deficit, taxation, health care, and education. And when all three candidates agree on the need to reduce the presidential staff, as they did in 1992, they ensure that the problem of presidential staffing is virtually eliminated from the campaign agenda.

The lack of serious discussion during the 1992 campaign about the complex problems of presidential staffing was, from an academic perspective at least, a little disappointing. It was a missed opportunity to elaborate on an issue of importance to students of government, and all three candidates, in an interesting departure from previous campaign practice, not only pledged to cut the White House staff but also urged Congress to cut its staff by the same amount.[2] For some of the candidates, this may have been nothing more than a tactical ploy (i.e. by making White House staff cuts dependent on similar reductions in congressional staff, the candidates hit on a formula for ensuring there would be no cuts at all in the White House staff). A less cynical interpretation could be that, in linking the size of the White House staff with the size of the congressional staff, the candidates were implicitly recognizing that the role of political staff in government was a general problem that was adversely affecting the performance of the presidency, the Congress, and, by implication, other institutions of government where political staffs were entrenched as well. Might they not have been suggesting that, although some of the many problems associated with the development of the White House staff may be unique to that institution, some of those problems may also be endemic in the very nature of political staffing?

There is, of course, a danger in reading too much into what was merely a one-sentence commitment in Governor Clinton's campaign platform, two sentences in the case of President Bush, and three sentences for Mr. Perot; even so, those statements stand as a clear indication that the presidential staff system has become a serious problem in American government. Although presidential staffing did not figure as an issue in the campaign and did not arouse the passions of voters, it did get established as part of the campaign agenda and reflected elite, if not mass, concern with the accumulation of problems and controversies that have accompanied the development of the staff system in recent decades. Furthermore, President-elect Clinton felt sufficiently committed to his pledge to reduce the White House staff that he reiterated the promise several times in the early days of the transition and even specified, after a meeting with congressional leaders, that he would achieve the reduction in size "right away."[3]

The presidential staff system is now a well-developed and very necessary resource for the occupant of the White House, and it is difficult, if not impossible, to imagine how post–New Deal presidents could have responded to the pressures and demands on them without such staff assistance. But it is also true that the development of the presidential staff system has become problematic and the size of the staff is only one part of that problem. The impact of the presidential staff over a relatively short period has been one of the most remarkable and controversial developments in modern American politics and, perhaps, one of the least understood.

It began as a cry for help from Franklin D. Roosevelt more than half a century ago. The President's Committee on Administrative Management, commonly known as the Brownlow Committee, was established by Roosevelt to publicize and legitimize presidential complaints about what would now be called an "overload problem." By the time Roosevelt entered the White House in 1933, the nature and function of the presidency were undergoing profound change. The horrors of the Great Depression had rendered theories of limited government and a limited presidency obsolete. Roosevelt dealt boldly and decisively with the economic and social problems facing twentieth-century America but found that he was doing so with an administrative capacity appropriate to the nineteenth century. Managing the activities of a rapidly expanding executive branch had grown beyond the capabilities of one man, a fact that the Brownlow Committee thought was so well understood that it was unnecessary "to prove again that the president's administrative equipment is far less developed than his responsibilities."[4]

Roosevelt felt much the same about the presidential condition. "The Committee has not spared me," he said when transmitting the report to Congress in 1937.

> They say what has been common knowledge for twenty years, that the president cannot adequately handle his responsibilities; that he is overworked; that it is humanly impossible, under the system we have, for him fully to carry out his Constitutional duty as Chief Executive because he is overwhelmed with minor details and needless contacts arising directly from the bad organization and equipment of the Government.... The plain fact is that the present organization and equipment of the Executive Branch defeat the Constitutional intent that there be a single responsible Chief Executive to co-ordinate and manage the departments and activities in accordance with the laws enacted by the Congress.[5]

The Brownlow report provided Roosevelt and future American presidents with an institutional framework designed to bring the principal managerial units of government firmly under presidential control. The "canons of efficient government," said Brownlow, "require the establishment of a responsible and effective chief executive as the center of energy, direction, and administrative management."[6] To achieve this, the report proposed the creation of an Executive Office of the President (EOP), which would house those agencies concerned with executive branch budgeting, efficiency, personnel and planning policies, and a slightly enlarged personal support staff for the president in what was to become known as the White House Office. At the beginning of the most famous passage of his report, Brownlow stated unequivocally: "The president needs help. His immediate staff assistance is entirely inadequate."[7]

The Brownlow Committee also made a number of other recommendations besides its staffing proposals. It urged a massive reorganization of government departments and agencies, a reform of civil service administration, an extension of the merit system, and a major overhaul of fiscal management in government, all part of a package of initiatives designed to strengthen the managerial capacity of the chief executive.

Brownlow's report was presented to President Roosevelt in January 1937. Just over two years later, on 3 April, the Reorganization Act of 1939 was signed into law, and Roosevelt was given the help he had requested. The recommendation on enhanced staff assistance was one of the few features of the report to survive the stormy legislative passage through Congress. Congress had not seen eye to eye with Brownlow on all the canons of efficient government. It did not sanction the reorganization of government departments and agencies or the reforms in fiscal management, and it was openly hostile to the committee's proposals on civil service reform. The opposition to Brownlow is considered further in the following chapter; all that needs to be said here is that the proposals on staffing emerged from Congress relatively intact.

An Executive Office of the President was established, which implemented the concerns of the Brownlow Committee that there be an appropriate staffing system to support the *institution* of the presidency. It did this by moving key managerial agencies, such as the Bureau of the Budget and the National Resources Planning Board, into the new Executive Office so that critical management functions would be performed by staff working directly under the president doing the routine tasks that had to be done by any occupant of the White House. The president's personal staff was also enlarged, just as Brownlow had recommended, by the addition of six executive assistants to the White House Office. The White House Office became a division of the Executive Office of the President (EOP) on the organization charts, but it has remained functionally distinct from the other units of the EOP as an intimate, immediate, and personal staff arm of the president.

Brownlow did not invent the concept of a presidential staff. As we see in the following chapter, the presidential staff is as old as the presidency. What the report did do was provide the catalyst for the first serious congressional response to the critical problem of the president's workload. Until Roosevelt's cry for help, the staffing needs of the president were dealt with haphazardly, belatedly, and sometimes grudgingly, by successive Congresses. There had been little apparent concern about what the real needs of the president might be, and additions to the presidential staff were generally inadequate in quantity and kind. Other presidents had complained before, but none had had a Brownlow to publicize those complaints so effectively.

The Brownlow Committee's report constituted the boldest and most comprehensive set of proposals for strengthening the presidency since the adoption of the Constitution. In terms of what it did for presidential staffing, the report is a significant landmark. Together with the Reorganization Act of 1939, it established the framework around which the Executive Office of the President was to be built. Yet it must also be stressed that neither the report nor the Reorganization Act provided the blueprint for the presidential staff system we see today. From its inception, the history of the Executive Office of the President has been a history of departures and deviations from the Brownlow design, and therein lies the root of the problem that this book addresses.

The presidential staff quickly broke loose from what, in retrospect, were the tight constraints of Brownlow's concerns about administrative management in government and his notions of the appropriate role for executive assistants in the White House. As early as 1949, Clinton Rossiter felt able to claim that "the Executive Office is no longer simply a staff that aids the president directly in the discharge of the most exacting of his major responsibilities, that of chief administrator. . . . From a purely staff service it is fast developing into an agency that also formulates and coordinates policies at the highest level."[8] More recently, Nelson Polsby has remarked that perhaps the most interesting political development of the postwar period "is the emergence of a presidential branch of government that sits *across* the table from the executive branch at budgetary hearings, and that imperfectly attempts to co-ordinate both the executive and legislative branches in its own behalf."[9]

The presidential branch currently consists of eleven separate divisions: the White House Office, the Office of Management and Budget, the Council of Economic Advisers, the National Security Council, the Domestic Policy Council, the National Economic Council, the Office of the U.S. Trade Representative, the Council on Environmental Quality, the Office of Science and Technology Policy, the Office of Administration, and the Office of National Drug Control Policy. Collectively, they constitute the Executive Office of the President, which has an annual budget in excess of $172 million and a full-time staff of over 1600. It is also physically bursting at the seams. The White House itself is small, cramped, and overcrowded,[10] and the Old Executive Office Building next door has long been unable to contain the remainder of the president's staff. A large part of the EOP is now geographically located some distance from the Oval Office.

In its early stages, the development of the Executive Office of the President aroused mixed feelings among the few who devoted time to the study of this particular innovation in American government. Some, like Clinton Rossiter, saw it as a vital creation that had "helped decisively to save the presidency from paralysis and the Constitution from oblivion."[11] He argued that it enabled the presidency to adapt itself to the exigencies of the modern state far more successfully than Congress had done and gave an incumbent "a sporting chance to stand the strain and fulfill his constitutional mandate as a one-man branch of our three-part government."[12] George Graham concurred with Rossiter's view. He spoke of the Brownlow report as "a plan of salvation by staff" and claimed that "experience under the plan ... has so well demonstrated its merits that commendation is superfluous."[13] Nevertheless, he was also somewhat critical of certain operational shortcomings evident during the first ten years of the life of the EOP and made a number of recommendations for reform. Others were more inclined to emphasize the problems, and even the potential dangers, of this rapidly developing institution. In a prescient article published in 1956, more than a decade before the turbulent days of Richard Nixon and Watergate, Stephen K. Bailey raised a number of serious questions about the role of the presidential staff and its value to American government. He suggested that the growth of the presidential staff system might deprive the president of the benefits of vigorous advocacy from the departments and agencies, that it might lower the prestige and influence of department heads, that it might adversely affect the recruitment of capable sub-Cabinet officials, that the institutionalization of the president's office might increase paperwork without effecting real coordination of policy, and that power struggles among the staff of the EOP might ultimately trap or immobilize a weak chief executive.[14]

For the most part, however, attitudes toward the presidential staff system during its first twenty years were generally benign. Staff support for the president was welcomed by many observers of the presidency; and although there was some awareness that such an innovation would not be without its problems, few commentators were as pessimistic as Bailey. In any case, concern about the Executive Office of the President was hardly a major preoccupation of political scientists during the 1950s and 1960s. Neither did it attract the attention of journalists beyond the unceasing endeavor to identify the president's alter ego, or the number-two man in Washington, or whatever label journalists wanted to apply to particular individuals on the White House staff. Least interested was Congress, which theoretically exercised oversight of the executive branch. It would not be unfair to say that, by and large, Congress ignored the rapid institutional development of the Executive Office of the President during these formative years.

By the end of the 1960s things had begun to change, and many of the fears expressed by Stephen Bailey were ultimately realized during the presidencies of Lyndon Johnson and Richard Nixon. By then the presidential staff had become a powerful force on the political stage and an indispensable institutional arm of the presidency that had radically changed the framework of presidential policy making and demonstrated a capacity to upset established working relationships among the more traditional institutions in Washington. The presidential branch began to attract more critical attention, not only from political scientists but also from journalists, politicians, and even some former presidential assistants. Once the excesses and abuses perpetrated by the Nixon staff came to light, the criticism became more strident and more voluminous, most of it lamenting the growth in the size and power of the Executive Office of the President. There was a widely shared feeling that the presidential staff system was out of control—too large, too powerful, too unaccountable, too inexperienced, too isolated, and counterproductive to the proper functioning of government. In 1937, Brownlow's claim that the president needed help was accepted almost without question, but by 1973 that presumption urgently needed reappraisal, according to Thomas Cronin. "Today the president needs help merely to manage his help," he wrote. "The swelling and the continuous expansion of the presidency have reached such proportions that the president's ability to manage has been *weakened* rather than strengthened. Bigger has not been better."[15]

By the 1970s, we were also beginning to get a less than flattering picture of the qualities of the presidential staff, a picture far removed from the kind of elite professional corps of civil servants that Brownlow had imagined. In a lively and vitriolic book, former presidential assistant George Reedy exposed the inner life of the White House as "a mass of intrigue, posturing, strutting, cringing, and pious 'commitment' to irrelevant windbaggery ... designed as the perfect setting for the conspiracy of mediocrity."[16] What may initially have been read as a highly personal and somewhat excessive reaction to Reedy's own experience as Lyndon Johnson's press secretary was very soon confirmed in the numerous memoirs of former aides to President Nixon. "Blind ambition," in the words of John Dean, appeared to be the principal motivating force behind the activities of senior presidential staff in that administration.[17]

The involvement of a number of Richard Nixon's aides in the bugging of the Democratic party's Watergate office building headquarters, and the subsequent attempted cover-up of that and related incidents, did much to stimulate demands for reform of the presidential staff system. To many observers, the unfolding drama of the Nixon years spoke for itself, and little more needed to be said about why a president was forced to resign his office to avoid certain impeachment, about why so many senior presidential assistants were writing their memoirs in prison cells, and about why the Cabinet had been downgraded and rendered impotent by a chief executive bent on concentrating power in the White House. The urgent and essential question was not so much how the presidential staff came to be in the condition it was in at the beginning of the 1970s; it was, instead, what remedies could be applied to correct what were seen as obvious institutional defects in the Executive Office of the President? In the debate about what precisely ought to be done, certain broad assumptions were taken for granted: Presidential staff growth should be curtailed, the staff should be made more accountable, the Cabinet ought not to be neglected any longer, and the flow of power from the departments to the White House ought to be reversed.

The post-Watergate demand for reform of the presidential staff was only part of a more broadly based attack on the presidency and the growth of presidential power during the Johnson and Nixon years. Critics also sought changes in the relationship between the president and Congress, between the president and the courts, and in his relations with his party, the mass media, and the public at large. At least a decade of conventional wisdom about the power of the presidency was in the process of being modified, revised, or even occasionally rejected, and commentators who were once vigorous advocates of a strong and dominant presidency spent the mid-1970s trying to extricate themselves from an intellectual dilemma that had highlighted the inadequacy of their earlier writings.[18] Yet, while there was widespread agreement that "the textbook portrait of the presidency," to use Cronin's phrase,[19] was no longer empirically accurate or normatively desirable, there was far less consensus about what ought to take its place and, consequently, considerable variety in the proposals that made up the post-Watergate reform agenda. Solutions to the crisis of the presidency ranged from major constitutional reform and the introduction of parliamentary government at one extreme[20] to warnings about the dangers of excessive reaction at the other.[21] Watergate created a crisis of the presidency, and the role of the presidential staff was an integral component of that crisis. Yet the immediate post-Watergate response contained its own confusions and contradictions as critics rushed into print to add their own remedies to a growing list of reforms that fell somewhere in between the two extremes.

These confusions and contradictions were compounded later in the 1970s when observers of the presidency directed their attention not to the excesses of presidential power under Johnson and Nixon but to the weaknesses of the presidency during the Ford and Carter years. The latter was a response to a different set of circumstances and conditions, reflecting concerns about the performance of the presidency that were qualitatively distinct from those of the Johnson and Nixon years. This new crisis of the presidency was less dramatic than Watergate, but no less urgent, and it too produced a reform agenda, an agenda on which the presidential staff once again featured prominently.

Typical of the post-Carter response was a report published in 1980 under the auspices of the National Academy of Public Administration entitled *A Presidency for the 1980s*.[22] The authors of the report hoped to do for the presidency in the 1980s what Brownlow had done for the presidency in the 1930s. They reviewed the operation and organization of the presidential staff system within the context of what they perceived to be "a crisis of public management," and their objective was to make the Executive Office of the President a more effective management unit equipped to meet the challenge of government in the 1980s. What was remarkable about the recommendations in the report was that most of them called for the establishment of new staff units, or the expansion of existing units within the EOP, to perform additional functions and responsibilities deemed necessary to improve the management capacity of the presidency—recommendations that came less than ten years after "the swelling of the presidency" was seen to be such an undesirable development in the history of American government!

Conclusions like those reached by the National Academy of Public Administration are a useful indicator of how perspectives on the presidency changed *during* the post-Watergate years, and they also remind us that much of the conventional wisdom on the presidency remains conventional for only a short time. Inevitably, commentators on the presidency often react, whether consciously or not, to specific events and short-lived circumstances. As it happened, the presidential staff was a major concern of the critics during the Johnson-Nixon years and the Ford-Carter years, but the literature emanating from each of those periods had quite a different focus and a very different message.

The Reagan administration marks another phase in the saga of the presidential staff system. Notwithstanding the usual tensions and controversies, the White House staff, under the joint direction of James Baker, Edwin Meese, and Michael Deaver, functioned relatively efficiently and effectively during President Reagan's first term. Indeed, given President Reagan's well-known work habits and his propensity to delegate to those around him, the presidential staff must be accorded some of the credit for the Reagan record and the spectacular reelection victory in 1984. Debates about reforming the presidential staff system temporarily disappeared from the public and academic agendas of concerns about the presidency, and there was a hiatus in the "crisis-of-the-presidential-staff" literature that had flowed from the pens of presidency watchers since the beginning of the 1970s.

The relative tranquility was abruptly shattered halfway through President Reagan's second term. In November 1986, revelations about his administration's arms sales to Iran, and the subsequent siphoning of the profits from those arms sales to support the Nicaraguan *contras*, focused critical attention on the presidential staff again. A disastrous policy initiative had been engineered by key members of the National Security Council staff, which eventually resulted in the dismissal of one member of the staff, Oliver North, and the resignation of President Reagan's fourth national security adviser, Admiral John Poindexter. A special presidential review board (the Tower Commission) was set up to investigate the activities of the NSC staff. Its report laid the blame for the Iran-*contra* episode with two national security advisers, John Poindexter and his predecessor Robert McFarlane, White House Chief of Staff Donald Regan, Central Intelligence Agency Director William Casey, and the president himself.[23] The publication of the Tower Commission report was also a catalyst for the reluctant resignation of Donald Regan.

As the Tower Commission was finishing its report at the beginning of 1987, both the House of Representatives and the Senate established select committees to produce their versions of the story. The two committees published a joint report at the end of 1987 that found the common ingredients of the Iran-*contra* episode to be "secrecy, deception, and disdain for the law." The authors of the report discovered, among other things, "a seriously flawed policy-making process," "confusion and disarray at the highest levels of Government," and "pervasive dishonesty and inordinate secrecy." They were emphatic that "the ultimate responsibility for the events in the Iran-*contra* Affair must rest with the president."[24] But the Iran-*contra* story did not end with the recriminations in congressional reports. Pressure from Congress led to the appointment of a special prosecutor to investigate the Iranian arms deal and the diversion of funds to the *contras* and that, in turn, led to criminal indictments against former White House staffers North, Poindexter, and McFarlane. Inevitably, these events also ensured a steady flow of academic articles and books on the presidential staff and the national security decision-making process, and by the end of Ronald Reagan's presidency, post-Watergate concerns about the power of the White House staff were well and truly back on the agenda.

Those concerns were carried over into the Bush administration. Despite the fact that President Bush had served an eight-year apprenticeship as vice president, an experience that would have given him an opportunity to consider the problems of presidential staffing from an exceptional vantage point, his administration also was plagued with difficulties over the White House staff, many of them stemming from the controversial appointment of John Sununu as the chief of staff. The troubles that befell Sununu were anticipated by some from the moment he assumed his responsibilities. Media profiles of the former governor of New Hampshire tended to emphasize attributes ill suited to high-level work in the White House, or, rather, ill suited in terms of Brownlow's design for the presidential staff. One such profile, in the space of fewer than thirty column-inches, identified Sununu as "impatient," "strong willed," "confrontational," "assertive," "dogmatic," "arrogant," "aggressive," and "single-minded,"[25] and that was not untypical of what appeared in the media in November of 1988.

During the following two years, until his forced resignation in December 1991, Mr. Sununu was seemingly determined to prove the media correct. His abrasive dealings with his own staff, with the media, and with members of Congress quickly became the hallmark of his style and, after the chief of staff had been in office for only eight months, one leading White House correspondent wrote of how "suspicions linger that Sununu's bluntness will ultimately truncate his stay."[26] Those suspicions proved to be well founded, although it was not just bluntness that brought about the downfall of John Sununu. His personal intervention in major policy decisions aroused a great deal of adverse criticism,[27] his management capabilities were called into question after a series of blunders emanating from the White House,[28] and, finally, the abuse of White House perquisites, which generated national headlines in June 1991, made him a liability and an embarrassment to the president.[29] When President Bush's popularity plummeted toward the end of 1991, leading Republicans began to worry about the 1992 election and cast the White House chief of staff as an electoral liability as well as a liability in government. By that time, Sununu's unpopularity was so great that he could no longer withstand the pressures for his removal.

Governor Sununu's performance during the two years he was White House chief of staff reawakened the very fears that Brownlow had expressed about the potential for abuse of presidential staff power some fifty years earlier. In essence, what Brownlow had said when he defined the role of the staff was that staff assistants in the White House would need a special combination of personal qualities and attributes in order to discharge their delicate functions appropriately. The Sununu experience was a sharp reminder of the dangers inherent in the presidential staff system when those attributes are missing.

The Bush administration followed what seems to have become a pattern over the past twenty years or so, where a new team in the White House succeeds a discredited one and begins with a great deal of goodwill after promising that things in this administration will be different and the mistakes of the previous administration will not be repeated. But the good intentions dissipate once the presidential staff gets established and once the political pressures begin to mount. President Clinton's five immediate predecessors had problems with the behavior, role, and function of their closest aides, and the experience of each of those presidencies has raised the same fundamental questions about how the presidential branch fits into the structure of American government, and how it ought to fit into the structure of government. Those questions are the major concern of this book. It seeks to take stock of what has happened to the presidential staff since 1939 and tries to put the various perspectives into some sort of order. But it attempts to do so, not in response to a particular dramatic event or specific crisis in the turbulent history of the Executive Office of the President, like Watergate or the Iran-*contra* episode, but on the basis of what is known of its evolution over the past fifty years and, even before, during the pre-Brownlow era.

Studies of the presidential staff system rarely trace its history prior to the Brownlow report. Chapter 2 looks at the state of the presidential staff before Brownlow in order to set the context for examining the ideas about presidential staffing embodied in the Brownlow report and to offer a broader perspective on the more recent problems of the presidential branch. Chapter 3 traces the institutional development of the Executive Office of the President from its origins in 1939 to the present and examines some of the assumptions about the growth of the presidential staff that constituted such an important feature of the post-Watergate critique. Chapter 4 deals with the power of the presidential staff and considers how and why it has deviated so far from the Brownlow design. Chapter 5 focuses on the nature of congressional oversight and scrutiny of the presidential branch, especially the White House Office. In particular, it attempts to explain why and how the presidential staff has been immune from the normal standards of oversight applied to other areas of the executive branch of government. Chapter 6 reviews what may loosely be called the post-Watergate critique of the presidential branch, but it covers reactions to Watergate and the later reactions to the Carter, Reagan, and Bush experiences. It also assesses the reform proposals generated by the succession of post-Watergate crises of the presidential staff. The final chapter, by way of conclusion, discusses what this writer thinks is the fundamentally ambivalent position of the presidential branch in the structure of American government.

2. THE PRESIDENTIAL STAFF: 1789–1939

Franklin Roosevelt was by no means the first American president to complain about his workload, nor the first to plead for more adequate staff assistance. George Washington, for example, had let it be known, even before he was formally inaugurated, that his presidential correspondence had become "an insupportable burden."[1] Similarly, President John Adams once confided to his wife that "business of all kinds, and writing particularly... press upon me severely" and jokingly offered to send her his "peck of troubles in a large bundle of papers."[2] Thomas Jefferson was similarly affected. Leonard White notes that Jefferson "frequently complained about the pressure of business and in 1806 put in one sentence a classic observation: 'It is not because I do less than I might do, but that I have more to do than I can do.'"[3] President Monroe suffered too. In 1824, John Quincy Adams, then secretary of state, recounted in his diary how Monroe had handed him two important documents that had been signed and should have been delivered some eighteen months earlier. Adams commented, "These irregularities happen for want of a system in the multiplicity of business always crowding upon the president, and above all, from his want of an efficient private secretary."[4]

THE ORIGINS OF THE PRESIDENTIAL STAFF

It is commonly believed that this "want of an efficient private secretary" during the early years of the presidency was attributable to the failure of Congress to appropriate funds for the provision of presidential staff until 1857.[5] That, however, is not strictly true. Congress, in fact, made the first appropriation for presidential staff in 1789, but included it in a single lump-sum payment to the president that covered both his salary and expenses. The feeling in Congress at the time was that it would have been inappropriate to itemize the expenses element of the presidential compensation, but it is clear from the record of the debate that took place in the House of Representatives on 13 July and 16 July 1789 that part of the expense allowance approved by Congress was intended to provide for presidential secretaries and clerks.[6]

There were a number of reasons why the allocation for presidential staff was hidden. One was constitutional. John Lawrence of New York had argued in the House that the clause in Article II, Section I, which forbade the president to receive "any other emolument from the United States," made it necessary for Congress to combine his salary and his expenses into a single compensation. Lawrence believed that a separate expense allowance would constitute "an emolument beyond the compensation contemplated in the Constitution."

Other arguments for not prescribing how the president should spend his compensation were also advanced. Lawrence set the tone for the debate when he claimed that "if we establish salaries for his secretaries and clerks, we establish them as officers of the Government; this will be improper, because it infringes his right to employ a confidential person in the management of those concerns for which the Constitution has made him responsible." James Madison of Virginia concurred. He said that "the Executive Magistrate ought not to have the power of creating officers; yet if he appointed his secretary and clerks, and they were recognized, either with respect to salary or official acts, they became officers of the Government."

Several members of Congress also expressed the view that the question of how the president chose to spend his compensation was no business of the legislature. Samuel Livermore of New Hampshire asked, "Why should we pretend to direct him in the style in which he shall live? ... Let him have a salary and expend it in the manner he shall think proper." Michael Stone of Maryland agreed. "The president ought to be at liberty to live in any style he thought proper ... no part of the Constitution gives us a right to dictate to him on this head." A motion to strike out specific reference to "secretaries and clerks" from the wording of the appropriation was carried at the end of the first day of the debate.

The record of the second day's debate, on 16 July, provides some evidence that members of the House were well aware of the president's staffing needs. Twice during the deliberations it was suggested that the assistance of two or more secretaries would be necessary to enable the president to discharge his duties properly. Elias Boudinot of New Jersey also insisted that "they must be men of abilities and information." Furthermore, there seemed to be general agreement that the president's compensation of $25,000 would provide him with a reasonable salary and cover his expenses.

The distinction between the salary component and the expenses component of the president's compensation was soon buried in the records of those congressional debates, and the fact that George Washington declined to accept his compensation, paying his secretary from his own pocket, helped to compound the confusion. Inevitably, compensation became equated with salary, and it appeared that presidents had to bear the expenses of their office from their own salary. In any event, what may have been an adequate sum to cover salary and expenses in Washington's time was decidedly insufficient for President Jefferson. During his first year as president, Jefferson spent over $16,000 on household and office expenses alone, including the salary of his secretary, and ended the year some $4000 in debt.[7]

What necessitated immediate staff assistance for the president, more than anything else, was the burden of official correspondence. As Leonard White points out in his classic study of government administration during the Federalist period, this was a laborious and time-consuming chore. There were no mechanical devices to obviate the need for handwritten copies of letters from the president, and presidents had to spend more time than they desired trying to decipher the illegible scrawls on much of their incoming correspondence.[8]

It was fairly common practice in the early days of the presidency for presidents to employ young relatives as private secretaries or clerks. George Washington's private secretary, Tobias Lear, was unrelated, but the president also employed his nephew, Robert Lewis, for "the recording of letters in books" and, later on, Robert's brother Howell for the same task, at the rate of $300 per year.[9] James Monroe employed his younger brother and two sons-in-law; John Quincy Adams and John Tyler used their sons as private secretaries; Andrew Jackson used a nephew and then his son; Polk and Buchanan recruited nephews; and Zachary Taylor had the services of his brother-in-law.[10]

It is apparent from the small amount of existing evidence that the early private secretaries were something more than mere presidential scribes. Tobias Lear acted as liaison between President Washington and the heads of departments. He carried papers from the president to the heads of departments, and, according to Leonard White, he was informally consulted by them on matters that were to come before the president.[11] Thomas Jefferson described the role of the private secretary as being "more in the nature of that of an aide de camp than a mere Secretary" when he wrote offering the post to William Burwell in 1804. The principal duties of the office, Jefferson said, were "the care of our company, the execution of some commissions in the town occasionally, messages to Congress, occasional conferences and explanations with particular members, with the officers, and inhabitants of the place where it cannot so well be done in writing."[12]

There can be little doubt that the early American presidents were administratively overburdened, although the task of handling voluminous correspondence in a prephotocopy age was only a symptom of a wider problem related to the way those presidents perceived their role in government. Washington and his immediate successors saw themselves as chief executive officers and took a close interest in the day-to-day business of the departments of the executive branch. It was, perhaps, too close an interest. The heads of departments functioned as presidential assistants, according to Leonard White, and the presidential desire to be undisputed master of the whole of the executive branch generated an ever-growing workload that took its toll on the incumbent.[13] Thomas Jefferson wrote, with two years of his second term to run, that he was tired of the office. "To myself, personally, it brings nothing but unceasing drudgery and daily loss of friends."[14] Andrew Jackson described his situation as "dignified slavery"; his successor, Martin Van Buren, found the office "one of toilsome and anxious probation"; and James Polk "heartily rejoiced that my term is so near to its close."[15]

The Development of the Presidential Staff in the Nineteenth Century

The reason Congress was so slow to respond to and alleviate the administrative burdens of the presidency is a matter for some conjecture. One possible explanation is that the suffering presidents suffered in silence, confining complaints about their workload to private correspondence. There is no evidence that any president actually asked Congress to provide money for additional secretaries or clerks prior to a request made by President Monroe in 1825. Furthermore, Monroe's request coincided with congressional attempts to reduce government expenditures consequent upon the heavy cost of the War of 1812 and the depression of 1819. One form of cost cutting initiated by Congress was an effort, albeit unsuccessful, to persuade heads of departments to reduce their clerical staff wherever possible.[16] Simultaneous requests for additional presidential staff during this period were hardly likely to be looked on favorably.

Monroe's request was made in a report to a select committee of the House of Representatives.[17] The essence of his complaint was that the amount of time a president had to spend on "inferior details" detracted from the attention he could give to "the higher duties" of the office, and this Monroe considered to be detrimental to the public interest. "Such neglect and loss must, of necessity," he wrote, "fall, either on the public interests, or on his [the president's] own, and if on the former, the greater will the injury be in proportion to the importance of the trust which he holds." The actual appeal for assistance, however, was made in a somewhat diffident manner. Monroe raised the issue for consideration, rather than directly requesting specific assistance:

> Whether the public interest does not require that provision should be made by law, by special organisation in aid of the Chief Magistrate, in the discharge of those duties, is a subject into which I do not enter—I well know that they are of great extent, of high importance, and heavy burden. The mere signature of patents, added to that of commissions for the army and navy, and of Mediterranean passports, consumes time, which, with one nearly exhausted by other duties, is severely felt.

Eight years passed before Congress responded to Monroe's message in any positive way, and then the response was a very limited one. In 1833 Congress authorized the appointment of a secretary to the president for the sole purpose of signing land patents on his behalf. As Monroe had indicated in his message, this task had hitherto been a significant administrative burden on the presidency, a point well illustrated by the huge backlog of some 20,000 patents awaiting the new appointee.[18] But Congress did not consider this post to be part of the president's immediate personal staff. The appointment was subject to the advice-and-consent power of the Senate and was established for four years only,[19] although, in fact, the position of land patents secretary was still being funded in 1870.

Not until 1857 did Congress overcome its constitutional scruples and approve a specific appropriation for a private secretary to the president. It also permitted the president to appoint a White House steward and a messenger. The salary of the private secretary was fixed at $2500 per annum.[20]

James Buchanan, the fifteenth president, was the first to benefit from this appropriation, but it seems to have had little immediate impact on the administration of the presidency or the quality of his staff. Buchanan continued the practice of many of his predecessors by appointing a relative, his nephew James Buchanan Henry, to fill the post, for reasons apparently unconnected with the young man's administrative ability. Thus, the appropriation made by Congress did not automatically widen the source of recruitment of presidential private secretaries, nor did it establish the post on a more professional footing. It merely allowed presidents to pay their hired relatives from the public purse instead of from their own pockets.

Conveniently, James Henry left a graphic description of his duties as private secretary in a letter to President Buchanan's nineteenth-century biographer, George Ticknor Curtis. Correspondence was the first order of business. "I had a set of books or records carefully prepared," he wrote, "in which could be briefly entered the date of receipt of any letter or communication addressed to the president, the name of the writer—subject matter condensed to the utmost—dates and substance of answer, if any, to what department referred, and the date of such reference.... Such communications as the president ought to see I folded and briefed and took them to him every morning at eight o'clock and received his instructions as to the answer I should make." Henry also wrote that he had responsibility for "the expenditure of the library fund, the payment of the steward, messengers, and also the expenditure of the household which were paid out of the president's private purse."[21]

Apart from administration, Henry's other major responsibility was a social one. He handled all the arrangements for dinners and parties at the White House including "the proper assigning of precedence to the guests" at state dinners.[22] He also attended many social functions on behalf of the president. In those days it was not considered proper for the president himself to accept invitations to private social events, so Henry attended, along with the president's niece, to avoid giving needless offense.[23]

James Henry's letter to Curtis also throws some light on the proclivity of presidents to recruit private secretaries from their own families. "Public policy clearly indicates the propriety and desirability of the president's private secretary being, if possible, a blood relation," Henry wrote, "upon the ground that the honor and interests of the president and his high office can be safely entrusted to one having an interest in his good name and fame, and therefore more guarded against temptation of any kind."[24] If that was in fact the case, then the 1857 appropriation of $2500 would have done little to enhance the status and quality of private secretaries. There is, as we see further on, reason to be a little skeptical of Henry's argument, and the practice almost ceased with Grant's administration. He was the last president, with the exception of Franklin D. Roosevelt, to employ a relative as private secretary, and by the end of the nineteenth century, presidents were primarily interested in recruiting professional administrators, rather than personal confidants, as their private secretaries.

Congressional funding for presidential support staff increased slowly and erratically during the latter half of the nineteenth century. Ten years after the first specific appropriation, an assistant secretary, a shorthand writer, and four clerks were added to the White House payroll.[25] In the 1870 appropriation, however, the size of the presidential staff was actually reduced by two clerks. Moreover, Congress also specified that the assistant secretary's post, first established in 1867, was to be occupied by a shorthand writer. At the same time, a sum of $4000 for "contingent expenses of the executive office" was approved.[26] In 1880 the president's household was expanded once again. It then consisted of a private secretary at a salary of $3250 per annum, an assistant secretary at $2250 per annum, two executive clerks at $2000, a stenographer at $1800, and three clerks at various salary grades. There were also a steward, three ushers, five messengers, two doorkeepers, one watchman, and one fireman to manage the work of the executive mansion.[27] In 1889 the salary of the private secretary was increased to $5000 and, in 1900, Congress funded a second assistant secretary, bringing the complement of administrative and clerical staff in the White House to thirteen.[28]

Despite the increased funding for the White House staff, presidential complaints continued. The status of the private secretary was low, and so was his salary, and presidents found it difficult to obtain competent people for the job. Rutherford Hayes offered the post to two experienced Ohio politicians and was turned down on both occasions because the gentlemen considered it to be beneath their dignity. Soon after his election, President Garfield confided to a friend that he was more "at a loss to find just the man for Private Secretary than for any [other] place I shall have to fill.... The position ought to be held in higher estimation than Secretary of State."

Grover Cleveland encountered similar problems and lamented not being able to offer his private secretary a sufficiently high salary. He wanted something more than a private secretary and spoke of the need for an assistant to the president, claiming that "as the executive office is now organized it can deal with the routine affairs of Government; but if the president has any great policy in mind or on hand he has no one to help him work it out."[29]

In the struggle for power between president and Congress after the Civil War, Congress clearly gained the upper hand, and its unwillingness to fund the presidential staff at realistic levels merely reflected a general view of the role of the executive branch and its relationship to the legislature. But this would not have been the sole reason why Hayes, Garfield, and Cleveland had difficulty recruiting secretaries. The unattractiveness of the position may have had something to do with the caliber of the post-1857 private secretaries who, with the exception of John Nicolay, President Lincoln's secretary, were either incompetent, irresponsible, or ineffective and never managed to establish the office as anything more than a clerkship in spite of its official recognition by Congress.

James Buchanan Henry was more interested in the social than the political aspects of life in Washington and showed little inclination to develop and strengthen the office he occupied. Notwithstanding his observations on why presidents desired to have relatives as their private secretaries, there is some reason to believe that President Buchanan wanted his nephew by his side primarily so that he could maintain a close watch on him and keep him away from the wrong sort of female companionship to which he was attracted.[30]

Andrew Johnson's first private secretary was W.A. Browning, who died after only seven months in the post. The disastrous decision to replace him with the president's son, Robert, undoubtedly contributed to that troubled presidency. Robert Johnson was an incurable alcoholic and a womanizer, and both pastimes seriously affected the administration of the presidency. His drinking became so uncontrollable that, in 1866, the president, the secretary of state, and the secretary of the navy conspired to arrange an "official" visit to Africa for Robert in order to remove him from Washington and give his father a chance to reorganize his office.[31] Unfortunately, Robert disappeared on a drinking binge when his ship was due to depart. The ship sailed without him, and the president's son eventually returned to the White House.

It was also one of Robert Johnson's female companions who tainted the Johnson administration with scandal. After the Civil War, Mrs. Lucy Cobb had gained a reputation in Washington as a "pardon broker" through her contacts in the White House. Presidential pardons for southerners were in great demand, and Mrs. Cobb made a lucrative living on the basis of her ability to obtain signed pardons at short notice. She was eventually entrapped and arrested, after which it was discovered that her only White

House contact was the president's son, who secured the pardons in return for sexual favors. The Cobb case not only brought scandal to the presidency but also reflected badly on the president's controversial and unpopular reconstruction policy. Given the problems encountered by the Johnson administration, Robert Johnson was a huge liability. Michael Medved concludes that his presence in the White House "prevented the emergence of the sort of effective co-ordinated staff that might have saved his father from the series of blunders that led to his impeachment."[32]

The nadir of the presidential staff system was reached, not surprisingly, during the administration of Ulysses S. Grant. Grant had three private secretaries during his tenure. He began with Robert Douglas, the son of Stephen A. Douglas, who served in that capacity until 1873 when he was replaced by Levi P. Luckey. Luckey died in a drowning accident in 1876, and for the remainder of Grant's term, the post was filled by the president's son, U.S. Grant, Jr. All three were competent administrators but were overshadowed by two of Grant's military secretaries, General Orville Babcock and General Horace Porter, with whom the real staff power resided. Babcock and Porter, officially on the staff of General William Sherman, had been assigned to the White House to work for Grant. Babcock, in particular, spent most of his time there extending his personal influence as far as he could, manipulating those around him, including the president, and building up his personal wealth. He was shrewd, ambitious, thoroughly corrupt, and a central figure in three major scandals of the Grant administration.[33] Grant finally removed him from the White House in 1876, but by then the damage had been done, and Babcock had established himself as a major contributor to the abysmal record of the Grant administration.

It is hardly surprising that Rutherford Hayes had difficulty filling the low-paid and tainted post of private secretary, but the eventual choice of his former classmate and law partner, William K. Rogers, proved to be unfortunate. Rogers was, in the words of Michael Medved, a "well-intentioned ... honest man hopelessly out of his depth."[34] He had failed in three careers before arriving at the White House and subsequently failed miserably as the president's private secretary. Hayes had a close personal relationship with Rogers and continued to employ him despite the enormous unpopularity that Rogers had generated in Washington. Neither could it be said that the president was unaware of his friend's deficiencies in the world of politics. Hayes once wrote in his diary that Rogers was "easily duped; trusts all men who profess friendship. He seems to lack a sense of duty and responsibility."[35]

There was, however, one beneficial development within the presidential staff system during the Grant-Hayes years. The increased number of positions approved by Congress after 1857, particularly at the executive clerk level, permitted the beginning of some degree of institutional continuity in the White House. Although President Hayes had installed his own man as private secretary, he retained President Grant's assistant secretary, C.C. Sniffen, and two executive clerks, O.L. Pruden and William H. Crook.[36] When Sniffen was later promoted to the post of paymaster in the army, Pruden became the new assistant secretary and remained in this position until his death in 1902, thus spanning nine presidencies. Crook had begun his career in the White House under President Lincoln and he too served through to the administration of Theodore Roosevelt.

The responsibilities of the assistant secretary and the executive clerks were primarily concerned with the routines and formalities of the presidency. They handled the paper flow in the White House, took messages to Congress, published executive orders, recorded all presidential appointments, commissions, and pardons, and enrolled legislation from Congress.[37] Whether the continuity in office of these officials was by design or by accident, it did establish a most important precedent, which has been followed to the present day. The basic duties of the executive clerks are now much the same as they were a hundred years ago, and it is customary for the staff in the Executive Clerk's Office continues to serve whoever occupies the presidency.

President Garfield, like his predecessor, was rebuffed in his initial choice of private secretary. He had hoped to secure the services of John Hay, who had already seen something of the job as Nicolay's assistant in the Lincoln administration. Unfortunately, for Garfield, Hay's reply to the job offer indicated that he had seen enough of it. "The contact with the greed and selfishness of office-seekers and bull-dozing Congressmen is unspeakably repulsive. The constant contact with envy, meanness, ignorance, and the swinish selfishness which ignorance breeds needs a stronger heart and a more obedient nervous system than I can boast."[38] Eventually, a twenty-two year-old stenographer, Stanley Brown, accepted the post that Hay could not stomach and later proved himself a more than able administrator when he virtually ran the presidency from the time Garfield was shot until his death ten weeks later.

Brown's tenure also marked a turning point in the quality of presidential private secretaries. Garfield's successors, with perhaps the exception of President Taft, managed to avoid any disastrous repetition of the Johnson, Grant, and Hayes appointments, and two of the later nineteenth-century private secretaries—Daniel Lamont, who served President Cleveland, and George Cortelyou, who served President McKinley—were particularly inspired choices, both making a significant impact on the administration of the presidency. Lamont's service with Cleveland had begun when Cleveland was Governor of New York, during which time Lamont was able to unveil an effective combination of talents as an administrator, politician, campaign manager, and master of public relations. In Albany Lamont had been called "the Other Governor," and in Washington newspaper reporters soon dubbed him "the Assistant President."[39]

George Cortelyou began his White House service as President Cleveland's stenographer and later became assistant to McKinley's very inadequate private secretary, John Addison Porter. McKinley's biographer, Margaret Leech, writes that Porter was ignorant of Washington and its public men, had no comprehension of office management, was lax and bad-tempered, and lacked judgment, humility, and discipline.[40] As a consequence, McKinley came to rely on Cortelyou more and more, and Cortelyou very soon became the de facto private secretary. Porter's insensitivity prevented him from seeing that he had been shunted aside, and his continuing presence in the White House was largely attributable to McKinley's unwillingness to deal with the problem.[41] Ill health eventually overtook Porter. He resigned as private secretary in 1900, and the superefficient Cortelyou took over the title of the job that he had already been performing for a number of years.

The title of the post was, in fact, changed during McKinley's presidency from private secretary to secretary to the president. According to Margaret Leech, this was done at the insistence of the president, who wanted to enhance the importance of the private secretary and give the office a new dignity.[42] Little else changed. The salary of the secretary remained at $5000 a year, the same as it had been ten years earlier, and Congress showed no inclination to improve the president's staff resources in any fundamental way.

Looking back from the McKinley era, one can begin to see a gradual evolution of the presidential staff system. By the end of the nineteenth century, the secretary to the president was much more than the clerk he had been at the beginning of the century. Once Congress had decided to fund additional presidential staff posts, as it did from 1867 onward, the private secretary was simultaneously freed from the most basic and routine clerical chores. This presented the opportunity to take on additional responsibilities within the White House, which some of the more adept private secretaries did. The professional late nineteenth-century secretaries, like Lamont and Cortelyou, were quite active as intermediaries between the president and key constituencies. They tended to regulate access to the president, draft speeches for him, and liaise with important party officials and the rapidly expanding world of political journalism, and in doing so they were beginning to display some of the characteristics that one usually associates with the post-Brownlow presidential staff.

The increased size of the staff in the last quarter of the nineteenth century essentially reflected developments in administrative technology. The advent of stenography, telegraphy, and, later, the typewriter and the telephone made communication tasks easier and more efficient but required trained personnel to be employed in the White House. Stenography, incidentally, provided presidents with a remarkable source for the recruitment of private secretaries. Stanley Brown, Daniel Lamont, George Cortelyou, and William Loeb, who served Theodore Roosevelt, all began their careers as stenographers. It was purely coincidental that these stenographers also turned out to be first-class political operatives in the White House and thus helped to fill a need that Congress had failed to provide for.

Another feature of the late nineteenth-century presidential staff was the difficulty of determining the exact number of White House employees. The presidential staff was supplemented at various times by officials formally on the payroll of government departments. The most obvious cases were the president's military secretaries, who were paid from the War Department's budget but spent the whole of their time in the White House. The practice seems to have started back in Andrew Jackson's time. His nephew and private secretary, Andrew Jackson Donelson, was paid from the budget of the General Land Office while working full-time in the president's office.

The Presidential Staff in the Early Twentieth Century

The size and shape of the White House staff hardly changed at all during the first decade of the twentieth century. In 1910, the salary of the secretary to the president was raised from $5000 to $6000, the first increase in twenty years, and to $7500 in 1922, but that was the only significant development. Some expansion of the staff took place in the early 1920s. By 1922, the official administrative and clerical staff in the White House totaled thirty-one, although all the increase in personnel had been at the lower end of the staff hierarchy. The relevant appropriation legislation for 1922 shows that the White House staff was composed of the secretary to the president, an executive clerk, a chief clerk, an appointments clerk, a record clerk, two stenographers, an accounting and dispersing clerk, two correspondents, and twenty-one other clerks.[43] The following year, Congress wrote a provision into the Independent Offices Appropriation Act permitting the president to borrow an unspecified number of executive branch employees "for such temporary assistance as may be necessary,"[44] thus legitimizing what had already become a common practice. Although this was a welcome relief, it did not satisfy the need for more high-level assistance in the White House. Finally, in 1929, Congress agreed to increase the number of secretaries to the president from one to three and raised the salary for that post to $10,000 per annum.[45] The addition of two senior aides allowed some division of labor and specialization among the president's staff and enabled Herbert Hoover to designate one of his three secretaries, George Akerson, press secretary—the first White House aide to have that title.

Perhaps the most noticeable change in the early twentieth-century presidential staff can be seen in the type of person recruited to the post of secretary to the president. As time passed, the penchant for stenographers was replaced by a preference for secretaries with prior political experience. Of the nineteenth-century secretaries, only Cleveland's Daniel Lamont had any substantial background in politics before his time in the White House. The twentieth-century trend was established by Woodrow Wilson, whose secretary, Joseph Tumulty, had served a tough political apprenticeship as a reform Democrat in the New Jersey legislature and then as secretary and adviser to Wilson during Wilson's governorship of New Jersey. George Christian, President Harding's secretary, also came from a political background, although his credentials were somewhat less impressive than Tumulty's. Christian's father was a leading Democrat in Marion County, Ohio, and George, Jr., began his life in politics with the Ohio Democratic Committee. He made an unsuccessful attempt to become a member of the Ohio legislature and in 1914 got the job of secretary to his next-door neighbor, the newly elected Republican senator from Ohio with whom he remained until the president's death in 1923. Christian's successor in the Coolidge administration, C. Bascom Slemp, was the most experienced politician to have filled the post of secretary to the president. Slemp, the son of a Virginia congressman, was chairman of the Virginia Republican party and a member of Congress in his own right for fifteen years. When he left the White House at the beginning of Coolidge's second term, he was replaced by another congressman, Everett Sanders. One of President Hoover's three secretaries, Walter Newton, was also a former congressman.

The need for a president to have a politically experienced assistant in the White House reflected the increasing responsibilities attached to the job of secretary to the president in the early years of the twentieth century. Joseph Tumulty, for example, did a lot more for Woodrow Wilson than merely direct the routine business. He was Wilson's liaison with politicians and journalists. He worked closely with the Democratic National Committee and, along with the president's unofficial adviser, Colonel House, handled all patronage matters. Tumulty was, in the words of Arthur Link, "the one totally political functionary in the Wilson group."[46]

Bascom Slemp's appointment as Coolidge's secretary clearly illustrated how political the job had become. Slemp had built up a Republican machine in Virginia based on the federal patronage he controlled in the South by virtue of being one of the very few southern Republicans in Congress at the turn of the century. It was a patronage scandal that eventually led to Slemp's voluntary retirement from the House of Representatives,[47] but his experience in Washington and in the Republican party was precisely what Coolidge needed to ensure the Republican presidential nomination in 1924. Coolidge's nomination was by no means certain when he succeeded to the presidency on Harding's death, but, as William Allen White notes, "less than four months after the new president had crossed the portals of the White House, his nomination seemed assured. When he chose Bascom Slemp as his Secretary, his choice was an announcement."[48]

As the secretary to the president was becoming more political in the twentieth century so he was also becoming more visible. One indicator of this was the public controversy that surrounded the appointments of Tumulty and Slemp respectively. In Tumulty's case, Protestant extremists were outspoken in their opposition to a Roman Catholic being so close to a president of the United States.[49] Opposition to Slemp came from the Democratic National Committee, which made the most of his questionable patronage practices while in Congress, and also from the National Association for the Advancement of Colored People, objecting to Slemp's establishment of a "lily-white" Republican party in Virginia.[50]

Given the heightened political role of the president's chief aides, it is perhaps not surprising that the men around the president in the early part of the twentieth century began to display some of the behavioral characteristics more commonly associated with modern White House staffs. For example, proximity to the president induced a preoccupation on the part of some secretaries with protecting their privileged position. Charles Dyer Norton, Taft's unfortunate appointment, went to great lengths to monopolize access to the president, even to the extent of attempting unsuccessfully to dismiss Taft's favorite stenographer. According to Michael Medved, Norton was unable to tolerate the idea that anyone else on the staff might enjoy a personal relationship with the president.[51] George Christian behaved in much the same way with respect to Harding, at the cost of denying Harding access to the kind of policy advice he so desperately needed.[52] When things got bad for Herbert Hoover, his White House staff, directed by Lawrence Richey, organized into a palace guard and "formed a buffer line around the president day and night," which brought complaints and criticism from the press.[53]

These years also witnessed the first of what are now fairly frequent power struggles among presidential aides. Colonel House, who had recommended to Woodrow Wilson that Tumulty be appointed secretary to the president, came to regret his advice and in 1915 led a campaign aimed at forcing Tumulty's resignation. The campaign was partially successful in that President Wilson did ask for his secretary's resignation, but Tumulty fought back and organized pressure on Wilson to change his mind. The president eventually did so, but the incident strained the relationship between president and secretary permanently.[54] Political infighting became more usual once Congress increased the number of presidential secretaries from one to three. There was considerable rivalry between Herbert Hoover's three secretaries: Lawrence Richey, George Akerson, and Walter Newton. Richey reportedly spied on Akerson and Newton, and Akerson eventually resigned his post before the end of Hoover's term of office after losing out in the power struggle with Richey.[55]

Prior to Franklin Roosevelt's inauguration in 1933, a rudimentary presidential staff system had already taken shape and was displaying some of the characteristics of the contemporary White House Office. The staff was expanding in size and function, it was supported by additional personnel borrowed from the departments and agencies, and it had just begun to organize its workload around specialized tasks. Roosevelt also inherited a staff system in which secretaries to the president had already crossed the line between administration and politics. It is, therefore, not surprising that precedents for many of the less desirable features of the "inner life" of the modern White House can be found in the pre-Brownlow presidential staffs. There are, indeed, many similarities between the contemporary and pre-Brownlow presidential staff systems.

There is also a great deal of difference. Brownlow provided Franklin Roosevelt and his successors with something more than a personal staff. He provided institutional support for the presidency, which was to operate in a vastly different political context and climate of expectations. The modern presidential staff system took off with the publication of the Brownlow report in 1937.

THE BROWNLOW REPORT

Franklin Roosevelt's New Deal aggravated the presidency's staffing difficulties. The enormous growth of government activity during those years, coupled with the proliferation of new government agencies to administer New Deal programs, magnified the existing structural defects within the executive branch. The need for efficient management in government became ever greater, yet seemingly ever more difficult to attain. During the 1932 election campaign, Roosevelt had pledged to reorganize the executive branch, and at his first presidential press conference he announced that reorganization would have top priority,[56] although the major reorganization initiative did not eventuate until his second term in office.

By that time, the problem of presidential staffing had become more closely bound up with wider issues about presidential management of the executive branch as a whole, and it was in this context that the Brownlow report was born. On 22 March 1936, President Roosevelt announced the appointment of a committee composed of three academic public administrators, Louis Brownlow, Charles Merriam, and Luther Gulick, to study the organization of the executive branch with the primary purpose of considering the problem of administrative management. The immediate impulse for reform was, as Clinton Rossiter noted, Roosevelt's "own candid recognition that an otherwise professional performance during his first term in the presidency was being severely hampered by the sheer multiplicity and complexity of his duties and by the want of effective assistance in their discharge."[57]

On 14 November, Brownlow and Gulick met with Roosevelt and presented him with an outline of the major recommendations to be made by the committee, most of which he approved.[58] After the changes required by the president had been incorporated, the final report was handed to him at the beginning of January 1937.

Brownlow and his colleagues had interpreted their mission broadly. Their inquiry, they said, was focused on "the organization for the performance of the duties imposed upon the president in exercising the executive power vested in him by the Constitution of the United States." Administrative management, as they defined it, "concerns itself in a democracy with the executive and his duties, with managerial and staff aides, with organization, with personnel, and with the fiscal system, because these are the indispensable means of making good the popular will in a people's government."[59]

The report opens with an essay on the vitality and centrality of the presidency in the American system of government. In many ways it stands as a twentieth-century restatement of Alexander Hamilton's case for the presidency published in *The Federalist* almost 150 years earlier, and, like Hamilton and the Founding Fathers, Brownlow was far from happy about the state of executive power in his America. In general terms, the committee thought that the presidency was not abreast of advances made in administrative management techniques and practices. In specific terms, the complaints Brownlow made were very similar to those uttered by various American presidents over the previous hundred years or so. "Where . . . can there be found an executive in any way comparable upon whom so much petty work is thrown? Or who is forced to see so many persons on unrelated matters and to make so many decisions on the basis of what may be, because of the very press of work, incomplete information? How is it humanly possible to know fully the affairs and problems of over 100 separate major agencies, to say nothing of being responsible for their general direction and coordination?"[60] The similarity between Brownlow's complaint and that made by President Monroe in 1825 is indicative of the lack of any substantial progress in meeting the president's staffing needs during the intervening 112 years.

The recommendations of the committee fell into five broad categories:

1. To deal with the greatly increased duties of executive management falling upon the president the White House staff should be expanded.
2. The managerial agencies of the government, particularly those dealing with the budget, efficiency research, personnel, and planning, should be greatly strengthened and developed as arms of the chief executive.
3. The merit system should be extended upward, outward, and downward to cover all non-policy-determining posts, and the civil service system should be reorganized and opportunities established for a career system attractive to the best talent of the nation.
4. The whole executive branch of the government should be overhauled and the present 100 agencies reorganized under a few large departments in which every executive would find its place.

5. The fiscal system should be extensively revised in the light of the best governmental private practice, particularly with reference to financial records, audit, and accountability of the executive to the Congress.[61]

The Brownlow report was greeted with both praise and criticism from academics, professional public administrators, and politicians. The director of the Public Administration Clearing House, Herbert Emmerich, called it "a beacon on the road to enlightened administration,"[62] whereas Princeton University's Edward S. Corwin thought the report was "thoroughgoingly Jacksonian," the strongest epithet he could muster at the time.[63] The academic criticism of Brownlow principally centered on what was seen as the committee's willingness to give Roosevelt the kind of report he wanted, a charge Brownlow admitted and stoutly defended,[64] and on what was viewed as the committee's misguided adherence to the principles of rational organization.[65] The political attack at the time was more concerned with the goal of the reorganization proposals. Roosevelt had been arguing for executive reorganization on the grounds of managerial efficiency, as opposed to the more traditional reorganization-for-the-sake-of-economy argument. Some members of Congress also saw the proposals for the reform of the Civil Service Commission, the Office of the Auditor General, and the merit system as a blatant power grab by the president, which led a number of them to complain that American government was headed toward dictatorship.

The legislative passage of the Brownlow proposals was difficult and complex, and the debate over the reorganization bill was often far from rational.[66] The legislation got dragged down with Roosevelt's unpopular bill to "pack" the Supreme Court. It also clashed with counterproposals on executive reorganization from a Senate select committee headed by Senator Harry Byrd and backed by the then conservative Brookings Institution. Furthermore, the reforms came under attack from interest groups and government bureaucrats who would have been disadvantaged by the reorganization proposals and from conservative opponents of the Roosevelt administration who had been able to generate intense opposition to Roosevelt's plans. Although the legislation cleared the Senate by a narrow margin in March 1938, it was defeated in the House the following month. A much watered-down version was finally signed into law on 3 April 1939, and the proposal to enlarge the president's personal staff was one of the few features of the Brownlow report to survive the legislative battle in Congress.

It should be noted, however, that the proposal to give the president additional staff assistance was never really at the center of the criticism of Roosevelt's reorganization bill and, apart from some journalistic cynicism, was generally accepted from the beginning. In any case, President Roosevelt already had a press secretary, an appointments secretary, a secretary for political affairs, and a total White House staff of thirty-seven before the publication of the Brownlow report.[67] Brownlow had merely recommended an additional six, and that largely as a consequence of other reforms proposed in the report.

Irrespective of how presidents have used their staffs since, Brownlow defined the role of the additional White House assistants in careful and narrow administrative terms. Their number was to be limited: "a small number of executive assistants ... probably not exceeding six," said the committee immediately following the statement that "the president needs help."[68] The report then went to some lengths to spell out strict limits to the role and function of the executive assistants. "These aides would have no power to make decisions or issue instructions in their own right," wrote Brownlow. "They would not be interposed between the president and the heads of departments. They would not be assistant presidents in any sense." Their function, according to Brownlow, was to assist the president "in obtaining quickly and without delay all pertinent information possessed by any of the executive departments so as to guide him in making his responsible decisions; and then when decisions have been made, to assist him in seeing to it that every administrative department and agency affected is promptly informed."

The Brownlow Committee placed special emphasis on the desired personal characteristics and qualities of the new assistants. "Their effectiveness in assisting the president will, we think, be directly proportional to their ability to discharge their function with restraint. They would remain in the background, issue no orders, emit no public statements. ... They should be men in whom the president has personal confidence and whose character and attitude are such that they would not attempt to exercise power on their own account." Brownlow then produced the sentence for which he became famous. The presidential assistants, he said, "should be possessed of high competence, great physical vigor, and a passion for anonymity."

What cynicism there was toward Brownlow's staffing proposal was partly attributable to Roosevelt himself. Luther Gulick noted that when the sentence describing the desired qualities of the staff was first read to the president, "he burst out chuckling and laughing and read the phrase out loud a second time."[69] And, when Roosevelt presented the report to a press conference on 11 January 1937, he told the assembled journalists "to sharpen your pencils and take this down. This is a purple patch, one you will never forget." Brownlow commented later: "The president got a laugh, as he had expected, but he also got a chorus of various audible expressions of cynical disbelief. In fact one man spoke up and said 'There ain't no such animal.'"[70] The press went to town with the "passion-for-anonymity" phrase and the journalists even ran a contest among themselves for the best poem lampooning the proposal.[71] On one level, at least, the staffing proposal was tainted from the start.

Brownlow, however, was most earnest about his design for the presidential staff. It was the product of discussions he had had with Tom Jones, once deputy to the head of the British Cabinet secretariat, Sir Maurice Hankey. Jones had used the phrase "passion for anonymity" to describe the attributes of Hankey and, in doing so, he recommended the British secretariat as the model for Brownlow to follow.[72] Indeed, Brownlow followed it very closely. One of his original recommendations was that Roosevelt should establish an administrative secretariat under one executive director, rather than the corps of executive assistants that appeared in the final report, but the president had rejected this recommendation prior to the publication of the report because he was strongly opposed to the idea of a chief of staff in the White House.[73] Brownlow had also suggested that some of the presidential assistants should be recruited from the executive departments, do a tour of duty in the White House, and then return to their former assignments. This proposal was included in the report and was analogous to the recruitment system adopted by the Cabinet Office in Britain where positions in the secretariat are usually held on the basis of a two-year secondment from the departments.[74] That Brownlow had been so impressed with the improvement in top management practices that followed the establishment of the Cabinet secretariat in Whitehall, and that the presidential staff was conceived, figuratively speaking, in London, not Washington, were to have an important bearing on the subsequent history of the White House Office.

THE BIRTH OF THE EXECUTIVE OFFICE OF THE PRESIDENT

The Reorganization Act of 1939 gave the president authority, subject to a number of conditions and a congressional veto, to submit plans for the reorganization of the executive branch. Title III of the act also authorized the president to appoint up to six administrative assistants, at a salary of not more than $10,000 each, to perform such duties as the president might prescribe.

The first reorganization proposal Roosevelt submitted under the terms of the act, Reorganization Plan No. 1. 1939, formally established the Executive Office of the President and provided for the transfer of the Bureau of the Budget and the National Resources Planning Board to that office. A more explicit statement of the structure and functions of the Executive Office followed in the shape of Executive Order 8248, issued by President Roosevelt on 8 September 1939, a landmark document in the history of the modern presidency.[75]

Executive Order 8248 established five divisions within the new Executive Office of the President: the White House Office, the Bureau of the Budget, the National Resources Planning Board, the Liaison Office for Personnel Management, and the Office of Government Reports. It also provided that, in the event of a national emergency, the president is permitted to establish an emergency management office as part of the Executive Office of the President.

The White House Office was the formal home of the president's personal staff and was "to serve the President in an intimate capacity in the performance of the many detailed activities incident to his immediate office." The executive order identified three kinds of staff in the White House Office. The first consisted of secretaries to the president, those senior presidential aides who had existed prior to Brownlow. They were "to facilitate and maintain quick and easy communication with the Congress, the individual members of the Congress, the heads of executive departments and agencies, the press, the radio and the general public." This job description merely recognized what the post of secretary to the president had become by the end of the nineteenth century and what all presidential secretaries had been doing during the twentieth century. The executive clerk and his assistants were the second group of White House staff detailed in the executive order and were responsible for clerical services and the orderly handling of documents and correspondence. The third category consisted of the six new administrative assistants. Their role was described in much the same way as it had been in the Brownlow report, which was hardly surprising given that Brownlow had also assisted in the drafting of the executive order. Once again he stressed the circumscribed role of the administrative assistants in the newly established White House Office.

> The Administrative Assistants shall be personal aides to the president and shall have no authority over anyone in any department or agency, including the Executive Office of the President, other than the personnel assigned to their immediate offices. In no event shall the Administrative Assistants be interposed between the president and any one of the divisions in the Executive Office of the President.

Their function, according to the executive order, was "to assist the President in such matters as he may direct, and at the specific request of the President, to get information and to condense and summarize it for his use." The work of the administrative assistants was certainly less grand than that of the secretaries to the president, who were responsible for liaising with the president's most important constituencies, and the functional distinction between the two categories of staff was quite evident in the text of the executive order. It was, however, a distinction that was to have little relevance to the subsequent history of the White House Office. The title of secretary to the president was eventually dropped by legislation passed in 1956.[76]

The other components of the Executive Office of the President were designed to provide an institutional support staff for the presidency and were intended to be quite distinct from the personal staff that occupied the White House Office. The most important of these was the Bureau of the Budget.

The bureau was originally established in the Budget and Accounting Act of 1921, and its primary responsibility was to prepare the annual budget that, henceforth, the president would be required to submit to Congress at the beginning of each session. Although the bureau had been located in the Treasury Department since its creation, its director and assistant director were appointed by the president, without the necessity of Senate confirmation, and were directly responsible to the president. The bureau was therefore a presidential agency before 1939, but one that had been lodged in a department as a result of a legislative compromise during the passage of the bill through Congress.[77] Such an arrangement, although politically expedient, did not make much organizational sense in 1921, or thereafter, and at least five separate studies prior to the Brownlow report had recommended moving the Bureau of the Budget from the Treasury Department.[78]

The Brownlow report proposed not only to move the bureau to the new Executive Office of the President but also to upgrade substantially its role in government. It advocated an increased appropriation for the bureau and a staff commensurate with the magnitude of its responsibilities. The major concern of the Brownlow Committee, however, was directed at the failure of the bureau to carry out certain functions assigned to it in the 1921 act, and the report highlighted the bureau's ineffectiveness as an instrument of administrative management.[79] The criticism was a just one. Budgeting had taken precedence over everything else during the early history of the bureau and its narrow focus was, in part, the result of a rather limited view of the role of the bureau held by a succession of budget directors in the 1920s and 1930s.[80]

Both the Brownlow report and Executive Order 8248, infused with the ideals of the scientific-management school of public administration, aimed to revive the importance of administrative management to the bureau's purposes. The executive order listed eight functions for the bureau. The first two related to the preparation and control of the budget. The third and fourth were about *management*. Specifically, the bureau was to "conduct research in the development of improved plans of administrative management" and to "aid the President to bring about more efficient and economical conduct of Government service." In fact, these new terms of reference differed little from those originally provided in Section 209 of the Budget and Accounting Act eighteen years earlier, but, this time, administrative management was being promoted with greater vigor and more intense commitment than ever before.

The fifth and sixth of the eight functions specified in the executive order recognized the legislative clearance procedures that had been adopted by the bureau in the mid-1930s. The order said simply that the bureau was

To assist the president by clearing and coordinating departmental advice on proposed legislation and by making recommendations as to presidential action on legislative enactments, in accordance with past practice.

To assist in the consideration and clearance and, where necessary, in the preparation of proposed Executive orders and proclamations, in accordance with the provisions of Executive Order No. 7298 of February 18, 1936.

The term "legislative clearance" belies the significance of this procedure as a mechanism for presidential coordination of policy development in the executive branch. The job of the Office of Legislative Reference within the Bureau of the Budget was to determine whether or not departmental and agency policy proposals and enrolled legislation were in accord with the president's program. As Richard Neustadt described it in his classic study of the development of legislative clearance, "here is presidential machinery to coordinate a vital aspect of executive policy development; machinery to control ... the means by which the diverse elements of the executive express and implement their own designs."[81]

The Brownlow report, and the consequent legislation, helped to revitalize what had become a moribund Bureau of the Budget. It did this by removing the bureau from the Treasury Department, placing it at the heart of the institutionalized presidency, and then highlighting the key functions of the bureau in the context of a comprehensive examination of administrative management in American government. But this was not the full explanation for why the Bureau of the Budget became the most important, and indispensable, presidential management agency. The staff whom Roosevelt appointed to the bureau in the immediate post-Brownlow years, especially the new director, Harold D. Smith, were qualitatively unlike their predecessors. They were men of vision, experience, and ability, strongly committed to the Brownlow proposals, and were willing and able to translate the Brownlow ideals into reality. They led what Larry Berman has called "the born-again Budget Bureau" into its golden age.[82]

The renaissance of the Bureau of the Budget was immediately evident. Before Brownlow, the bureau had operated with a staff of forty-five on an annual budget of $187,000. Following the publication of the report, President Roosevelt asked Congress for a 70 percent increase in the bureau's appropriation, which enabled him to more than double its staff. By the mid-1940s the bureau's staff totaled over 600 and its annual appropriation stood at more than $3 million.[83] There was also a notable change in staff-recruitment practices in the Roosevelt years. During the 1920s, career military officers dominated the top positions in the bureau. The first two directors, Charles Dawes and Herbert Lord, were army generals, and the third, J. Clawson Roop, was a colonel. Their key subordinates tended to view their jobs as steppingstones to greater things in the army, and, as Edward Hobbs notes, this military monopoly of top jobs affected civilian morale in the bureau.[84] But by the end of the 1930s the bureau had begun to recruit staff from state and local government, and from the universities, and had attracted some leading professional public administrators. This had a profound effect on the immediate future of the Budget Bureau.

The National Resources Planning Board (NRPB) was the product of Section IV of the Brownlow report, which had argued the need for a presidential staff skilled in the analysis and interpretation of national planning policies. The language of the report was bold. It called for "social vision in the fusion of American interests, techniques, and ideals into sounder and more satisfactory modes of conversing and expanding our national resources and facilitating their equitable award." In Executive Order 8248 this was translated into four broad functions:

1. To survey, collect data on, and analyze problems pertaining to national resources, both natural and human, and to recommend to the president and Congress long-time plans and programs for the wise use and fullest development of such resources.
2. To consult with federal, regional, state, local and private agencies in developing orderly programs of public works and to list for the president and Congress all proposed public works in the order of their relative importance with respect to (1) the greatest good to the greatest number of people, (2) the emergency necessities of the Nation, and (3) the social, economic, and cultural advancement of the people of the United States.
3. To inform the president of the general trend of economic conditions and to recommend measures leading to the improvement or stabilization.
4. To act as a clearing house and means of coordination for planning activities, linking together various levels of planning.

Program planning was a central feature of Brownlow's approach to administrative management. The National Resources Planning Board was intended to do for planning what the Bureau of the Budget was to do for budgeting. The NRPB had a much less happy existence than the Bureau of the Budget and was terminated by Congress after only four years. The reasons for the early demise of this particular presidential staff unit were many and various, but the idea of a planning agency never commanded wide support in an increasingly conservative Congress. The original proposal for a National Resources Planning Board was omitted from the House version of the reorganization bill, and the agency was eventually created through a reorganization plan device that did not require the specific approval of Congress.[85] On two occasions, in 1941 and 1942, President Roosevelt had to intervene to protect the board from an even earlier death, but congressional suspicion of planning, public works programs, and the breadth of the board's terms of reference were too much for even Roosevelt to defend. The board was eventually abolished on 26 June 1943.[86] The termination of the NRPB was an early reminder of the ability of Congress to affect the shape and nature of the presidential staff when it chose to do so, even if it decided to take a position contrary to that of the president.

The Office of Government Reports, intended to be a clearing house for government information, servicing state and local government bodies and citizens' organizations, hardly fared any better. In 1942 President Roosevelt signed an executive order that transferred the functions of the Office of Government Reports to the Office of War Information. In 1946 it became part of a division within the Office of War Mobilization and Reconversion. The following year Congress severely curtailed its functions, and then finally abolished it on 30 June 1948. The Office of Government Reports was, however, the least important division within the new Executive Office of the President, and its fate was nowhere near as consequential as the demise of the National Resources Planning Board.

The Bureau of the Budget and the National Resources Planning Board were two of the three principal presidential management agencies within the Executive Office of the President. The third was the Liaison Office for Personnel Management, which was what President Roosevelt managed to salvage from the wreckage of Brownlow's civil service proposals. Brownlow had recommended radical reform of the management of the civil service. One of the most contentious reforms was that the Civil Service Commission be replaced by a Civil Service Administration, to be headed by a single executive officer and housed in the Executive Office of the President. This aroused grave fears that the merit system would be threatened, that the civil service administrator would no longer be nonpartisan, and that too much authority would be vested in one person.[87] An array of important interest groups opposed the measure, including the National Civil Service Reform League, and it went down to defeat in the House of Representatives, along with many of the other reorganization proposals, in April 1938. When Roosevelt presented his second reorganization bill in 1939, civil service reform had been dropped.

It reappeared, somewhat diluted, in Executive Order 8248 in the guise of the Liaison Office for Personnel Management. One of the six new administrative assistants to the president was to be designated liaison officer for personnel management and would head the office. His responsibilities were to assist the president with personnel management and to "liaise with all agencies dealing with personnel matters." This, of course, meant that the Civil Service Commission, which had successfully withstood the Brownlow reform proposals, remained a power unto itself outside the Executive Office of the President. For this reason, the Liaison Office for Personnel Management never functioned as an effective personnel management unit and was eventually abolished by President Eisenhower in 1953.[88]

One further feature of Executive Order 8248 needs to be considered. The provision for the establishment of an Office of Emergency Management in the event of a national emergency aroused little comment when the executive order was published in 1939. Within the space of a year, however, Roosevelt utilized this authority to establish the Office of Emergency Management, the first of a series of temporary but vitally important emergency management agencies in the Executive Office of the President. The provision enabled the president to coordinate the war effort in a manner more suitable to his style of government and thus avoid many of the inevitable jurisdictional disputes over control and direction with the regular departments and agencies. The full benefits of the emergency management provision were realized when the Office of War Mobilization was created in May 1943. It was headed by former Supreme Court Justice James F. Byrnes and proved to be a very successful coordinating agency during the crucial years of World War II.

The Brownlow report, the Reorganization Act, Reorganization Plan No. 1, and Executive Order 8248 together were a watershed in the history of presidential staffing. It is difficult to imagine how the presidency could have survived as an effective institution in American government without the addition of an enhanced presidential staff. The Brownlow report stands as the first successful attempt in the history of the presidency to publicize the problems of the president's workload, and it found, not surprisingly, that the president was remarkably ill equipped to perform the functions of a chief executive. Brownlow's significant contribution was to recommend the establishment of a support staff for the *institution of the presidency* to assist with the principal managerial functions of government. Even though many of its specific recommendations were rejected or short-lived, the report succeeded in establishing a broad framework for an Executive Office of the President that was to become a vital part of government in the second half of the twentieth century.

Of lesser immediate significance in 1939 were the Brownlow proposals relating to the president's personal staff. Another six assistants were to be added to the White House Office to help the president handle the new management structure that had been established in the Executive Office of the President. There was nothing new about the concept of a personal staff for the president. A rudimentary one had existed ever since 1789. By the end of the nineteenth century, the size of the president's entourage was expanding, its character was less amateur than it had been during the first half of the century, and it was beginning to carve out an important place for itself in the system of government. What Brownlow did was to devise a tightly constrained administrative role for the new administrative assistants that gave few clues to the way the White House Office would develop in the post-

Brownlow years. The cynicism about Brownlow's "passion for anonymity"—his "purple patch," as Roosevelt called Brownlow's phrase—has been shared by many observers since. They tend to agree with the journalist at FDR's press conference who said "there ain't no such animal"; and subsequent White House staff deviations from the Brownlow design may well have proved them right. The Brownlow report was not the blueprint for the presidential staff system we see today. Yet, without reference to Brownlow, one cannot properly explore how the presidential staff has become what it is today, and how it fits into the American system of government. We return to Brownlow further on.

3. THE DEVELOPMENT OF
THE EXECUTIVE OFFICE
OF THE PRESIDENT

The early demise of three of the five original units of the Executive Office of the President was a pointer to the way this new institution would develop during the postwar years. Once established, agencies within the EOP were not necessarily fixed there for all time. They could be disbanded when they had outlived their usefulness and new presidential staff units, serving different purposes, could be added to the EOP when they were needed. A variety of offices, more than forty in all, have been housed in the Executive Office since 1939, and only a small proportion have outlived the administration that created them.[1] In this respect, a great virtue of the structure that Brownlow had proposed was its capacity to meet the staff needs of a succession of different presidents, operating in different circumstances, with different ideas about managing the government of the United States.

It must be noted, however, that the president is not the sole determinant of the structure of the EOP. More than once, Congress has demonstrated its capacity to shape the presidential staff system, and it has done this not just by disbanding agencies, as it did with the National Resources Planning Board, but also by creating new units and new staff functions within the EOP. The final form of the Council of Economic Advisers, for example, was constructed in the corridors of Congress rather than in the White House, as was the National Security Council, and in neither instance was President Truman noticeably enthusiastic about the congressional product. Similarly, what is now the Office of U.S. Trade Representative was originally foisted on a reluctant President Kennedy by Congress in 1962. This is not to suggest that Congress can effectively force advice on the president against his will: Its attempts to shape the the Executive Office will always be tempered by the fact that nothing can compel the president to take advice from a source that he does not wish to consult. A staff arm of the presidency created by congressional initiative will be effective only if the president chooses to make it so. Some presidents may do so, whereas others may not, and that is the principal reason why the most important divisions of the EOP, like the Council of Economic Advisers, the National Security Council, the Office of Management and Budget, and the Office of the U.S. Trade Representative have had such a checkered history.

Congress made its major impact in shaping the structure of the Executive Office during the decade following the passage of the Reorganization Act when it added the Council of Economic Advisers and the National Security Council to the two principal staff units, the White House Office and the Bureau of the Budget. Together, these four divisions have formed the core of the Executive Office and have been in continuous operation, despite the many additions and modifications to the EOP, since the 1940s. Each has changed significantly during this time, particularly the Bureau of the Budget, which underwent a major reform in 1970 and had its name changed to the Office of Management and Budget, but they have remained the most important units within the presidential staff system. During particular presidencies, other EOP units have sometimes shared the stature of the big four, and it is very likely that President Clinton's innovation, the National Economic Council, will be of major importance within the EOP during his administration.

STRUCTURING THE EOP: THE LEGAL FRAMEWORK

There are several methods by which new units can be added to the Executive Office of the President. About one-third of all the divisions of the EOP since 1939 were established directly by an act of Congress. In most of these instances, the new staff unit was related specifically to new policies or programs incorporated in major legislation. The Council of Economic Advisers, for example, was devised as part of the Employment Act of 1946, which committed the government of the United States to a policy of maintaining full employment and gave the president broad responsibilities in the area of economic management. Among other things, the act required the president to report to Congress each year on the state of the economy and to make recommendations for implementing the policy goals of the legislation. The Council of Economic Advisers was to advise the president on the complex and technical issues of economic policy and to assist in the preparation of the annual Economic Report. The Office of Science and Technology Policy was also the direct production of legislation. It was mandated by the National Science and Technology Policy Organization and Priorities Act of 1976 to be a scientific think tank for the president, in much the same way as the Council of Economic Advisers functions as an economic policy think tank.

Congress has its best opportunity to stamp its mark on the Executive Office of the President when new divisions are established by statute. The complex and tortuous legislative process automatically subjects any institutional innovation to the pressures of a variety of interests, and the interest of the president is only one of several that Congress must take into account. Thus it is not surprising to learn that additions to the presidential staff system might well reflect the needs of Congress as much as the needs of the president. The creation of the Council of Economic Advisers illustrates this point nicely. Certainly this innovation was a recognition by Congress that expert economic analysis and advice had to be made available to presidents in view of their new economic policy responsibilities, but the way in which the council was structured as part of the Employment Act was also a reflection of congressional concern about the increasingly dominant role of the president in economic policy making. In part, the establishment of the council was an attempt to curb and counterbalance presidential power. By specifying that its members would be subject to Senate confirmation, by stipulating the necessary qualifications that its members should possess, and, by establishing a joint congressional committee that would oversee the work of the council, Congress hoped to broaden the scope of economic policy advice reaching the president and thus reverse the trend toward presidential supremacy in this important policy arena.[2] Similarly, the establishment of the National Security Council in 1947 has been interpreted by some as a congressional vote of no confidence in presidential management of national security during the war years.[3]

A second method by which new units have been established in the Executive Office of the President is through the presidential submission of a reorganization plan to Congress. This is done on the basis of a broad grant of reorganization authority delegated to the president by Congress in statute law, usually for a specified period and with conditions attached, which was how the EOP was set up in the first place. The Reorganization Act of 1939 gave President Roosevelt the *authority* to reorganize the executive branch, but the establishment of the original divisions of the EOP was achieved through Reorganization Plan No. 1 issued on the basis of that authority. When the reorganization authority has expired, the president must seek a renewal from Congress before any further reorganization plans can be submitted.

In the past, reorganization plans usually took effect after sixty days, unless Congress specifically disapproved of the president's submission, by either a concurrent resolution (a resolution passed by both houses) or a simple resolution (a resolution passed by one house), depending on the reorganization authority in force at the time.[4] President Roosevelt, for example, was given reorganization authority subject to a concurrent resolution of disapproval, whereas President Carter's reorganization authority was subject to a one-house resolution.

The reorganization plan procedure was an accommodation between the president and Congress. Presidents who wanted the authority to make organizational changes to the executive branch had to accept the conditions imposed by Congress and the ultimate power of veto by Congress, but what they got in return was a method of bypassing the regular legislative process, which meant that it was possible for their reorganization initiatives to take effect without having been considered by Congress at all. Because the reorganization authority did not require Congress to approve a reorganization plan—only to disapprove of it if it was so moved—it allowed presidents, in most cases, to restructure the Executive Office without subjecting the specifics of their plans to all the interests, pressures, bargaining, and compromising that the legislative process entails. Furthermore, even if Congress wanted to reject the plan, the president still had the advantage because the onus was on Congress to mobilize the necessary opposition within a relatively short period of time. Among the present divisions of the EOP, the Office of Management and Budget and the Office of Administration were both established through reorganization plans.

The accommodation between president and Congress over reorganization authority broke down in the 1980s as a result of a legal challenge to the constitutional validity of the disapproval mechanism contained in most of the authorizing legislation since 1939. Both the concurrent and simple disapproval resolutions are examples of what is more commonly known as the legislative veto, a practice the Supreme Court ruled to be unconstitutional in the *Chadha* decision of 1983.[5] To comply with the Supreme Court's ruling, Congress had to modify the arrangements regarding the reorganization authority it delegates to the president. In extending the reorganization authority to President Reagan in 1984, Congress changed the procedure so that a reorganization plan would take effect only when both houses *approved* of it by means of a joint resolution (a resolution that has to be signed by the president, or his veto of it overridden, before it becomes effective) within a ninety-day period. These new arrangements reverse the advantage that the reorganization plan device traditionally afforded presidents. Now, the president's proposals must be scrutinized in both houses of Congress under a time limit that imposes a tight deadline by which the president must win congressional approval. Under this procedure, there is no longer any incentive for presidents to seek reorganization authority because the regular legislative process at least avoids the ninety-day deadline. No presidential reorganization authority has been requested since the last expired in 1984.

About 40 percent of all the divisions of the EOP since 1939 have been established by executive order, much the easiest of the three devices from the president's point of view. An executive order is a presidential directive relating to the affairs of the executive branch and based on the president's constitutional authority as chief executive. The power to issue executive orders is not defined in the Constitution or in statute law. It is an implied power and, like most other implied presidential powers, has been stretched to its limits and even beyond.[6] In respect of the organization of the EOP, however, executive orders have been used most where there is already reasonably clear authority for creating new units or altering existing ones, or where there is tacit agreement between the president and Congress on the changes to be made. Executive orders can be overridden by statute law or challenged in the courts, but, so far, restructuring of the EOP by executive order has not been sufficiently controversial to generate those kinds of challenges. It is likely, however, that presidents who do wish to reorganize the EOP will now make greater use of the executive order to achieve their ends, given that the reorganization plan device is no longer a realistic option. It is interesting to note that President Clinton's first addition to the EOP—the National Economic Council—was established by executive order.

Each of the methods of establishing new units in the EOP can also be used to terminate older ones. Reorganization authority and the executive order, in particular, have given presidents a fairly efficient and effective tool with which to undo, without too much difficulty, the staffing structures initiated by their predecessors. They also allow occupants of the White House the opportunity to experiment with different staffing structures in the knowledge that they can just as easily terminate their own institutional initiatives without too much cost and without a prolonged battle with Congress.

THE EXPANSION OF THE EOP

The relative ease with which presidents have been able to restructure the Executive Office partially accounts for the expansion that has occurred there since 1939. If every organizational change to the EOP had to be subjected to the rigorous legislative process in Congress, then one might reasonably assume that far fewer units would have been added and presidents would have been less inclined to experiment with different staffing arrangements. Some presidents have been more prone to expanding the EOP than others. Six new divisions were created during the Truman administration, although not all of them at the initiative of the president. President Johnson added three new units and abolished none of those he had inherited, and when he left the White House, there were nine divisions in the EOP. By the end of President Nixon's term of office, there were fifteen. President Ford abolished a number of the Nixon agencies, but established six of his own during his short tenure and thus handed over fifteen divisions to his successor. President Reagan terminated two and created one, and two new divisions were established during the administration of President Bush. Presidents Eisenhower and Carter both reduced the total number of units during their presidencies, while President Kennedy maintained the same number as his predecessor. To date, President Clinton has established one new unit, changed the name of another, abolished two units, and failed in his efforts to abolish another because of opposition in Congress.[7]

The increase in the number of divisions within the Executive Office, particularly during the Johnson and Nixon years, was also accompanied by an increase in the number of personnel employed there. A report produced by the Post Office and Civil Service Committee of the House of Representatives in 1972 revealed that the number of employees in the EOP had risen from 1403 to 2236 between 1955 and 1972. This amounted to a 59 percent increase in the size of the presidential staff compared with a 19.2 percent growth rate in the departments and agencies during the same period. The report noted that almost half of that increase had occurred during the Nixon years.[8] Not all of the reported increase in EOP personnel was attributable to the creation of new divisions within the Executive Office because the most significant expansion took place in older, more established offices such as the White House Office, the Bureau of the Budget, and the staff of the National Security Council. According to the Post Office and Civil Service Committee's report, the size of the National Security Council staff trebled between 1955 and 1972, the number employed in the Bureau of the Budget rose from 435 to 684 during the same period, and the White House Office doubled in size during the Johnson to Nixon years alone.[9]

Other aspects of the expansion of the EOP also worried the House Post Office and Civil Service Committee. Its report noted that the annual salary bill for the presidential staff was increasing at a dramatic rate. In 1955 it stood at just under $10 million per annum. By 1973 the budget for EOP staff salaries was over $41 million and rising at an annual average rate of $4.45 million. The report also revealed that as the size of the staff increased, so did the number of senior positions in the EOP. Between 1955 and 1972, there was a 106 percent increase in the number of staff employed at the GS13–GS18 levels and a 175 percent increase in those on the executive-level pay scale.

In the post-Watergate literature on the presidency, much was made of the sheer size of the presidential staff, particularly the dramatic growth rate during the presidencies of Lyndon Johnson and Richard Nixon. Countless writers echoed Thomas Cronin's view that size, itself, was a major problem of the modern presidency and agreed with Stephen Hess that the prodigious growth of the presidential entourage was the most significant characteristic of the history of the EOP.[10] Critics of the expansion of the presidential staff system were given even more ammunition when it became apparent in the early 1970s that "official" figures seriously understated the real size of the Executive Office.

It was discovered, for example, that some EOP personnel were "detailed" to the presidential staff from the departments and agencies, and although they worked in the Executive Office, their salaries were paid out of the budget of the department from which they had been borrowed. This meant that they were officially counted as departmental staff and not EOP staff. There was, of course, nothing new in the practice of detailing personnel to work in the White House. As was pointed out in the previous chapter, the practice appears to have started way back in Andrew Jackson's time, but, like many other established practices, this one took on a more sinister aspect during the Watergate period. It was also discovered that some members of the presidential staff were paid for, not from the regular EOP staffing budget, but from a variety of little known and little understood special funds that had been allocated to the president during the 1940s and 1950s.[11] This, too, was a method of hiding a large number of presidential aides from the official personnel count and came to be regarded as another dubious practice at the time of Watergate.

Not surprisingly, there was some confusion about just how large the Executive Office of the President had become by President Nixon's period in the White House. Totals very much depended on which set of statistics were used. The House Post Office and Civil Service Committee report based its calculations on the number of permanent staff positions as given in the regular EOP budget. It arrived at a figure of 1766 for fiscal year 1970. Yet, data published in the *Congressional Record* just two months after the committee's report was issued, derived from U.S. Civil Service Commission statistics, reported that 4265 people were employed in the EOP during 1970.[12] A second report from the House Post Office and Civil Service Committee, prepared six years later by the staff of the Congressional Research Service, calculated the "actual manpower" of the EOP for 1970 to be 4806.[13]

Calculating the real size of the Executive Office in terms of manpower has always been, and remains, a difficult task. We return to this problem in the next chapter in the context of the White House Office, the particular division of the EOP to which much of the concern about size was directed. But, whether there were 1766 or 4806 people employed in the EOP in 1970, a remarkable unanimity existed among post-Watergate critics that, whatever statistics were used, the size of the EOP was big, that it had expanded too much, and, some thought, that its growth had become uncontrollable.

There is no doubt that that the Executive Office of the president has expanded since 1939 and that the expansion during the Johnson and Nixon years appeared to be particularly dramatic, but there is some debate about whether the Watergate-induced focus on the Johnson and Nixon periods has distorted the developmental history of the EOP. John Helmer, for one, has argued vigorously that too much has been made of the expansion of the EOP under Nixon. His view is that a number of the Nixon additions to the Executive Office, like the Council for Urban Affairs, the Council for Rural Affairs, and the Office of Intergovernmental Relations, were small, cheap, and short-lived operations; that others, like the Council on Environmental Quality and the Council on International Economic Policy, were placed in the EOP against President Nixon's wishes; and that, in budgetary and manpower terms, the expansion during the Nixon years accounts for a very small percentage of the size of the Executive Office.[14]

Helmer's perspective on the expansion of the EOP is a useful one. He urges those discussing the growth of the presidential staff to focus particularly on the White House Office and the Office of Management and Budget, which have accounted for a significant share of the overall expansion of the EOP. (In fact, 60 percent of the total personnel in the EOP is employed in these two units alone, which also take over 55 percent of the total funding for the EOP; see table 3.1). These, Helmer suggested, are qualitatively far more significant than the sheer quantity of new units or aggregate manpower. Helmer also pointed out that during the 1970s, the growth of the EOP, as measured by budgetary outlays, was significantly lower than the rate of staff growth in some executive branch departments (he singled out Transportation, Labor, and Commerce), and much lower than the rate of staff growth in Congress. His point is that, in many respects, the expansion of the EOP has been quite modest relative to comparable political bodies.[15]

Just as there is some debate about the extent of the expansion of the Executive Office of the President, so commentators are also now beginning to argue about the causes of the enlargement of the EOP. Little had been written on this subject before the Watergate-generated concern over the growth of the presidential staff, but, since then, various attempts to identify the expansionary pressures on the EOP have undoubtedly added to our understanding of the institution. Initially, explanations for the expansion of the presidential staff were cast in terms of broad and very significant developments within the American political system that had occurred since World War II. The best-known exponent of this type of explanation was Thomas Cronin, whose ideas are worth reviewing here.[16]

The most significant factor in the expansion of the presidential staff, Cronin claims, was "the accretion of new presidential roles during national emergencies." Congress and the public have turned to the president in times of crisis, and presidents have tended to respond by increasing the presidential staff to deal with such emergencies. Cronin cites as examples the addition of science advisers to the EOP following the Soviet Union's successful entry into space with the launching of Sputnik in 1957 and the increase in the national security staff by President Kennedy after the Bay of Pigs fiasco in 1961. There are other examples. The Council of Economic Advisers was an institutional response to the massive levels of unemployment during the Great Depression, and the National Security Council was a response to the crisis of the Cold War.

A second explanation for the growth of the presidential staff, in Cronin's view, has been "the belief that critical societal problems require that wise men be assigned to the White House to advise ... on appropriate solutions and to serve as agents for implementing them." He notes that Congress often acts on the basis of this belief and now insists on more and more technical information from the president on these critical problems. Such an explanation implicitly recognizes the growing complexity of public policy as a cause of presidential staff growth in the postwar years and the

TABLE 3.1.
EXECUTIVE OFFICE OF THE PRESIDENT:
BUDGET AND PERSONNEL, 1994

Division	Budget for F.Y. 1994		Staffing level as of 1 Oct. 1994	
	In dollars	% of total	Number	% of total
Office of Management & Budget	$56,539,000	(32.8)	572	(34.0)
White House Office	$38,754,000	(22.5)	430	(25.5)
Office of Administration[a]	$25,010,000	(14.4)	189	(11.2)
Office of U.S. Trade Representative	$20,600,000	(11.9)	191	(11.3)
Office of National Drug Control Policy	$11,687,000	(6.8)	25	(1.4)
National Security Council	$6,648,000	(3.9)	147	(8.7)
Office of Policy Development[b]	$5,122,000	(3.0)	50	(3.0)
Office of Science & Technology Policy	$4,450,000	(2.6)	46	(2.7)
Council of Economic Advisers	$3,420,000	(2.0)	35	(2.1)
Council on Environmental Quality[c]	$375,000	(0.2)	0	(0.0)
Total	$172,596,000		1685	

SOURCES: Budget totals from *Treasury, Postal Service, and General Government Appropriations Act, 1994* (Public Law 103-123); *Departments of Commerce, Justice, and State, the Judiciary, and Related Agencies Appropriations Act, 1994* (Public Law 103-121); *Departments of Veterans Affairs and Housing and Urban Development and Independent Agencies Appropriations Act, 1994* (Public Law 103-124). Staffing totals are based on the Clinton administration's estimated number of staff as of 1 October 1994. They include all detailees, assignees, interns, and White House Fellows. See U.S. House of Representatives, Committee on Appropriations, 103d Cong., 1st sess., *Treasury, Postal Service and General Government Appropriations for Fiscal Year 1994, Part 3* (Washington, D.C.: Government Printing Office, 1993), 482.

a. The appropriation for the Office of Administration includes $160,000 for the Office of National Service, a newly created section within OA.

b. The appropriation and staffing levels for the Office of Policy Development cover the National Economic Council, the Domestic Policy Council, and the Office of Environmental Policy (a section within the White House Office).

c. The Clinton administration intended to abolish the Council on Environmental Quality so no provision was made for staff in its estimated staffing total for 1 October 1994. Congress refused to abolish CEQ and voted a small appropriation to keep it in existence through 1994, which allowed CEQ up to seven staff positions.

fact that the president of the United States can no longer be a master of all trades.

A third cause of staff growth identified by Cronin is the general abdication of responsibility by Congress for critical decision making. Thus presidents acquire additional responsibilities by default, and that, too, generates a need for more staff in the Executive Office.

The complexity of public policy and the growth of government in the twentieth century are other underlying reasons for the increase in the size of the presidential staff. The task of controlling and coordinating policies and programs, where more than one, and sometimes many, departments and agencies have an interest, can no longer be left to the departments or even to the Cabinet. Coordination has to be done at the highest level, hence more presidential staff.

Cronin also points to the deep suspicion and distrust of the permanent bureaucracy by occupants of the White House. From the presidential vantage point, this permanent government in Washington is often perceived to be hostile to presidential leadership, and so presidents respond by expanding their own staffs to do what the departments and agencies ought to be doing in the first instance.

Finally, Cronin sees "the addition of interest-group brokerage to the more traditional staff activities" as an important cause of the expansion of the presidential staff. This was a response to increasing demands from key interests in the 1960s and 1970s for greater access to presidential attention. Indeed, as Cronin noted, "it now appears essential to interest groups to have their own man (or woman) right there in the White House."

Stephen Hess, another noted contributor to the post-Watergate debate on the presidency, offers a similar, but even broader, explanation for the growth of the presidential staff. He points to increased U.S. participation in international affairs since World War II, an expanded concept of the role of the government in society, the failure of state and local governments to respond to the legitimate needs of the people and the consequent shift of responsibilities to the federal government, popular support for an increasingly activist concept of the presidency, complicated interrelationships among government programs, new offices in the EOP imposed by Congress, and dissatisfaction on the part of the White House with the performance of existing departments and agencies.[17]

The causal factors identified by Cronin and Hess at once make it clear that the expansion of the Executive Office of the President has been brought about by a myriad of complex forces beyond the total control of any one individual or institution and reflects profound changes in the nature of American politics during the twentieth century. For that reason, the growth of the presidential staff cannot simply be blamed on successive presidents or on presidents and Congress combined. This, of course, has important implications for those who felt that, in the aftermath of Watergate, there was an urgent need to reverse this expansion and reduce the size of the Executive Office.

Such explanations, however, are not altogether satisfactory. They are very generalized, and they do tend to understate the involvement of the president and the Congress in the expansion of the EOP since 1939. They also sit uneasily with developments in presidential staffing during the post-Watergate period, when there have been periods of contraction in the size of the EOP. Although it is impossible to be precise about how many people are employed on the presidential staff, there have been reductions from the peak of the Nixon years, yet few, if any, of the expansionary forces described by Cronin and Hess have disappeared from the American political scene. This does seem to suggest that either there are limits to the impact of such forces or other broad pressures have compelled some presidents to reduce the size of their staffs. Alternatively, it could indicate that presidents can reduce the size of the presidential staff by choice. President Clinton's announced reduction of 350 staff positions in just his third week in office, for example was motivated not by any external pressure but by his own desire to send a symbolic message to the American public as part of his overall attempt to reduce the budget deficit.[18]

Attempts have been made to explain the expansion of the EOP in less sweeping terms than Cronin or Hess have used. John Helmer, for instance, identifies four main sources of EOP growth, placing greater emphasis than either Cronin or Hess on the roles of the president and Congress. The first source, Helmer claims, has been the president's desire to have a highly visible base for launching, coordinating, and implementing his policy initiatives. Second, the EOP has grown because Congress wanted and insisted on particular new units at the center of power. The third cause of growth, according to Helmer, has been the president's judgment of the resources needed to mobilize public opinion and wage campaigns for reelection. Finally, Helmer points to the growth of the federal budget as a source of the growth of the EOP because, he says, it is reasonable to link the size of the federal budget to the size of the Office of Management and Budget, the largest single agency in the Executive Office.[19]

Helmer views the growth of the EOP from a different perspective than that of Cronin and Hess and places less emphasis on the broad causal factors they have identified. Another contributor to the discussion, Hugh Heclo, has attempted to narrow the explanation even further by arguing that the growth of the Executive Office has ultimately depended on what would be countenanced by Congress. He believes that presidential attempts to improve coordination of the executive branch have been accepted only because they satisfy the needs of Congress and that any presidential management device that fails to meet this test is doomed to extinction.[20]

There is one further perspective that ought to be considered, and this involves a shift from very general explanations to highly specific ones. Given that the Executive Office of the President is a large and very complex institution, composed of many functionally specialized units, some of which have existed over a long period, it is not unreasonable to assume that different and particular factors have contributed to the development and expansion of the various component parts of the EOP and that what applies to one specific area of activity does not necessarily apply to all. Stephen Hess recognizes this when he moves from the general to the particular in discussing President Kennedy's expansion of the Executive Office. He notes, for example, that some growth in the EOP under Kennedy was caused by the need to find a face-saving position for an official who had been removed from another post, the need to find a useful activity for the vice president, and the need to satisfy the personal interest of the president's wife in the arts.[21] This author's own study of the expansion of the congressional liaison staff, an important division of the White House Office, at the beginning of the Kennedy administration also suggests that the causes of presidential staff growth cannot be explained satisfactorily without detailing a very specific set of circumstances and conditions relating to a particular area of responsibility at a particular time.[22]

Identifying the causes of presidential staff growth helps us to understand the role of the Executive Office of the President in modern times, but it is only part of the story. The forces that have been responsible for the establishment of staff units in the EOP are not necessarily those that sustain the particular staff function or determine how staff is utilized by successive presidents. There may well be limitations on a president's ability to restructure his Executive Office, and Congress might well give him the kind of staff he would prefer not to have. But the president does have considerable freedom to use the component parts of the EOP in the manner he chooses, irrespective of the reason they were ordained in the first place, especially if he wants to ignore them. Different presidents have used the EOP in different ways. A division of the Executive Office, like the Council of Economic Advisers for example, might be at the very center of presidential decision making, as it was during the Kennedy and Johnson administrations, and then find itself virtually ignored, as it was during the Reagan years. The development of the EOP, then, is not just a history of growth and expansion in size but also a history of experimentation in presidential decision making reflecting a variety of styles, approaches, and purposes over more than fifty years as determined by eleven dissimilar presidents. For that reason, we must now examine the dynamic nature and function of the Executive Office.

THE NATURE AND FUNCTION OF THE EXECUTIVE OFFICE

The complexity of the institution, the varying importance of its component parts, and the diverse areas in which the presidential staff work make it very difficult to generalize about the nature of the Executive Office; nevertheless, some generalizations about its development can be made.

First, the EOP now operates in a far broader range of areas than the Brownlow Committee had originally planned. Brownlow's proposed Executive Office was designed as a tool to aid the president in personnel management, fiscal management, and resource management. Personnel management has never been a major function of the EOP, resource management was given short shrift by Congress, and the work of the presidential staff today goes beyond fiscal management.

Second, whereas Brownlow's Executive Office was intended to be an agency for centralized administrative management essentially concerned with coordination tasks, today's EOP is very much involved in policy advice, policy making, policy implementation, and political strategy, as well as in coordination of executive branch activities. *Management,* except perhaps in the broadest application of the term, is an inadequate description of what is actually done in the present-day Executive Office of the President.

Third, because its concerns extend across the whole spectrum of public policy, the work of the Executive Office necessarily overlaps, second-guesses, and often conflicts with the work done in the departments and agencies. This, together with the budgetary control exercised by the Office of Management and Budget over the departments and agencies, is the principal source of the adversarial relationship between the presidential branch and the executive branch.

Fourth, as the Executive Office has developed, so the White House Office has become the directing force and the most powerful division within the EOP. To a great extent, the major Executive Office units operate as satellites of the White House Office, with key political appointees directing the work of the various staffs. One consequence of this has been that the distinction made in the Brownlow report between an institutional staff for the presidency and the president's personal staff has been somewhat eroded over the years.

As with most large and complex institutions, the principal functions of the Executive Office of the President do not correspond exactly to neat little boxes on organizational charts. There is some overlapping of responsibilities among the various units of the EOP and a necessary degree of cooperation among them on particular issues, so, rather than focus exclusively on each compartmentalized division, this and the next chapter explore the nature of the Executive Office under eight broad headings corresponding to the major areas in which the EOP staff operates: economic policy, national security policy, budgeting and management, domestic policy, science and technology policy, trade policy, operations and administration, and political strategy. This approach allows us to take into account various attempts to develop and experiment with different staff structures in each of these particular areas throughout the history of the EOP, which would not be possible if we confined our survey to the present offices.

Economic Policy

Advising the president on economic policy presents a major challenge to the presidential staff system. Not only must coherence emerge from the fragmentation of economic policy responsibilities between the various divisions of the EOP, but the EOP must also coordinate the input from the large number of departments and agencies whose views on economic issues have to be taken into account. Since 1939, a variety of different staff structures have been utilized by presidents to help them cope with economic policy,[23] but no president seems to have discovered a system that his successor has found entirely adequate and satisfactory. Perhaps the only generalization one can make about the pattern of economic policy advice to presidents over the past five decades is that there has been no pattern. It has all very much depended on the mode of operation of each particular occupant of the White House.

Formally, the principal source of economic advice to all presidents from Harry Truman to George Bush was the Council of Economic Advisers because it was the only unit within the EOP that had a charter to be, in the words of an early CEA chairman, Leon Keyserling, "an overall general economic advisory staff."[24] The council was established under Section 4 of the Employment Act of 1946.[25] Its statutory duties are (1) to assist and advise the president in the preparation of the economic report he is required to transmit to Congress at the beginning of each regular session; (2) to collect and analyze economic data in the light of the policy objectives of the Employment Act; (3) to monitor federal government programs to determine whether they are consistent with full-employment policy objectives; (4) to recommend to the president national economic policies to promote free competition, to avoid economic instability and to maintain employment, production, and purchasing power; and (5) to provide the president with whatever advice he requests.

The Council of Economic Advisers is composed of three members appointed by the president with the advice and consent of the Senate. The Employment Act specifically requires that appointees be recruited from among those who are "exceptionally qualified" by virtue of their "training, experience and attainments" to analyze economic developments, appraise government programs, and recommend national economic policy. In practice, "exceptionally qualified" has meant a proven record in academia. Of the thirty-two members who served on the council from 1946 to 1976, all but three held economics Ph.D.s, and all but four came to the council from university posts.[26] The three members of the council also have the support of a small staff, consisting mainly of younger academic economists who serve a short stint with the council and who are supplemented by a few part-time consultants.

The requirement that members of the CEA be distinguished professional economists implied, to some observers at least, that the council was meant to dispense advice to the president in a thoroughly detached, objective, scientific, and nonpolitical manner, a view shared by its first chairman, Edwin G. Nourse. In his letter to President Truman accepting the appointment as chairman, Nourse described the council as "a scientific agency of the Federal Government" whose "prime function is to bring the best available methods of social science to the service of the Chief Executive and of Congress." He went on to say that there would be "no occasion for the Council to become involved in any way in the advocacy of particular measures or in the rival beliefs and struggles of different economic and political interest groups."[27] Experience was to prove that this was not the most appropriate conception of the council's role if it were to be an effective presidential advisory body. Professional experts would need to come to terms with the political context in which economic policy is made. As Walter Heller, chairman of the CEA under Presidents Kennedy and Johnson, once remarked, "the detached, Olympian, take-it-or-leave-it approach to presidential economic advice—the dream of the logical positivist—simply does not accord with the demands of relevance and realism and the requirements of the Employment Act."[28]

The success of the Council of Economic Advisers ultimately rests above all else on its relationship with the president. The council has no client other than the president, it has no operational responsibilities, and it does not usually act as a coordinating body within the economic policy-making machinery of government. Its sole commodity is the expert advice it can offer a president, and in making that commodity available it has to compete with a host of other staff units, departments, agencies, and interagency committees for presidential attention. As Edward Flash concluded in his major study of the CEA under Truman, Eisenhower, and Kennedy, the council's powers "have been so transitory, peripheral and intangible that ... its competitive position has been consistently weak."[29] Consequently, the most effective councils have been those that have tempered their advice and their methods of operating to what seemed to have a reasonable chance of acceptance. "The Council's access to the President is potential, not guaranteed," wrote Walter Heller. "Unless personalities click; unless the economic adviser is both right and relevant; unless he gets off his academic high horse without falling obsequiously to the ground—his usefulness will be limited and his state of proximity to the president will gradually wither away."[30]

Members of the council and its staff must constantly tread the fine line between expert advice and political reality. Some have failed in this endeavor, and, as a result, the history of the council has been a very mixed one. It got off to an inauspicious start under Nourse's leadership when it quickly gained a reputation for its internal discord and its distant relationship with President Truman.[31] Nourse complained bitterly in his memoirs about Truman's attitude toward the council and about the impossibility of securing an effective intellectual relationship with the president, charges that have been strenuously denied by the vice chairman of the Nourse council, Leon Keyserling.[32] Keyserling succeeded to the chairmanship when Nourse resigned in 1949 and thereupon launched a more active, aggressive, and effective phase in the council's life. Keyserling firmly believed in policy advocacy, was more aware than his predecessor of the competitive situation in which the council operated, and was more politically in tune with the general policy orientation of the Truman administration. Keyserling was a vigorous and consistent advocate of expansion economics, although this was an approach the administration was less willing to accommodate once the Korean war became a significant factor in economic policy making.[33]

The fragmentation of economic policy staff work within the EOP was evident even in Truman's time. From its beginnings, the Council of Economic Advisers had to relate to the Bureau of the Budget, the National Security Council, the now defunct National Security Resources Board and its successor, the Office of Defense Mobilization, which President Truman established in 1950 to coordinate the mobilization program for the Korean war. During the Truman years there was substantial "interpenetration" among EOP agencies, according to two members of the CEA staff, Bertram Gross and John Lewis, "and the desirability of structural reorganization was a subject of recurring speculation." But Gross and Lewis also point out that the overlap in the economic policy arena was "much less extensive than is often supposed" and, "in the degree to which it existed, often made for a more balanced net appraisal of a problem than if it had been analyzed exclusively within a budgetary, national security, or economic perspective."[34]

Notwithstanding its brief period of effectiveness under Keyserling before the outbreak of the Korean war, the continued existence of the CEA was very uncertain by the end of the Truman administration. The Hoover Commission on the organization of the executive branch, which reported in 1949, had little sympathy with this particular form of economic advice to the president. The well-publicized internal disagreements, particularly during the Nourse years, had obviously colored the commission's view of the short history of the CEA, and it recommended abolishing the council and replacing it with a single economic adviser.[35] Criticism also extended beyond the Hoover Commission. Keyserling came to be regarded by some as too political, and his brand of Keynesian economics was unpopular with a number of Republicans in Congress. The Republican-controlled 80th Congress drastically slashed the council's budget for two successive fiscal years—one of the rare occasions when Congress has seriously interfered with presidential staff agency budgets—and so arranged things that funding would run out on 1 March 1953.[36] It was a tempting invitation for incoming President Eisenhower to abolish the council permanently.

Eisenhower resisted that temptation in spite of the feelings of some Republican leaders in Congress. Instead, he revived the council, mainly at the insistence of Gabriel Hauge, whom the president had appointed his personal economic adviser in the White House Office.[37] Hauge was also responsible for recommending the appointment of Dr. Arthur Burns, who formally took up his position of chairman of the Council of Economic Advisers once congressional funding for the council had been restored.

With the revival of the council came reform. On 1 June 1953, President Eisenhower sent a special message to Congress accompanying Reorganization Plan No. 9, which was designed to strengthen the internal administration of the council and improve its relationship with the president.[38] This was achieved simply by transferring the functions vested in the council to the chairman of the council, so that the chairman would be responsible for the council's operations, including its staff, and he, not the council as a whole, would communicate with the president. The reforms were intended to avoid any repetition of the troubles that dogged the council in its early years under Truman when the three members were coequals. The position of vice chairman was abolished, and President Eisenhower recommended that the chairman's compensation be increased to take account of his additional responsibilities.

One of those additional responsibilities was to chair a new body, the Advisory Board on Economic Growth and Stability, foreshadowed in Eisenhower's message to Congress in June 1953. The board formalized the council's liaison with other EOP divisions and with the economic departments and relevant regulatory agencies outside the EOP. It had no coordinating function. Its purpose, according to the president, was to keep him "closely informed about the state of the national economy and the various measures necessary to aid in maintaining a stable prosperity."[39] In that sense, the board was little more than an extension of the Council of Economic Advisers and an attempt to achieve better integration of economic advice to the president. It was the brainchild of Arthur Burns and effectively ceased to exist when Burns left the council at the end of 1956, but it was a forerunner of subsequent attempts in future administrations to deal with the same problem.

Apart from reviving the Council of Economic Advisers, Eisenhower's most important addition to the economic machinery of the EOP was the appointment of Gabriel Hauge as a special assistant for economic affairs, the first time this responsibility had been designated within the White House Office. Obviously, such an appointment set up potential conflict between the special assistant and the chairman of the CEA, but that never materialized in the Eisenhower administration. Hauge was essentially an economic troubleshooter for the president, rather than an economic analyst like Burns, and the relationship between the two men was a complementary one.[40] Perhaps one reason for the harmony between Burns and Hauge was that neither had responsibility for coordinating the economic machinery of the EOP, but some of Eisenhower's successors, particularly Nixon and Ford, were attracted to the idea of a White House economic assistant who would be a coordinator or process manager, doing for economic policy what the national security assistant did for national security policy.[41] President Clinton was not only attracted to the idea of having an economic policy assistant in the White House, he also wanted to replicate the National Security Council in this policy area and did so just five days after taking office when he signed Executive Order 12835 establishing the National Economic Council.

The Council of Economic Advisers functioned effectively during the Eisenhower years, notably in dealing with the economic recession of 1953 and 1954.[42] Burns, and his successor as chairman, Raymond Saulnier, maintained a lower profile than Keyserling had done in the Truman administration and advocated a more conservative position in keeping with their own and the administration's conservative economic philosophy. Burns, in particular, seems to have had a better appreciation than Keyserling of the constraints on the role of the economic adviser in an expanding Executive Office and has been credited with rehabilitating the role of economists in government.[43]

President Eisenhower saved the Council of Economic Advisers from early extinction, but Presidents Kennedy and Johnson witnessed its halcyon days. Neither before nor since has the council played such a significant role in economic policy making in the United States. It was "the most important single creative force in the development of a new approach to economic policy," claims Flash,[44] and had a profound effect on the economic thinking of both presidents.

When President Kennedy announced the nomination of Walter Heller to be chairman of the council, he spoke of the need for the council "to return to the spirit as well as the letter of the Employment Act" and said that he expected the CEA "to take its place as a key element within the presidential office."[45] But, it must be doubted that even Kennedy foresaw at the time the degree to which Heller and his colleagues would fulfill their mandate.

The economic record of the Kennedy administration has been well documented, and there is no dispute about the crucial part played by the Heller CEA in bringing what has been called "the new economics" into the White House.[46] The CEA was instrumental in a number of major initiatives during the Kennedy and Johnson years, especially the tax cut that President Kennedy announced during his State of the Union message of January 1963. Concluding his study of the CEA under Kennedy, Flash isolates four fundamental reasons for the council's impact on the policy-making process. First, the state of the economy, particularly the uncertainty of the economic recovery begun in 1961, strengthened the force of the council's arguments and gave them an added sense of urgency. Second, President Kennedy established a harmonious relationship with the council and was educable and receptive to the council's views. Third, Heller maintained excellent relations with

Douglas Dillon, the secretary of the treasury, despite the very different economic views held by Dillon. The council and its staff also worked "in a spirit of rapport and mutual assistance" with the Treasury, the Bureau of the Budget, and the Federal Reserve Board. Fourth, the council and its staff were strong; it was well-led, aggressive, hardworking, and productive. In short, says Flash, "the Heller Council was in harmony with its times."[47]

The effectiveness of Heller and his colleagues did not imply that competition for the president's attention during the Kennedy-Johnson years was any less than it had been in previous administrations. The Council of Economic Advisers was not the only EOP agency to be revitalized under Kennedy. The Bureau of the Budget also took on a new appearance after 1961, and its director was to play a much more more substantial role in the making of economic policy than ever before. The National Security Council's role in foreign economic policy issues was also strengthened under Kennedy by the appointments of Carl Kaysen and Francis Bator to the NSC staff. These two were to become key White House staffers on such issues as the balance of payments, trade negotiations, foreign aid, and international monetary problems.[48] Then there were Theodore Sorensen and his two assistants, Lee White and Myer Feldman, in the White House Office. They covered a broad range of economic issues by virtue of their responsibilities for translating policy proposals into concrete programs. In addition to the above, President Kennedy also created within the White House Office the position of Special Representative for Trade Negotiations in January 1963, following the passage of the Trade Expansion Act in 1962.

Coordination of economic policy advice during the Kennedy administration was done very informally, in keeping with Kennedy's preference for a less structured style of operation. The principal coordinating machinery was a body popularly known as "the Troika," consisting of the chairman of the Council of Economic Advisers, the secretary of the treasury, and the director of the Bureau of the Budget. Under President Johnson, it was expanded to include the chairman of the Federal Reserve and became known as "the Quadriad." But the essence of successful coordination of economic policy advice in the EOP during the Kennedy years was to be found not in structures, formal or informal, but in the individuals who were occupying the key positions. Their compatibility made coordination possible, without which no structure, however informal, would have been able to integrate the views of these key officials. David Bell, director of the Bureau of the Budget for the first two years of the Kennedy administration, pinpointed the secret of success:

> We had in those days an extraordinarily easy situation. We were all very much heirs of the post-war policy worked out largely under Mr. Truman. We all carried those ideas forward. Furthermore, we were a group that was

extremely compatible. You could almost say by hindsight that we were too similar. The group in the White House—principally Sorensen, Feldman, and Lee White on the domestic side and Bundy and Kaysen on the international side, the group in the Council of Economic Advisers, which was Heller, Tobin, and Kermit Gordon to begin with, myself and Bob Turner and Ken Hansen in the Budget Bureau—you could almost switch any of these people around to any of the other jobs in that set of related responsibilities and hardly miss a stitch.[49]

The combination of conditions that permitted the Council of Economic Advisers to operate as it did during the Kennedy and Johnson years has not recurred, and the council has declined in influence since the Nixon administration, reaching its nadir under President Reagan, who, it was reported, seriously considered abolishing it at the end of his first term.[50] In fact, from the Nixon administration onward, there have been a remarkable number of additional presidential structures concerned with economic policy making and a variety of experiments with economic policy coordinating machinery within and outside the Executive Office of the President. One consequence is that the Council of Economic Advisers has faced much greater in-house competition for the president's attention than it did in the pre-Nixon days.

One of the new Nixon staff units competing with the Council of Economic Advisers was the Domestic Council, established in 1970 and intended as a domestic policy equivalent of the National Security Council. The Domestic Council's membership consisted of the heads of the domestic policy departments and key EOP officials. A staff, initially of around fifty, formally assisted the council, but the council itself quickly became the formality, leaving a larger and more structured domestic policy staff working for the president in the EOP. President Carter dispensed with the pretense of collegiality, redesignating the council as the Domestic Policy Staff. President Reagan changed its name yet again to the Office of Policy Development, and President Clinton returned to something like the original Nixon model when he opted for a Domestic Policy Council. Irrespective of the changes of name, there has now been a large staff unit in the EOP operating in the domestic policy arena for more than twenty years, and given the impossibility of separating economic policy from domestic policy, it is hardly surprising that the domestic policy staff gets involved in economic policy. During the Carter years, that involvement was extensive. To some Treasury officials, the Carter Domestic Policy Staff was overinvolved and overextended in economic issues, particularly in the 1978 tax-reform program. This seriously undercut the authority of Secretary of the Treasury Michael Blumenthal, and stories of bitter conflict between Blumenthal and Carter's domestic policy assistant, Stuart Eizenstat, were widespread at the time.[51]

Another Nixon innovation was the establishment of a Council on International Economic Policy in January 1971.[52] This body consisted of the secretaries of state, treasury, agriculture, commerce, and labor, together with the director of the Office of Management and Budget, the chairman of the Council of Economic Advisers, the assistant to the president for national security affairs, the executive director of the Domestic Council, and the special representative for trade negotiations. It had a broad mandate in the field of international economic policy and responsibility for ensuring consistency between foreign and domestic economic policies. The Council on International Economic Policy was given a secretariat, headed by an assistant to the president, and, like most of the Nixon-created EOP units, the staff rapidly grew in size. By the time Nixon left office in August 1974, the staff was as large as that of the Council of Economic Advisers. The Council on International Economic Policy existed alongside a Cabinet committee on economic policy during the Nixon administration, but neither body functioned to the satisfaction of the president; as his administration progressed, he turned toward individuals, rather than councils or committees, to coordinate economic policy.[53]

Secretary of the Treasury John Connally was the first economic overload in the Nixon administration and was succeeded by George Shultz in 1972. Shultz created a precedent in the history of the presidential staff when Nixon made him assistant to the president for economic affairs in addition to his position as secretary of the treasury; he thus became the first White House aide also to head a department.

Shultz's control over economic affairs was reinforced in January 1973 when President Nixon announced a new command structure in the White House so that responsibility for all executive branch policy making would be channeled through five assistants to the president, of whom Shultz was one.[54] This scheme represented the ultimate in centralizing power in the White House staff and the furthest any president has gone in coordinating the diffuse economic policy machinery of the Executive Office. But it is difficult to assess its impact. Within four months of Nixon's announcement of his reorganization scheme, two of the five presidential assistants, H.R. Haldeman and John Ehrlichman, were forced to resign over their part in Watergate, and the new command structure effectively collapsed as President Nixon spent the next year and a half preoccupied with the Watergate crisis. Schultz eventually became discouraged by the state of the economy and disillusioned with Nixon's handling of Watergate. He left the government early in 1974, pleading exhaustion.[55] For the remainder of the Nixon administration, the posts of assistant for economic affairs and secretary of the treasury were in separate hands.

Whether or not economic policy coordination by one person worked for President Nixon, it certainly had little appeal for President Ford, who had been urged by his advisers to restore policy-making responsibility to the heads of executive branch departments. Ford's contribution to the art of rationalizing the economic policy machinery was to return to a more collegial approach by establishing the Economic Policy Board (EPB) in September 1974. The board was made responsible for providing advice to the president on all aspects of domestic and international economic policy and for the formulation, coordination, and implementation of all economic policy. It was to serve as "the focal point for economic policy decision making."[56] The board was chaired by Secretary of the Treasury William Simon, who was designated principal spokesman for the executive branch on matters of economic policy. It was also given an executive director, the president's assistant for economic affairs, William Seidman, who was to be responsible for coordinating the implementation of economic policy and to serve as deputy chairman of the board. The membership of the board consisted of the secretaries of all the departments, except Defense and Justice, together with the director of the Office of Management and Budget, the chairman of the Council of Economic Advisers, and the executive director of the Council on International Economic Policy.

The Economic Policy Board was in keeping with the post-Watergate spirit in that it attempted to restore to the departments, and their heads, a meaningful role in the policy-making process, but it did not constitute a complete rejection of previous staffing tendencies. Even though the EPB was not formally part of the Executive Office, key EOP staff maintained control over the board by dominating its executive committee. The full board was considered inappropriate as a forum for dealing with the great majority of economic policy issues because of its size, said Porter.[57] An executive committee was established and met almost daily, but apart from the secretary of the treasury, its membership was entirely EOP personnel until it was expanded a year later to include the secretaries of state, commerce, and labor.

The significance of President Ford's Economic Policy Board was that it consolidated responsibility for all economic policy into one body.[58] Within that body, however, there was an important division of responsibility between the chairman (policy advice and formulation) and the executive director (policy coordination), and much would depend on the working relationship between the two.[59] Opinion from insiders, at least, was that the relationship worked reasonably well. In his important study of the board, Roger Porter, then a member of the EPB's secretariat, claimed that the good relationship enhanced the quality of the decision-making process, it strengthened the president's influence and presence throughout the executive branch, it provided an open system of policy advice that exposed the competing arguments and viewpoints, it established a reasonable degree of consistency among policies on related issues, it encouraged a sense of collective responsibility for broad economic advice among board members, and it helped to remove any justification for reopening and reversing decisions after they had been considered by the board. In short, the operation of the Economic Policy Board fitted a multiple-advocacy model of presidential decision making, with the executive director and the staff committed to the role of honest broker.[60] President Ford described the board as "the most important innovation of my administration," and Porter's own conclusion was that the EPB represented "the most sustained, comprehensive, successful collegial attempt ever to advise a president on economic policy."[61]

Another addition to the economic policy machinery of the EOP during the Ford administration was the Council on Wage and Price Stability, established by Congress two weeks after President Ford took office. In essence its responsibility was to monitor inflationary pressures in the American economy, such as wages, costs, profits, and prices. It was an institutional response to the high rate of inflation in the 1970s, in much the same way as the Council of Economic Advisers was a response to the high levels of unemployment in the 1930s. The Council on Wage and Price Stability survived the transition to the Carter administration, but was eventually pushed into the background when President Carter appointed a White House adviser on inflation in 1978. The new presidential adviser took over the chairmanship of the council from the chairman of the Council of Economic Advisers and he, rather than the council, became the principal spokesman on inflation. The impact of the Council on Wage and Price Stability was slight, but it did provide a vehicle for adding a vast number of additional staff to the EOP payroll.[62]

By the end of Gerald Ford's presidency, the economic policy structure in the Executive Office was fairly specialized. The Office of Management and Budget was primarily concerned with budgetary policy. The Council of Economic Advisers looked at macroeconomic issues and took responsibility for economic forecasting and analysis. Inflation was the preserve of the Council on Wage and Price Stability. Foreign economic issues were handled by the Council on International Economic Policy, and trade policy got a voice of its own in the form of the Office of Special Representative for Trade Negotiations, which was formally established as a division of the EOP in 1974. The Domestic Council staff, the National Security Council staff, and the president's political advisers in the White House Office also had an input into the economic policy-making process. Inevitably, in such a fragmented structure, there were overlapping responsibilities, duplication, and conflict, all to be minimized by the pivotal body, the Economic Policy Board.

President Carter promptly abolished the pivot, along with the Council on International Economic Policy. The staff of the National Security Council became an important focus for foreign economic policy advice,[63] but there was no effective equivalent to the Economic Policy Board in the Carter administration. The Board was replaced with a body known as the Economic Policy Group (EPG), but this differed from the Ford version in several important respects. The chairmanship of the Carter EPG was shared between the secretary of the treasury and the chairman of the Council of Economic Advisers, whereas, under Ford, the chairmanship of the EPB was firmly in the hands of the secretary of the treasury. Furthermore, Carter's EPG had no base in the Executive Office of the President. It was staffed out of the secretary of the treasury's office, and its executive director had no effective access to the White House. Thus, the EPG could not easily play the role of honest broker in the economic policy-making process that had been such a vital ingredient in the success of the Ford Economic Policy Board. Indeed, in the Carter White House, there was no presidential assistant for economic affairs. The Economic Policy Group failed to coordinate. It was a large, unwieldy body without an executive steering committee, which met only rarely in the all-important early days of the Carter administration and got little support from the president himself.[64]

The absence of any effective coordinating machinery, together with the plethora of economic policy units under President Carter, added to the intractable problems of economic management during his administration. Although there can be no guarantee that a properly coordinated structure will produce the right economic policies, the structural disarray in the Carter administration was hardly conducive to the emergence of any economic strategy.[65]

President Reagan's principal means of coordinating economic policy advice during his first term was the Cabinet Council on Economic Affairs, one of the seven subcommittees of the Cabinet through which policy issues were handled at the top level. The council was chaired by the secretary of the treasury and managed by an executive secretary from the Office of Policy Development. The secretaries of state, commerce, labor, and transportation were members of the council, along with the director of OMB, the U.S. trade representative, and the chairman of the Council of Economic Advisers. The vice president, the counselor to the president, the White House chief of staff, and the assistant for policy development were ex officio members of the council. At the beginning of President Reagan's second term, the Cabinet Council on Economic Affairs became one of two subcommittees of the Cabinet under a revamped decision-making structure in the White House. President Reagan did not have an assistant for economic affairs in his White House Office, but the counselor to the president (Edwin Meese during Reagan's first term) was responsible for the work of all the Cabinet councils, including the Council on Economic Affairs. The council met two or three times a week during the first two years of the Reagan administration and established what Roger Porter described as "a phalanx of subcabinet level working groups" to develop issues for the council's consideration.[66]

Despite the coordinating responsibilities of the Cabinet Council, competition, and often open conflict, characterized the economic policy machinery in the Reagan administration. One serious embarrassment, the public disclosure in 1982 of a plan to tax unemployment benefits on which the president's staff was badly divided, was attributed directly to inadequate consideration of the political implications of the policy in the Cabinet Council itself.[67] But the most important disputes were about the budget deficit, and these were more than an embarrassment. Conflicts between the director of the Office of Management and Budget and the secretary of defense over cuts in defense expenditures, and a public row between the secretary of the treasury and the chairman of the Council of Economic Advisers over tax increases to reduce the budget deficit, damaged the administration by substantially undermining its position in Congress. One Republican Senator claimed that these disagreements "made it easier for Congress to compromise" Reagan's objectives because he had "encouraged all sorts of opinions in the White House that have been voiced outside the White House as if the President was talking in multi-voices."[68]

The disorder that marked the Reagan administration's handling of economic policy was overshadowed in the second term by the disaster that had befallen national security policy in the form of the Iran-*contra* episode, but once George Bush had taken over the reins of power, it seemed, on the basis of early press reporting, that the new president had got a grip on the economic policy apparatus of the EOP and was about to undo the damage that had been done by his predecessor. His appointment of Roger Porter as assistant to the president for economic and domestic policy augured well. Porter had extensive White House staff experience, having previously served Presidents Ford and Reagan in senior policy positions. Moreover, as a professor at Harvard's Kennedy School of Government and the author of two book-length studies about the problems of coordinating economic policy, he had a major professional interest in, and great sensitivity toward, the complexities of economic policy management in the EOP. Above all, Porter's title constituted an important new development. He was the first White House domestic policy coordinator to have responsibilities for economic policy coordination as well, and that, at least, had the potential to end the turf wars between the two policy areas within the presidential staff system.

President Bush also attempted a resurrection of the Council of Economic Advisers. In September 1989, the *New York Times* published a report on the CEA entitled "Happy Days for Economic Advisers" in which journalist Robert Hershey noted that some people in Washington were suggesting that the revival of the council in the Bush administration "may soon be inviting comparisons with the halcyon days of Walter Heller."[69] There were significant differences between the Bush and Reagan administrations with respect to the CEA, due not only to the president's willingness to make greater use of the council's expertise, but also because of the political adroitness of Bush's CEA chairman, Michael Boskin, and the manner in which he cultivated a close personal relationship with the president.[70] Once again, the council was being seen as an effective and influential player within the EOP. Robert Hershey cited its critical input on such diverse issues as steel import quotas, incentives to reduce air pollution, job training, and the rights of the disabled. In fact, so great was the improvement in economic policy making within the Bush administration that the *New York Times* ran a page-one story under the headline "Tight White House Control Marks Bush Economic Policy" within just two months of President Bush's taking office.[71]

Those early press reports proved to be premature and very wide of the mark. Economic policy making in the Bush administration degenerated into a chaotic state of bitter infighting and personal animosities between key players in the White House in which President Bush refused to intervene until it was too late. In a revealing exposé of the economic policy-making process in the Bush White House, published in the *Washington Post* just one month before the 1992 presidential election, Bob Woodward described the relationship between the chairman of the Council of Economic Advisers (Boskin), the director of the Office of Management and Budget (Richard Darman), former White House chief of staff (John Sununu), and secretary of the treasury (Nicholas Brady) as that of "warring feudal chiefs vying for the attention and favor of the king, jealously guarding their own territory and at times belittling each other in private conversations."[72] The originally designated economic policy coordinator, Roger Porter, was well out of the picture by the time the infighting began in earnest during the summer months of 1991. Among other things, it was reported that the chairman of the CEA found that Sununu and Darman were cutting off his direct access to the president and excluding him from key economic meetings. Relations between Darman and Secretary of the Treasury Brady were also appalling. Woodward reports that Darman had told other colleagues that "Brady is a dolt who could not pass an introductory economics exam at any American university," and Brady had described his relationship with Darman as "one of the most complicated and difficult he has ever had in his life." It was not until October 1992, and less than a month before election day, that President Bush responded to the widespread criticism of his economic team and announced publicly that, if reelected, he would replace Darman, Boskin, and Brady,[73] but by then it was too late to redress the damage that had been done.

In a book on the presidential staff system, John P. Burke has argued forcefully that staff structures alone do not make for a successful institutional presidency and that the management style and practices of the president are vitally important in making the structure work. Organizational structure and presidential management style are independent variables in the equation, says Burke.[74] Bush's economic policy machinery was a classic illustration of the problem Burke addresses: a case of personalities overpowering the structure and the failure of the president to exert the necessary management and leadership to remedy the defects.[75] The arrangements for economic policy making within the EOP have varied enormously over the years, and the defects the system has sometimes displayed have been a cause of consternation to many observers of the modern presidency. During the 1970s that consternation increased as the state of the economy worsened.

Rising unemployment, high rates of inflation, uncontrollable budget deficits, and the fall in the value of the dollar all added impetus to those seeking new institutional solutions to the problem of economic management. At the risk of oversimplifying a vast body of literature, what bothers critics most with respect to the economic policy machinery of the EOP is its apparent inability to coordinate advice and produce coherent economic policy recommendations.

The quality and quantity of economic advice available to the president has not been an issue. Fragmentation of policy responsibility within the EOP ensures that plenty of advice from a multitude of perspectives will be on hand constantly, and there have always been a number of high-caliber professional economists on the presidential staff to dispense their expertise. While one has to face the fact that economics is an inexact science and economists can make mistakes, the problem is not the availability or the correctness of advice, but the willingness of the president to utilize it. Past experience demonstrates that this is a most unpredictable variable. The Council of Economic Advisers, for example, was a vital institution in the economic policy-making machinery of the Kennedy and Johnson administrations, but President Reagan rendered it impotent and ineffective simply by ignoring it and delaying replacement of council members when they resigned. One can assume that it was only the CEA's statutorily mandated duty to provide an annual economic report that saved it from total extinction at the end of Reagan's first term of office.[76]

The problems of coherence in a highly fragmented economic advisory structure are immense, and all are attributable to the fact that economic policy transcends almost every activity in the Executive Office. After more than fifty years of experience and experimentation, there remain many unresolved questions about the nature of economic policy making within the presidential branch. One concerns the relationship between domestic policy advice and economic policy advice and has never been satisfactorily settled. Two reform commissions in the 1980s recommended that an economic affairs staff be established within the EOP, along with a reconstructed domestic affairs staff minus its present economic policy responsibilities,[77] but neither report explains just how, in practice, economic issues are to be removed from domestic policy considerations, and until that is resolved, the practicality of such suggestions is questionable. The same problem was considered ten years later by yet another reform commission cosponsored by the Carnegie Endowment for International Peace and the Institute for International Economics. It recommended that the president establish a Domestic Council and an Economic Council to coordinate those respective policy areas in the same way that the National Security Council coordinates foreign and national security policy. In making the proposal for separate councils, the report noted that "responsibilities, functions, and personnel will inevitably overlap, but a majority of this commission believes that creating two councils—one focused on economic policy and the other on domestic—offers the best structure to manage these issues." But, in a footnote following that sentence, minority dissent was recorded, indicating that several members of the commission believed that the two councils should be merged into one, under a single assistant to the president for domestic and economic affairs, on the grounds that there would be considerable overlap, and on many issues complete overlap. The majority rejected this because they felt it created "too broad a span of issues for one person to handle."[78]

Another major difficulty concerns the relationship of international economic issues to domestic economic issues and whether the one should be treated independently of the other. On many occasions they have been. Eisenhower and Nixon had a Council on Foreign Economic Policy and a Council on International Economic Policy respectively. Under Kennedy and Carter, key aides on the National Security Council Staff were the principal operators in the international economic policy arena. President Ford attempted to integrate foreign and domestic economic policy under the auspices of the Economic Policy Board, but notwithstanding its considerable achievements as a coordinating body, the board rarely commanded the cooperation of Secretary of State Henry Kissinger, who frequently bypassed it and dealt with the president alone on international economic issues.[79]

There is within any administration a natural tendency to keep foreign and domestic economic policy in separate hands. Presidential advisers are conditioned to protect their turf in the fiercely competitive life of the Executive Office, but that is not the only reason. Perspective also matters. Some aides will inevitably see foreign economic policy primarily as foreign rather than economic, and, as long as foreign economic policy is treated by national security and foreign policy advisers as a strategic and diplomatic tool, then there is little point in arguing over the complex relationship between domestic and international economics. But the distinction between foreign economic and domestic economic issues has become so blurred over the past few decades that the weight of opinion now firmly supports the coordination of foreign and domestic economic policy under one senior presidential assistant for economic affairs with overall responsibility for all economic policy.[80] Yet, how one gets the foreign policy staff to consent to that proposition is another unsettled question.

A third unsettled issue affecting coherence in economic policy concerns the different perspectives of the president and his staff on one hand and the departments and agencies on the other. The problem revolves around the extent to which the views and advice from representatives of the departments, who themselves may be representing vast and complex issue networks,[81] can be reconciled with the perspective of the president, who has a different and a unique constituency to speak for. The president's perspective on economic issues is not simply the aggregate of departmental perspectives, and the difference between the two necessitates an important but ill-defined role for the presidential staff if policy coherence is to be achieved. The problem, however, is a general one and not just confined to economic policy making. It raises questions about the appropriate relationship between the presidential staff and the members of the Cabinet that are a central element of the post-Watergate critique of the Executive Office. For that reason, the problem is better considered in its broader context and must be set aside for the present.

There is less uncertainty in the post-Watergate literature about the most desirable means of coordinating economic policy within the Executive Office. The various experiments with coordinating mechanisms since the Eisenhower administration have provided plenty of lessons about coordination and the lack of it, and there is a consensus in the reform literature that what presidents need is a senior White House assistant responsible for managing the process of providing economic advice to the president, to facilitate, to coordinate, to be an honest broker between the advisers, but not to be a policy advocate or policy maker. Economic advice would come from the departments and agencies and the Council of Economic Advisers; coordination would be the responsibility of the assistant and his staff in the EOP. On paper, it appears to be an ideal arrangement, but the practicality of dividing the functions of policy advice and policy management, particularly in the economic sphere, is another matter, and a recurring problem in the study of the functions of the Executive Office.

Much of what has been said above may become redundant if President Clinton's innovations in economic policy making prove to be successful. Clinton moved very swiftly after taking office to address a number of the most fundamental problems of economic policy coordination in the EOP. Just five days after his inauguration, he signed Executive Order 12835 establishing a National Economic Council under the direction of an assistant to the president for economic policy. The functions of the council, listed in Section 4 of the Order, are extensive: (1) to coordinate the economic policy-making process with respect to domestic and international economic issues; (2) to coordinate economic policy advice to the president; (3) to ensure that economic policy decisions and programs are consistent with the president's stated goals, and to ensure that those goals are being effectively pursued; and (4) to monitor implementation of the president's economic policy agenda.[82] The assistant was given the authority to take such actions as may be necessary or appropriate to implement such functions and was also designated to chair the council in the absence of the president and the vice president. In addition to the president, vice president, and assistant for economic policy, the membership of the council consists of the secretaries of state, treasury, agriculture, commerce, labor, housing and urban development, transportation, energy, and the administrator of the Environmental Protection Agency, along with the chairman of the Council of Economic Advisers, the director of OMB, the U.S. trade representative, the national security adviser, the assistant to the president for domestic policy, and the assistant for science and technology policy.

When President Clinton announced the formation of the council, he said he believed that "this will enable us to make economic policy in a much more specific, clear, and effective way than the Federal government has in quite a long while."[83] He may well see his hopes fulfilled. The executive order is quite unambiguous about where the responsibility for policy coordination rests, and Section 4(b) requires all executive departments and agencies to coordinate economic policy through the council. It also gives the council and the assistant for economic policy responsibility for coordinating domestic and international economic policy, and it notes the need for cooperation between the assistant for economic policy, the assistant for domestic policy (President Clinton did not see fit to merge these two positions into one), and the assistant for national security. As the Bush administration demonstrated, however, organizational structures mean little without the right personalities and management practices to go with them, and President Clinton addressed this problem by appointing as his assistant for economic policy Robert Rubin, a Wall Street investment banker with well-established managerial credentials who, the *New York Times* said, "has an "ability to make things happen," and, according to the *Washington Post,* "gets things accomplished without histrionics."[84] But, with memories of Donald Regan still fresh, no one can guarantee that Mr. Rubin's highly successful Wall Street background will equip him to cope with the problems of coordinating economic policy in Washington; still the Clinton-initiated economic policy machinery gives Rubin the framework within which to address the major defects of the system and his personality and temperament seem suited to the important coordination role assigned to him.[85] If the Clinton innovation in economic policy coordination works as intended, it will stand as one of the most significant developments in the history of the Executive Office of the President.

National Security

There has been greater thematic coherence to the development of the national security machinery within the EOP than is true of the economic policy structure, and, unlike economic policy, there is a clear focal point for national security policy making in the form of the National Security Council (NSC) and, more particularly, its staff.

The National Security Council was established by the National Security Act of 1947. Its function is "to advise the President with respect to the integration of domestic, foreign, and military policies relating to the national security." Its statutory membership, which has been changed at various times since 1947, at present consists of the president, the vice president, and the secretaries of state, defense, and treasury, the U.S. ambassador to the United Nations, and three senior members of the White House staff—the assistant to the president for national security affairs, the assistant to the president for economic policy, and the White House chief of staff. The chairman of the Joint Chiefs of Staff is the statutory military adviser to the NSC, and the director of the Central Intelligence Agency is its intelligence adviser. The NSC was given a staff, to be headed by a civilian executive secretary, and responsibility for the Central Intelligence Agency, which had been established under the NSC by the 1947 Act. In 1949, the National Security Council was formally placed in the Executive Office of the President through a reorganization plan submitted to Congress by President Truman.[86]

The origin of the National Security Council is a long and complex story,[87] but the salient points must be recounted in order to understand the council in its present form. The idea of a national security council developed as a reaction to the highly personal, ad hoc style of decision making adopted by President Roosevelt during World War II.[88] The alleged administrative chaos and confusion that resulted from the Roosevelt method was an experience that a number of wartime officials believed should not be repeated, and when President Truman, who shared those views, took office, the government moved quickly to remedy what was seen by some as a weakness in the policy-making system.[89] The principal reform on the agenda was the unification of the armed services within a single Department of Defense, and this was finally achieved when the National Security Act Amendments of 1949 became law. The hitherto separate Departments of the Army, Navy, and Air Force became military departments within the Department of Defense and operationally subordinate to the overall direction of the new secretary of defense.

The Navy, particularly Secretary James Forrestal, had favored a different method of achieving unification of America's defense structure. Forrestal had long been impressed with the British Committee of Imperial Defence and became a strong proponent of a similar kind of collegial coordinating mechanism for the United States. Once President Truman had agreed to establish a unified Department of Defense, Forrestal was even more determined to fight for his coordinating committee as a way of guaranteeing that the president would consult key officials on national security matters and of protecting the Navy's interests by giving it the voice it was otherwise to lose by no longer having representation in the Cabinet.

There was some sympathy in Congress for Forrestal's position, and acting on a suggestion from the chairman of the Senate Naval Affairs Committee, Forrestal commissioned a study of the alternatives to departmental unification. The study was prepared by a close associate of the secretary, Ferdinand Erberstadt, and was completed by late summer of 1945.[90] It reinforced Forrestal's views and made several recommendations for policy coordinating mechanisms as an alternative to departmental unification, including the establishment of a national security council to formulate and coordinate policy in the political-military arena. From that point onward, the Erberstadt report became part of the agenda of reform measures being considered by Congress, even though it was not originally included in the president's plans. Forrestal eventually succeeded in getting his collegial body written into law, alongside the administration's departmental unification plan.

The National Security Council was "a creature of compromise" in the words of Anna Kasten Nelson. It was "part of the price Truman had to pay to gain support within his own administration for his unification proposal."[91] From the president's perspective, it could have been a heavy price because the proponents of the council idea were clearly attempting to institutionalize national security advice to the president to ensure collegiality, rather than perpetuate a one-man decision-making process. Erberstadt's report had even envisaged the council as a collective decision-taking body because, although it recognized that the council was formally advisory, the authors thought "the fact that the President himself heads the Council would for all practical purposes insure that the advice it offered would be accepted."[92] It is no wonder that the NSC was quickly labeled "Forrestal's revenge."[93]

The revenge, if any, was short-lived. The National Security Council turned out to be much less of a constraint on the president than its advocates had hoped and has never succeeded in establishing itself as a collective decision-taking body. In fact, the hopes of Forrestal and Erberstadt were frustrated from the start by a series of developments that put aside any doubts that the NSC would be anything other than a presidential agency.

Perhaps the most important of these was the intervention of the Bureau of the Budget during the drafting of the administration's version of the national security bill. What the bureau did was resist attempts to give the NSC statutory powers that would have forced the president to take decisions in the council itself. It was the bureau, representing the presidential perspective, that ensured the council would be only an advisory body and would not be given authoritative functions in the proposed legislation.[94]

President Truman also played an important part in defining the role of the National Security Council as a presidential agency by assiduously protecting the prerogatives of the chief executive in the early days of the council's life. Prior to the outbreak of the Korean war, Truman attended only twelve of the fifty-seven meetings of the NSC because he felt his presence might imply a delegation of authority he did not intend.[95] Moreover, the president's memoirs make it abundantly clear that the existence of the NSC was not going to alter his ultimate responsibility for the nation's security. Truman wrote:

> I used the National Security Council only as a place for recommendations to be worked out. Like the Cabinet, the Council does not make decisions. The policy itself has to come down from the president, as all final decisions have

to be made by him. A "vote" in the National Security Council is merely a procedural step. It never decides policy.[96]

A third important development concerned the staffing of the National Security Council and the choice of its first executive secretary, Sidney Souers. Souers, who had been recommended for the post by Forrestal, was a former naval officer, a member of Erberstadt's committee, and a friend of Forrestal's, but he declined to adopt Forrestal's conception of the role of the council and instead sided with Truman's view that it was an advisory body only.[97] Souers also made an important decision to house himself and the staff of the NSC in what is now the Old Executive Office Building next door to the White House, rather than accept the offer of accommodation in the Defense Department that Forrestal, then secretary of defense, had made.[98] The physical proximity of the council's staff to the president, together with Souers's view of the place of the Council within the executive branch, made it all the more difficult for the NSC to be captured by the defense establishment.

In a seminal article on the development of the National Security Council, I.M. Destler identifies three principal ways in which the NSC structure has been used by postwar presidents:

> It has served as an advisory forum of senior officials reviewing foreign policy issues for the President, usually in his presence. It has provided a focal point for the development of formal policy planning and decision processes. It has provided the umbrella for the emergence of a presidential foreign policy staff. Its founders mainly conceived it as the first: the last is what it has most importantly become.[99]

The potential of the NSC to be a meaningful advisory forum was first realized when the Korean war broke out in 1950. That caused Truman to change his attitude to the council. He directed that it meet regularly each week and that all major national security advice be coordinated through it, and he made an number of organizational changes to rid the council of some of the weaknesses that had become apparent in the early years of its existence. The president also began presiding over council meetings on a regular basis, missing only nine of the seventy-one NSC sessions from the end of June 1950 to January 1953.[100]

Eisenhower used the National Security Council as an advisory forum even more extensively than Truman. It suited Eisenhower's style to hear arguments over national security issues in a large formal committee with all key officials present, backed up by highly organized staff work and a system of subcommittees designed to prepare the council as thoroughly as possible on matters brought before it. The Eisenhower NSC system—the council, supported by a Planning Board, an Operations Coordinating Board, a newly appointed presidential assistant for national security affairs, and an enlarged staff was the most elaborate development of the basic NSC idea that any president has put into practice.[101]

What all this achieved in terms of genuine deliberation has been a matter of some dispute. Critics of the Eisenhower NSC have argued that the council's membership was too large for any meaningful discussion, that the presence of the president inhibited the free expression of views, and that participants at council meetings were spokesmen for their departments so that advice to the president was the product of bargaining and horsetrading rather than deliberation. Critics have also claimed that the council was primarily concerned with general and long-range policy, leaving Eisenhower to go elsewhere for advice on immediate day-to-day problems. They also claimed that policy papers prepared by a bureaucratized and rigid staff structure swamped the Council with formality and detail.[102]

In the wake of recently released archival material at the Eisenhower Library and the spreading influence of Eisenhower revisionism among scholars, some are now challenging the conventional wisdom about the role of the Eisenhower National Security Council. Phillip Henderson, for example, has produced a detailed account of two particular meetings of the NSC, based on NSC papers, to show that there was genuine deliberation at council meetings, that real differences of opinion were aired before the president, and that the council was able to refine issues and help the president resolve complex problems. He concludes that, under Eisenhower's leadership, the National Security Council became the principal forum for the formulation and implementation of national security policy in the Eisenhower administration.[103] In a rather more qualified evaluation, Anna Kasten Nelson has also tried to correct the record. She found that there were candid discussions within the council that were important to the president, but she also notes that although "some critical problems were fully debated in Council meetings; others were never presented to the Council."[104] Burke and Greenstein's detailed study of Eisenhower's decision not to intervene in Vietnam in 1954 provides support for Nelson's position. They stress that the "NSC machinery was part of a larger advisory process, a significant part of which was informal, in which Eisenhower himself was the ultimate decision maker," and they note that Eisenhower made a critical decision against a surgical air strike in 1954 without an NSC debate.[105]

The Eisenhower administration also demonstrated the capacity of the National Security Council to be a focal point for the development of formal policy planning and decision processes. Regularized procedures were established late in the Truman years, and Eisenhower built on those procedures extensively. The Planning Board he established was an interdepartmental coordinating committee consisting of the relevant assistant secretaries. It was concerned with the development of policy papers covering a wide range of foreign policy problems and met regularly three times a week from anywhere between three and five hours at a time.[106] The Operations Coordinating Board was an interdepartmental committee at undersecretary level essentially concerned with the implementation of NSC decisions. In addition, Eisenhower created the post of special assistant for national security affairs within the White House Office to act as the principal executive officer for the NSC system and as chairman of the Planning Board. The executive secretary of the council became, in effect, a staff assistant to the president's assistant.

There is no doubt that Eisenhower created a highly ordered and systematic process for considering national security problems, but it was also a cumbersome, slow-moving, and bureaucratic structure that attracted a great deal of criticism in the later years of his administration. The most important criticism came from Senator Henry M. Jackson's Subcommittee on National Policy Machinery, which had been established in 1959 to study and review the national security policy process. The subcommittee's views on the Eisenhower NSC were encapsulated in one paragraph of a staff report that firmly concluded the Council lacked effectiveness as a policy advisory body.

> The root causes of difficulty are found in over-crowded agenda, overly elaborate and stylized procedures, excessive reliance on subordinate interdepartmental mechanisms, and the use of the NSC system for comprehensive coordinating and follow-through responsibilities it is ill suited to discharge. The philosophy of the suggestions that follow can be summed up in this way to "deinstitutionalize" and to "humanize" the NSC process.[107]

The Jackson subcommittee view was shared by John F. Kennedy, who discontinued the Eisenhower system when he took office. Kennedy promptly disbanded the Planning Board and the Operations Coordinating Board and made far less use of the council as a forum for policy advice. Large, formal group meetings were anathema to Kennedy's operating style. He preferred a less structured, more flexible approach to seeking advice. The National Security Council was only one of several traditional structures that did not suit the new president and although meetings of the council were held, this was done, according to Theodore Sorensen, partly to put the views of key officials on the record who might otherwise have complained that they had not been consulted, and to silence outside critics who equated machinery with efficiency.[108] Kennedy was not alone. None of Eisenhower's successors attempted to resurrect the NSC in the Eisenhower fashion.

What Kennedy and the presidency did inherit from Eisenhower was the post of special assistant for national security affairs. From Kennedy onward, the role of the special assistant and the NSC staff as a tool of presidential policy making expanded significantly. This transformation of the NSC apparatus from a collegial body of key advisers into a national security staff arm of the president has been the most remarkable development within the national security policy-making machinery and has completely defeated the intent of those reformers who designed the council to constrain the president and to counter the centralization of decision making that had characterized the administration of Franklin D. Roosevelt.

Several factors contributed to this transformation. One of the most important was Eisenhower's decision to establish the position of special assistant for national security affairs within his personal staff and then place that assistant in charge of what was originally intended to be a career staff working for the National Security Council. By downgrading the role of the executive secretary of the NSC, an immediate consequence of bringing in the special assistant, Eisenhower signaled as clearly as any president has done that the NSC system was there to serve the president's purpose. By doing this, he also put an end to any hope that a professional, nonpartisan, career national security staff might develop within the Executive Office.

Moreover, in creating the post of special assistant for national security affairs, Eisenhower provided a most convenient structure within which two key functions—process management and policy advice—could be performed by one individual. It may not have been Eisenhower's intention to do this, and his national security assistants did not exercise a policy advocacy function to any significant degree,[109] but Henry Kissinger and Zbigniew Brzezinski made no distinction between these two functions when, during the presidencies of Richard Nixon and Jimmy Carter, they filled the post that Eisenhower had invented. The experience of Kissinger and Brzezinski subsequently led many critics to argue that these two functions are incompatible when in the hands of one person.[110] The integrity of the staff assistant as custodian of the policy process, as an honest broker between competing advisers, is undermined when he, too, is one of those advisers.

Another important contribution to the development of the national security staff was the recruitment of policy specialists to fill key positions, particularly the position of special assistant for national security affairs. Under Truman and Eisenhower, none of those who held the position of executive secretary of the NSC or special assistant had broad expertise in the substance of foreign policy and were there primarily because of their management skills. But that changed with Kennedy's appointment of McGeorge Bundy, the first of a succession of national security assistants with proven foreign policy credentials to be recruited from academia. Henry Kissinger and Zbigniew Brzezinski were both men with distinguished academic records in the field of international politics, and both were known proponents of strong foreign policy views. These policy specialists recruited other policy specialists to fill senior posts in an expanding NSC staff, and hence it is understandable why the national security assistant and the NSC staff became more concerned with policy advice and less concerned with the process of coordinating outside advice in an impartial way.

One other important explanation behind the transformation of the NSC apparatus after Eisenhower can be found in the very meaning of the term *national security*. In the Cold War years it became a synonym for *foreign policy* and was used less and less in its narrower defense context. The preeminent position of the NSC staff and the national security assistant, which was reached by the end of the 1960s, amounted to preeminence over the whole foreign policy process, not merely over defense or security issues.

The rise to prominence of the national security assistant and the NSC did not happen overnight, but a quantum leap occurred during President Nixon's first term of office when Henry Kissinger acquired dominance in the foreign policy-making process. This was manifested in Kissinger's high public profile, his role as President Nixon's principal spokesman on foreign policy, his monopoly of U.S. negotiations with Vietnam to end the war, and subsequently with China to reestablish Sino-U.S. relations, and, as Destler pointed out, his identification "as the architect and actual builder of a particular set of policies."[111] Nixon eventually appointed Kissinger secretary of state in September 1973, in addition to his job as Assistant for National Security Affairs, marking the completion of the transformation of the NSC process begun in the Eisenhower administration.

Kissinger did not see his role in the White House as merely one of policy coordination. As he candidly admits in his memoirs, "Like the overwhelming majority of high officials I had strong views and did not reject opportunities to have them prevail."[112] He also had little passion for anonymity and welcomed publicity, which he received in abundance. He was supported by the largest-ever NSC staff, over fifty professionals, and had a penchant for operating in secret in order to neutralize potential sources of opposition within the administration.[113] Moreover, Kissinger's rise to power met little real opposition from a weak secretary of state, William Rogers, the official who had most to lose from a White House centralized decision-making system, and that, too, was an important factor in Kissinger's command of foreign policy making. But, ultimately, Kissinger's influence derived from the confidence the president placed in him and Nixon's own determination to conduct foreign policy from the White House.[114]

There was a short break in the developmental pattern of the national security process during the Ford administration, when the new national security assistant, Brent Scowcroft, took a back seat to Secretary of State Kissinger, but the pattern reasserted itself under President Carter with Zbigniew Brzezinski as the Assistant for National Security Affairs. Brzezinski, like Kissinger, was primarily interested in policy advocacy, even though he declared on taking up his appointment that his was not a policy-making job. As with Kissinger, so Brzezinski became the president's principal foreign policy spokesman and gradually asserted his dominance within the administration. He also conducted sensitive diplomatic negotiations on the president's behalf (on the normalization of relations with China), much to the annoyance of Secretary of State Cyrus Vance.[115] Brzezinski simply took up the job of national security assistant where Kissinger had left off, except that Brzezinski was not secretary of state as well. In his memoirs, Brzezinski describes his role as that of the president's "stand-in on national security matters,"[116] something no national security assistant would have said in the days before Kissinger.

Not one of the six national security advisers who served Ronald Reagan during his eight years in office attained the dominance and control over foreign policy that Kissinger and Brzezinski had achieved, although two of them, Robert McFarlane and Admiral John Poindexter, gained greater notoriety for their part in building that monument to Reagan's national security decision-making process, the Iran-*contra* affair. Reagan began with a weakened national security adviser, Richard Allen, whose role had been deliberately downgraded and who reported to the president, not directly, but through the president's counselor, Edwin Meese. It was, according to Meese, an effort to restore the honest-broker role of the national security assistant "in keeping with the traditional (i.e., pre-Kissinger) nature of the position."[117] But Allen failed in the role, and so did the attempt to turn the clock back. Allen's replacement, William Clark, came in as a very senior White House assistant, reporting directly to the president, and presided over what proved to be a very dangerous development in the national security advisory machinery—the involvement of the NSC staff in operational matters and, ultimately, in covert operations.[118] It began with the involvement in Lebanon in 1982 and culminated in the secret arms sales to Iran and the illegal diversion of the profits from those sales to support the Nicaraguan *contras,* a policy that began to unravel in November 1986.

The Iran-*contra* affair shattered the credibility of the administration's foreign policy, particularly its hard line on international terrorism. For the first time in six years, Ronald Reagan's detachment from the business of government became a huge liability as his popularity tumbled and the most serious crisis of his presidency unfolded. Iran-*contra* resulted in the resignations of the national security adviser, Admiral Poindexter, a member of the NSC staff, Oliver North, and, subsequently, White House Chief of Staff Donald Regan. A presidential commission and then two congressional committees were set up to investigate the affair, and an independent counsel was appointed after an investigation by the then Attorney General, Edwin Meese, failed to satisfy the critics. Indictments were subsequently brought against Poindexter, North, Robert McFarlane (Poindexter's predecessor), and eight other executive branch officials including Caspar Weinberger, former secretary of defense. There were accusations of a cover-up, heightened by President Bush's Christmas Eve pardon of Weinberger and others in the dying days of his presidency, by which time the president himself had become a subject of investigation by the independent counsel. At the root of the Iran-*contra* affair was the arrogance, zealotry, unaccountability, and contempt for the law and the political process by presidential staffers doing things that the National Security Council staff was never intended to do and ought not to do. Iran-*contra* not only resulted in a disastrous policy initiative, but also constituted, as the author of one postmortem has argued, "a nearly successful assault upon the constitutional structures and norms that underlie [the] postwar national security system."[119]

Once the perpetrators of the Iran-*contra* affair had left the White House, their replacements began to remedy the defects in the national security advisory system, and by the end of Reagan's second-term the national security operation was getting good marks from the press. In an editorial in July 1988, the *New York Times* declared that "after all the mess of the first seven years, the foreign policy team is now running smoothly. It's a belated blessing for this president and a good example for the next one."[120] The next president, George Bush, followed that example and restored some coherence and integrity to the National Security Council staff. His national security adviser, Brent Scowcroft, was one of only two occupants of that position who came to the job with previous experience in the post, having served in the same position under President Ford. Phrases like "low key," and "behind the scenes" have been used to describe Scowcroft's operating style, a style that went with a "quiet, calm, conciliatory, [and] self-effacing" personality.[121] Implicitly contrasting him with Kissinger and Brzezinski, a *National Journal* profile of Scowcroft opened with this sentence: "Brent Scowcroft believes that national security advisers should be seen and not heard."[122] He did have a clear concept of his role as national security adviser, which was not surprising given his previous experience and the fact that he was one of the three members of the Tower Commission set up by President Reagan to investigate the Iran-*contra* affair. "It is my job," he said, "to ensure the integration of advice, to fill in where there are holes, and hopefully, to help provide a strategic concept which covers the whole field of national security."[123]

Scowcroft was responsible for establishing the elaborate hierarchy of NSC subgroups described in document NSD-1, issued by President Bush on the day of his inauguration.[124] Below the NSC itself was a body known as the Principals Committee, chaired by Scowcroft and consisting of the then statutory members of the NSC, minus the president and vice president, but including the White House chief of staff. Its purpose was to "review, coordinate, and monitor the development of national security policy." Below the Principals Committee was the Deputies Committee, made up of the deputies to each of the principal members of the NSC and chaired by the deputy assistant to the president for national security affairs. Its task was to "review and monitor the work of the NSC interagency process and make recommendations concerning the development and implementation of national security policy." The Deputies Committee was also required to "ensure that all papers to be discussed by the NSC or the NSC/PC fully analyze the issues, fairly and adequately set out the facts, consider a full range of views and options, and satisfactorily assess the prospects, risks, and implications of each." At the base of the NSC structure were ten Policy Coordinating Committees, six focused on geographical regions and four on key policy areas—defense, international economics, intelligence, and arms control. The membership of these committees included a representative of each of the executive departments represented on the NSC and an NSC staff member serving as the executive secretary of the committee. The Policy Coordinating Committees had responsibility for "identifying and developing issues for consideration by the NSC" and were seen as "the principal inter-agency forum for the development and implementation of national security policy for [the] regional or functional area."

Although not a great deal is known about the way this bureaucratic structure operated in practice, and probably will not be known until the relevant documents are declassified and made available to researchers, there may be a parallel with the Eisenhower NSC system here. It is possible that critics of the Bush version might also see a cumbersome, unwieldy, and rigid system that may have contributed to the caution that marked President Bush's approach to foreign policy. One thing that is known about the NSC system under Scowcroft's direction is that it required vast numbers of personnel to staff the structure. In 1992, the NSC had budget authorization for a staff of sixty, but, that same year, the executive secretary of the NSC told a House Appropriations Subcommittee that the NSC employed approximately 170 individuals, 110 of them detailed from the State Department, the Pentagon, or the CIA.[125]

There has been some criticism that President Bush's style of operation and his close relationships with his national security team may have effectively cut out the institutional capacity of the NSC system. It has been suggested that the Bush national security team was too tightly drawn and too homogeneous, with an absence of creative tension that makes for innovative foreign policy.[126] Terry Eastland has also argued that Scowcroft was more a personal adviser than an institutional manager or strategic thinker and that "the temptation for those presidents who regard themselves as especially capable in national security affairs is that they will effectively dispense with the NSC and rely instead on their own contacts and skills." Eastland suggests that this was one reason why the Bush administration misread the intentions of Iraq's Saddam Hussein in the months leading to Iraq's invasion of Kuwait in 1990.[127]

President Clinton essentially adopted the Bush NSC structure when he took office in January 1993, but he broadened the membership of the council itself in order to bring economic policy concerns more directly into the consideration of national security issues. He added the secretary of the treasury, the assistant to the president for national security affairs, the assistant to the president for economic policy, the White House chief of staff, as well as the U.S. ambassador to the United Nations, as full members of the council and made the deputy assistant for national security affairs a member of the Economic Council to ensure close coordination between the NSC and that body.[128] When President Clinton's national security machinery became the target of media criticism in October 1993, after a trio of foreign policy mishaps over Somalia, Bosnia, and Haiti, it was reported by one journalist that there had been just eight full meetings of the NSC since Clinton's inauguration, about one per month.[129] While it might be premature to claim that this points to a decline in the role of the council as a focus of policy making in Clinton's White House, it does raise questions about what the president was hoping to do by expanding the membership of a body that was destined to meet so infrequently.

From Truman to Clinton, the national security machinery within the Executive Office of the President has not changed a great deal and certainly has not been subject to the sort of structural experimentation that has characterized the economic policy process. A reasonably consistent pattern of development in national security advice has evolved, and although each president has modified the NSC system, those modifications have generally been confined to operating procedures within the NSC and to the subcommittee structure of the NSC. They have not been substantial.

Another important difference between the national security policy structure and the economic policy structure within the EOP is that national security responsibilities have been far less fragmented than economic policy responsibilities, making for less internal competition among the president's staff. With the single exception of the Reagan administration, the authority to coordinate the national security policy process within the EOP has rested with the president's national security assistant. During Reagan's tenure, that authority was subject to periodic challenge and constant oversight from a higher level, from the counselor to the president during part of the first term and from the White House chief of staff during most of the second.

The costs of this White House-centered national security policy-making system have been high and have been felt beyond the confines of the Executive Office. The most visible defect of an advisory structure that gives the president's national security assistant a dominant policy-making role is the potential for conflict between the assistant and the secretary of state. As Henry Kissinger notes in his memoirs: "If the security adviser becomes active in the development and articulation of policy he must inevitably diminish the Secretary of State and reduce his effectiveness."[130] A dominant national security assistant, such as Kissinger was, does not become a de facto replacement for the secretary of state. Instead, the two officials compete to assert their authority, usually from different policy perspectives, which leads to contradiction and incoherence in the public enunciation of American foreign policy. The consequences are serious. To quote Henry Kissinger again: "Foreign governments are confused and, equally dangerous, given opportunity to play one part of our government off against the other; the State Department becomes demoralized and retreats into parochialism."[131] This is not a hypothetical consequence or even a remote possibility. It happens, as Cyrus Vance records in his account of the turbulent relationship between Zbigniew Brzezinski and himself:

> I supported the collegial approach with one critical reservation. Only the president and his secretary of state were to have the responsibility for defining the administration's foreign policy publicly. As time went on, there developed an increasingly serious breach of this understanding. Despite his stated acceptance of this principle, and in spite of repeated instructions from the president, Brzezinski would attempt increasingly to take on the role of policy spokesman. At first, his public appearances, press interviews, and anonymous "backgrounders" to journalists were simply a source of confusion. Eventually, as divergences grew wider between my public statements and his policy utterances, Brzezinski's practice became a serious impediment to the conduct of our foreign policy. It also became a political liability, leaving Congress and foreign governments with the impression that the administration did not know its own mind.[132]

When the authority of the secretary of state is challenged and undermined by a dominant national security assistant supported by a strong NSC staff, so too is the influence of the Department of State. If this happens to any consequential degree, the foreign policy-making process is then denied the input of policy specialists with operational responsibilities. That is also a heavy price to pay because the NSC staff simply does not have the resources and capability to fill this particular vacuum and the danger is that more policy is formulated without due regard to the problems of implementation.

It has also been suggested that when the national security assistant and the NSC staff function primarily as policy advocates, the very purpose for which the NSC was established—the coordination and integration of national security policy—tends to be neglected. This was the central criticism of one study of President Carter's national security apparatus commissioned for the President's Reorganization Project. The author of the report, Philip Odeen, thought that the Carter NSC staff was so preoccupied with making policy that it ignored other "institutional" responsibilities, particularly the responsibility of identifying in advance major issues that would require the president's attention, the responsibility of managing the decision process, and the responsibility of ensuring that the president's policies and decisions were implemented.[133]

Unless recent presidents have been oblivious to the defects of a White House-centered national security policy-making process, one can only assume that, notwithstanding its costs, they think it has served their purpose well. That certainly seems to have been so with Nixon and Carter, as neither made any attempt to change the structure in spite of the public criticism it engendered. Yet precisely what purpose does it serve? Destler suggests that "it responds to the president's immediate needs and caters to his personal convenience," but it "does not serve his broader, long-term need to lead a strong, loyal and responsive government."[134] Most of the proposals for improving the national security apparatus within the EOP, which will be considered further on, depend on getting presidents to look at longer-term benefits instead of considering only their personal convenience. Even Henry Kissinger has now disowned the dominant, national security-assistant style of decision making of which he was the archetype.[135]

Budgeting and Management

Budget control and management improvement were two cornerstones of the Brownlow Committee's conception of the institutionalized presidency. Both tasks were entrusted to the revitalized Bureau of the Budget under the terms of Executive Order 8248 and the subsequent turbulent history of the bureau was closely tied to the way successive presidents have regarded these two functions.

The golden age of the Bureau of the Budget coincided with the tenure of its first two post-Brownlow directors, Harold D. Smith (1939–46) and James E. Webb (1946–49).[136] Thereafter, the performance of the bureau increasingly became the target of criticism. Its structure and organization were scrutinized by a succession of internal reviews and external reform commissions, and its status as an objective, nonpartisan, expert career staff arm of the presidency was eroded. In 1970, the bureau underwent a major upheaval when it formally became the Office of Management and Budget (OMB). During the Reagan-Bush years, OMB was an overtly political institution and the very center of policy making, led by two of the most controversial directors in the agency's history.

Budget control by the Office of Management and Budget is built around a complex routine of agency submissions, budget previews and reviews, and detailed evaluation of agency programs by a staff of about 200 budget examiners.[137] All this is designed to ensure that departmental and agency spending plans are in accordance with the president's goals and objectives. These very routines were a source of Budget Bureau power, according to Allen Schick, because they guaranteed the bureau's place in the presidential scheme of things and assured it a prominent role for which it did not have to fight year after year.[138] But Schick also argues that, from Kennedy onward, presidents were less willing to accept the routines and timetables imposed on them, which they saw as a constraint on their ability to act quickly and reshape the budget to their own purposes, and this partly explains the decline of the bureau's influence and its preeminent position during the 1960s and 1970s.[139]

The importance of budgeting as a tool of presidential control and leadership, however, was not lost on presidents during this period, and a number of initiatives were taken to strengthen the president's hand. Lyndon Johnson, for example, initiated a major reform of the budget process in the mid-1960s by instituting the Planning-Programming-Budgeting System (PPBS), which was an attempt to replace incremental budgeting with a system emphasizing cost-benefit analysis and clearly defined program goals and objectives, leading to greatly improved presidential control over priority policies. The implementation of this presidential branch initiative subsequently proved to be more difficult than President Johnson's staff had anticipated, and successful executive branch resistance limited the impact of PPBS. The system was abandoned in 1971.[140] President Carter was also determined to make his mark on the budgetary process. During the 1976 election campaign, and in his 1977 budget message to Congress, he promised to implement zero-based budgeting (ZBB), which required departments and agencies to justify all their programs each year, not just new programs that constituted increments to the previous year's budget. Given the size of the federal budget and its complexity, ZBB would have been a monumental task for most government departments to perform and would probably have overloaded completely the budget review capacity of OMB. The scheme never got off the ground, and little more was heard about ZBB from President Carter after the early days of his administration. Had PPBS or ZBB been implemented successfully, they might have made the budget process a more effective management tool for presidents and the presidential branch. As it was, the failure of these initiatives merely reinforced the views of those who believed that budgeting had had its day as a management device.

During the Reagan and Bush years, the budget became much more an instrument of policy than of management. President Reagan arrived in Washington with an ideological commitment to reducing the domestic component of the federal budget and achieving a balanced budget because he wanted to get government "off the backs of the people" and, in common with many other conservatives, believed that budget deficits were immoral. The Office of Management and Budget became the focal point for the development of the Reagan administration's budget policy and the architect of drastic reductions in domestic expenditure, under the initial leadership of the controversial David Stockman. President Bush inherited not only the presidency from Ronald Reagan but also an alarming and seemingly uncontrollable budget deficit brought on by the 1981 tax cuts and Reagan's failure to control total spending.[141] Deficit reduction thus became a major concern during the Bush years, and consequently the Office of Management and Budget assumed a central policy making role in the administration that reinforced its identity as a political arm of the president, rather than a career staff agency of neutral experts supporting the office of the presidency.

As a consequence of its heightened policy responsibilities, the reputation of OMB as a budgeting agency was damaged during the Reagan-Bush years. The politics behind the policy problems of deficit reduction began to affect OMB's budgetary assumptions, projections, and forecasts. Creative accounting and overoptimistic scenarios about the level of anticipated revenues and economic growth clouded the budget presentation, and as a result the politicized product of OMB's work had less and less credibility, especially in Congress where every budget that Reagan submitted after 1981 "was promptly announced 'dead on arrival' and almost completely ignored on Capitol Hill."[142] No single incident better symbolizes the changed nature of the budgetary process within OMB than the revelations by Washington journalist William Greider about the behavior of Reagan's OMB director, David Stockman. When Stockman assumed office, he programmed a computer to predict the budgetary consequences of President Reagan's three-year tax-reduction proposal and increases in defense expenditures. The computer projection shocked Stockman. It predicted a series of unprecedented budget deficits with consequent adverse effects on interest rates, long-term inflation, and confidence in the financial markets. Stockman's response was simply to change all the assumptions built into the original computer model so that the outcome would appear much less disastrous. Moreover, Stockman later confessed to Greider that even he did not really understand the numbers in his budget calculations.[143] Little wonder that, when President Clinton's nominee as director of OMB, Leon Panetta, testified to Congress at his confirmation hearing, his central theme was the restoration of integrity to OMB and the budget process, claiming that "the American people need to be told the truth about the federal budget."[144]

Aside from the criticism of OMB as a budgeting agency, there has also been much dissatisfaction concerning its persistent weakness as a management agency.[145] Despite the intent of the Brownlow report, the post-1939 Bureau of the Budget never did succeed in establishing its managerial credentials, and it was essentially this failure that prompted President Nixon to reform the bureau in 1970. The Nixon reorganization was the culmination of many attempts over the previous two decades to get the Bureau of the Budget to take its management responsibilities seriously.

"Management" can mean a number of things in government. On the one hand, it can refer to the task of improving administrative procedures and organization, and this was the kind of management activity that the post-Brownlow Bureau of the Budget successfully engaged in during its early years. In 1939, a Division of Administrative Management was established within the bureau that was essentially concerned with the internal management of operating agencies in government. It functioned as a management consultant for the rest of the executive branch, giving advice but unwilling to force its recommendations on any department or agency. When government departments and agencies subsequently acquired their own management staffs, or began to use outside management consultants, the Division of Administrative Management became somewhat redundant. The bureau never moved much beyond this narrow interpretation of its management responsibilities, and Schick asserts that it failed to adapt to the new kinds of administrative problems that were reaching the president's desk in the 1950s. These were principally the problems of coordinating government programs that cut across departmental and governmental jurisdictions, as has so much government activity from the New Deal onward.[146] The problem of coordination represented a broader sense of the term "management."

President Nixon expanded the meaning of "management" even further. To him, it stood for nothing less than policy implementation, ensuring that what the president wanted done was done. During his first year in office, President Nixon established an Advisory Council on Executive Organization under the chairmanship of Roy Ash. Its advice to the president on the Bureau of the Budget was embodied in Reorganization Plan No. 2, submitted to Congress the following year. The plan proposed a significant upgrading of the bureau's management functions and a reduced emphasis on its budgetary responsibilities. The Bureau of the Budget was to be formally replaced by an Office of Management and Budget, whose major purpose would be to ensure greatly improved executive branch responsiveness to presidential priorities. Such was the Ash council's concern with management improvement that it originally proposed to call the new body the Office of Executive Management. It was only congressional insistence that forced "Budget" back into the title.

There was much more to the new Office of Management and Budget than merely a change of name. Its staff was increased significantly, it was structured to reflect the primary importance of its management functions and, most significantly, political appointees were placed in charge of the major divisions of OMB to perform line functions that were traditionally the preserve of career officials. Nixon was following the advice of one of his principal advisers on management, Fred Malek, who once told him, "You cannot achieve management policy or program control unless you have established political control."[147] The new associate directors and assistant directors were President Nixon's political agents within OMB. They possessed considerably less expertise than the careerists and much less experience in government. Most were recruited from outside government for what turned out to be short-term appointments, and they brought with them a distrust of career officials and a lack of understanding of the processes of government. They established a barrier between the career staff and the director of OMB which, according to Louis Fisher, "resulted in delays, frustration and poor communication" and led to the departure of many senior career staff from OMB.[148] But what they did possess was loyalty to the president, and they brought to OMB a degree of political responsiveness that had not been part of the ways of the former Bureau of the Budget.

The heightened political responsiveness of OMB under Nixon was also reflected in the status of its director. Both Kennedy and Johnson had brought the director of the Bureau of the Budget into the White House circle of policy advisers, but Nixon went even further. He gave his first director of the new OMB, George Shultz, an office in the White House and regarded him as a key member of the White House staff. Roy Ash, who became the third director of OMB under Nixon, not only had an office in the White House but was also given the formal title of assistant to the president in addition to his title of director of the Office of Management and Budget. The directorship of OMB is now firmly recognized as a political post and the likelihood of its ever again being held by a career civil servant must be regarded as remote. In 1973, Congress moved to make the appointment of the director and deputy director of OMB subject to Senate confirmation and succeeded in doing so the following year.

In the Nixon administration, all the principal functions of OMB were regarded as management functions, and in the president's reorganization message to Congress, "management" was clearly defined as "implementation." Nixon not only announced plans for reforming the Bureau of the Budget but also his intention to establish a Domestic Council to be the focus of domestic policy making and a domestic policy equivalent of the original version of the National Security Council. In his message to Congress, the president explained that "the Domestic Council will be primarily concerned with *what* we do; the Office of Management and Budget will be primarily concerned with *how* we do it, and *how well* we do it."[149]

The Nixon reforms did not fare as well as the president must have hoped. Larry Berman surveyed all OMB employees in 1976 and 1977 and found that only 3 percent of the professional staff believed that Nixon's reorganization plan had worked as intended and that well over 50 percent of those who responded to his questionnaire gave OMB a "fair" to "poor" rating when asked to assess the agency's management performance. In fact, 86 percent of his respondents thought that budgeting remained the high-priority function of OMB, compared with only 14 percent who saw management as the highest priority.[150] These findings were quite consistent with other published critiques of OMB, and it was not long before reformers were proposing, yet again, plans for strengthening the management functions of OMB.[151]

The Nixon reform did a lot to erase the distinction between institutional staff support for the presidency and personal staff support for the president in what was meant to be the principal institutional staff agency within the Executive Office of the President. The Office of Management and Budget was "politicized," and, consequently, "neutral competence" was compromised. As Hugh Heclo points out, concerns about the responsiveness to presidential leadership are perfectly legitimate, but so too are the claims of neutral competence, which he defines as "a continuous, uncommitted facility at the disposal of, and for the support of, political leadership" that provides "the best independent judgement of the issues to partisan bosses" and is "sufficiently uncommitted to be able to do so for a succession of partisan leaders."[152] What OMB lost as a result of its politicization was a certain degree of institutional memory and continuity, a lot of expertise because of the high staff turnover that resulted from the 1970s reforms, its nonpartisan credibility with the departments and agencies and Congress, and morale among career officers unused to political executives operating so far down the OMB command structure.

All of President Nixon's successors have continued to regard OMB in much the same way. President Carter, particularly, accelerated the partisan development of OMB by increasing the number of political executives and by nominating his close personal friend, Bert Lance, to be director. The additional political executives were given the title of executive associate director and formed a new layer in the OMB hierarchy between the assistant directors and the associate directors, thus removing the career officials one step further away from the director. Carter's choice of Bert Lance, a Georgia banker with no previous experience in government, smacked of cronyism, and the subsequent scandal that forced Lance's early resignation did little to help the image of OMB.

Presidents Reagan and Bush further politicized the Office of Management and Budget by enhancing its role in the area of regulation review. Prior to Reagan, OMB had responsibility to review government agency regulations in much the same way as it reviewed and cleared proposed legislation to make sure it was consistent with the president's program. But Reagan and Bush did the same to the regulatory review process as they had done to the budget process: They transformed it from a management tool into an instrument of policy. Within days of taking office, President Reagan set up a Task Force on Regulatory Relief, chaired by Vice President Bush, and a few weeks later issued Executive Order 12291, which considerably broadened presidential control over agency regulations, primarily by making them subject to cost-benefit analysis and to what, in effect, was a White House veto of government regulations through a new staff unit, the Office of Information and Regulatory Affairs (OIRA), established as a division of OMB.[153] The Office of Information and Regulatory Affairs quickly became the implementer of Reagan's deregulation policy and did this with some success.[154] Not surprisingly, there was considerable controversy relating to the secrecy with which it conducted the regulatory review process and the constitutionality of the executive order that mandated the cost-benefit analysis on all new government regulations. Subsequently, when Bush became president, he gave the drive for deregulation an even higher profile by establishing a Council on Competitiveness, under the chairmanship of Vice President Quayle, specifically charged with reducing the regulatory burdens on free enterprise in the United States.[155] The Quayle council generated even more criticism and hostility than the Reagan initiatives had done, not only because it seemed to be operating in greater secrecy, but also because it was highly successfully in overturning government regulations, particularly in the areas of health, occupational safety, and environmental protection.[156] Subsequently a number of Senators, led by John Glenn, introduced legislation—to be known as the Regulatory Review Sunshine Act—designed to curb the power of the Quayle council.

The Office of Management and Budget today is clearly identified as a politically responsive staff unit and can no longer be regarded as a career staff unit serving the longer-term interests of the presidency by confining its functions to established review routines and providing objective, nonpartisan advice to whomever occupies the White House. The latter was what Brownlow wanted the Executive Office of the President to be, and what the Bureau of the Budget—more than any other component of the EOP—was intended to represent. As time passes, OMB seems to be moving farther away from the Brownlow ideal, an ideal that has been incrementally undermined by a succession of presidents, beginning with Eisenhower and his decision to appoint a noncareer official to head the Bureau of the Budget in 1953. This may be nothing more than a reflection on Brownlow's misplaced optimism in assuming that the Bureau of the Budget could satisfy the needs of a president by serving the longer-term interests of the presidency, and certainly none of President Nixon's successors has shown much remorse over the death of the Bureau of the Budget, nor any willingness to put the clock back and return to the Brownlow ideal.

Domestic Policy

For the first thirty years of the EOP's existence, the White House Office and the Bureau of the Budget shared the major staff responsibilities in the domestic policy arena. Senior aides in the White House Office acted as the president's immediate policy advisers and assisted in developing priority policies. This was done through the preparation of presidential speeches, messages to Congress, other public statements, and the drafting of legislation to be sent to Congress. The involvement of the Bureau of the Budget was directed toward coordinating policy proposals emanating from the departments and agencies, although, beginning with Kennedy, the directors of the bureau became more overtly involved in policy advice. In 1970, the domestic policy machinery of the Executive Office was expanded when President Nixon established within it the Domestic Council, a body that has been reshaped a number of times by his successors and now exists in the Clinton EOP as the Domestic Policy Council supported by a staff under the direction of the assistant to the president for domestic policy.

President Nixon's Domestic Council was, in part, a development of the domestic policy machinery in the White House Office. From Roosevelt to Kennedy, the number of domestic policy staff was small. In the Truman administration, for example, the special counsel (initially Samuel Rosenman, who was succeeded by Clark Clifford and then Charles Murphy) managed staff work on the president's legislative proposals, speeches, messages to Congress, the preparation of executive orders, final review of enrolled bills, and agendas for Truman's meetings with congressional leaders. In the later years of the Truman administration, Charles Murphy had the support of two administrative assistants and his own personal assistant, who were, in the words of one them, "general purpose associates, operating very intimately and very flexibly, working jointly or severally on anything and everything that came along."[157]

In Eisenhower's White House, domestic policy staff work, like so much else, was firmly in the hands of the assistant to the president, Sherman Adams, and his deputy, Wilton B. Persons. The functions of the special counsel during Eisenhower's presidency were primarily confined to legal matters, and although he did participate in domestic policy formulation, his role was nowhere near as important as that of his predecessor in the Truman administration.[158]

President Kennedy reverted to the Truman model. Domestic policy was handled by Special Counsel Theodore C. Sorensen, with the assistance of Lee White and Myer Feldman. Richard Goodwin, a speechwriter, was also attached to Sorensen's office. But when President Johnson succeeded President Kennedy, the size of the White House domestic policy staff expanded significantly, and control was fragmented among several key aides. Joseph Califano was generally recognized as the principal domestic policy assistant in the Johnson White House, but, as John Kessel has pointed out, three other senior White House staffers, Bill Moyers, Harry McPherson, and Douglass Cater, had significant domestic policy responsibilities, and each had his own staff. Including the principals, Johnson had a staff of twenty-one White House aides working on domestic policy, and Califano alone had seven assistants working directly under him. Some of this expansion was attributable to the large number of domestic policy initiatives undertaken by the Johnson administration, but it was also, in part, a consequence of Johnson's freewheeling style and his habit of handing out staff assignments to whoever happened to be with him when the issue arose.[159]

The expanding White House domestic policy staff became a new and separate division of the EOP in July 1970 when the Domestic Council was established. The council was set up as a Cabinet-level body intended to be a forum for discussion and action on policy matters that cut across departmental jurisdictions. It was to be chaired by the president, and its membership consisted of the vice president, all the members of the Cabinet except the secretaries of state and defense, and the director of the Office of Economic Opportunity. The council was to be supported by a staff, headed by an executive director. In his message to Congress proposing the establishment of the Domestic Council and the reform of the Bureau of the Budget, President Nixon complained that, hitherto, there had been no "organized, institutionally staffed group charged with advising the president on the total range of domestic policy." He intended that the Domestic Council staff would fill that gap and would also be responsible for integrating the various aspects of domestic policy into a consistent whole.[160]

The Domestic Council was seen as a parallel body to the National Security Council, and its development under Nixon was remarkably similar to that of the NSC. Like the NSC, the Domestic Council was little more than a formality. It rarely met as a group and most of its work was done in smaller committees directed by a senior member of its staff. Because the council met so infrequently, the president had little involvement with it, and the management of the council's business was left to John Ehrlichman, its executive director. Ehrlichman was also the president's principal White House adviser on domestic policy issues and the effective contact between the president and the Domestic Council. It soon became apparent that the Domestic Council's staff, rather than the council itself, was really the significant force and, just as the NSC had become a staff arm of the president, so too did the Domestic Council. "Nixon never seems to have meant it as a collegial body," notes Stephen Hess,[161] and in his brief references to the Domestic Council, John Ehrlichman himself has made it very clear that the staff worked for the president, not the council.[162]

The Domestic Council staff grew in numbers and power. Kessel lists the names of twenty-six professional staffers working with the Domestic Council and the report of the growth of the EOP from the House of Representatives Post Office and Civil Service Committee indicates a total staff of fifty-two in 1971, rising to seventy the following year.[163] The staff operated at the highest level of the policy-making process. On the basis of extensive interviews with members of the Domestic Council staff, Kessel shows that staff work was "concentrated on clarifying choices to be made by the president, and making the much larger number of decisions that were not important enough to be referred to the chief executive." Only a small part of the staff's work was devoted to such routine tasks as collecting information and monitoring agency activity.[164]

With Ehrlichman at the helm, the Domestic Council staff was very much an extension of the president and far too obviously the personal instrument of Richard Nixon to be regarded as an institutional staff in the Brownlow sense. When Ehrlichman was forced to leave the White House on 30 April 1973 because of his involvement in Watergate-related activities, the influence of the Domestic Council began to wane. Ehrlichman's successor, Kenneth Cole, did not enjoy the same close relationship with the president, nor was he able to exert the same level of influence within the council.[165] Moreover, because the council staff was so closely identified with the staffing needs of Richard Nixon, it became a victim of the president's preoccupation with Watergate during the final eighteen months of his presidency. When Richard Nixon ceased to concern himself with anything except Watergate, there was correspondingly little purpose behind Domestic Council staff activity.

For a short time, the Domestic Council staff had been a very influential body within the EOP and had partially eclipsed the power of the Office of Management and Budget. Nixon's idea that the Domestic Council would be responsible for "what we do" and OMB for "how we do it" created tension and competition between the two units. The division of responsibilities was never as clear-cut in practice as Nixon made it out to be on paper,[166] and, as long as a powerful figure like Ehrlichman ran the Domestic Council, the position of OMB, particularly in the area of program planning, was constantly under challenge. In this sense, Watergate eased the competition for OMB, and the Domestic Council was never again to be the force that it had been under Ehrlichman.

The problems of the Domestic Council staff continued into the Ford administration. Although attempts were made to turn it into a longer-range domestic policy planning unit, it failed to make any real impact in this regard. A number of problems plagued the Ford Domestic Council staff, including weak direction at the top, reduction in staff numbers, and a major challenge to its jurisdiction from the newly created Economic Policy Board.[167]

The Domestic Council staff gained a new lease on life during the Carter administration. President Carter formally abolished the Council in 1977, thus doing away with the pretense of collegiality that had existed since 1970, but held on to the staff, which was renamed the Domestic Policy Staff (DPS). It was placed under the direction of the president's domestic policy adviser, Stuart Eizenstat, whose relationship with Carter was as close as that of Ehrlichman to Nixon and who became one of the most influential White House aides in the Carter administration.[168]

The size of the Domestic Policy Staff increased substantially during the Carter years, to more than double that of its counterpart in the Ford administration. It came to play a dominant role in domestic policy making, particularly from April 1978, following the first signs of President Carter's dissatisfaction with "Cabinet government" and his subsequent concentration of policy-making responsibility in the hands of the presidential staff.[169]

Eizenstat structured the enlarged Domestic Policy Staff around ten "issue clusters" covering the whole range of government domestic policy, including economic policy.[170] Each cluster was headed by an associate director, and each associate director reported to Eizenstat through his two deputies. The function of the Domestic Policy Staff was emphasized as a coordinating one, "as shepherding policy along, developing it in tandem with the agencies," in the words of Eizenstat,[171] but that coordinating role gave the DPS a "pervasive influence on every major White House policy proposal."[172] No government department or agency was outside the purview of the DPS's issue clusters and its associate directors.

The Domestic Policy Staff represented a substantial strengthening of the presidential branch over the executive branch during the Carter administration. It continued to operate during the Reagan administration under a different name, the Office of Policy Development (OPD), but it did not match the prominence and influence of its predecessor. President Reagan gave the OPD a number of administrative support responsibilities, such as servicing the newly established Cabinet councils, which proved to be something of a diversion from the policy analysis and advisory role that preoccupied the DPS under President Carter. Furthermore, the Reagan OPD operated within a different political environment from its Carter counterpart and encountered stronger competition from other EOP agencies, principally OMB and the White House Office, for a dominant voice in domestic policy making.[173] But there were also internal weaknesses within the OPD that lowered its prominence in President Reagan's first term. Ineffective leadership, ideological rigidity, lack of experience, and high levels of staff turnover (Reagan had three Assistants for Policy Development in his first term) characterized the OPD in its early days and limited its effectiveness as an advisory body. This was compounded by the fact that the Assistant for Policy Development did not have direct access to the president. He reported through senior White House aide Edwin Meese, which marked a downgrading in the status of the office he represented in the hierarchically conscious presidential staff system.

During Reagan's second term, the role of the Office of Policy Development was circumscribed by the presence of a powerful White House chief of staff who took an active role in policy formulation. In the Bush presidency, it was circumscribed by a powerful combination of White House Chief of Staff John Sununu and Director of OMB Richard Darman. This is not to say that OPD was redundant during the Reagan-Bush years, but rather, that it operated at one remove from the president, and in neither presidency was the assistant for policy development able to attain the kind of status that John Ehrlichman or Stuart Eizenstat enjoyed in the Nixon and Carter administrations. In any case, Roger Porter, who served as director of OPD for President Bush, was not particularly interested in emulating Ehrlichman or Eizenstat, or engaging in power struggles with Sununu and Darman. Porter was the quintessential honest broker in the White House, the process manager who, according to a *New York Times* profile, was "skilled at taking the issue of the moment, finding out where everyone stands, clarifying and organizing their positions and presenting them to the president in a fair way."[174] He seemed willing to leave the broad lines of policy and legislative strategy to Sununu and Darman,[175] but when Sununu and Darman themselves became a major problem, Porter's process-management skills were not enough. Sununu was replaced as chief of staff at the end of 1991 when President Bush's approval ratings were beginning to plummet and domestic policy was seen to be a major reason for his decline in popularity. The new chief of staff, Samuel Skinner, saw an urgent need to improve the domestic policy-making operation in the White House and brought in Clayton Yeutter as counselor to the president to oversee domestic policy and, it was widely reported, to exert some policy control over Darman.[176] Porter remained in his position as assistant to the president for economic and domestic policy, but junior to Yeutter in a bizarre arrangement that lasted until Secretary of State James Baker reluctantly returned to the White House, replacing Samuel Skinner as chief of staff in August 1992. Yeutter had been ineffective as domestic policy overlord and departed at the same time as Skinner. Porter survived the second upheaval in the Bush White House, but, by that time, the 1992 election result had made questions about his position and status as assistant for economic and domestic policy moot.

President Clinton's version of the Office of Policy Development is the most complex to date. The Office of Policy Development has become merely an umbrella term in the Clinton administration covering three distinct staff units: the National Economic Council, the Domestic Policy Council, and the Office of Environmental Policy. Each is headed by an assistant or deputy assistant to the president. Clinton's Domestic Policy Council appears to be a return to the Nixon model of a Cabinet committee supported by a staff unit that prepares and coordinates advice to the president on domestic issues, and if the Clinton version works like the Nixon model, then one would expect the staff to be rather more prominent in the policy-making process than the council itself. The third arm of the Office of Policy Development under Clinton is the Office on Environmental Policy, charged with providing advice to the president on all domestic and international environmental issues, coordinating all interagency efforts on environmental matters, and working with the National Security Council, the National Economic Council, and the Domestic Policy Council to address what the White House calls "cross-sectoral environmental concerns."[177]

There is no single assistant to the president in charge of the Office of Policy Development in the Clinton White House. There is an assistant for economic policy (Robert E. Rubin), an assistant for domestic policy (Carol Rasco), and a deputy assistant for environmental policy (Kathleen McGinty), each with their own staffs. President Clinton has also appointed a "Senior Adviser for Policy Development" (Ira Magaziner), who operates semi-independently within OPD structure, and a "Senior Adviser for Policy and Strategy" (George Stephanopoulos), who works directly for the president, with no intermediary. The president has also given the First Lady, Hillary Rodham Clinton, a major role in coordinating the administration's efforts to develop a health-care policy. In addition, Clinton has sought advice on policy matters from a number of former campaign aides who are not members of the White House staff and are acting as consultants to the president under the aegis of the Democratic National Committee.[178] There were, however, one or two signs that the staff working under the umbrella of OPD will be the engine room of domestic policy making in the Clinton administration. In testimony to the House Appropriations Subcommittee that handles the OPD budget request, Patsy Thomasson, director of the Office of Administration in the EOP, reported that President Clinton had changed the mix of policy staff to support staff within OPD so that there would be a greater number of policy people and fewer clerical and administrative staff. Out of a total staff of forty, Clinton had a ratio of three policy to one support staff in his OPD. Moreover, he had moved the responsibility for the administration of the three staff units within OPD to the Office of Administration because, according to Thomasson, he did not want the OPD staff distracted from policy work by management and administration.[179]

The fragmentation of policy advice in the early days of the Clinton administration makes it difficult to foresee how the domestic policy-making machinery will perform, and much will depend on the ability of the various White House staffers with responsibilities in this area to coordinate activities among themselves as well as coordinating the input from the departments and agencies. Since its establishment as a separate division within the Executive Office of the President, the domestic policy staff has been most influential when the Assistant for Domestic Policy has been a trusted member of the president's inner circle of White House advisers. At other times, it has been vulnerable to competition from other EOP units and its position within the presidential branch somewhat more uncertain. The Clinton machinery is rather more unpredictable than corresponding structures in previous administrations because of the larger number of senior staffers under the umbrella of the Office of Policy Development (two assistants to the president and at least five deputy assistants in three distinct staff units, plus the "Senior Advisers"), creating the potential for considerable in-house competition and conflict. On the other hand, the structure does offer the possibility of genuine policy coordination across overlapping jurisdictions, especially across the economic policy/domestic policy divide, which no previous president has been able to do satisfactorily.

In addition to the Office of Policy Development, other EOP agencies have also played a role in the domestic policy arena in recent administrations. Two of them, the Council on Environmental Quality and the Office of National Drug Control Policy, advise the president in specific policy areas. The third, the Office of Management and Budget, has an important across-the-board process function.

The Council on Environmental Quality (CEQ) was established within the EOP by the National Environmental Policy Act of 1969. The council consists of a chairman and two other members appointed by the president, subject to the advice and consent of the Senate, and a staff that has fluctuated in size quite dramatically over the life of the council. When President Nixon left office, the CEQ had a staff of over sixty. That had been reduced to nine by the end of Ronald Reagan's term, but was expanded to just over thirty in the last few months of the Bush presidency. Among its responsibilities, the CEQ is charged with recommending to the president national policies to improve the quality of the environment and to make an annual report to Congress on the state of the environment. But its work has been rather peripheral to the day-to-day concerns of most presidents, particularly in the Reagan administration, where there was little empathy with environmental policy. The council and its staff were even located peripherally in a small office in Jackson Place, not in the Old or New Executive Office Buildings, and, but for the fear of offending the environmental lobby, the Council's functions could have easily been absorbed within the Department of the Interior, the Environmental Protection Agency, or the Office of Policy Development in the EOP.

Ironically, it was the strongly pro-environment Clinton administration that moved to abolish the CEQ shortly after taking over the White House. On 8 February 1993, President Clinton pledged to elevate the Environmental Protection Agency to a Cabinet-level department and proposed replacing the Council on Environmental Quality with an Office of Environmental Policy that would have "broader influence and a more effective and focused mandate to coordinate environmental policy."[180] The new Office of Environmental Policy was intended to ensure that environmental issues got much fuller attention than they had under previous administrations and to be a central, rather than a peripheral player in the policy development process within the White House. A further irony is that most major environmental groups quickly came out in opposition to the abolition of the Council on Environmental Quality, even though the reform was intended to strengthen the voice of environmental concerns within the White House. They were worried about the loss of a statutory body within the EOP that has served as a bulwark against antienvironmental policy in the past and would be able to do so again if a less friendly administration succeeded that of President Clinton.[181] Because the Council on Environmental Quality was created by statute, it can only be abolished by legislation passed by Congress. Thus the decision to reorganize environmental policy making in the Clinton White House is not totally in the hands of President Clinton. Congress refused to go along with the president in this case. In fact, several members of the House of Representatives successfully threatened to block the legislation elevating the Environmental Protection Agency to Department status in order to salvage the CEQ, and Congress subsequently funded a scaled-down council for the 1994 fiscal year.[182]

In its origin, the Office of National Drug Control Policy (ONDCP) was not unlike the Council on Environmental Quality. Both agencies were set up by Congress in response to difficult policy problems when there were no obvious policy solutions to those problems. The Office of National Drug Control Policy was established under Title I of the Anti-Drug Abuse Act of 1988 and came into effect on the first full day of the Bush presidency. It represented a very substantial addition to the number of staff in the EOP and the policy-making and coordination responsibilities of the presidential branch. In fact, the ONDCP quickly took on the appearance of a small government department. The 1988 act provided for four presidentially appointed officials: a director, two deputy directors, and an associate director, all subject to Senate confirmation. Measured by the size of its budget, the ONDCP became the third-largest unit in the Bush EOP, after OMB and the White House Office, and the size of its staff more than doubled during President Bush's term.

The ONDCP was given substantial responsibilities for coordinating federal, state, and local efforts to control illegal drug abuse and devising national antidrug strategies, which the director was required to present to Congress through the president. But ONDCP met with little success during the Bush administration. It had problems with its basic mission of coordinating antidrug activities, and there was little to show in other areas.[183] Furthermore, as its staff numbers grew, ONDCP began to be seen as a dumping ground for political supporters. There was, for example, considerable controversy when it was revealed that Digger Phelps, a former Notre Dame basketball coach, had been appointed to a $104,000-a-year job in ONDCP at the insistence of Vice President Dan Quayle. Representative Charles Rangel, chairman of the House Select Committee on Narcotics Abuse and Control, told the *Washington Post* that ONDCP was "top heavy with political rejects" and claimed that "there were few people over there who knew an interdiction program from an eradication program."

In 1993, the incoming Clinton administration identified forty-six staff positions in the drug-control office that had been occupied by political appointees. The new president's response was to reduce the level of ONDCP's staff from the 146 that Bush left behind to 25, and although Clinton did propose to elevate the director of the ONDCP to full membership of the Cabinet, that did not prevent the drastic staff reductions being read as a downgrading of ONDCP.[184] According to White House Chief of Staff Thomas McLarty, who briefed the media after President Clinton announced the reorganization of ONDCP, the president believed that "resources to fight the drug problem should go to education, to treatment and to enforcement at the state and local level." McLarty also told the media that "the real essence here is not to pull everything into the White House, but to get those functions out in the Cabinet levels where you have the resources."[185] The staff reductions in ONDCP were announced by President Clinton as part of a broader package of reform designed to fulfill his campaign promise to reduce the overall size of the presidential staff by 25 percent, an initiative greeted with some cynicism by the media but, nonetheless, an expression of the president's disinclination to have such a large staff unit, essentially involved in operational matters, dumped by Congress in the Executive Office of the President.

The principal responsibilities of the Office of Management and Budget in the domestic policy arena, aside from budgetary policy, center on the legislative clearance process, briefly described in the previous chapter, and on what is known as legislative programming. Legislative clearance is a routine process, carried out by the Legislative Reference Division of OMB, that involves reviews of departmental and agency legislative initiatives and of enrolled legislation to determine if they are in accord with, or consistent with, the president's position. When this is not the case, OMB advises departments or agencies to revise their proposals accordingly or recommends that enrolled legislation be vetoed by the president.[186] Legislative programming is another coordinating activity conducted by OMB on behalf of the president. Essentially, it involves identifying in advance departmental and agency ideas for legislation, relating them to budgetary considerations, and working with the White House staff to build the ideas into the president's legislative program. This is less of a routine, and more of a political activity, than is legislative clearance, and for that reason the degree of OMB involvement in legislative programming can fluctuate, depending on the style of the president and the way in which the White House staff is deployed. Generally, the White House staff depends far more on OMB for legislative clearance work than it does on its legislative programming processes.[187]

Science and Technology Policy

Since 1933, when Franklin D. Roosevelt established a Science Advisory Board, science and technology have had a voice in or around the White House. It has not always been a very powerful voice, at times only a faint whisper, but it is heard periodically, and the Office of Science and Technology Policy is now a statutorily established source of analysis and advice within the Executive Office of the President.

Science advice first got a foothold inside the EOP when President Roosevelt signed an executive order in June 1941 establishing an Office of Scientific Research and Development as a subdivision of the Office of Emergency Management. Its major responsibility was to advise the president on scientific and medical research in relation to the war effort, and the office was eventually absorbed within the National Military Establishment (the forerunner of the Department of Defense) in 1947.

President Truman reestablished a science advisory mechanism in the EOP by creating a Science Advisory Committee in the Office of Defense Mobilization, under the chairmanship of Dr. Oliver Buckley. It was not a great success. Buckley, who declined to serve directly as the president's science adviser, had a very limited vision of what the committee should do, and, according to one of its members, "the committee languished in desuetude."[188] President Eisenhower kept the committee in existence and gave it a number of useful assignments, but it took the launching of the Soviet Union's Sputnik in October 1957 to bring science advisers closer to the president. Shortly after the launch, Eisenhower announced that he was creating the post of special assistant to the president for science and technology within the White House Office, to be filled by the then president of MIT, Dr. James Killian. Two weeks later, Eisenhower also announced that he was removing the Science Advisory Committee from the Office of Defense Mobilization and installing it in the White House Office as an enlarged and renamed President's Science Advisory Committee.[189]

Thanks to the Soviet Union, science and technology advice was upgraded significantly in the presidential staff hierarchy under Eisenhower. The launching of Sputnik had undermined America's claims to leadership in scientific and technological development and had aroused widespread concern about the state of American military security. Consequently the role of the new science adviser was seen primarily in terms of weapons development and the space race. The headline in the *Boston Herald* the day after Eisenhower announced the appointment of the new science adviser read "Killian Named Missile Czar," and even Killian saw the president's initiative as "a calculated political act to fend off attacks on his defense policies."[190] Yet the upgrading of science advice in the White House was not just a symbolic response to a national crisis demanding an immediate presidential initiative. Killian and his successor, George Kistiakowsky, played an important part during the last three years of the Eisenhower administration in evaluating and advising on high-technology defense programs. As Killian modestly admits in his memoirs, "Under Eisenhower the science adviser had acquired unusual power for a staff member, especially in the domain of military technology."[191]

The function of President Eisenhower's special assistant for science and technology was essentially analytical and advisory. Policy coordination was to be handled outside the EOP by a Federal Council for Science and Technology, which Eisenhower had established by executive order on 13 March 1959. President Kennedy retained the Eisenhower structure for just over one year, then moved to expand the science and technology advisory mechanism and to add coordination responsibilities to its functions. In March 1962, the president submitted a reorganization plan to Congress that established a new Office of Science and Technology as a separate unit within the Executive Office of the President, to be headed by a director who would be appointed with the advice and consent of the Senate. The special assistant would thus perform a dual role as adviser to the president and director of what Kennedy saw as a permanent staff resource in the field of science and technology.

In his accompanying message to Congress, Kennedy specified the responsibilities of the director. The first was concerned with policy advice, especially the relationship of science and technology to national security. This had always been the principal and overriding purpose of the science adviser's function since Eisenhower had established the post, and it remained the principal focus throughout the Kennedy administration. The second responsibility was analyzing and evaluating selected scientific and technical developments in relation to their impact on national policies, and the third major responsibility was the new one of "review, integration and co-ordination of major Federal activities in science and technology."[192] The Federal Council for Science and Technology, which was nothing more than an interagency committee, continued to operate, but Kennedy had made clear that overall coordination of science and technology would be centered in the EOP.[193]

Kennedy attached much importance to the role of the science adviser. The 1962 reorganization, and the subsequent increase in staff, were indications of enhanced status in the presidential staff system. Furthermore, the range of concerns being addressed by the Office of Science and Technology was broadened and no longer confined to military and space issues.[194] Among the nonmilitary matters studied by Kennedy's science advisers were such diverse problems as waterlogging and salinity in West Pakistan, narcotic abuse, biomedical research, and manpower needs in science and technology.

Under Eisenhower and Kennedy, presidential science advisers had a significant impact on public policy. The executive secretary of the president's Science Advisory Committee, David Beckler, has claimed that a remarkable series of scientific and technological initiatives was directly traceable to the new staff mechanism. Among them he listed the establishment of the National Aeronautics and Space Administration (NASA), major improvements in the long-range ballistic missile program and in ballistic missile early-warning capabilities, advances in technical capabilities of antisubmarine warfare, recommendations that led directly to the establishment of the Arms Control and Disarmament Agency, and assessment of the technical feasibility of a nuclear test ban that culminated in the Nuclear Test Ban Treaty of 1963.[195]

The impact of presidential science advisers during this period depended on a number of factors. The circumstances of the time, particularly the launching of Sputnik, were obviously a major catalyst in making two presidents aware of the need to bring the special expertise of science advisers into the policy-making process at the highest level. The close relationships that Eisenhower and Kennedy had with their science advisers were also critical factors. Killian, Kistiakowsky, and, later, Jerome Weisner, had access to presidents who were genuinely keen to utilize high-level technological expertise. Yet another important variable, and one to which Beckler attaches a great deal of weight in his account of science in the White House, was the relationship between the science advisers and other key presidential staff, especially the national security adviser.[196] Because so much of what the science advisers did concerned national security and overlapped the responsibilities of the national security staff, Eisenhower's decision to bring science advisers into the White House created the potential for considerable intrastaff conflict. This conflict never materialized under Eisenhower, largely because Robert Cutler, the national security assistant, was supportive of the new science advisory mechanism and welcomed the participation of the science adviser at meetings of the National Security Council.

Tensions between the science adviser and other elements of the presidential staff system began to surface toward the end of the Kennedy administration when McGeorge Bundy, the president's special assistant for national security affairs, with the support of an enlarged NSC staff, assumed a more prominent role than had his predecessors. This made it more difficult for the director of the Office of Science and Technology, Jerome Wiesner, to have direct access to Kennedy on national security issues,[197] and David Beckler attributed the declining influence of the science adviser under Johnson and Nixon directly to the growth of the NSC staff and its concern with detailed national security policy formulation.[198]

The status of the science advisory mechanism deteriorated rapidly during the Johnson and Nixon years, and in 1973 President Nixon submitted a reorganization plan to Congress to abolish the Office of Science and Technology and the President's Science Advisory Committee (PSAC). Lurking behind the president's claims about the need to streamline the White House was the inherent structural weakness of the science and technology staff. There was nothing in the constitution of the Office of Science and Technology to counter the antipathy of Johnson and Nixon toward scientists who were out of sympathy with the political direction of the administration they were advising. Science advisers came to be regarded by both presidents as symbolic of the academic and intellectual community's hostility toward the conduct of the Vietnam war. They also began to be a source of opposition to other presidential policies, especially during the Nixon years when members of the PSAC opposed a number of important Nixon initiatives including the antiballistic missile program and the development of a supersonic airplane.[199] There was also little the science adviser could do to fend off bureaucratic competition from within the EOP. Top White House aides tended to share Nixon's suspicion about the loyalty of science advisers, the NSC staff was concerned about protecting its turf and successfully denied the science adviser access to NSC meetings, and OMB deprived the Office of Science and Technology of the budgetary clout necessary to do its job properly.[200] Moreover, during the Johnson and Nixon years, a number of new and very specialized staff units were added to the EOP, such as the National Council on Marine Resources and Engineering Development, the Council on Environmental Quality, and the Energy Policy Office, and these took away a number of responsibilities from the Office of Science and Technology.

Although there was hardly any congressional opposition to President Nixon's dismantling of the Office of Science and Technology and the President's Science Advisory Committee, there was enough subsequent pressure by the scientific community to mobilize congressional support for the eventual restoration of a science advisory mechanism three years later.[201] In May 1976 Congress passed, and President Ford signed into law, the National Science and Technology Policy, Organization and Priorities Act, which established a new Office of Science and Technology Policy (OSTP) in the EOP.

Under Presidents Carter and Reagan, the Office of Science and Technology Policy operated as a second-level staff unit, providing advice both to the president and other units in the Executive Office, particularly the Office of Management and Budget. Indeed, the budgetary aspects of science and technology policy have been an important preoccupation of the post-1976 science advisers, who have been forced to reconcile federal support for scientific research with far tighter budgetary constraints than were imposed on their counterparts in the Eisenhower and Kennedy administrations. In this respect, both Frank Press, President Carter's science adviser, and George Keyworth II, who held the position during the first term of the Reagan administration, made significant gains in defending the levels of science research funding at a time of ever-increasing budget deficits.[202]

Neither under Frank Press, George Keyworth, nor Keyworth's successor in Reagan's second term, William Graham, did the Office of Science and Technology Policy achieve the prominence that the science advisers had during the Eisenhower and Kennedy years. President Bush did try to give the post a little more profile and importance. He appointed Allan Bromley as director of OSTP and also as assistant to the president for science and technology, thus elevating the science adviser to the senior ranks of the White House staff. The size of the Office of Science and Technology, which had contracted dramatically under Reagan, was increased substantially by President Bush.[203] In addition, Bush established a President's Council of Advisers on Science and Technology, under Bromley's chairmanship, which was intended to be the science policy equivalent of the Council of Economic Advisers.[204] Because the council was set up over halfway through his presidency, however, there was really little time for it to make its mark and have any clear impact on science policy making. Bromley himself played a part as well by revitalizing the Federal Coordinating Council for Science, Engineering and Technology, a body established by the National Science and Technology Policy, Organization and Priorities Act to be the principal technology policy coordinating mechanism in the executive branch, but which had been dormant during the Reagan presidency.[205] But, as Bruce Smith concludes in his historical survey of presidential science advising, despite the enhanced status of the science adviser under George Bush, the office was still a fragile and precarious one and subject to endemic jurisdictional conflicts with other presidential staff and the "vagaries of life at court."[206]

Under President Clinton, the responsibilities of the Office of Science and Technology Policy have been expanded slightly to include some of the functions previously performed by the National Space Council and the National Critical Materials Council. The National Space Council was another of those presidential staff units established by Congress but unwanted by the president. Its authority derived from Title V of of the National Aeronautics and Space Administration Authorization Act passed by Congress in 1988 and was established by Executive Order 12675 signed by President Bush on 20 April 1989. The council was meant to be both an advisory and a coordinating body on space policy, but it rarely met and was allocated just a handful of staff. The National Critical Materials Council was established by Congress in 1984 to advise the president on policies related to strategic and critical materials. It was chaired by the president's science adviser and had therefore been effectively subsumed into the Office of Science and Technology Policy before President Clinton announced his intention to do so formally. No funding for the National Space Council or the National Critical Materials Council was included in President Clinton's budget request for fiscal year 1994, and the White House announced it would be submitting legislation to Congress to terminate the authorization for these staff units.

One important departure from tradition in the Clinton administration has been the appointment of a nonresearch scientist to head the Office of Science and Technology Policy. Clinton's choice for the position, John Gibbons, was a nuclear physicist by training but was recruited from the congressional Office of Technology Assessment where he had been director for the previous fourteen years. Gibbons had a reputation as an effective consensus builder with extensive knowledge and experience of the workings of government in Washington and had been credited with transforming the Office of Technology Assessment from an ineffective agency to a respected information-gathering arm of Congress.[207] Such an appointment might indicate a more substantial role for the Office of Science and Technology Policy as a policy coordinator, rather than just a policy adviser. At the least, the appointment of Gibbons sends a clear message to the science community that the president's science adviser is a member of the presidential staff rather than the science community's spokesman inside the White House, the latter being a perception of the science adviser's role that may have contributed to the weakness of the science advisory mechanism in some previous administrations.

The future of scientific advice in the White House will always be uncertain, despite the fact that the Office of Science and Technology Policy was reestablished by statute law in 1976, which makes disbanding it difficult, should any future president wish to do so. But the statutory basis of the office is no guarantee that the voice of the science adviser will be heard in the competitive environment of the Executive Office. In the past, science advisers have been most effective when scientific and technological issues have been at the forefront of public policy concerns and when presidents themselves have genuinely wanted to make use of science advice at the highest level. At other times, science advice, in the words of David Beckler, has had "a precarious life in the White House."[208] Scientific and technological advice is essentially specialized, objective, nonpolitical (at least in the eyes of scientists), and future oriented, which makes the science adviser's office a very different outfit from most of the other EOP units. Like the Council of Economic Advisers, the Office of Science and Technology Policy has no program responsibilities and few routine functions that might automatically give it a higher profile. Without strong presidential patronage and a crisis like the one generated by the launching of Sputnik, the Office of Science and Technology Policy can easily become a peripheral staff unit within the presidential branch. Given what happened to the Council of Economic Advisers during the Reagan administration, this might well be a fate common to any think-tank staff unit in the EOP.

Trade

Trade policy has had a separate voice in the Executive Office of the President for over thirty years and, although the Office of the U.S. Trade Representative (USTR) is now well established, it is also the most politically delicate of all the presidential staff units. This is partly because USTR was created by Congress, rather than the president, and since its inception, key members of Congress have continued to maintain an almost proprietary interest in its work. It is also partly because USTR is, as I. M. Destler has put it, an organizational anomaly. Its primary function, that of negotiating international trade agreements, is more akin to the day-to-day operational activities normally located in the executive branch departments, and its work can be somewhat removed from the immediate concerns of the president.[209] Furthermore, because USTR does not quite fit with the usual kind of presidential staff activity, its continued existence in the EOP is frequently questioned, more often than not through suggestions that USTR be elevated into a Department of Trade.

The origin of what is now called the Office of the U.S. Trade Representative is found in Section 241 of the Trade Expansion Act of 1962, a major piece of legislation initiated by President Kennedy to provide authority for the negotiation of sweeping new tariff reductions, popularly known as the Kennedy Round. Before the passage of that legislation, the Department of State had carried the major responsibility for international trade negotiations, but there had been considerable dissatisfaction over the way State had been handling trade negotiations, and with new tariff reductions imminent, pressure was put on Congress to remove that responsibility from State. Farm groups, in particular, believed that the State Department had been overly concerned with foreign political interests, to the detriment of domestic economic considerations, and had been "selling the country down the river for years."[210] The then chairman of the House Ways and Means Committee, Wilbur Mills, shared that view and it was he who added to the Kennedy trade bill a provision creating a new post of special representative for trade negotiations.[211] Mills also wanted to place the new trade negotiator in the Executive Office of the President. Kennedy, however, was reluctant to accept congressionally imposed staff units, and so a compromise was arrived at in which the president informally agreed to establish the special trade representative in the EOP at a later date under his own terms through the flexibility of an executive order.[212]

Section 241 of the 1962 Act made the appointment of the special representative for trade negotiations subject to the advice and consent powers of the Senate and gave ambassadorial rank to the holder of the post. But it said little about the responsibilities of the office except to require that the Trade Representative seek the advice of the relevant industry, agricultural, and labor interests before any negotiation on tariff reduction. No other presidential staff unit has been under a comparable statutory duty to consult interest groups, and perhaps it is not surprising that interest groups themselves are now particularly sensitive to this presidential agency and especially to the choice of who is to lead it.

President Kennedy fulfilled his part of the compromise with Ways and Means Chairman Wilbur Mills when, on 15 January 1963, he issued Executive Order 11075 establishing an office of the special representative for trade negotiations in the Executive Office of the President. By implementing Section 241 of the 1962 act by executive order, Kennedy had preserved presidential prerogative to shape his staff system as he desired without undue congressional interference, and, at the same time, satisfy the desire of Congress to remove responsibility for Kennedy Round trade negotiations from the State Department. The major statutory responsibility of the special representative for trade negotiations was, as the title of the post implies, the negotiation of trade agreements and tariff reductions consequent on the 1962 act. Executive Order 11075 elaborated a little on the statute, but President Kennedy was careful to define the role of the trade negotiator in a low-key manner. He gave the holder of the office responsibility for advising the president on the operation of the trade agreements program, coordinating the views of other departments and agencies, and acting as principal administration spokesman on trade legislation before Congress. It is important to note, however, that the responsibilities of the special trade representative related mainly to trade negotiations conducted under the authority of the Trade Expansion Act, and there was nothing in the legislation or the executive order to guarantee that there would necessarily be a longer-term purpose for this unit after the Kennedy Round had been concluded.

In the beginning, the strength of the special representative for trade negotiations came not so much from the statutory powers and responsibilities attached to the office, which were not particularly extensive, but from President Kennedy's choice of a former secretary of state in the Eisenhower administration, Christian Herter, to be the first occupant of the post. Herter, together with his two deputies, William Roth and Michael Blumenthal, instituted an effective operating unit for multilateral trade negotiations and worked in harmony with other departments, including State, which still carried responsibility for trade negotiations outside the Kennedy Round,[213] and with other White House staff who had responsibility for advising the president on trade policy generally and on its implications for both domestic and foreign policy.[214] Herter and his deputies established the new staff unit with a degree of restraint and with the recognition that the creation of the Office of Special Representative for Trade Negotiations had not completely centralized a hitherto fragmented policy-making process. It had merely provided the potential for better coordination of trade negotiations for the duration of the Kennedy Round.

Being essentially an operational staff unit in the EOP, the fortunes of the Office of the Special Trade Representative tended to rise and fall in relation to the importance of the work it had to do. Shortly after the Kennedy Round had been completed in June 1967, the office "went into eclipse,"[215] notwithstanding the efforts of William Roth, who had succeeded Christian Herter at the beginning of 1967, to broaden his responsibility by getting involved with bilateral trade questions in the hope of developing a more comprehensive approach to trade issues.[216] The eclipse of the special trade representative coincided with the first three years of the Nixon presidency and can be attributed to the change in administration combined with the absence of ongoing multilateral trade negotiations. The experience under Nixon, in contrast to the Kennedy-Johnson years, illustrates the degree to which a change of president can drastically alter the function and status of a presidential staff agency without any change in its statutory basis.

President Nixon's new special trade representative, Carl Gilbert, was not confirmed by the Senate until July 1969. In the interim, the Office of Special Trade Representative came close to being abolished after an attempted power grab by Secretary of Commerce Maurice Stans, who wanted the responsibility for coordinating trade policy placed in his department. Pressure from interest groups prevented Stans from getting his way, but the secretary of commerce did manage to exert considerable influence in the choice of the new special trade representative, an appointee who turned out to be an ineffective leader of a staff unit that, without any prospect of immediate trade negotiations, was peripheral to the trade policy making machinery in the Nixon White House.[217] In the words of I. M. Destler, the Office of the Special Trade Representative "became a bureaucratic backwater, weakly led and devoid of presidential support."[218] Furthermore, it encountered challenges to its potential jurisdiction over trade policy from other more powerful staff units in the Nixon White House. Initially, the National Security Council staff, under Henry Kissinger, had interests in the development of trade policy and had several international economists on its staff, but, more significantly, Nixon's creation of the Council on International

Economic Policy in January 1971 effectively relegated the Office of Special Trade Representative to a purely operational unit, albeit with little operational work to do at the time.

The weakness of the special trade representative's position was, ironically, partly responsible for its revival in the latter years of the Nixon administration and, indeed, its institutionalization in the EOP from then on. A proposal to have the office subsumed within the Council on International Economic Policy—in effect the second attempt during the Nixon administration to abolish the unit—worried some members of Congress, who reacted by strengthening the statutory base of the Office of Special Trade Representative in the course of putting together the Trade Act of 1974. Again, it was the House Ways and Means Committee that inserted into the administration's legislation a stronger foundation for the trade unit by technically abolishing the Office of Special Representative for Trade Negotiations, which President Kennedy had created under Executive Order 11075, and re-creating it under the same name as a statutorily based entity in the Executive Office of the President. The immediate consequence of this was that no future president would be able to abolish the office or move it to some other location in the executive branch without congressional assent in the form of an amendment to the 1974 act.

Prospects for a new round of trade negotiations became brighter in 1972, by which time Carl Gilbert had been replaced as special trade representative by William Eberle, who was able to breathe life into his office and restore some of its credibility within the administration. The Trade Act of 1974 did not give any significant additional powers to the Trade Representative. Essentially, Section 141 incorporated the provisions of the 1962 legislation and President Kennedy's executive order, but with two significant differences. The 1974 act dropped the requirement that the special representative for trade negotiations consult with relevant interest groups before each negotiation, but it introduced a new requirement that this presidential assistant would have to report and be responsible to Congress, as well as the president, for the administration of trade agreements negotiated under this act, the Trade Expansion Act of 1962, and the Tariff Act of 1930. In this respect, the office was unique. No other presidential staff agency has had this dual obligation and allegiance placed on it, and while it gave a potentially vulnerable body a strong base of support in Congress, that could also be used as an excuse by future presidents for putting some distance between themselves and the special trade representative.

The Office of the Special Representative for Trade Negotiations was strengthened significantly during the Carter administration. Carter's appointment of Robert Strauss as special trade representative brought in a politically experienced, former Democratic National Committee chairman, and well-known Washington personality, whose negotiating skills and sensitivity toward members of Congress were instrumental in securing the passage of the Trade Agreements Act of 1979, a major legislative achievement that ratified a further round of multilateral tariff reductions in the face of growing protectionist sentiment in Congress.[219] Strauss's high profile and his success in the job enhanced the position of his office within the trade policy-making machinery of American government.

It was further enhanced by a restructuring of the international trade functions of the executive branch announced by President Carter in September 1979.[220] In part, Carter's reorganization proposal was designed to stave off pressure from some quarters in Congress to consolidate all trade policy functions in a new Department of Trade, modeled along the lines of the Japanese Department of International Trade and Industry.[221] As a consequence, the Office of Special Representative for Trade Negotiations was renamed as the Office of the U.S. Trade Representative (USTR), was given responsibility for "international trade policy development, co-ordination and negotiation functions," thus establishing it as the lead agency within the executive branch for trade policy formulation, and was allowed to expand the number of staff in the unit quite significantly.[222] In his reorganization message to Congress, President Carter recognized the deficiencies in the trade policy-making machinery that had generated the congressional pressure for reform. He admitted that "current arrangements lack a central authority capable of planning a coherent trade strategy and assuring its vigorous implementation" and claimed that his reorganization would correct these deficiencies by establishing "an efficient mechanism for shaping an effective, comprehensive, United States trade policy."[223]

The Carter reorganization did not completely eliminate potential competition over trade policy making. As Destler points out, it gave policy-making functions to USTR while leaving policy implementation to the Department of Commerce, an arrangement that would work only if USTR and Commerce cooperated, with Commerce deferring to USTR direction.[224] The arrangement did seem to work adequately during the remainder of the Carter administration, but not so in the Reagan administration.

Reagan's first secretary of commerce, Malcolm Baldrige, had as strong a desire to run trade policy as did his counterpart in the Nixon administration, Maurice Stans. The new U.S. Trade Representative, William E. Brock, assumed office not only fending off Baldrige's power plays but also having to deal with Baldrige's powerful ally on the White House staff, Counselor to the President Edwin Meese. Meese supported Baldrige in an attempt to merge the Office of the U.S. Trade Representative with the Department of Commerce as a new Department of International Trade and Industry and was successful in persuading President Reagan to endorse the proposal, which was also being advocated in Congress by Senator William Roth, then chairman of the Senate Governmental Affairs Committee. The legislation never reached the floor of either chamber for a vote.[225]

Brock was weakened in his position of U.S. Trade Representative by

President Reagan's support for the abolition of his office. He was also weakened by the system of Cabinet councils established during Reagan's first term, in which presidential policy making was formally structured through seven Cabinet subcommittees whose work was tightly managed by senior White House staff. Although the Trade Representative had Cabinet status, trade issues were covered by the Cabinet Council on Commerce and Trade, and Baldrige, rather than Brock, was given the chairmanship of the group. Brock's greatest problem, however, was his lack of a close personal relationship with President Reagan, a situation that was even more acute with his successor, Clayton Yeutter, who served as U.S. Trade Representative in Reagan's second term. A *New York Times* profile of Mr. Yeutter after a year in office emphasized his lack of direct access to President Reagan, "his exclusion from the elite circle of trade policy makers close to the President," and, in one instance, his obvious lack of knowledge about the Reagan administration's trade policy toward South Africa.[226] In President Reagan's second term, the principal players changed. Secretary of Commerce Malcolm Baldrige lost some of his influence over trade policy when his ally, Edwin Meese, left the White House in 1985 to become Attorney General, and Yeutter replaced Brock as Trade Representative, but it was the former White House Chief of Staff James Baker, in his new position as secretary of the treasury, who emerged as the dominant figure in trade policy making from 1985.[227]

What kept the U.S. Trade Representative in the picture was the increasing importance of trade policy among White House priorities during the 1980s, inspired primarily by growing dissatisfaction on Capitol Hill with the administration's efforts to protect American manufacturers from foreign imports, and by a desire on the part of the Reagan administration to head off tougher protectionist measures from Congress.[228] The protectionist sentiment in Congress was well entrenched in the major piece of trade legislation during the Reagan years, the Omnibus Trade and Competitiveness Act of 1988, which, among other things, strengthened the statutory authority of the U.S. Trade Representative by transferring from the president to the USTR the power to take action against foreign nations engaging in unfair trade practices under Section 301 of the Trade Act of 1974. Previously, the Trade Representative could only recommend action to the president, who was under no compulsion to accept the recommendation.[229] The 1988 act effectively gave that discretion to a presidential subordinate, and in doing so it said a great deal about how Congress regards this anomalous presidential agency.

The revision of Section 301 after 1988 provided President Bush's U.S. Trade Representative, Carla Hills, with a vehicle for establishing her credibility within the new administration, which she exploited very successfully.[230] But, like most of her predecessors, she was not part of the inner circle of the White House system. As I.M. Destler has suggested, had Bush and his trade representative had a closer relationship on broad trade policy issues, the president might have been saved from the political blunders he made on his disastrous trade mission to Tokyo in January 1992.[231]

The continued existence of the Office of U.S. Trade Representative within the presidential branch owes more to Congress than it does to the various occupants of the White House since 1962. Two presidents, Nixon and Reagan, attempted to get rid of USTR, but each time Congress responded by shoring up its institutional foundations, thus making it more difficult for presidents to change the functions and location of this agency. The organizational flexibility that Kennedy insisted on when he created the forerunner of USTR no longer exists and now no president can contemplate removing the Office of U.S. Trade Representative from the EOP without a fight in Congress. Furthermore, it is not only Congress that wants to influence what the president does with his own staff agency. Interest groups also get involved. During President-elect Clinton's transition to the White House, intense battles broke out over possible nominees for the job of U.S. Trade Representative, with some trade and business lobbies launching public campaigns for or against prominent individuals who may have been under consideration.[232] While it is not known whether these campaigns influenced the president-elect's choice, there were no similar interest-group efforts with respect to any other positions within the presidential staff.

While Congress maintains its strong interest in the Office of U.S. Trade Representative, there is not likely to be significant change in the structure, function and location of this presidential staff unit. But, no matter how much Congress strengthens the powers of USTR, it cannot force the president to make the USTR more powerful than he wants it to be, and if trade policy is a low presidential priority, then it is likely that the Trade Representative will be a marginal player within the EOP. If trade policy is a high priority for the president, then one can expect that he or she will face competition from other players in the president's administration. In the past, there has been significant rivalry from the secretary of commerce, which is inevitable as long as trade remains the most important policy responsibility of the Department of Commerce. The Treasury has also been a powerful force in trade policy despite congressional attempts since 1962 to reduce its influence. Rivalry can come from inside the White House as well, and the Clinton administration may well be vulnerable to intrastaff conflicts over trade policy. The establishment of a National Economic Council to co-ordinate all economic policy provides one potential challenger to the USTR, and President Clinton's choice of Laura D'Andrea Tyson, an academic economist with expertise in trade policy, to head the Council of Economic Advisers certainly provides another. What will also undoubtedly continue is the debate over the organization of trade policy making within the executive branch, and one can expect further proposals for centralizing all trade functions in a new Department of Trade,[233] for although USTR has been an institutional success in many respects, it nevertheless remains an institutional anomaly. After thirty years of existence, USTR is still an operational agency located in the EOP as a political expediency. Political expediency keeps it there.

Operations and Administration

There exists within the EOP an Office of Administration. It was established by President Carter in 1977 to supply basic administrative and management support services to all units within the EOP, and it deals with such matters as information and data processing, financial management, records maintenance, library services, general office operations, equipment procurement, and EOP personnel matters. The Office of Administration is headed by a political appointee and is now the third largest unit in the EOP, with a full-time staff of 189 under President Clinton. However, the Office of Administration has very little consequence for intra-EOP politics because its functions are purely routine and administrative in nature.

The establishment of the Office of Administration was regarded by some as a devious method of shifting a large number of White House staff off the White House Office payroll, thus creating the impression that President Carter was fulfilling his promise to reduce the size of the president's personal staff.[234] The functions performed by the Office of Administration are little different from those performed by the administrative staff formerly located in the White House Office, and some observers still prefer to count the staff of the Office of Administration as part of the White House staff.[235] However, as the Office of Administration was created by a reorganization plan and is a separate line item in the EOP budget, it is a formally distinct unit of the EOP and not part of the White House Office. That distinction is now a necessary one, since President Bush established a small staff unit within the White House Office known as the Office of Management and Administration that handles various miscellaneous administrative and management chores relating to the White House Office and the Executive Residence. That staff unit has been continued in the Clinton White House and operates in conjunction with the Office of Administration in the EOP.

As it currently functions, the Office of Administration is probably not of any great consequence for the student of political science. It does, however, have the potential to become more than it is at the moment. If any future president decided to separate the budget and management functions at present within OMB, then the Office of Administration could be an existing base on which a revitalized executive branch management unit might be built. The management functions performed by the Office of Administration are primarily organizational and procedural, rather than coordinating and control. They are quite different from what OMB does today, but not unlike the kind of management role undertaken by the Bureau of the Budget in the immediate post-Brownlow phase of its development. It is also interesting to note that the first director of the Office of Administration in Reagan's White House also had the title of assistant to the president for management and administration.

In addition to the Office of Administration, there is a sizable operations, administrative and support staff within the White House Office who manage functions such as the White House mail room, the visitors' office, the correspondence unit, the White House Central Files and the telephone, telegraph, and transportation services.[236] Traditionally, many of these positions have been regarded as nonpolitical and were, at one time, under the direction of the executive clerk, the most senior nonpolitical official in the White House. Currently, most of these support units are responsible to a political appointee, either the president's assistant for management and administration or the staff secretary.

The executive clerk's office still functions around the same routines and formalities that it did in the late nineteenth century and with much the same minimal staff, at present an executive clerk, a deputy executive clerk, and four assistants. The executive clerk handles the "official" side of presidential decision making. He has the responsibility for receiving enrolled bills from Congress and making sure they are processed within the ten-day constitutional limit, for the formal delivery of presidential messages to Congress, for presidential commissions and appointments, and for the publication of executive orders. The executive clerk's office also acts as a repository of the statutory powers of the president. It is the only unit in the White House that maintains a compendium of every item of legislation that gives powers, responsibilities, and duties to the president.

The importance of the executive clerk's office and the operations staff must not be overlooked. They keep the White House running, and the executive clerk is the only real "institutional memory" in the structure of the presidency, particularly since the Bureau of the Budget ceased to be an institutional staff unit after 1970. Yet very little gets written about the executive clerk, and the office has been ignored, not only by students of the presidency but also by politicians. Incoming administrations have shown surprising ignorance about the role and status of the permanent White House staff, and as a consequence its existence has, at times, been in jeopardy. Some presidents and their top aides have had difficulty accepting that anyone working in the White House in a previous administration can be loyal to the new regime. At the very time when the executive clerk's office is most valuable to a new president, it is also at its most vulnerable.

The executive clerk and his staff are strictly nonpartisan officials, but they are not career civil servants in the sense of being protected by the merit system. Presidents are perfectly at liberty to dispose of all the permanent White House staff if they desire to do so, and on occasions some presidents have had to be persuaded that a permanent administrative and operations staff can serve the presidency in a thoroughly professional way irrespective of which party and which individual occupies the office at any one time. After twenty years of Democrats in the White House, the Eisenhower staff required a lot of persuading. William Hopkins, appointed as an assistant clerk under Franklin Roosevelt, managed to hold on to his job as executive clerk in 1953 only by convincing Sherman Adams that he first joined the White House staff during Herbert Hoover's administration.[237] Hopkins continued as executive clerk under three more presidents, eventually retiring in 1971 after forty years of service in the White House, ten years less than his predecessor, Maurice Latta, who served from 1898 until 1948. The current executive clerk, Ron Geisler, has completed twenty-nine years service and has now worked for seven presidents—four Republicans and three Democrats.

As the White House staff has expanded, so the executive clerk has tended to lose functions and some status. William Hopkins, for example, had an office in the White House, attended President Truman's morning staff meetings and, occasionally, Cabinet meetings during the Johnson administration. Today, the executive clerk has little direct contact with the president. He reports to the president's staff secretary, shares one small office in the Old Executive Office Building with his staff, and no longer has any responsibility for the operational units in the White House.

Most presidents eventually come to recognize the value of the permanent staff of the White House. President Johnson, for example, upgraded Hopkins's title to executive assistant to show his appreciation, and President Nixon awarded him the Presidential Medal of Freedom. The executive clerk's office is a professional, institutional administrative staff and perhaps the only unit in the White House that still adheres to Brownlow's notion about a passion for anonymity. The executive clerk and his staff can provide three vital services to any new occupant of the White House: information, memory, and continuity, each of which is vulnerable to any incoming administration that fails to make the distinction between institutional and personal staff. The politicization of the presidential staff has to stop at the door of the executive clerk's office.

Political Strategy

The last of the eight EOP staff functions identified at the beginning of this chapter related to political strategy. That is the preserve of the president's senior staff in the White House Office, the most important unit of the Executive Office and the directing force for all other divisions. For that reason, the development of the White House Office since Brownlow must be dealt with in a separate chapter.

4. THE WHITE HOUSE STAFF

Brownlow's 1937 blueprint for an enlarged White House staff was designed to provide presidents with much needed additional administrative capacity and to ensure that an enhanced personal staff unit could be made to fit into the existing structure of the executive branch of government without disrupting the traditional, established relations between the president and members of his Cabinet. The fit was to be achieved, or so Brownlow had hoped, by confining presidential staff members to a tightly defined role and relying ultimately on their self-constraint to keep them within the limits of that role. The concern expressed in the Brownlow report and Executive Order 8248 about the character, attitude, and professionalism of the White House staff, and about its ability to discharge functions with restraint, was a vital element of the blueprint.

With hindsight, it now appears that Brownlow was somewhat unrealistic about how presidential assistants might behave in office. He seems to have adopted a morality of public administration that was either short-lived or never existed in the United States, and he had not fully come to terms with the essential differences between the British Cabinet Office, on which he modeled his staffing proposals, and the White House. The self-restraint that may have been characteristic of those who made up the Cabinet secretariat in London was not easily transposed to Washington. President Truman observed the lack of it among his own staff. He once referred to them in his diary as "prima donnas" and commented that "some of my boys who came in with me are having trouble with their dignity and prerogatives. It's hell when a man gets in close association with the president."[1]

Nowadays, senior White House staffers regularly do what Brownlow said they should not do. They quickly become prominent figures in every administration. They do make decisions, issue instructions, and emit public statements. They do interpose themselves between the president and the heads of departments. They do exercise power on their own account, and, on occasions, certain members of the White House staff have not discharged their functions with restraint. In recent years, some have clearly lacked the high competence Brownlow thought essential, and few have displayed much passion for anonymity. The reality of life in the White House is far removed from the Brownlow Report.

As a consequence of these departures from Brownlow's vision, the enlarged White House staff has not fitted easily into the existing structure of relationships within the executive branch. What was essentially intended to be a conduit between the president and the enhanced management capacity in the Executive Office has instead become the management itself. The White House Office is now the directing force of the presidential branch, and the important units within the EOP are very much satellite agencies of the White House Office. Today there are very few traces of a truly institutional presidential staff in the Executive Office of the President, and few of the senior staffers within the White House Office would see themselves as "executive assistants" in the sense that Brownlow used the term.

The Brownlow report has influenced generations of political scientists who have studied the organization of the presidency, and its concern with improved administrative management has permeated almost all the major presidential reform commissions since 1945. But Brownlow's ideas about the president's personal staff have been discarded and ignored. They have been seen to be rooted in untenable assumptions about the separation of politics and administration, and as they have had little bearing on the actual development of the White House Office, they are considered to be of no real analytical value. Given the nature of the American presidency since the New Deal, most contemporary observers would seriously doubt that any senior staff assistant working in the White House could be confined to the rigid administrative role that Brownlow devised, and they would probably agree with the journalist at Roosevelt's press conference who exclaimed that "there ain't no such animal."[2]

Yet the Brownlow report ought not to be discarded in the context of discussions about the White House staff because it still has a lot to say about the problem of controlling those aides in close proximity to the president, and because it is a useful basis for examining the development of the White House Office during the postwar years. The most significant and controversial aspects of that development are to be found in the departures and deviations from the Brownlow design.

The Size of the White House Office

In much of the immediate post-Watergate literature, the size and growth of the White House Office was identified as one of the most significant causes of the abuse of presidential power associated with that period. Almost all the government officials who went to jail for their part in Watergate-related events were either on the White House Office staff or worked under the direction of senior members of the White House staff. Those jail sentences, plus the flood of apologetic memoirs that followed, made it easy for observers to locate blame. There was a general feeling that the president's personal staff had grown too large to be controlled by the president himself and that many presidential aides had gone into business for themselves to establish their power and status in a ruthlessly competitive political environment. The consequences of this expansion are considered further on, but, as a preliminary, it is necessary to examine one question to which the post-Watergate literature has failed to provide a definitive answer: How big is the White House staff?

As was pointed out in the previous chapter in the context of the Executive Office as a whole, the exact size of the presidential staff is difficult to calculate. One example was given where, within the space of two months, two different sets of figures were published by Congress, with one set showing the EOP two and a half times as large as the other. Not only has there been confusion about actual numbers, but the statistics have also been subjected to quite differing interpretations, some arguing that the expansion of the EOP was nowhere nearly as serious as a number of post-Watergate critics made it out to be.

The same problems and uncertainties arise in the specific context of the White House staff. Before the publication of the Brownlow report, there were thirty-seven full-time staff officially working in the White House Office. The Reorganization Act of 1939 authorized another six positions. In the thirty years from 1944 to 1974, the number of people officially employed in the White House Office increased tenfold, from about 58 to approximately 560, but one can do little more than talk about trends in growth and a rough approximation of staff numbers during this period because the available data are so inexact and no two sets of published statistics agree on any one figure for any one year.

Concern about the size of the White House staff was, and is, a Watergate-related phenomenon. The first attempts to quantify the expansion of the presidential staff began to appear in the early 1970s. A report from the House of Representatives Post Office and Civil Service Committee, referred to in the previous chapter, was the pioneer in this endeavor,[3] soon to be followed by the work of political scientist Thomas Cronin.[4] The data on staff growth in both of these contributions were derived from the annual *Budget of the United States Government.*

The annual budget provides two indicators of White House staff size: the total number of full-time permanent positions and what it calls "full-time equivalent employment."[5] The latter is the more realistic figure, as it accounts for part-time employees as well. On the basis of these budget statistics, the House Post Office and Civil Service Committee and Cronin produced the data on the growth of the White House staff shown in table 4.1.

Both the Post Office Committee's report and Cronin note that the budget figures did not include the number of staff "borrowed" by the White House from the departments and agencies to work in the White House Office while remaining on the payroll of the department or agency. If these "detailees" had been included, it would have boosted the official budget

TABLE 4.1.

THE GROWTH OF THE WHITE HOUSE OFFICE STAFF:
TWO EARLY CALCULATIONS

Year	House Post Office and Civil Service Committee figures	Cronin's figures
1944	*	48
1952	*	252
1955	262	*
1960	*	275
1963	*	263
1965	255	*
1968	*	202
1970	250	*
1971	533	*
1972	540	*
1973	510	510
1975	*	540

SOURCES: U.S. House of Representatives, Committee on Post Office and Civil Service, 92d Cong., 2d sess., *A Report on the Growth of the Executive Office of the President 1955–1973* (Washington, D.C.: U.S. Government Printing Office, 1972), 15; Thomas E. Cronin, *The State of the Presidency* (Boston: Little, Brown, 1975), 119.
  * Figures not reported for year shown.

total of White House staff considerably. Cronin suggests adding another 20 percent to the figures he supplied.[6]

The inadequacy of the budget figures was not just related to the omission of the number of detailees. The budget also disregarded those White House Office staff whose salaries were paid, not from the White House Office appropriation, but from various other general appropriations to the president, such as the Special Projects Fund, the President's Emergency Fund, and the Management Improvement Fund. The Special Projects Fund, for example, had been an important source of funding for White House staff posts ever since it was established in 1955, and more so than Cronin or the House Post Office and Civil Service Committee were aware of at the time. It enabled Eisenhower, Kennedy, Johnson, and Nixon to hide a significant number of White House staff from the official budget figures. For example, in 1959, Maurice Stans, the director of the Bureau of the Budget, revealed in testimony to a House of Representatives subcommittee that 101 White House staffers were being carried on the Special Projects Fund, in addition to the 272 who were paid for from the regular White House Office appropriation.[7] In 1973, a Senate subcommittee managed to extract from the Nixon administration a list of all White House staff members on the Special Projects payroll during that fiscal year. The list had 148 names on it, and although slightly more than half were secretaries or summer interns, it also included 20 staffers at a salary of $30,000 a year or more, some of whom, like Donald Rumsfeld and Kenneth Cole, were very senior members of the Nixon staff.[8]

The White House Office budget request for fiscal year 1971 is sometimes called "the honest budget" as a result of the Nixon administration's decision to consolidate into one single budget the funding of all full-time detailees, Special Projects staff performing full-time continuous functions, and "official" White House staff.[9] This explains the large increase in staff between 1970 and 1971 shown in the staffing statistics provided by the Post Office and Civil Service Committee (see table 4.1). It does not represent a significant real increase in the size of the White House staff because it was largely an accounting exercise. It did, however, make the budget a slightly more realistic guide to White House staff size from 1971 onward. Even so, a number of White House Office employees were still not included in the budget totals, and as the example in the previous paragraph illustrates, that number can be quite significant. The figure of 148 staffers still on the Special Projects payroll two years after "the honest budget" suggests that the budget was not so honest after all.

The point is that the *Budget of the U.S. Government* does not provide an accurate reflection of the number of personnel employed in the White House Office. Prior to 1971, budget figures were particularly unreliable, seriously understating the real size of the staff and consequently exaggerating the extent of staff expansion that took place during the first term of the Nixon presidency. Column A of table 4.2 shows the number of full-time equivalent posts in the White House Office as specified in the budgets from 1939 to 1976. It stands in comparison with more realistic attempts to determine the true size of the presidential staff, based not on budget figures but on the Federal Civilian Workforce Statistics published by the then U.S. Civil Service Commission. Apart from the budget statistics, these were the only "official" figures on the size of the White House Office. They are still released monthly (by the U.S. Office of Personnel Management) and show the number of staff employed in every department and agency of government. The Executive Office of the President is broken down into its component parts, and the staffing total for the White House Office is listed separately from other units.

In 1978 the House Post Office and Civil Service Committee produced another, and much more substantial, report on presidential staffing prepared by Louis Fisher and Harold Relyea of the Congressional Research Service. In the report the authors provided a series of figures on White House Office staff levels from 1939 to 1976 that they called "actual manpower," in contrast with the number of budgeted positions in the White House Office.[10] The "actual manpower" figures were drawn from the Federal Civilian Workforce Statistics with 31 December as the chosen base for each calendar year. These figures

TABLE 4.2.
FOUR MEASURES OF THE SIZE OF THE
WHITE HOUSE STAFF, 1939–76

Year	A Budget	B (Fisher-Relyea)	C (Wayne)	D (King-Ragsdale)
1944	47.5	58	192	50
1945	48.6	66	215	61
1946	51.5	216	213	61
1947	210	219	217	293
1948	245	209	268	210
1949	241	243	246	223
1950	238	313	248	295
1951	258	246	297	259
1952	272	248	283	245
1953	287	247	290	248
1954	250	262	273	266
1955	272	366	300	290
1956	273	372	392	374
1957	271	399	423	387
1958	277	395	403	394
1959	282	406	384	405
1960	274	416	388	446
1961	276	439	476	411
1962	282	338	432	467
1963	279	376	429	388
1964	278	328	431	349
1965	262	292	448	333
1966	266	270	475	295
1967	261	271	497	272
1968	260	261	456	344
1969	252	337	546	344
1970	252	491	632	311
1971	538	583	572	660
1972	544	583	584	660
1973	515	524	520	542
1974	525	560	552	583
1975	548	525	523	625
1976	515	534	497	541

SOURCES: Column A compiled by the author from *Budgets of the U.S. Government* show-ing the number of *budgeted positions* from 1939 to 1941, *man-years* from 1942 to 1950, and *full-time equivalent employment* from 1951 to 1976. Column B from U.S. House of Representatives, Committee on Post Office and Civil Service, 95th Cong., 2d sess., Committee Print 95-17, *Presidential Staffing: A Brief Overview* (Washington, D.C.: Gov-ernment Printing Office, 1978), 57. Column C from Stephen J. Wayne, *The Legislative Presidency* (New York: Harper & Row, 1978), 220–21. Column D from Gary King and Lyn Ragsdale, *The Elusive Executive: Discovering Statistical Patterns in the Presidency* (Washington, D.C.: CQ Press, 1988), 206–9.

are reproduced in column B of table 4.2 and present a much more realistic guide to the size of the staff than do the statistics derived from the budget data. Among other things, they reveal a quite significant difference between the number of budgeted staff positions and the "actual manpower" in the White House Office during the second term of the Eisenhower administration.

There are, however, one or two problems with the Federal Civilian Workforce Statistics. First, they do not adequately account for the number of detailees assigned to the White House, and, in fact, the Fisher-Relyea study admits that it is impossible to discover from the public record the actual number of detailees in the White House Office for the years 1950 to 1969.[11] Where figures are available, they suggest that the actual manpower total would increase substantially if detailees were included, although there is still some confusion about the exact numbers.[12]

A second problem with the Fisher-Relyea data is that it takes the size of the White House staff to be that given by the Civil Service Commission for 31 December each year. What it discounts is the sometimes considerable monthly variation in the size of the White House staff over any one year. For example, if Fisher and Relyea had taken 30 June instead of 30 September as their base, the actual manpower total for 1975 would have been 625, rather than 525, nearly 20 percent more.

In the same year that the Fisher-Relyea report was released, Stephen Wayne published a different, but very comprehensive, set of statistics on White House staff size in an appendix to his book *The Legislative Presidency*. This showed the number of staff on the official budget for the White House Office, the number paid for from the Special Projects Fund, and the number of detailed employees. Wayne added them together and provided a "grand total" of White House staff for each year from 1934 to 1976.[13] The "grand total" figure is reproduced as column C of table 4.2. The source of Wayne's data was James Connor, a member of President Ford's White House staff, but no details are provided on how each set of figures was derived. There is a reasonably close correlation between the Wayne and the Fisher-Relyea totals for some years (e.g., 1947, 1949, 1972, and 1975) and a significant discrepancy between them for others (e.g., 1944, 1950, 1962, and 1964–70). The differences might be explained away if the base figure for each year came from a different month, or they might be related to the way the Ford White House accounted for the number of detailees,[14] but one can only speculate about the reasons for the variation.

Subsequent to the publication of the first edition of this book, yet another data set on the size of the White House staff appeared in a handbook of statistics on the presidency compiled by Gary King and Lyn Ragsdale.[15] Their figures have been added to the original table 4.2 as column D. Needless to say, they do not match up with any of the other sources cited here. Like Wayne, King and Ragsdale provide little information on how their staff totals were calculated. They say their figures were derived from the *Statisti-*

cal Abstract of the United States (which is based on the Federal Civilian Workforce Statistics figures) and the *Budget of the U.S. Government,* but they give no indication on how or why they blended the two sets of data, nor do they indicate whether detailees, temporary, and part-time staff have been accounted for.

As the Fisher-Relyea, Wayne, and King-Ragsdale sets of data purport to be measuring the same thing, the different results obtained suggest that one must tread warily when making statements about the exact numbers in the White House. The four sets of data reproduced in table 4.2 are useful as a rough guide to the growth of the White House Office over four decades. They show quite clearly that it got bigger, but, beyond that, it is difficult to be any more specific. They become especially problematic if one tries to relate staff growth to particular presidencies. Different patterns emerge according to which set of figures one uses. The budget statistics, for example, show a major increase in the size of the staff under Truman, almost insignificant variations from Eisenhower through Johnson, and then another huge increase halfway through Nixon's first term. On the other hand, Wayne's figures show an increase in the size of the staff during the Kennedy-Johnson years, whereas the King-Ragsdale data show an equally significant decrease over the same period. Perhaps the most interesting common feature of the Fisher-Relyea, Wayne, and King-Ragsdale figures is that although the numbers differ, they all reveal a much larger White House staff under Eisenhower than conventional wisdom, based on budget data, had established, and they suggest that Richard Nixon may not have been the only president to make substantial and significant additions to the size of the White House staff during his term of office.[16]

A new source of official data on presidential staff size was provided for in the White House Personnel Authorization-Employment Act, a little-known piece of legislation signed by President Carter in 1978. This act requires the president to submit a report to Congress at the end of each fiscal year specifying the number of employees in the White House Office during that fiscal year.[17] As well as showing the permanent (full-time and part-time) staff numbers (under three different categories related to salary levels), the reports also have to specify the number of individuals detailed to the White House for more than thirty days, the number of days worked in excess of thirty, the number of consultants employed by the White House, and the number of days their services were used. The circumstances that gave rise to this legislation are examined in the next chapter; so, too, are the weaknesses of the act, of which the reporting requirement is just one. But, for the present purposes, our attention is directed to the data the reports have yielded since the first was sent to Congress in 1979. These are reproduced in table 4.3, and they provide a basis for calculating an aggregate total of White House Office staff that includes categories of staff omitted from the budget data and from some of the data sets reported in table 4.2.

TABLE 4.3.

WHITE HOUSE OFFICE STAFF TOTALS (1979–93) REPORTED
UNDER SECTION 113 OF THE WHITE HOUSE PERSONNEL
AUTHORIZATION-EMPLOYMENT ACT OF 1978

Fiscal year	Cumulative number of staff and (actual staff at 30 September)		Detailees and (total number of days worked)		Part-time consultants and (total number of days worked)	
1979	478	(not given)	44	(6,294)	6	(193)
1980	489	(not given)	205	(30,075)	13	(677)
1981	663	(351)	221	(21,670)	3	(7)
1982	416	(315)	50	(5,326)	0	(0)
1983	383	(313)	61	(8,369)	0	(0)
1984	387	(321)	55	(11,999)	0	(0)
1985	444	(319)	48	(11,486)	0	(0)
1986	431	(313)	42	(7,759)	3	(180)
1987	422	(317)	135	(25,023)	14	(672)
1988	404	(325)	83	(9,365)	6	(357)
1990	398	(342)	80	(20,153)	5	(277)
1991	417	(335)	78	(19,006)	12	(546)
1992	475	(353)	60	(11,021)	8	(288)
1993	871	(401)	65	(4,997)	16	(340)

SOURCE: The White House Office, "Aggregate Reports on Personnel Pursuant to Title 3, U.S. Code, Section 113," 1979–93.

First, a word of explanation is necessary about the data reported under the terms of the White House Personnel Authorization-Employment Act. Since the act requires the president to report the number of *all* individuals employed in the three categories (permanent full-time and part-time staff, detailees, and consultants) in any fiscal year, the totals given are *cumulative,* so where one member of the White House Office staff is replaced by a new recruit during a fiscal year, this shows up in the report as two employees, even though only one staff position was being filled. This creates problems in any fiscal year in which a new administration takes charge of the White House. The report for that year will show the staffs of the outgoing and incoming presidents in one combined, meaningless total, as in the figure given for 1981. To overcome this problem, the Reagan administration voluntarily added to its 1981 report the total number of staff employed in the White House Office on 30 September, the last day of the fiscal year, and this practice has been continued ever since. Thus there is now one figure for all permanent White House Office staff for one specific day of the year irrespective of which budget their salaries came from.

A second defect with the data reported under the terms of the 1978 act is that the reports do not include all detailees, only those who have worked for more than thirty days in each fiscal year. Thus it will never be possible to derive from these data the full extent of detailing to the White House Office staff. However, as the act does require the president to report the number of days in excess of thirty worked by the detailees included in the total, it provides an incomplete but the nearest possible measure of the impact of detailees on White House Office staffing. In table 4.3, the days worked in excess of thirty by all detailees covered by the reporting requirement have been totaled, and thirty days have been added on for each detailee. This produces a figure for the total number of days worked by all detailees included in the report.[18]

The reports made to Congress under the terms of the White House Personnel Authorization-Employment Act do provide another reasonably acceptable source of data on the real size of the White House Office staff, even though the reporting requirement has a number of shortcomings in the quality of the data it yields. Moreover, since 1981, they also provide a basis for calculating an aggregate total of White House Office staff that includes detailees and consultants. This can be done by converting the number of days worked by detailees and consultants into the equivalent of full-time employment and then adding that figure to the total of permanent staff given for 30 September, provided that one is content to accept the 30 September figure as reasonably typical of the size of the permanent staff for that fiscal year. For example, in fiscal year 1983, detailees in the White House Office worked a total of 8369 days, the equivalent of 22.9 years. If we take those 22.9 years as equal to 22.9 permanent full-time employees for one year, and add that to the 303 permanent staff employed on 30 September, we get a rounded total of 326 White House Office staff for 1983 (there were no consultants employed that year). The major shortcoming of this formula is that, apart from excluding the number of detailees who worked for less than thirty days, it does not include the category of personnel in the White House who are labeled "assignees" and who, in some areas of the Executive Office, constitute a significant addition to the official staff. In the last few years, the Appropriations Committees in both the House and the Senate have questioned this recently discovered category of staff in the presidential branch.[19]

One of the by-products of President Clinton's commitment to deliver on his campaign promise to cut the White House staff by 25 percent was the compilation of the only completely accurate figures on EOP staffing levels to be published publicly. As a result of some intense questioning about the proposed staff cuts, the House Appropriations Subcommittee that has major responsibility for the EOP budget managed to extract from the Clinton administration the statistics on which the planned reductions were to be based. These turned out to be the actual number of people working in each EOP division on 7 November 1992, the end of the week of the 1992 presidential election. The count covered all permanent full-time and part-time employees and all "other government employees" working in the White House on that day, which included all detailees, assignees, and even interns and White House Fellows.[20] On that one day, President Bush had a total of 470 staff working in the White House Office, which, incidentally, was 78 more than the figure reported in the Federal Civilian Workforce Statistics for that month.[21]

The reports mandated by the White House Personnel Authorization-Employment Act are never going to settle the question of exactly how big the White House staff is or was; nor are they likely to lead to one common and agreed official data set on White House Office size.[22] They are imperfect in a number of respects, but at the moment they constitute the least imperfect official data on White House staff size. But beyond the problem of how bodies are counted by those responsible for compiling statistics, there is another and more complex issue of which bodies to include under the umbrella of the White House staff.

Part of the problem stems from the unfortunate fact that terms like "White House staff," "presidential staff," and "Executive Office staff," are often used loosely and interchangeably, and as a consequence confusingly—particularly when staff size is being discussed. It happens even at the highest level. For example, when President Clinton addressed the White House press corps on this subject on 9 February 1993, he had this to say:

> During the recent campaign I pledged to reduce the White House staff by 25 percent below the size left by my predecessor. Today I am announcing a reorganization of the White House that keeps that commitment to the American people.

That was more or less exactly what he had promised in the campaign,[23] and if by "White House staff," candidate Clinton had meant the president's immediate personal staff who work in the White House Office, then this would have constituted a more than symbolic staff reduction and a very significant reversal of the "swelling of the presidency" in the postwar age. But it transpired that this was not quite what President Clinton did mean. He continued:

> These cuts come as part of a quite significant reorganization of the *Office of the President*. The reorganization will reduce the size of *the President's Office,* including *the White House* and the *Executive Office of the President* by some 350 people ... *not counting, of course, OMB and the Trade Representative's Office.* (Author's italics.)[24]

The result of President Clinton's very broad and loose definition of the White House staff was confusion, and later cynicism, that marked almost all media reporting of the staff-cutting exercise from then on. Under Clinton's definition, cuts applied not only to the White House Office but to the whole of the Executive Office of the President, with the unexplained exception of OMB and USTR, two of the three largest units in the EOP. Nevertheless, included in the 25 percent reduction target was the Executive Residence (what President Clinton apparently meant by "the White House" in his statement to the media). That included the gardeners and housekeeping staff, who were not the kind of personnel that most critics tended to think about when they contemplated the size of the presidential entourage. Clinton never recovered. "What the cuts have become," wrote Ann Devroy, the *Washington Post*'s White House correspondent, some eight months after the president announced the plan, is "a study in creative definitions of what constitutes the White House staff."[25]

One authority, Bradley Patterson, has defined the White House staff in even broader terms than President Clinton did and, in 1987, discovered 3366 full-time employees working in what he called the "White House staff community."[26] Patterson incorporates into his definition large numbers of support staff, like the U.S. Secret Service, the domestic staff who work in the Executive Residence, the National Park Service staff who look after the grounds of the White House, the engineering and maintenance staff, and 1300 military personnel whom, he claims, are attached to the White House Military Office. Many of those included in Patterson's total would be classified as "assignees" to the White House, doing the work of their home agency (see note 19), and are not counted in any of the official statistics. In utilizing such a broad umbrella, Patterson appropriately draws attention to the large number of personnel working at the White House in a support capacity who are on the payroll of some other department or agency, and there has, subsequently, been much concern in Congress to force public disclosure of the true costs of running the White House.[27]

But one must ask whether or not the inclusion of National Park Service groundsmen, or the crew who fly Air Force One, or the engineers who fix the air conditioning in the White House, or the florists who place fresh flowers around the White House contributes to or confuses discussion of the kinds of problems about presidential staffing that have been identified in the post-Watergate period.

Making sense of the size of the White House staff needs to go beyond mere quantification. Although Patterson's total does not differentiate between support staff and those doing political work, this is also the case with the official statistics (budget figures, Federal Civilian Workforce Statistics, and the White House reports mandated by the White House Personnel Authorization-Employment Act). If one assumes that the expansion of clerical, secretarial, and other support and maintenance staff is not of the same qualitative significance as the growth of the professional staff, in the context of the criticisms being made about the size of the presidential staff since Watergate, then some distinction ought to be made. When one does take into account the proportion of support staff in the White House Office itself, then it is obvious that aggregate totals overstate one aspect of the problem of White House staff growth.

One experienced presidency watcher has estimated that, in 1977, roughly half of the White House staff was secretarial and half was professional, commenting that it is "really not the monstrous absurdity that it's often depicted to be."[28] Similarly, Richard Neustadt mentions a figure of 180 professionals in the Carter White House in 1978,[29] which would be slightly less than half of the monthly average staff level reported for that year in the Federal Civilian Workforce Statistics. One study has estimated that President Johnson's professional staff numbered about fifty.[30] None of the official statistics on White House Office staff size match staff numbers to staff functions, so it is difficult to get any accurate measure of the proportion of professional to support staff, but there was one occasion when the White House did release this information. At the height of the Watergate crisis in 1973, the House Appropriations Subcommittee that deals with the White House Office budget requests insisted that it be supplied with a list of all persons working in the White House Office, together with a short job description. This list was subsequently published as part of the subcommittee hearings on the White House Office appropriation. It revealed a White House Office consisting of 500 staff, of whom only 100 were professional or political staff. The other 400 were clerical, secretarial, and other support personnel. The list showed, among other categories, 160 secretaries in the White House Office, 27 staff in the mail room, 21 in the telephone office, 49 in the correspondence section, and 27 employees working on accounts, purchases, and personnel matters.[31]

Another factor that ought to be taken into account when considering the expansion of the White House staff is that the data exaggerate the number of assistants working directly for the president by not distinguishing between presidential aides and the staffs of presidential aides. The growth of aides' staff has been an important feature of White House Office development for the last twenty years; today no self-respecting senior White House aides lack their own staff apparatus. The assistant for national security affairs, the assistant for domestic policy, and the assistant for economic policy have large, formal staffs as separate entities in the Executive Office of the President. Other senior aides, such as the press secretary, the director of communications, the assistant for legislative affairs, and the assistant for public liaison, have their own teams within the White House Office itself. Some of those staffs are fairly large. The congressional liaison team working for President Reagan in 1981, under the direction of Kenneth Duberstein, consisted of twenty-eight full-time staff in all.[32] Thus, in the context of arguments about presidential span of control becoming weaker as staff size expands, one must recognize the hierarchical pattern of White House staff development and the fact that many of those in the White House Office report to the president indirectly, if at all, through a senior aide. One of President Carter's top assistants, who resigned after a year on the White House staff, commented that "even many of those at the highest levels—assistants, deputy assistants, special assistants—don't see the president once a week or speak to him in any substantive way once a month. There are dozens of $40,000-a-year assistants who have less personal contact with the president than many folks in Aliquippa, Pa., or Yazoo City, Miss."[33]

If there is a problem about the size of the White House staff, then it is considerably less of a problem than aggregate staffing statistics might, on first inspection, lead us to believe. The data on White House staff growth need to be treated cautiously, qualitatively as well as quantitatively. In general, the post-Watergate critics handled that data rather casually, using crude statistics as the basis for their diagnosis of what was wrong with the presidency and as an argument for a drastic reduction in the size of the White House staff, which they saw as a necessary precondition for improved executive government in Washington.

Numerically, the present size of the White House Office staff does appear to be a departure from Brownlow. The Brownlow report was quite specific about the number of executive assistants to be added to the presidential staff. At the beginning of the section on the White House staff, it proposed "a small number of executive assistants ... probably not exceeding six...."[34] This was to be in addition to the existing secretaries to the president, of which there were three at the time. In contrast, the reported statistics on the size of the presidential staff during the Nixon era, some showing in excess of 600, appeared horrendous. But there was nothing in the Brownlow report to suggest that the White House staff was to remain at three secretaries and six executive assistants for all time. Indeed, the thrust of the report was that the president ought to be given staff support to match the changing nature of government and the increased responsibilities thrust upon the presidency. It follows, therefore, that if the responsibilities of the presidency expanded even more, Brownlow would not have been averse to some additional increase in the presidential staff. Furthermore, Brownlow was able to talk in terms of a small presidential staff, and even determine an optimum number, because the functions he had intended the staff to perform were limited, reasonably specific, and very different from those the White House staff has since acquired.

Those who use Brownlow as a yardstick to criticize the present extent of the White House staff are implicitly saying something about changing political circumstances and changing staff functions, rather than making a statement about size itself. Aggregate totals of White House staffs since 1939 do not, in themselves, indicate a great deal about the development or the present state of the White House Office. The size of the staff is not so much the cause of the organizational problems of the modern presidency; rather it is a consequence of other political developments that have occurred since Brownlow, and it is to the causes of White House staff growth that we must now turn.

The Development of the White House Staff

The White House Office staff has grown in both size and function since 1939, but we ought not to forget that it was growing in size and function before 1939 as well. Brownlow did not invent the president's personal staff; instead he attempted to fix its developmental direction on a path quite different from that taken since the late nineteenth century, and he was singularly unsuccessful in doing so. The post-Brownlow White House staff continued to evolve much as the pre-Brownlow staff had done, except that the post-1939 development resulted in a significant increase in the power of the staff within the executive branch of government. That accretion of power has been consequent on the evolving functions of the White House Office rather than its expanding size. Similarly, the problems of the presidential staff system are primarily problems of what the staff does, not of how many staff there are to do it.

The functional evolution of the White House Office is not attributable to any one single factor. A number of forces have been at work to make the presidential staff what it is today. In the previous chapter, some general explanations about the growth of the Executive Office as a whole were examined, and we can now add to that by looking more specifically at the White House Office by itself.

Many attempts to explain the development of the White House staff emphasize its role as a coordinator of executive branch activity, a role assumed as a direct result of the weakness of the Cabinet as a coordinating mechanism. In the mid-1950s, John Steelman, President Truman's de facto chief of staff, commented that "the size of the White House staff ... grows in direct relationship to the inability of the more rigid cabinet system to meet growing complexities in the management of government programs."[35] Similarly, Richard Fenno thought that the growth of the staff was "an inevitable response to the new dimensions of governmental activity, but also in part ... an adverse reflection on the ability of the Cabinet in coping with the difficult problems of co-ordination involved."[36] Cronin made the same point as part of his more general perspective on the evolution of the EOP.[37] The fact is that as government has expanded during the twentieth century, so the presidential perspective and the perspectives of his heads of departments are more liable to be different. The presidential perspective on government now requires that the executive branch be coordinated by the presidential branch, and as Pressman and Wildavsky remind us, where there is an absence of common purpose, then coordination is another term for coercion, and thus it becomes a form of power.[38]

A second important explanation is to be found in the changed and more complex nature of the constituencies to which a president must relate. It was noted in the previous chapter that both Cronin and Hess had emphasized, as a source of staff expansion, the demands of interest groups to be represented inside the White House. But all of the president's constituencies have become more demanding over the last few decades. As Richard Neustadt has pointed out:

> Yet Reagan's people find, as Nixon's and Carter's, that they call for more manpower now than fifteen years ago or than Ford chose to use in the immediate aftermath of Watergate. In part this is attributable to the media, especially TV and its developing technology. In part it is responsive to the growth of staff elsewhere, all calling for White House contact. In part it is a tribute to the president-as-clerk, with cabinet members, congressmen, mayors, governors and private leaders, also local press, now looking to his staffs to help them do a lot of things they once did on their own (or not at all).[39]

A significant proportion of White House staff activity and of the post-1939 expansion of the professional staff has occurred in precisely those areas identified by Neustadt. A number of functionally specialized units now exist within the White House Office to connect with, service, and manipulate important elites in the political system. "Outreach" is one of the principal concerns of the contemporary White House Office staff.

White House staff have dealt with presidential constituencies since the beginning of the presidency. As noted earlier, George Washington's private secretary, Tobias Lear, acted as a liaison between the president and his heads of departments, and Jefferson used his private secretary as a link between members of Congress and himself. In the later nineteenth century, the more politically astute private secretaries handled presidential relations with the press and with party leaders as an important area of their work.

The earliest formal recognition of the use of the White House staff as a link to a key presidential constituency did not occur until Herbert Hoover's presidency when, having been given two additional senior White House staff by Congress, he designated one of them to be his press secretary. Since then, every president has had a press secretary in his White House Office, and the press secretary's staff has expanded steadily over the years. President Carter's press secretary, Jody Powell, had two deputy press secretaries, three associate press secretaries, one press assistant, and eleven other professional staff working for him. One journalist reported that Powell had a total of forty-six employees in his office.[40] This expansion must, however, be partly set against the growth and development of the media over the last three decades. No longer is it possible for the president to meet the whole of the White House press corps for an informal chat in his office. Today, about 2000 reporters have White House press credentials, and the White House press corps (the regular reporters who have assigned seats at the press secretary's daily briefings) number about sixty.[41] Neither is it possible for the president and the press secretary to rely on a relatively tame and compliant media in Washington. The Vietnam war, credibility gaps, Spiro Agnew, and Watergate resulted in fundamental changes in presidential-media relations and gave birth to a new type of aggressive and adversarial White House correspondent, who became the star of the network news on television screens each evening. Television, of course, made a profound difference. The size of its audience, its technical capacity to cover the president wherever he happened to be, and the fact that it conveyed an image as well as a message made the media a more demanding and more difficult clientele to handle than ever before.

President Nixon extended the White House media management machinery when he appointed a director of communications to handle the wider public relations effort; that position, too, has been maintained by each of his successors.[42] Under President Reagan, the director of communications ran a large outfit that encompassed the president's speechwriting staff, a media relations and planning unit, an Office of Public Affairs, and the Office of Public Liaison.

Liaison with Congress has also become an important staff function over the past forty years, particularly in the aftermath of Watergate when Congress became more difficult for presidents to handle. Every president since Eisenhower has had a congressional relations staff within his White House Office, and each has made small additions to the size of the staff bequeathed by his predecessor.[43] The congressional relations staff acts as the president's eyes and ears on Capitol Hill, as lobbyists, as providers of vital services to members of Congress, and sometimes as policy advisers within the White House. A skillful White House Office of Congressional Relations (or Office of Legislative Affairs, as it is now known) can be a major asset to a president. An incompetent one can be very costly, as President Carter found out.[44]

Another formal link to presidential constituencies, the White House Office of Public Liaison, was established by President Ford. Its function is to lobby the lobbies. It reaches out to important nongovernment constituencies such as business, labor, ethnic, religious, and women's groups to sell the president's policies and build coalitions in support of them.[45] The influence and status of the Office of Public Liaison has declined since its heyday in the Carter administration under Anne Wexler. In President Reagan's second term, it was subsumed within the empire of the White House director of communications, but was returned to the status of an separate unit under President Bush and remains so under President Clinton. By the Bush presidency, the Office of Public Liaison had become an established function within the White House Office and a mini empire with at least sixteen staff assistants including, in addition to the assistant to the president for public liaison, three deputy assistants, six special assistants, and three associate directors.

In the Reagan White House, there was a noticeable development of the smaller liaison and outreach operations headed by assistants for intergovernmental relations, political affairs, and Cabinet relations. The Office of Intergovernmental Relations had twelve professional staffers to deal with governors, mayors, and state and local government organizations. President Reagan established the post of assistant for Cabinet affairs during his first term with a staff of eight, which grew to fifteen under President Bush. During the Carter administration, Cabinet affairs and intergovernmental relations were handled by one unit, with a staff of five, and there was no Office of Political Affairs.

President Reagan's establishment of an Office of Political Affairs within the White House Office is also a reflection of the way in which the post-1968 reforms of the presidential nomination process have affected the nature and function of the White House staff. The political affairs unit is a formal recognition of the need for first-term presidents to maintain an experienced and professional campaign organization during the first term to cope with the demands of the new rules of the nomination game. With the choice of the party's presidential nominee now beyond the control of party leaders, and with a system so open that it positively encourages challenges to the front-runner, incumbent presidents can no longer enjoy the luxury of automatic renomination after four years. Presidents who desire a second term in office must now give far more continuous attention to electoral politics during their first term than ever before.

Even before the creation of an Office of Political Affairs, the White House was becoming a dumping ground for campaign specialists, who were given make-work jobs to keep them occupied for the years between elections. One doubts, for example, that the jobs and titles President Carter bestowed on White House staffers Peter Bourne (special assistant for health issues), Joseph Aragon (ombudsman) and Greg Schneiders (special assistant for special projects) had much to do with the day-to-day work of the White House Office, but all three had played an important part in Carter's election success in 1976.

The electoral connection now looms large in the work of the presidential staff and not only because presidents are compelled to keep their campaign organization intact to manage the next election. The new nomination process has made the campaign organization a more prominent source of recruitment for the whole range of White House staff jobs than in the past, simply because the process of selecting a party's presidential nominee tends to isolate the successful candidate from party elites and effectively restricts the candidate's options over the choice of his staff.

The reason for this is that the nomination struggle is no longer mediated in private by party leaders who value party unity and coalition building in the process of selecting the nominee. Today's mediators are the mass media, which tend to encourage conflict, competition, and maximum party disunity in their attempt to make the very public contest for the nomination attractive to readers and viewers. By the time a candidate has run the gauntlet of caucuses and primaries and the party convention, he has little point of contact with the party leadership and often considerable antagonism to other factions in the party built around similar candidate-centered campaigns and candidate-centered organizations. Given the difficulty of winning a party's presidential nomination, it is not surprising that party nominees choose the same candidate-centered campaign organization to fight the election proper. Neither is it surprising that success in November seems to convince presidents-elect that what is good enough to win the nomination, and then win the election, is also good enough to govern the country with. Presidents tend to recruit their immediate personal staff from among those they know best. By the time a candidate has won his way to the presidency, it is his campaign staff with whom he is best acquainted and who inevitably end up with White House staff jobs.

Although the practice of recruiting White House staff from the ranks of campaign aides predates the McGovern-Fraser reforms, the new nomination process has the potential to put a very different kind of campaign aide into the White House. There is little incentive for today's campaign organizers to be skilled in the arts of compromise and coalition building because there are no party mediators to compromise with and there is no need to build coalitions to win nominations. As Nelson Polsby has pointed out, the strategic imperative lies not in forming a broad coalition within the party, as used to be the case, "but in mobilizing a faction by emerging first in rank-order among the numerous presidential candidates who put themselves forward."[46] Faction fighting requires different sorts of skills from coalition building; yet, although the route to the White House may have changed dramatically in the 1970s and 1980s, what it takes to be a successful president has not, and in government there is still every incentive to compromise and seek supporting coalitions for presidential initiatives. White House staff recruited from today's campaign organizations may well find the transition from electioneering to governing a difficult one to make, and they may also be unwilling to make it even when they are ensconced at their White House desks.

In one respect, however, the modern presidential campaign organization shares a common characteristic with the contemporary White House Office. Both operations now require and depend on a functionally specialized division of labor among their staff to cope with the nature of the tasks before them. Today, typical White House staffers are much less jacks-of-all-trades than their predecessors forty years ago, and they are now much more likely to be identified with one particular area of staff work. Indeed, only the very senior presidential aides in the White House Office have responsibilities that traverse the fairly well defined functional divisions of the White House Office.

The need for specialization in the White House was an inevitable consequence of several developments in American government, particularly the increased responsibilities heaped on the president in the years after World War II, the way successive presidents have moved to concentrate power in the White House, and the more demanding nature of the constituencies the president must deal with. The workload of the presidential staff is too heavy, too complex, and too specialized to permit individual staffers to range too widely. One person can no longer advise on policy, draft legislation, write presidential speeches in support of legislation, lobby on Capitol Hill, and negotiate compromises to head off hostile amendments, as, for example, Thomas Corcoran did for Franklin D. Roosevelt.[47] There is no equivalent to Corcoran on the White House staff today, and almost all the senior staff are known for a particular jurisdiction, be it congressional liaison, media handling, domestic policy advice, national security management, public relations, intergovernmental affairs, or whatever.

Specialization has both positive and detrimental effects on the performance of the White House Office. On the one hand, it has, at least, enabled the presidential staff to keep pace with developments in other parts of the political system and thus enabled the presidency to respond to an increasingly complex political environment. Congress, for example, demands more sophisticated attention from the White House today than it did thirty years ago. The weakness of party leadership, the fragmentation of power, procedural reforms, the pull of constituency interests on Capitol Hill, and the post-Watergate reaction to the imperial presidency have combined to make Congress harder to manage from the White House perspective.[48] A weekly meeting of the president and the congressional leadership no longer suffices as the method by which the White House gets what it wants from Congress. Legislators now demand individual attention on a regular basis from White House aides, who must have detailed knowledge and understanding of the political circumstances in which each of those individuals operates. Consequently, ad hoc contacts between the White House and Congress have now given way to a much more structured and strategic approach that utilizes significantly more staff, computerized records on every member of Congress, a carefully organized allocation of responsibilities among the liaison staff, and the coordination of the congressional liaison units in the departments and agencies. What the president's congressional liaison staff does today could not be done by one general-purpose assistant whose time was divided among several responsibilities. Handling Congress today has become a specialist matter, and the same is true with respect to the other presidential constituencies.

On the other hand, when staff functions are differentiated and each is defined as a specialized task managed by specialist aides, then, inevitably, subunits within the White House Office tend to develop separate identities and unique perspectives on staff tasks. That in turn can lead to internal competition, empire building, and divided loyalties among the staff as a result of close identification with the specialist constituency being served.

Distinct subunits of the White House Office are forced to compete for the president's attention within the various coordinating mechanisms that have been established to bring together what specialization has forced apart. The very existence of these coordinating mechanisms, such as the Legislative Strategy Group established during President Reagan's first term of office, is testimony to the different interests and perspectives to be coordinated and reconciled in the process of White House decision making. Inclusion in key staff meetings and in the flow of important papers has become a measure of status in the White House staff hierarchy; conversely, exclusion can be the cause of frustration and alienation.

Specialization has also helped accentuate the intensely competitive atmosphere within the White House by forcing staffers to engage in activities designed to increase their influence and defend the interests and jurisdictions of their particular areas of staff work. Invitations to attend high-level staff meetings are not the only symbols of power. As John Dean noted in his memoir of the Nixon White House, the size of one's office, the quality of the furnishings in it, and its proximity to the president's office were vitally important signs of prestige and status. "Movers busied themselves with the continuous shuffling of furniture from one office to another as people moved in, up, down or out. We learned to read office changes as an index of the internal bureaucratic power struggles."[49]

Empire building can easily become a necessary exercise for the aspiring White House staffer. It manifests itself not only in terms of office space and proximity to the president but also in the growth of staffs' staff and the expansion of staffs' functions. When Jeb Magruder, one of President Nixon's more notorious aides, commented on the phenomenal ascendancy of his colleague Charles Colson, he noted simply, "He arrived in the White House with one secretary and by the time he left he had dozens of people reporting to him."[50] As a measure of his own success in the Office of Communications while an assistant to Herbert Klein, Magruder commented, "Eventually I built up Klein's office from four assistants to about twelve."[51] Similar examples of empire building were seen in the Carter administration. Zbigniew Brzezinski, Carter's national security adviser, expanded his staff to prevent other White House staff units from invading his turf. Clearly dissatisfied with what he called "the occasionally sputtering overall White House co-ordination with Congress," Brzezinski appointed his own congressional liaison assistant quite independently of the Office of Congressional Relations. He also appointed his own press secretary because he felt that Jody Powell, the president's press secretary, did not know much about foreign affairs and that Powell's office needed reinforcement.[52]

The expansion of White House staff functions is also partly attributable to the specialized division of labor, one of the classic characteristics of any bureaucratic structure. Yet, in some respects, as Lewis Dexter has argued, the White House Office resembles not so much a bureaucracy, but a court whose courtiers are loyal to the person at the top, rather than a set of organizational norms and values.[53] In a court, advancement depends primarily on pleasing the ruler and making oneself indispensable to the person, not the organization; but in the White House court, the opportunities for most of the courtiers to do this are constrained by the limits of the specialized tasks they are given to perform. Hence court politics and bureaucratic organization combine to produce an almost inevitable tendency among ambitious staffers (courtiers) to expand their specialized tasks as far as possible. John Dean, appointed Counsel to President Nixon, has given a graphic account of how the process worked in his case:

> Before I hired my first assistant, I had formulated a plan of advancement.... I knew Fred [Fielding] wanted to succeed at the White House as badly as I did, and I explained my ideas for doing it.... "Fred, I think we have to look at our office as a small law firm at the White House.... But to convince the president we're not just the only law office in town but the best, we've got to convince a lot of other people first. Haldeman, Ehrlichman and the others who surround the president."[54]

Dean then explains his strategy. He wanted to work on the conflict-of-interest problems of other members of the White House staff:

> We put in long gruelling hours, and word soon got around that the counsel's office was eager to tackle anyone and everyone's problems and do it discreetly.... Although our work was technical and legal, we discovered that we could use it to get a foothold in substantive areas. If we were alert in conflict-of-interest reviews and investigations, we would have a small say in presidential appointments.... The staffers we helped recommended us to their bosses, and the bosses seemed satisfied with our work. It did not take long for Haldeman ... to learn that business was booming at the counsel's office. He gave his blessing, which meant that I was soon enjoying some of the coveted White House status symbols.... The small law firm grew; within six months my professional staff was up to three lawyers, plus Caulfield. We enjoyed neither the power nor the spectacular growth of Chuck Colson's office, but we became known as a steady ground-gainer.[55]

A further way in which specialization can affect the development of the White House Office is by its consequent tendency to tie individual staff members more closely to presidential constituencies than would be the case if there existed a more flexible method of distributing staff assignments. The risk is that a White House staffer who deals with one specific constituency all day every day will identify so closely with that constituency that he or she eventually becomes an advocate for its interests inside the White House. The danger of this has been recognized in the past. According to White House aide James Rowe, President Franklin Roosevelt opposed the establishment of a formal congressional liaison staff because he felt that as soon as his staff began to deal with congressional requests and complaints, they would be working for members of Congress as well as for him. Roosevelt thought that if his staff then failed to respond to the demands of legislators, they would soon lose the confidence of their constituents; either way, the aides' usefulness to the president would quickly wear out. In his view, the idea of a specialist congressional liaison staff carried with it built-in obsolescence.[56] The point was iterated by Richard Neustadt in an advisory memorandum to President-elect John F. Kennedy on the White House congressional liaison office. "Go slow on staffing up Congressional liaison," he urged Kennedy. "An over-organized White House liaison operation—like the one Eisenhower built in his first term—tends to turn Presidential staffers into chore-boys for congressmen and bureaucrats alike. From this the President has more to risk than gain, in my opinion."[57]

Given the development of outreach units in the contemporary White House Office, the risk of divided loyalties among presidential staff must be a significant one. Lawrence O'Brien was frequently accused of overly representing the interests of Congress in the Kennedy White House. But the problem is not just confined to congressional relations. President Reagan's first assistant for intergovernmental relations also seems to have become too closely identified with his constituents. According to one authoritative reporter, Rich Williamson had gone too far in defending the interests of state and local governments against a proposed round of budget cuts, and he lost his White House job as a result.[58]

So far the evolution of the White House Office has been described mainly as a response to external pressures and a consequence of inevitable bureaucratic behavior deriving from the specialized division between the staff. Ultimately, however, the White House Office is the president's personal staff unit and he is free to shape it as he pleases. Although not a great deal is known about how presidents put together their White House Office, it is highly improbable that they always respond to external pressures and never initiate new directions in White House staffing. Since 1939, different presidents have responded to similar external circumstances in different ways, and no two presidents have organized the White House in exactly the same manner.[59] Eisenhower, for example, decided to create a formal congressional liaison staff after his two immediate predecessors conducted congressional relations without one. Kennedy managed his White House Office without a chief of staff, not wishing to have another Sherman Adams as the single top aide. Ronald Reagan installed a three-man team of Meese, Baker, and Deaver to do what H.R. Haldeman alone did for Richard Nixon. Some presidents have seen a need to have economic policy coordinators on the staff; others have not. Some presidents attach great importance to particular staff functions, whereas others relegate the very same functions to a low order of priority. Some presidents have enlarged the White House staff more than others, and depending on what set of figures one uses, one or two have actually reduced staff size during their tenure. So presidential choice must also be taken into account when considering the development of the White House Office.

Some of those choices have had a major impact on the evolution of the post-Brownlow White House staff. Eisenhower's decision to create the post of assistant for national security affairs, for example, and, later, Kennedy's decision to fill that post with a foreign policy specialist were instrumental in establishing a foreign policy-making capacity in the White House that now routinely dominates the policy-making process. When Richard Nixon established a White House Office of Communications, ostensibly to enable him to go over the heads of what he considered to be an unsympathetic White House press corps,[60] he laid the foundation for a significantly enhanced public relations machinery in the White House and, more important, elevated public relations concerns to the forefront of White House staff work. President Kennedy left a permanent mark on the way in which the modern White House deals with Congress as a consequence of his personal decision to reject advice from two of his advisers on how to handle congressional relations. One thought there was no necessity for a formal congressional liaison staff, and the other urged caution in building up such a staff. Neither had liked what Eisenhower had done in this respect, but Kennedy saw the necessity for a congressional liaison staff, and under the direction of Lawrence O'Brien, there was little reticence in developing a staff operation quite different from Eisenhower's into what was to become the model of how a contemporary president deals with Congress.[61] The boldest of all staffing innovations must be credited to President Nixon, whose decision in January 1973 to establish five senior White House aides as executive branch policy overlords to whom Cabinet members would report had a profound impact on the White House Office. This episode was so important that it warrants further discussion in the next section of this chapter dealing with the power of the White House staff.

Finally, when explaining the evolution of the post-Brownlow White House staff, one must consider the role of Congress, a role that has been one of almost total noninvolvement. In striking contrast to the way in which Congress has actively participated in shaping the structure and functions of the Executive Office generally, the White House Office has remained immune from all but the most perfunctory congressional oversight of its activities. Long-standing traditions of comity and courtesy between the two branches preclude the one from interfering in the other's housekeeping matters, and Congress regards the president's personal staff as a housekeeping matter. Consequently, at no stage since 1939, even in the aftermath of Watergate, has Congress done anything to restrict the president's freedom to develop his personal staff as he wishes. Indeed, by unquestioningly voting appropriations for the White House Office year after year, Congress has acquiesced in the way successive presidents have used that freedom.

THE POWER OF THE WHITE HOUSE STAFF

There is, in the history of the pre-Brownlow White House staff, considerable evidence of the increasingly prominent role played by the private secretaries and, from the McKinley administration onward, the secretary to the president. Lamont, Cortelyou, Loeb, Tumulty, and Slemp did far more on behalf of the presidents they served than their formal titles might have suggested, and by any standard they were powerful political operators. But their operations were confined to political activities, using the word *political* in its more popular sense. They liaised with party leaders and party organizations, handled patronage matters, managed election campaigns, and manipulated the press, as far as they could, to promote the image of the man they served. None of them got overtly involved in matters of policy. Generally speaking, nineteenth- and twentieth-century presidents sought policy advice from elsewhere—from members of the Cabinet, from kitchen cabinets like the one Andrew Jackson created, or from individual confidants like Colonel Edward House, who served unofficially as Woodrow Wilson's policy adviser.

Brownlow was concerned about checking the growth in power of the White House staff and, particularly, ensuring that it did not spill over into the policy-making arena. As noted in chapter 2, both the report and Executive Order 8248 went to great lengths to constrain the role of the new administrative assistants in policy matters by specifically stating that in no event would the administrative assistants be interposed between the president and the heads of departments. That, of course, turned out to be wishful thinking. It was premised on a concept of administrative management that presupposed a separation of politics and administration, which could not be sustained at the highest level of American government. The post-Brownlow White House staff has continued to enhance its power in the political arena, but it has also accrued significant power in the policy-making arena.

The power of the contemporary White House staff derives from its political and policy functions. It advises and advocates, and does so from a privileged and most advantageous position. It coordinates and thus attempts to control the activities of the executive branch departments and agencies on behalf of the president, and it represents the president in all the political and governmental arenas in which he operates. Such an accumulation of power constitutes a major departure from the Brownlow design and has been viewed critically by many post-Watergate commentators, some of whom have interpreted the power of the White House staff as an almost illegitimate development in American government. Yet, for many of those critics, it was not the functions performed by the White House staff that were at issue, but the fact that the White House staff performed them. It became apparent to many of those trying to make sense of Watergate that the power of the presidential staff had grown at the expense of more traditional institutions of government, especially the Cabinet. The White House Office had become a force in the policy process, had interposed itself between the president and Cabinet members, and had usurped functions that properly belonged to the Cabinet. The growth of White House staff power was thus seen in terms of the decline of the Cabinet, a process many thought it highly desirable to reverse.

Such a view was hardly surprising. The declining prestige, status, and authority of Cabinet members was a very visible manifestation of the increasing power of the White House staff. It had happened gradually, with no obvious single point of origin, but by the end of President Nixon's first term, the subordination of the Cabinet to the presidential staff could not be denied. Shortly after the commencement of the second term, it was quite open and official, and the nature of White House staff–Cabinet relations during the Nixon administration was central to the post-Watergate critique of the institutionalized presidency. So, too, was the Eisenhower experience, which was equally important in setting the context for the post-Watergate debate about the expanding power of the presidential staff.

The Cabinet derives its existence from custom, not from the Constitution or from statute law. It is a creature of the president, and presidents are at liberty to make considerable use of it as a source of advice, or they are free to neglect it completely. Andrew Jackson did the latter. Lincoln, Theodore Roosevelt, and Woodrow Wilson neglected their Cabinets only a little less so.[62] Other presidents, however, have used their Cabinets more positively, and Eisenhower was one of those. As Richard Fenno has noted, "probably the best example of a decision-making procedure with extensive, built-in Cabinet reliance is that of President Eisenhower."[63] Edward Corwin went even further in asserting that "to a far greater degree than any of his predecessors President Eisenhower has endeavored to employ the Cabinet as an instrument of collective policy making."[64] Greenstein claims that the importance Eisenhower attached to Cabinet meetings is evident from their profusion, an average of thirty-four meetings a year over his two terms,[65] and certainly no president since has emulated Eisenhower in his use of the Cabinet. But what should have been regarded as just one of the various ways in which a president can use his Cabinet has come to be celebrated as a model of responsible government from which Eisenhower's successors have more or less departed. The power and prominence of the White House staff have thus become a measure of deviation from the Eisenhower "norm."

At the other end of the spectrum is the Nixon presidency. No president in modern times has done more to puncture the status of the Cabinet collectively or its members individually and, correspondingly, to enlarge the power of the White House staff. Despite the president-elect's preinaugural declaration about not wanting a Cabinet of "yes-men" and about how every Cabinet member would participate in all the great issues of his administration,[66] Richard Nixon proved to be much the same as his two immediate predecessors in his disregard of the Cabinet. Both Kennedy and Johnson had opted for more flexible and informal advisory mechanisms, in preference to the large and rigid formal gathering of heads of all the departments. The Cabinet was convened only thirty-one times during the Kennedy administration. Arthur Schlesinger Jr. reports that Kennedy found Cabinet meetings "simply useless," and Theodore Sorensen claims that "no decisions of importance were made ... and few subjects of importance, particularly in foreign affairs, were ever seriously discussed. The Cabinet as a body was convened largely as a symbol."[67] One member of Lyndon Johnson's White House staff thought that "the Cabinet became a joke, it was never used for anything near what could be called presidential listening or consultation."[68]

The difference between Nixon and his two predecessors, however, was that whereas Kennedy and Johnson were not enamored of the Cabinet as a collective entity, they did make use of the advisory talents of Cabinet members in an individual capacity. Nixon, on the other hand, moved determinedly toward a state of affairs in which heads of departments were frozen out of the White House processes of policy advice. The abnormally high turnover of Cabinet members during the Nixon years seemed calculated in part to replace politicians with organization and management specialists whose jobs would be to manage the vast bureaucracies under them and to implement policies that had been settled by others in the White House.[69] It is interesting to note that when announcing his new Cabinet at the beginning of his second term in January 1973, President Nixon emphasized the organizational talents of his new team—"the eleven men whom I have chosen as department heads in the new Cabinet are one of the strongest executive combinations ever put together here in Washington, in terms of management ability, personal integrity, and commitment to public service"[70]—but said nothing about their political wisdom or experience. This was in striking contrast with the fanfare that announced his first Cabinet in December 1969. Nelson Polsby has summed up Nixon's exercise in Cabinet building thus: "Mr. Nixon increasingly appointed people with no independent public standing and no constituencies of their own. In this shift we can read a distinctive change in the fundamental political goals and strategies of the Nixon administration from early concerns with constituency building to a later preoccupation, once Mr. Nixon's re-election was assured, with centralizing power in the White House."[71]

President Nixon's contributions to the declining status of the Cabinet went beyond merely ignoring heads of departments in White House policy deliberations. He also initiated two institutional changes that significantly enhanced the power of the presidential staff. The first was the establishment of the Domestic Council in 1970.

In his memoirs, John Ehrlichman notes that, when the members of President Nixon's Cabinet were briefed on the Domestic Council plan, one of them, George Romney, voiced an objection to what he saw as another White House staff apparatus because he feared it would only make it more difficult for Cabinet members to meet with the president, one on one, for substantive discussions.[72] Romney's fears were correct. The real intent behind the establishment of the Domestic Council was to create a staff operation in domestic policy, similar to the one Henry Kissinger had built up around the National Security Council. And just as Kissinger was dominating the national security policy-making process, so Ehrlichman would come to dominate the domestic policy process. It was Ehrlichman and his staff who called the meetings of the Domestic Council, who prepared the agenda and the discussion papers for those rare occasions when the council met. It was also Ehrlichman who conveyed the results of the council's deliberations to the president.

The Domestic Council was also a convenient device to restrict the range of policy issues on which members of the Cabinet could express their views. It was what might be called a *specific-issue cabinet,* confined to matters of domestic policy and with no brief to discuss foreign policy or national security issues. Moreover, the creation of the Domestic Council marked the beginning of a propensity on the part of presidents to use such devices more and more. President Ford, for example, established the Economic Policy Board in addition to the Domestic Council, and this effectively took many economic matters away from the full Cabinet. President Reagan extended the concept of specific-issue cabinets even further. During his first term of office, he established seven Cabinet councils (economic affairs, human resources, natural resources and environments, food and agriculture, commerce and trade, legal policy, management and administration),[73] thus fragmenting the full Cabinet as far as one possibly could.

One final point about specific-issue cabinets is that when they do function, they tend to focus on details rather than broad policy directions. This was certainly so in the Reagan administration, where, as an analysis of the Cabinet-council system concluded, the councils operated at a secondary level of policy making, directing their efforts toward facilitating the implementation of policy agendas rather than policy development.[74] This kind of work is far removed from the type of activity that one might expect the full Cabinet to engage in. In specific-issue cabinets, detailed technical work, managed by senior White House staff, takes the place of broad political debate on future policy directions.

The second important institutional development during the Nixon administration was the president's announcement, on 5 January 1973, of a revamped White House staff structure. This had its origin in a presidential proposal to Congress two years earlier to restructure the executive branch of government by abolishing the Departments of Agriculture, Labor, Commerce, Housing and Urban Development, Transportation, Interior, and Health, Education, and Welfare and consolidating their functions into four new superdepartments: Human Resources, Natural Resources, Community Development, and Economic Affairs.[75] Consequent on the failure of Congress to enact the executive reorganization plan, President Nixon announced at the beginning of his second term that he would restructure the White House Office around five assistants to the president, to be responsible for foreign affairs (Henry Kissinger), economic affairs (George Shultz), domestic affairs (John Ehrlichman), executive management (Roy Ash), and what was euphemistically called White House administration (H.R. Haldeman). Under these five White House assistants (of whom Shultz and, later on, Kissinger were also heads of departments) were three Cabinet members "elevated" to the status of White House Counselors. Their job was to undertake responsibility for policy coordination in those areas that would have been the focus of the new superdepartments had Congress enacted Nixon's plan of executive reorganization. This brought Earl Butz (natural resources), Caspar Weinberger (human resources) and James Lynn (community development) into the White House policy circle, but they were to operate under the direction of John Ehrlichman. Nixon also stated that other department heads would report to him "via the appropriate assistant to the president."

There was no ambiguity in Nixon's 5 January statement about the subservience of Cabinet members to the White House staff. Moreover, the restructuring had created a three-tiered Cabinet. Two Cabinet members had the highest status of assistant to the president, three more were counselors to the president, and the remainder were consigned to third-class citizenship. The Cabinet itself became totally redundant, even as a symbol of unity in an increasingly fragmented executive branch. Under the restructured system, unity was symbolized by strong, centralized control from the White House.

The Nixon system soon fell apart, as a casualty of Watergate, when Haldeman and Ehrlichman were forced to resign their White House posts at the end of April 1973 and when, in order to appease criticism that the president was ignoring his Cabinet, the three Counselors turned in their dual portfolios and returned to the rank of ordinary Cabinet members. Nevertheless, Nixon, unlike any of his predecessors, had publicly exposed the very tenuous and fragile basis underlying the president-Cabinet relationship in American government and had given an unequivocal presidential imprimatur to a less prominent role for the Cabinet collectively and heads of departments individually as sources of policy advice.

It is not possible to quantify the extent of the long-term damage done to the status and authority of the Cabinet and its members by the Nixon initiatives, but that damage was not erased by Nixon's premature departure from the White House. It has been claimed that President Ford did more to restore a sense of purpose to the Cabinet as a deliberative, meaningful advisory body than any postwar president except Eisenhower,[76] but Ford had much the same view about the role of Cabinet members as Nixon. "What I wanted in my Cabinet," he said, "were strong managers who would control the career bureaucrats.... I would leave the details of administration to them and concentrate on determining national priorities and directions myself."[77] There were, however, few overt signs of White House staff–Cabinet problems during Ford's brief tenure, and his presidency may well mark a short hiatus in the ascendancy of the staff over the Cabinet. But President Carter soon succeeded in reestablishing the pattern of dominance.

Despite the protestation at the beginning of his term of office that "there will never be an instance while I am President when the members of the White House staff dominate or act in a superior position to the members of the Cabinet,"[78] Carter's presidency illustrated the reverse. There was a permanent and serious problem of White House staff–Cabinet conflict throughout the Carter administration, which has been well documented from one side of the fence by former Secretary of Health, Education, and Welfare Joseph Califano.[79] A weekend meeting of the Cabinet, the White House staff, and the president in April 1978 did nothing to stop the situation from deteriorating, and when President Carter discovered a "crisis of the American spirit" during his famous retreat at Camp David in July 1979, his only tangible response was to dismiss five members of his Cabinet and to enhance the power of his top White House aide, Hamilton Jordan, by designating him chief of staff. What became known as "the July massacre" elicited the response from one Congressman: "Good grief! They're cutting down the biggest trees and keeping the monkeys."[80] From that point on, there was no doubting the supremacy of Carter's White House staff in the policy-making process.

White House staff–Cabinet tension and conflict continued during the Reagan and Bush presidencies. Sometimes it resulted in clear winners and losers, as with Reagan's Secretary of State Alexander Haig and Health and Human Services Secretary Margaret Heckler, both of whom lost out in fights with the White House staff and eventually resigned their Cabinet positions. At other times, the tensions and conflict persisted throughout the years in power, with neither side giving way. Such was the case in the Bush presidency with the key economic policy makers in the White House fighting a permanent and, eventually, a very public war against Secretary of the Treasury Nicholas Brady.[81] But by then the media, at least, seemed to show less interest in White House staff–Cabinet conflict. Perhaps such behavior had become part of the normal expectations about any post-Nixon administration in Washington and consequently was less newsworthy. Perhaps Cabinet secretaries in the Reagan-Bush years were so constrained by the overriding importance of the budget deficit that there was little scope for initiative and action on their parts and thus less potential for conflict with the White House staff. Perhaps it was because the expectations of members of the president's Cabinet had finally adjusted to the realities of centralized direction from the White House, and they were more willing to accept the treatment they received from White House staffers. Whatever the reason, attention seems to have shifted during the last decade to the conflict and tensions within White House staffs, rather than those between the staff and members of the Cabinet, and that in itself might be taken as a measure of the extent of centralization of power within the White House. There is now an abundance of evidence, albeit anecdotal, that presidential policy making can be seriously affected by the intrigue, the ambition, the personalities, and the power plays that have now become a regular feature of life among the presidential staff.[82]

Although post-Watergate critics observed the increasing power of the White House staff and the declining status of the Cabinet as an empirical fact, and drew certain conclusions from it, the historical context of this development got less attention than it deserved. Rarely was it pointed out that the Cabinet's role as a deliberative body, indeed its very identity as a collectivity, was the result of a historical accident in the constitutional scheme of things. The intent of the Founding Fathers was that the Senate would be the body to perform Cabinet-type functions as a dispenser of collective advice to the president.[83] As Woodrow Wilson noted at the beginning of this century: "There can be little doubt in the mind of any one who has carefully studied the plans and opinions of the Constitutional Convention of 1787 that the relations of the President and the Senate were intended to be very much more intimate and confidential than they have been."[84] The accident occurred early in the history of the presidency. When President Washington went to the Senate in August 1789 to confer over an Indian treaty, the Senators were reluctant to discuss the matter in his presence and postponed debate for two days, at which point Washington left the chamber in anger.[85] The Founding Fathers' conception "broke down the first time it was put to the test," notes Corwin,[86] and thereafter Washington turned to the heads of the executive departments as an alternative source of advice and consultation.[87]

Not all of Washington's successors followed his precedent, and the fortunes of members of the Cabinet began to decline almost as soon as the Federalist era was over. As the nineteenth century progressed, American presidents demonstrated greater willingness to seek advice in a more flexible way, often turning to personal acquaintances outside the executive branch. Yet, even though the Cabinet has no constitutional basis, and individual members of the Cabinet have no constitutional claim to be the sole source of policy advice to the president, the notion of the Cabinet as an advisory body managed to survive, endowed with some semiconstitutional sanctity, as a theoretically important element in the structure of executive government. That survival can be partly attributed to the absence of any credible alternative institution within the formal framework of government that might have challenged the privileged advisory position of the members of the Cabinet. So long as the Senate showed no desire to fulfill the privy council role that the Founding Fathers had intended it to have, the heads of departments collectively constituted the only feasible institution to fill the vacuum. But the creation of the White House Office changed the situation. Given the flexibility of the Constitution with regard to presidential advisory mechanisms, together with the preferences of most postwar presidents about where to get advice, it was not too difficult for the White House staff to mount a successful challenge to the hitherto privileged position of the Cabinet. The White House staff replaced the Cabinet in much the same way as the Cabinet had once replaced the Senate, and there is nothing constitutionally illegitimate about a president choosing to take advice from his White House staff in preference to his Cabinet. It might be unwise for a president to rely on his White House staff to the exclusion of the members of his Cabinet, but that is another question.

The constitutional structure of American government is therefore one important explanation for the growing power of the White House staff. By not writing into the Constitution any provision for a cabinet, an executive council, a privy council, or any other type of presidential advisory mechanism, the Founding Fathers left a vacuum to be filled as circumstances and necessity dictated. When necessity eventually did dictate that the White House staff assume a more prominent position in American politics, its move to center stage was made easier by the absence of any fixed institutional barrier in its path. The Cabinet proved to be no real obstacle.

It is not the case, however, that the White House staff acquired power by usurping the functions of the Cabinet. Presidents call on their staff to do things that the Cabinet and the heads of departments individually are ill suited to do. As Richard Neustadt pointed out a long time ago, presidents and Cabinet members do not share the same vantage point in government, nor the same risks, and presidential choices cannot be made by anyone but the president.[88] However much Cabinet members profess loyalty to the president, they quickly become enmeshed in a network of institutional relationships, each of which commands a certain degree of allegiance from the Cabinet member if he is to operate successfully within it. Multiple allegiances inevitably result in divided loyalties, and members of the Cabinet are as much an object of the president's powers of persuasion as are all the constituents with which a president must deal.

The White House staff, as Neustadt has emphasized, must also be persuaded.[89] Only the president can see his personal stake in the choices he makes, and he begins to risk his power prospects as soon as he depends on others. Nevertheless, necessity obliges that presidents depend on others to perform the numerous and demanding chores of office, and in that sense the presidency has long been too big a job for one person to handle. Presidential staffs have become powerful because they are, functionally, an extension of the president and because the functions they perform place them in a strategically commanding position relative to other actors in the political process, particularly executive branch officials.

Those functions are broadly of three kinds: coordinating, gatekeeping, and promotion. The coordinating function relates primarily to those policy-making, budgeting, and other activities within the executive branch in which the president has an interest. The object here is to bring those activities into line with the president's desires. Consequently, the White House Office becomes the arbiter of what is, and what is not, in accord with the president's position. As gatekeeper, the White House staff determines who and what gets access to the president, a function necessitated by the obvious fact that the president cannot physically satisfy all the demands made on his time. As the principal promoter of the president, the White House Office is responsible for ensuring that the president and his presidency appear to his various publics in the best possible light, the objective being to create and sustain public support for the president in office and, eventually, for the president as a candidate for reelection. All of these functions are control functions, giving the White House staff the final say, short of the president himself.

The White House Office has acquired power because it is a functional necessity of the modern presidency. The decline of the Cabinet is merely a manifestation of that power, not the cause of it, and the impact of White House staff power extends far beyond the members of the Cabinet and other political appointees in the executive branch. Necessity and proximity to the president make staff power formidable, and in most of the recent well-publicized battles between the White House staff and other key political actors, the White House staff has emerged victorious. It is not, however, an absolute power, nor is the White House staff guaranteed to emerge as the dominant force in any particular power struggle in which it is engaged. The staff, like the president, must compete for power in a pluralistic system of government, although, of course, they compete from a most advantageous position.

The power of the White House staff has also been strengthened by one very significant development during the past twenty years or so, the *deinstitutionalization* of the Executive Office of the President.[90] As was emphasized in the previous chapter, the EOP is no longer the institutional staff that it once was, or that Brownlow envisaged. It is not a permanent, professional, nonpartisan, expert staff, serving the office of the presidency irrespective of who holds that office at any one time. The senior echelons of the Executive Office are now filled by noncareer, highly partisan, presidential loyalists, many of whom do not possess professional expertise in government. In 1980, for example, the top ten positions in the Office of Management and Budget went to political appointees, nine of whom were without any prior experience in the executive branch.[91]

The Executive Office of the President has been politicized, and in place of neutral competence it now provides the president with what Terry Moe has called "responsive competence."[92] Whether that is a good or bad development in American government is the subject of much current debate elsewhere and need not be considered at this juncture. The immediate point is that, whatever its policy implications, deinstitutionalization enhances the power of the president's personal staff to control the apparatus of the presidential branch by removing the potential obstacle of a career civil service inside the EOP possessed of expertise, experience, and institutional memory. This leaves senior White House staffers as the unchallenged directors of the Executive Office. It means that EOP units are more responsive to the needs of the political leadership of the day as defined by senior presidential aides in the White House Office. This is particularly the case with the four principal divisions in the Executive Office, namely the Office of Management and Budget, the Domestic Policy Council, the National Economic Council, and the National Security Council, where deinstitutionalization (or politicization) has been most apparent. In recent years, each of these divisions has been run by senior White House staff or, in the case of OMB, by a political appointee close to the president.

POWER AND BEHAVIOR

In giving direction to the activities of the presidential branch, the White House staff has come to be associated with a set of behavioral characteristics that, like most other aspects of presidential staffing, became a cause of concern in the aftermath of Watergate. The worst of the behavioral defects associated with those around the president was their utter disrespect for the law, as revealed during the Nixon years when senior White House staff were involved in a range of criminal acts that included breaking and entering into private premises, burglary, bugging and telephone tapping, misusing campaign funds, and obstructing justice. For their crimes, senior White House aides H.R. Haldeman, John Ehrlichman, John Dean, and Charles Colson went to jail.

Other behavioral problems associated with the White House staff were of a non-criminal nature and were not confined to the Nixon administration. Perhaps the most serious of these was the alleged tendency of staff to isolate the president from the world outside the White House. As gatekeepers, they determined which people and what information penetrated the Oval Office, and terms like "palace guard," "praetorian guard," and "the Berlin Wall" (specifically applied to Nixon's three senior aides, Haldeman, Ehrlichman, and Kissinger) were frequently used in the 1970s to emphasize the power of top aides to close off access to the president.[93] In the Bush administration, White House Chief of Staff John Sununu performed a similar role. "His domineering style," as one Bush White House staffer wrote of Sununu, "increasingly meant that Bush was deprived of oxygen."[94]

White House staff were also accused of bringing problems to the White House that did not belong there. George Reedy, for example, cited as examples the number of labor disputes that President Johnson was called on to resolve personally. Reedy believed that the steel strike of 1965 and the maritime strike of 1966 were not serious enough to warrant settlement in the Oval Office, but the fact that they were resolved there paved the way for presidential intervention in the 1966 airline strike, which turned out to be a disastrous setback for Lyndon Johnson.[95] Such things happen because staff members make judgments about what might impress the president primarily to enhance their individual positions in the White House pecking order. If problems are solved satisfactorily, then the president benefits politically and the staff assistant responsible gains some personal credit. Reedy, on the other hand, suggests that there is little incentive for the White House aide engaged in such behavior to think about the longer-term implications of his action on the president and the presidency.

Another much-criticized feature of White House staff behavior is its excessive loyalty to the president, sometimes bordering on sycophancy. It results, we are told, in an unending quest to please the boss by telling him only what he wants to hear and shielding him from the bad news he ought to hear.[96] Few White House staffers, conventional wisdom has it, are willing to incur the wrath of the president in this way, and the wise presidential assistant, George Reedy tells us, develops the facility to maintain close proximity to the president coupled with the ability to disappear at the right moment.[97]

Arrogance has also been a hallmark of White House staff behavior. Anecdotal evidence and general impressions over recent years suggest that some White House aides have not accepted the power bestowed on them with sufficient humility and sensitivity toward other key actors in the political system. Sometimes they can be openly arrogant and cause offense, as Hamilton Jordan did during the Carter administration by rarely returning telephone calls from Cabinet members,[98] or when a member of President Kennedy's congressional liaison staff was overheard on Capitol Hill asking, "Anyone have a dime? I want to buy a Congressman."[99] At other times, the energy, ambition, aggressiveness, and loyalty of the White House staff combine to produce an arrogance of power that more established political figures in Washington find offensive. Indeed, a survey conducted by Thomas Cronin showed that presidential staff themselves perceived their own insensitivity toward departmental officials as the single most important White House source of conflict between the staff and the executive branch departments.[100]

The most frequently mentioned manifestation of this arrogance is the tendency of White House staffers to use the president's name to legitimize their own actions and authority, often when there is little justification for their doing so. A presidential assistant who can tell someone else that the president wants something done has considerable leverage over one who might be inclined to object or argue about it. Moreover, the expanding size of the White House staff has also meant that a larger number of individuals than ever before are in a position to use the words "the president wants," and the president has less and less control over what is being said and done in his name.[101]

Finally, there is ambition. The White House Office can be a ruthlessly competitive environment in which individuals engage in an unending struggle to increase their influence and get as close to the Oval Office as possible. Once there, they engage in an equally demanding effort to protect their privileged positions, and so the gamut of staff behavior can range from the empire-building activities of a John Dean or Charles Colson, alluded to earlier in this chapter, to power struggles at the very top of the staff hierarchy, like those that characterized the first term of the Reagan administration and were endemic in the Bush White House team.

The behavioral problems of White House staffers started to be well publicized at the beginning of the 1970s. George Reedy, formerly press secretary to President Lyndon Johnson, set the tone for many of the subsequent commentaries with a damning indictment of the inner life of the White House in his book *The Twilight of the Presidency*. The White House, he said, was "an ideal cloak for intrigue, pomposity and ambition" and went on to charge that it "provides camouflage for all that is petty and nasty in human beings and enables a clown or a knave to pose as Galahad and be treated with deference."[102] Elsewhere in the book, Reedy variously described the inner life of the White House as a "barnyard," "a pressure cooker," and "the perfect setting for the conspiracy of mediocrity" and urged that no one be permitted to work there until they had achieved at least forty years of age and suffered major disappointments in life.[103] There may have been a little exaggeration in his analysis, as Reedy himself admits, but the book had a significant impact on the way critics came to view the presidential staff in the post-Watergate period. When the Watergate saga subsequently provided abundant evidence to support Reedy's picture of the presidential staff system, it was easy to argue that the growth of White House staff power, and the behavior that power engendered, was what got the Nixon administration involved in Watergate, and it was equally easy to propose a whole set of remedies designed to reduce staff power and check its worst behavioral defects, and many post-Watergate critics did precisely this.

But although this unflattering image of the White House staff was something of a revelation in the late 1960s and early 1970s, the defects it exposed certainly predated the Nixon administration. Haldeman and Ehrlichman, for example, were not the first White House aides to isolate the president they worked for. As was pointed out in chapter 2, Charles Dyer Norton successfully isolated Taft, George Christian closed off access to Harding, and Lawrence Richey did much the same to Herbert Hoover. There were also power struggles and intrigue in pre-Brownlow White House staffs: Witness William Loeb's eagerness to step into Cortelyou's shoes,[104] or Tumulty's battles with Colonel House, or the never-ending friction between the first White House staff troika of Richey, Akerson, and Newton in Hoover's administration, or in Louis Howe's fierce jealousy of his standing with Franklin Roosevelt.[105] Pre-Brownlow White House staffs also had their share of ambitious assistants, and if one goes back to the nineteenth century, some corrupt, dishonest, and deceitful presidential aides as well. The behavioral defects of the White House staff have a long history and tradition and predate the postwar expansion in the size of the presidential staff.

The very public exposure of the seamy side of White House staff behavior during the Watergate crisis raised questions about the accountability of the staff—questions that had not merited much attention until then. If, as James Madison once claimed, American government was built upon the principle that "ambition must be made to counteract ambition,"[106] then Watergate was fairly concrete evidence that the ambition of the White House staff had not been counteracted very well. The fact that many of President Nixon's top aides went to jail for the worst of their behavioral sins, or that the president eventually suffered for what his staff had done in his name by forfeiting his presidency, failed to satisfy the critics. They saw a strong and unhealthy relationship between the size, power, and the behavior of the presidential staff and called for institutional reform, not just individual punishment, to correct the situation. A great deal was written on what ought to be done, a lot less on why the White House staff had escaped the usual checks and balances of the American political system. A large part of the answer to that question can be found in the subject matter of the next chapter, which examines the role of Congress in the development of the presidential staff system.

5. CONGRESS, COMITY, AND THE PRESIDENTIAL BRANCH

For most of its history, the presidential branch has been allowed to move to center stage of American politics with few barriers in its path. Until the early 1970s, the development of the Executive Office of the President was of little interest to many observers of the Washington scene, with the single exception of a handful of political scientists who kept an academic eye on what was going on in the west wing of the White House and the Old Executive Office Building. The Washington press corps was more concerned with individuals and personalities than with political institutions, and Congress was hardly concerned at all. In fact, until Watergate, the presidential branch appeared to be almost totally immune from even the most mundane forms of congressional oversight.

The lack of congressional interest in the oversight of the Executive Office during its first thirty years of life is somewhat at odds with the periodic eagerness of legislators to shape the structure and functions of the presidential staff system by placing new units in the EOP, sometimes against the wishes of the president. Why Congress has been so keen to create new presidential staffs, but at the same time unwilling or unable to oversee the operations of the staff system, calls for some explanation. So does the fact that congressional attitudes toward oversight of the presidential branch hardly changed at all during and after Watergate.

The congressional response to a political institution whose members were at the center of many Watergate-related activities was minimal, and although a president was forced to resign his office under the threat of impeachment and a number of his senior aides were sent to jail, institutionally speaking, the presidential staff system survived Watergate intact, untouched, and unscathed by Congress. Moreover, the way Congress responded to the institutionalized presidency was also quite different in effect from the general congressional response to the growth of presidential power following the Johnson and Nixon presidencies. On a broad front, Congress made a determined effort to regain some of the power and authority it had lost to what Arthur Schlesinger, Jr. labeled "the imperial presidency."[1] It moved to strengthen its authority with respect to the war power, the power of the purse, the control of foreign policy, the conduct of intelligence agencies, the information monopoly possessed by the executive branch, and the administrative discretion exercised by the departments and agencies. The reaction amounted to a short-lived resurgence of Congress within the American political system and shifted the imbalance of power between the two branches more toward Congress than it had been for a long time.[2]

The presidential staff system, however, was virtually excluded from the post-Watergate resurgence of congressional authority by a legislature seemingly reluctant even to apply for a search warrant to examine the home of so many of the Watergate villains.

THE THEORY AND PRACTICE OF OVERSIGHT

To anyone familiar with the literature on congressional oversight, it will come as no surprise to learn that Congress showed little interest in oversight of the presidential branch because, in general, Congress has neglected its oversight responsibilities, and there is a broad consensus that its performance of oversight since the passage of the 1946 Legislative Reorganization Act has been inadequate.[3] In fact, the weakness of congressional oversight was the most persistent criticism made to the Select Committee on Committees (the Bolling Committee), established in 1974 to consider structural reform of the House of Representatives.[4] Research has suggested that the performance of oversight very much depends on the motivations of members of Congress to engage in such activities and has found that, despite a general consensus in Congress that oversight ought to be conducted, "few members felt any strong stimulus to fulfill this obligation."[5] Morris Fiorina has argued that there is little electoral incentive for members of Congress to do so,[6] and much of the evidence given to the Bolling Committee also emphasized that many members found the oversight function to be politically unrewarding in relation to the time and effort required.[7]

Research also suggests that there are limits to what one can say generally about congressional oversight. The degree of oversight exercised by Congress varies according to the particular area involved, the nature of the committee and the committee chairman with jurisdiction in that area, the attitudes of members to the particular department or agency under scrutiny, the priorities of members of Congress in terms of competing legislative responsibilities, and whether or not Congress and the White House are controlled by the same party.[8] Hence the quality and quantity of oversight in any particular instance cannot be predicted from generalizations about the aggregate oversight exercised by Congress. Paradoxically, while much of the general criticism of congressional oversight relates to the lack of systematic, comprehensive, and coordinated oversight by Congress as a whole, Congress has also been accused of micromanagement or, in less neutral terms, excessive meddling in the details of administration.[9]

One cannot, therefore, explain congressional attitudes toward the presidential staff solely in terms of the general weakness and ineffectiveness of the oversight process. In any case, even if a general explanation for the lack of congressional oversight in this area would have been acceptable prior to Watergate, it certainly would not adequately account for the post-Watergate period. Watergate was a crisis of such gravity, and the presidential staff was so central to that crisis, that some kind of congressional response was called for. That response was not forthcoming, despite the fact that on a general level Congress was more diligent about its conduct of executive branch oversight in the post-Watergate period. Recent research has identified a dramatic increase in the amount of congressional oversight from the mid-1970s, "reaching and sustaining very substantial levels."[10]

There is also a third reason for examining congressional scrutiny of the presidential branch as a special case of oversight. The major constraint on Congress in this particular area—the historic tradition of comity—is a unique one and applies to no other agency of the executive branch of government.

Formal congressional oversight of the executive branch is conducted in a number of ways. The most senior personnel in the executive branch, excluding the president and the vice president, are subject to Senate confirmation before their appointments are made official, and having been appointed, they are then frequently required to testify before congressional committees about their performance in office. Authorizing, or legislative, committees are free to conduct investigations, commission reports, and hold hearings on any issue arising within their jurisdiction. Fiscal oversight is effected through the appropriations process, which ensures an annual review of the departments and agencies. In addition, the Government Operations Committee in the House and the Governmental Affairs Committee in the Senate are primarily oversight committees with wide-ranging remits to examine any government agency quite independently of the legislative or appropriations process.[11] Congressional committees and individual members of Congress can also call upon the resources and expertise of the General Accounting Office, an independent agency with more than 5000 staff and a mandate to audit the activities of the executive branch including the Executive Office of the President. Ultimately, of course, Congress can legislate to ensure accountability in government and has the power to pass legislation over a presidential veto if necessary.

The Executive Office of the President is formally part of the executive branch. It is funded directly by Congress, just like any other department or agency, and it does not, in theory, stand beyond any of the formal techniques of oversight mentioned above. As a division within the EOP, the White House Office is no exception, notwithstanding its very special relationship to the president. In practice, however, the EOP has been treated quite differently from other departments and agencies, which is another reason for making an analytical distinction between the presidential and executive branches of government. Congress has traditionally been most reluctant to bring the presidential branch into the same mode of oversight that applies to the executive branch in general.

THE FRAMEWORK OF CONGRESSIONAL OVERSIGHT

Before examining the application or nonapplication of the formal methods of oversight to the presidential branch, a brief description of the framework of congressional oversight in this particular area is in order.

Regular oversight responsibility is within the jurisdiction of four congressional committees: the House Post Office and Civil Service Committee, the Senate Committee on Governmental Affairs, and the House and Senate Appropriations Committees. Within these bodies, the effective responsibility is delegated to subcommittees. Within the House Post Office and Civil Service Committee, the Subcommittee on the Civil Service has been a major forum for presidential staffing matters, although the Subcommittee on Human Resources was also active in this area until it was abolished at the beginning of 1993. In the Senate Governmental Affairs Committee, oversight responsibilities are handled by the Subcommittee on Federal Services, Post Office, and Civil Service, whose jurisdiction spans the whole area covered by the full House Post Office and Civil Service Committee. Within the House and Senate Appropriations Committees, fiscal oversight is conducted principally through the Subcommittees on Treasury, Postal Service, and General Government, which handle the EOP budget submission each year.[12]

Beyond these four committees, intermittent oversight of the presidential staff can be performed through many other committees. The House Government Operations Committee, for example, has a wide mandate to inquire into the economy and efficiency of government operations and a specific legislative and oversight mandate in the area of executive branch reorganization. Other committees can also investigate aspects of presidential staffing when an issue touches on their jurisdiction. In the aftermath of Watergate, for example, the Subcommittee on the Separation of Powers of the Senate Judiciary Committee held hearings on the issue of the presidential staff and the claim of executive privilege, and the Senate Foreign Relations Committee examined the role of the president's national security adviser and how he might be made more accountable to Congress. Congress can also establish select committees to inquire into aspects of presidential staffing should it wish to do so, as it did in both the House and the Senate in 1987 in response to the Iran-*contra* episode.

In practice, the degree of intermittent oversight of the presidential branch has been negligible, and the amount of oversight exercised by those committees with specific jurisdiction over the staff has varied considerably. The House Post Office and Civil Service Committee has been very active since the beginning of the 1970s and has been at the forefront of congressional efforts to make the presidential branch more accountable to the legislature. Most of the initiatives that Congress has taken in this regard have emanated from the Post Office and Civil Service Committee. The House Appropriations Committee also responded to Watergate by casting a more critical eye over the EOP budget for a short time in the mid-1970s, and terminating one or two abuses in presidential staff funding, but the committee has since reverted to a more passive role. The Senate Governmental Affairs Committee and the Senate Appropriations Committee have maintained a consistent lack of interest in oversight of the presidential staff and have even been unwilling to support initiatives taken by their counterparts in the House of Representatives.

The reason why the House Post Office and Civil Service Committee became active in oversight of the presidential branch at the beginning of the 1970s, but not before, is not solely attributable to the catalytic effect of Watergate. Part of the explanation can be found in the nature of the committee prior to 1965 and in two significant developments affecting the committee's behavior and jurisdiction that took place in 1965 and 1970.

Richard Fenno's study of the House Post Office and Civil Service Committee between 1955 and 1965 showed it to be a low-energy, low-influence, and low-prestige body whose members were not very interested in the work of the committee and, for the most part, wanted to leave it as soon as they could.[13] Morris Ogul discovered much the same when he studied the committee during the 89th Congress.[14] The committee was dominated by its chairman, Tom Murray, and its principal concerns were postal rates and pay rates for postal workers.[15] The majority of the committee were sympathetic to the committee's clientele, the postal workers and civil servants, from whom they derived significant electoral support,[16] but Murray was not, and he found himself in fundamental disagreement with the majority over what Fenno has called the committee's strategic premises.[17] As well as being in disagreement with his committee on policy, Murray was also very reluctant to engage in any oversight of the executive unless there was a strong case for it.[18]

In 1965, members of the House Post Office and Civil Service Committee moved successfully to challenge the power and dominance of Chairman Murray by adopting a new set of committee rules, which had the effect of devolving power to subcommittee chairmen, increasing the number of subcommittees from four to eight, and limiting the power of the chairman in the full committee.[19] The challenge to Murray was a necessary pre-condition for any increased oversight activity from the committee.

The second development affecting the House Post Office and Civil Service Committee was the passage of the Postal Reorganization Act of 1970, as a result of which the U. S. Postal Service became an independent establishment within the executive branch, and the Post Office and Civil Service

Committee lost its jurisdiction over postal rates and postal employees' salaries. That changed the orientation of the committee and weakened the links between committee members and clientele groups.[20] It left the committee searching for a role or, to put it more simply, for something to do, and one can reasonably assume that any new area of interest on the part of committee members would have been welcomed.

The 1965 and 1970 changes did not result in all members of the committee suddenly becoming eager to investigate the presidential branch, but they did offer an opportunity to those few individuals on the committee who wanted to do so, and the oversight effort in this instance is probably best explained in terms of individual members' concern about the presidential staff, unrelated to the committee's strategic premises or any obvious publicity or electoral benefits.

Unlike its counterpart in the House, the Senate Subcommittee on Civil Service, Post Office, and General Services has not had members who have felt strongly motivated to get into oversight of the presidential branch. Even if it had, the broad jurisdiction of the subcommittee and its limited staff resources would have been a major constraint on what the subcommittee could have done.

To its credit, the House Post Office and Civil Service Committee made the first serious study of the post-1939 expansion of the presidential staff. Under the direction of Representative Morris Udall, the full committee commissioned a report on the growth of the Executive Office of the President which it published in 1972. Udall's report concentrated on the growth in the number of employees in the EOP since 1955 and the budgetary costs of that increase, but its major concern was with the expansion that had taken place during the Nixon presidency. As noted in chapter 3, the report showed that half of the percentage increase in staff since 1955 had occurred under Nixon. The report contained no specific recommendations for change, but it drew attention to the centralization of power in the White House at the expense of the executive departments. It also highlighted the difficulty of obtaining useful data about the presidential staff, particularly on the functions being performed by senior EOP staff, and concluded by emphasizing the need for more information to "enable Congress to consider objectively the staffing needs of the executive departments and agencies on the one hand and the executive offices of the President on the other."[21] Since then, the House Post Office and Civil Service Committee has been involved in a continuous effort to obtain that information and has not been entirely successful in its endeavor.

The framework for fiscal oversight of the presidential branch needs less preliminary explanation. The Appropriations Committees in the House and Senate are better known than the Post Office and Civil Service Committees. They are considerably more powerful and prestigious bodies, and membership on the Appropriations Committee is eagerly sought in both chambers.

Thanks to the work of Richard Fenno and Stephen Horn, we also have very detailed accounts of how these two committees operate and how they relate to each other.

From these studies, three general points are worth extracting in the context of the framework of fiscal oversight of the presidential branch. First, the House Appropriations Committee functions with a complex set of informal rules which makes it very difficult for individual members to challenge the accepted norms of committee behavior. One of those norms is intensive subcommittee specialization, giving each subcommittee considerable autonomy over its particular jurisdiction.[22] Second, the House Appropriations Committee has adopted as its principal strategic premise that it should reduce executive budget requests and does, in fact, do so.[23] Fenno has shown that between 1958 and 1965, 91.5 percent of all appropriations bills were affected by committee-imposed cuts on the requested budget and that in more than one-quarter of the cases the cuts were in excess of 20 percent.[24] Third, the Senate Appropriations Committee is much more favorable to the executive than is its counterpart in the House and, according to Fenno, acts as "a lenient appeals court" against House-imposed budget cuts.[25] As a result, members of the House Appropriations Committee tend to see a Senate Appropriations Committee–executive branch alliance against their efforts to save money.[26] This study shows that the Senate Appropriations Committee has behaved quite consistently with its strategic premises in respect of the presidential branch. The House Appropriations Committee, in contrast, has deviated from the norm very significantly.

Having thus identified the principal committees with regular responsibilities for oversight of the presidential branch, we can now examine how the more common techniques of oversight have been applied in this particular case. The following discussion concentrates mainly on formal oversight procedures such as the Senate's advice-and-consent power, committee hearings and investigations, the appropriations process, and legislative authorization, but two qualifications need to be made before this analysis proceeds any further.

First, recent literature on congressional oversight has adopted a more expansive view of the concept and function of oversight, distinguishing between formal and informal techniques, or between what Morris Ogul calls "manifest" and "latent" oversight. As Ogul points out, "Things are not always what they seem. Substantial oversight is performed when apparently that is not the case. What is intended is not always achieved; what is achieved may not be what is intended."[27] Walter Oleszek, for example, notes that a great deal of oversight can be conducted through informal contacts between legislators and bureaucrats and that these contacts "can enable committees to exercise public influence in areas where statutory methods might be inappropriate or ineffective."[28]

The difficulty faced by the student of congressional oversight is that those informal contacts are both so private and so intangible that they are beyond the reach of any systematic analysis. Informal oversight, according to Oleszek, can be effected by executive officials being "attuned to the nuances of congressional language in hearings, floor debate, committee reports, and conference reports."[29] Dodd and Schott suggest that oversight can be an outcome of "understandings between agency officials and members or staffs of Congress."[30] Hence, although the emphasis of what follows is on formal oversight, one cannot ignore the possibilities of informal oversight of the presidential branch, however difficult they might be to detect.

The second qualification is that not all of the regular or formal methods of oversight can be applied to the presidential branch. For example, a significant amount of congressional scrutiny of the executive branch is achieved through program oversight. Programs are probably the easiest and most convenient vehicle by which Congress can maintain "continuous watchfulness" over departments and agencies,[31] but as the presidential branch has no program responsibilities, an important tool of oversight is denied to Congress in this instance. Casework is another example of an oversight mechanism that cannot be used by Congress with respect to the presidential branch. Because the presidential branch has no program responsibilities, it is far less likely than executive branch agencies to be the target of constituent complaints, and therefore members of Congress are not given the same sort of opportunity to assess the performance of any particular division of the EOP. Yet another formal method of oversight that is not always available to Congress insofar as the presidential staff is concerned is apparent in the following section.

Oversight by Senate Confirmation

The Senate's advice-and-consent power is the first weapon in the armory of congressional oversight. The confirmation process enables the Senate to scrutinize presidential nominations to senior positions in the executive branch in as much detail as it wishes, and ultimately it gives the legislative branch of government the power to deny the president his choice of officeholder. Although only a very small number of presidential nominees are rejected by the Senate, or voluntarily withdrawn because of the possibility of rejection, the effects of the confirmation process go far beyond the power to deny consent. The impact of the advice-and-consent power "is more complex and more deliberate than is commonly believed," argues Calvin Mackenzie, and he emphasizes that "the opportunities for using the process ... to shape the direction of public policy are more abundant and more sophisticated than the mere calling of the roll on a nomination."[32] In recent years, particularly since the Nixon administration, the Senate has treated the confirmation process more seriously than ever before and has broadened the scope of its investigations of nominees beyond merely checking on character and qualifications. Senators now regularly attempt to extract guarantees from nominees on policy matters within their jurisdictions and on their willingness to cooperate with Congress when in office.[33]

The presidential branch differs from the executive branch with respect to the advice-and-consent power. Traditionally, the confirmation process has not been applied to the president's personal staff because the relationship they have with the president is considered to be a privileged one. That precedent was established in the very first Congress in the course of debates on presidential compensation. As was noted in chapter 2, when members of the House of Representatives discussed presidential staffing in 1789, several of them, including James Madison, stated unequivocally that presidential aides should be regarded as confidential assistants and not be classified as officers of the government. The principle that the president's personal staff ought to be treated as an extension of the president himself is thus well established and has held firm since the earliest days of the republic. What has caused some confusion, however, is precisely what constitutes the president's personal staff, and Congress has recently answered that question by effectively defining the personal staff as those with appointments in the White House Office.

Prior to the Nixon administration, Congress had been reluctant to apply the confirmation process to senior personnel in the Executive Office of the President. The three members of the Council of Economic Advisers were the first EOP officials to be subject to the advice-and-consent power in 1946. When the National Security Council was established in the EOP in 1949, the directorship of the Central Intelligence Agency (an office formally responsible to the NSC, but not usually regarded as part of the president's staff) was also subject to Senate confirmation, but the executive secretary of the NSC was not. During the 1950s and 1960s, most senior EOP posts were excluded from the advice-and-consent requirement, but congressional pressure to extend its oversight through confirmation to other presidential staff began to build up during the Nixon years. This was partly a symptom of the general conflict between President Nixon and a Democratic-controlled Congress, but it was also partly because presidential advisers were seen to be behaving more and more as surrogates for departmental heads, which required that the basis of the privileged relationship be questioned.[34]

In 1973 legislation was introduced in Congress to amend the Budget and Accounting Act of 1921 to require Senate confirmation of the director and deputy director of the Office of Management and Budget. Congressional determination to include OMB in the advice-and-consent provision was intensified by the high profile of its then director, Roy Ash, who also carried the title assistant to the president. Because the legislation was effectively retrospective and would have applied to Ash, and because a close confidant of the president was targeted in the legislation, President Nixon vetoed the bill, and the veto was subsequently sustained in the House.[35] A new bill was eventually enacted in 1974 applying only to future OMB directors and deputy directors.

The director and deputy director of OMB thus joined the members of the Council of Economic Advisers and the Council on Environmental Quality as officials of EOP units subject to Senate confirmation. Subsequently, the advice-and-consent provision was extended to the executive director of the now defunct Council on International Economic Policy, to the administrator of the Office of Federal Procurement Policy (a division within OMB), to the director of the Office of Science and Technology Policy, to the director, two deputy directors, and the associate director of the Office of National Drug Control Policy, and to the three members of the National Critical Materials Council. It would now appear that Senate confirmation of senior appointments in divisions of the Executive Office of the President is the rule, rather than an exception, and future presidents must expect it to be applied to any new EOP units that Congress has a hand in creating.

The Nixon administration offered Congress every incentive to extend the confirmation process even further. Henry Kissinger's control of foreign policy in his capacity as Nixon's national security adviser, and his unwillingness to testify before congressional committees, was beginning to put foreign policy making beyond the reach of congressional oversight. Kissinger had usurped the traditional role of the secretary of state and established himself as the dominant foreign policy maker in a government where officials with far less power and authority than he had are routinely subject to the advice-and-consent requirement. The argument for subjecting the national security adviser to Senate confirmation was reinforced during the Carter administration when national security adviser Zbigniew Brzezinski appeared to model himself on Kissinger. During the 1970s, a number of bills were introduced in Congress to make the national security adviser and his deputy subject to Senate confirmation, and, in 1980, the Senate Foreign Relations Committee held hearings on the issue. Those hearings were significant in exposing the limits of the reach of the advice-and-consent clause with respect to the president's personal staff.

The argument for making national security adviser subject to Senate confirmation is complicated by the fact that there is no statutory position of national security adviser within the Executive Office of the President. Ever since President Eisenhower chose to appoint a member of his staff to be his national security adviser, every president has done the same and has also used that assistant to direct the work of the National Security Council staff. But presidents are not compelled to have a national security adviser at all, and there is nothing in any law to direct the president as to the manner in which he receives advice on national security issues. This makes things difficult for Congress because, before such a position could be made subject to the Senate confirmation process, it would first have to be formally established and the weight of expert opinion is against doing so.[36] By making the post of assistant for national security affairs one that is established by law, Congress would, in effect, be telling presidents how they must organize their personal staff. Such an action would also be tantamount to declaring that the relationship between the president and his closest advisers is no longer a privileged one. So far, Congress has been reluctant to break a 200-year-old tradition that how and from whom a president seeks advice is, ultimately, a matter to be determined by the president alone.[37]

Congress would have to discard this tradition if it seriously wished to extend its advice-and-consent power to the White House Office. No positions within that office are statutorily or formally established, and the complexities of making the national security adviser subject to Senate confirmation would apply equally to other members of the president's personal staff. The only possible way that Congress could bring the most senior and powerful presidential aides into the confirmation process, without dictating how the president should organize his personal staff, would be to legislate a blanket provision covering all White House Office employees, irrespective of their function and seniority. That is an unlikely possibility.

Other limits to the degree of oversight can be effected through the confirmation process. However useful the device may be in bringing to light existing conflicts of interest, or in extracting policy commitments from future government officials, or in making them aware of the importance of cooperating with Congress, it is, as James Sundquist has emphasized, a form of "before-the-fact control,"[38] and it is very difficult for Senators to predict the behavior of nominees before they actually take office. As Sundquist points out, many of those officials implicated in Watergate were confirmed in office by the Senate in 1969, and even in the post-Watergate period, President Carter's nominee to head OMB, Bert Lance, survived the confirmation process only to resign his office within a year because of new information about his previous activities in the banking world.[39] Senators cannot unconfirm nominees after their initial judgment, says Sundquist, and in the absence of this power (which Sundquist does not advocate) "the confirmation process can never be more than a weak instrument for controlling the executive branch."[40]

It would be difficult to claim that the presidential branch has become more accountable to Congress because of the confirmation process. Although the advice-and-consent provision now covers a number of senior positions in the EOP, its reach has not yet been extended to the White House Office from which most of the most important people on the president's staff operate, and the likelihood that it will be extended to cover White House Office staff must be considered very remote. But even if this did happen, there would be immense difficulties in making this an effective form of oversight. To demonstrate that the confirmation process was meaningful, the Senate would, at some stage, have to show that it had the will to reject a nominee when circumstances demanded, thus denying the president his choice of personal staff. Although it is accepted that the Senate may reject a Cabinet or a sub-Cabinet nominee, and even a nomination to an Executive

Office position subject to the confirmation process,[41] the rejection of a senior member of the president's personal staff would be very likely to generate considerable ill will, and possibly conflict, between president and Congress at the outset of a new administration. Presumably few members of Congress would think it worth the cost.

Oversight by Hearings and Investigations

Hearings and investigations are the most visible forms of congressional oversight and one of the primary means by which Congress holds accountable the officials who manage the departments and agencies of the executive branch. Those whose appointments in government are established by law are expected to testify before congressional committees when asked to do so, and their testimony, and the information it provides, is considered vital to the effective performance of the oversight function. Presidential staffs have been treated as an exception in this respect, because of their close relationship to the president, and the doctrine of executive privilege is invoked to exclude them from the requirement to testify before Congress. The rationale for this is simply that presidents need the best available advice, and that advice might not be given so freely if advisers were denied the protection of confidentiality and were ultimately forced to account in a public forum for the advice given.

That rationale is less applicable, and claims of executive privilege more questionable, when presidential aides become policy makers in their own right, as has happened in recent decades. There is little point in a congressional committee receiving testimony from a secretary of state, for example, if the real architect of foreign policy is the national security adviser in the White House. Neither can Congress exercise effective oversight if presidential staff with major policy responsibilities avoid testifying on matters of national importance by hiding behind the executive privilege doctrine. Henry Kissinger did just this while he was President Nixon's national security adviser. His refusal to go before the Senate Foreign Relations Committee while directing a controversial policy in Southeast Asia was perhaps the most blatant example of a policy maker evading accountability to Congress. The situation, exacerbated by Kissinger's high public visibility, led Senator Frank Church to remark that "we have to wonder whether it is appropriate for a person who is immune from congressional inquiry to act as a principal spokesman for the United States in matters of foreign policy.... If he can appear on 'Meet the Press,' why can't he appear before the Foreign Relations Committee? Why should he be accountable to what is often called the fourth branch of government when he is not accountable to the first branch?"[42]

As Louis Fisher has noted, "The claim of executive privilege sets the stage for a confrontation between two 'absolutes,' the power of Congress to investigate and the power of a president to withhold information."[43] As in so many other instances, that confrontation was heightened during the Nixon years, and the use of executive privilege was at the heart of the conflict between President Nixon and the Senate Select Committee on Presidential Campaign Activities set up to investigate Watergate. Nixon's refusal to make available to Senator Ervin's committee secretly taped conversations with White House aides was the beginning of the end of his presidency. The response of Congress to what it saw as the excessive use of executive privilege came in the form of extensive hearings in the 92d, 93d, and 94th Congresses on the executive privilege doctrine,[44] but no congressional action followed. Those contesting the broad claims of privilege emanating from the White House were given scholarly support by the publication of Raoul Berger's influential treatise in 1974, which argued that the doctrine had no constitutional basis at all,[45] but shortly afterward the Supreme Court in *U.S. v. Nixon* (1974) argued to the contrary, although it also said that the claim of privilege was not an absolute one.

Berger's study and the Supreme Court's opinion in *U.S. v. Nixon* represent only two of the many contributions to the continuing debate on executive privilege, but that debate has tended to obscure the very real powers possessed by Congress to compel attendance and testimony at committee hearings. Existing law (2 U.S.C. 192) makes it a misdemeanor, punishable by a fine and imprisonment, for anyone to refuse to appear as a witness if summoned by Congress and to refuse to answer any pertinent question. There is no specific exemption in the law for the presidential staff, not even for the president's personal staff in the White House Office. In terms of the strict letter of the law, it would seem that presidential staffers have no right to refuse to attend a congressional committee hearing, and if they refused to answer any pertinent question on the basis of executive privilege, then, because a misdemeanor would have been committed, the matter would have to be resolved in the courts and it would be up to the courts to determine the claim of executive privilege. But Congress has been reluctant to push the issue into the courts, and the effect of that reluctance has left the White House staff as the sole arbiters of when the doctrine of executive privilege should be invoked.[46]

Congress itself must carry some responsibility for the present situation. Although it would not want to deny the president any claim of executive privilege for his staff, neither can it be content with a blanket claim of privilege any time it seeks to question a presidential aide. There have been opportunities when it may have been worthwhile for Congress to enforce its subpoena power with respect to the president's personal staff, but it has chosen not to do so. For example, in 1981, Martin Anderson, who was then President Reagan's assistant for policy development, refused to appear before an appropriations subcommittee considering the budget request for the Office of Policy Development. The White House claimed executive privilege, even though Anderson's predecessor in the Carter administration had appeared each year for the same purpose. Instead of testing the privilege claim, however, the House Committee on Appropriations responded with a futile gesture by denying the budget request of nearly $3 million in its entirety.[47] The cut was later restored by the Senate Appropriations Committee, and in the end almost the full request was granted to the Office of Policy Development in a continuing resolution, so the committee's protest came to nothing.

The Anderson incident is instructive because, on this occasion, a member of the president's personal staff was being asked to testify about the budget request for a staff unit in the Executive Office that he directed, not about any confidential advice he might have given the president in his capacity as domestic policy adviser. Neither was the White House claiming that Congress had no right to hear testimony on the Office of Policy Development budget request because two officials from the Office of Administration were sent along to do just that.[48] What was being claimed was that Congress had no right to hear testimony from Martin Anderson himself, and thus the doctrine of executive privilege was invoked in this instance solely on the basis of Anderson's position on the president's personal staff, irrespective of the subject matter of the congressional inquiry. The Anderson incident aroused little publicity and was soon forgotten by all concerned, but it constituted as broad a claim of executive privilege as one could imagine.

The Nixon years and the traumas of Watergate made very little difference to the ability of Congress to gain information from those who exercise a high degree of power within the presidential branch. Even though it increased its staff resources in the immediate post-Watergate period and dramatically stepped up the level of oversight activity in the 93d and 94th Congresses,[49] it failed to tackle the very serious problem of executive privilege and the presidential staff at a time when it had every incentive to do so.

The Nixon administration also gave Congress, if not an incentive, certainly a very good excuse to hold hearings and use its investigatory powers to inquire into the state of the presidential branch. The doctrine of executive privilege and the noncooperation of presidential staff can only limit the amount of information Congress receives; Congress cannot be prevented from asking questions and seeking answers to those questions in a public forum. The legislative branch is quite free to investigate any aspect of the presidential branch and hold hearings if it chooses to do so.

The Watergate hearings, conducted by Senator Sam Ervin's Senate Select Committee on Presidential Campaign Activities in 1973, were undoubtedly the most significant of all oversight hearings on the presidential branch because they were instrumental in bringing down a president of the United States. If Richard Nixon's resignation can be said to have been brought about by any single incident, it surely must have been the revelation by Alexander Butterfield, first in a closed session and later in a public hearing held by the Ervin Committee, that the president had been secretly taping conversations in the Oval Office. Those hearings exposed the extent of the

Watergate cover-up and provided compulsive television viewing for millions of Americans. The effect they had on public opinion and on subsequent events, such as the House Judiciary Committee's impeachment proceedings against the president and the post-Nixon resurgence of Congress, was substantial, and they clearly demonstrated the capacity of congressional oversight mechanisms to hold the president and the presidential branch accountable in the last resort. But one must emphasize that this was oversight of the last resort, exercised in unusual circumstances by a select, not a standing, committee. Very rarely does Congress have to direct its attention to a criminal conspiracy among the president and the White House staff to subvert the course of justice.

Aside from Watergate itself, two aspects of the workings of the presidential branch stand out in particular as serious concerns of Congress and were the subject of congressionally initiated hearings and investigations during the post-Watergate period. The most time-consuming was the issue of executive privilege. This went beyond the question of immunity for presidential staff, and the concern of Congress was broadly directed at the use of the executive privilege doctrine by executive branch officials generally. In April and May 1973, three separate Senate subcommittees took the unusual step of holding joint hearings on executive privilege, secrecy in government, and freedom of information.[50] The hearings were accompanied by a number of bills and resolutions, most attempting to ensure that Congress, not the president, was the final arbiter in any dispute over executive privilege. But those attempts served only as a focus for the hearings and had no impact on the future use of the executive privilege claim. In 1980, the Senate Foreign Relations Committee was still debating executive privilege when considering proposals to make the appointment of the national security adviser subject to Senate confirmation.

The second aspect of the presidential branch subject to congressionally initiated hearings and investigations has been its growth and size. That concern began with the publication of the Udall report by the House Post Office and Civil Service Committee in 1972 (see page 153) and culminated in the passage of the White House Personnel Authorization-Employment Act of 1978. As that legislation was the principal post-Watergate congressional response to the institutional problems of the presidential staff system, it is considered separately further on in this chapter.

Just as the memory of Watergate was beginning to fade and congressional interest in the activities of the presidential branch abating, so the Reagan administration provided another test for the oversight capacity of Congress in the form of the Iran-*contra* affair. Congressional reaction was swift. The secret arms sales to Iran were reported in a Lebanese newspaper at the beginning of November 1986, verified by President Reagan in a nationally televised address on 13 November, and reviewed by Attorney General Edwin Meese beginning 21 November. On 25 November, Meese revealed that the proceeds from the Iran arms sales had been "diverted" to assist the Nicaraguan *contras*.[51] When the new Congress convened at the beginning of January 1987, both the House and the Senate immediately established separate select committees to investigate the Iran-*contra* affair. Subsequently, the two committees created a precedent in the history of congressional investigations by agreeing to share resources and information, by conducting joint hearings, and producing a combined report which was completed and published by mid-November 1987. In the course of the investigation, the staffs of the committees reviewed more than 300,000 documents and interviewed more than 500 witnesses, culminating in forty days of public hearings and an extremely detailed report of 690 pages.[52]

Staff members of the National Security Council were at the very center of the Iran-*contra* affair. The congressional report was largely an indictment of the behavior of one particular member of the NSC staff, Lieutenant Colonel Oliver North, and two national security advisers, Robert McFarlane and his successor, John Poindexter, and of the process of foreign policy decision making that these individuals had established. But it was most definitely not a indictment of any perceived institutional weakness in the presidential staff system. The conclusion of the majority of members of the two congressional committees was that "the Iran-*Contra* Affair resulted from the failure of individuals to observe the law, not from the deficiencies in existing law or in our system of governance."[53] Only four of the twenty-seven recommendations in the report relate to the functioning of the National Security Council, and each is remarkably mild given the enormity of the abuses in which the Reagan NSC officials engaged. Recommendation 11 counsels that the members and the staff of the NSC "not engage in covert actions," although it also points out that there is no express statutory prohibition on the NSC "engaging in operational intelligence activities." Given the zealotry that guided the behavior of Oliver North, one must wonder whether he, or others like him in a similar situation, would appreciate the linguistic differences between "covert actions" and "operational intelligence activities." Recommendation 12 calls for Congress to legislate, requiring the president "to report to Congress periodically on the organization, size, function, and procedures of the NSC staff," a recommendation that Congress has so far ignored. Recommendation 17 urges that presidential findings on covert action should be made known to all statutory members of the NSC, which, in itself, is a damning indictment of the relationship of the NSC to the NSC staff in the Reagan years. Recommendation 23 proposes that, as a matter of policy, the national security adviser should not be an active military officer and that there should be a limit on the time spent by military officers on the NSC staff. In this respect, it is interesting to note that, less than one month after the report was published, an active military officer, Lieutenant General Colin Powell, was sworn in as President Reagan's sixth national security adviser.[54]

The congressional report provides a very detailed narrative of the events of the Iran-*contra* affair and uncovered a vast amount of information that was not known publicly at the time. But because the aim of the committees was to locate blame and place responsibility on an individual basis, their exercise of oversight failed to expose and remedy the underlying institutional and constitutional weaknesses in the foreign policy-making process. As Harold Hongju Koh has argued in his analysis of the Iran-*contra* affair and its aftermath, the committees virtually ignored "the crucial legislative portion of their institutional mandate ... and never fully grasped either the constitutional moment or the legislative opportunity that the Iran-*contra* affair presented to them."[55]

Koh also points to numerous weaknesses in the way the Iran-*contra* committees conducted their business, especially the disjointed questioning of witnesses in public and televised hearings that enhanced the opportunities for individual grandstanding.[56] But his basic indictment of the process rests on the committees' decision to conduct a quasi-judicial prosecution rather than a study of foreign policy decision making.[57] As a consequence, the Iran-*contra* committees never grappled with fundamental questions about the structure of authority in foreign policy decision making and, eight years after the Iran-*contra* revelations, have thus far not modified the institutional base that permitted North and his colleagues to act as they did. In Koh's view, the opportunity offered Congress by Iran-*contra* has been "almost entirely squandered."[58]

Perhaps the most unfortunate measure of this particular exercise of congressional oversight was that the villain, Lieutenant Colonel Oliver North, emerged from the congressional hearings as a hero, at least in the view of some of the media and part of the public at large. Although convicted of three of the twelve counts brought against him, his performance in those hearings led to a lucrative contract for the publication of his memoirs and huge fees for numerous speaking engagements. Moreover, it established North's political credentials within the Republican party, and at this time of writing he is the leading candidate for the Republican nomination to contest the Senate seat in Virginia in 1994. Should he succeed in getting elected, the voters in Virginia will have upstaged those in Florida in 1992 who returned an impeached federal judge as member for the 23d District in the U.S. House of Representatives.

Oversight through the Appropriations Process

The Appropriations Committees of Congress took a long time to come to terms with the post-Brownlow presidential staff system, especially the president's personal staff in the White House Office. It would be no exaggeration to say that during the first fourteen years of the EOP's existence, there was little scrutiny of its budget at all, and until the Watergate years, a great deal of ignorance was shown by members of the Committees on Appropriations about the financing of the presidential staff system. In fact, until the 1950s, the only part of the president's staff budget discussed at Appropriations Subcommittee hearings was the proposed expenditure on the upkeep of the Executive Mansion and grounds. The White House chief usher regularly testified before the House Appropriations Subcommittee, along with a representative of the National Park Service, which had responsibility for the maintenance of the White House grounds. Discussion at those hearings was usually confined to matters within the jurisdiction of the officials present, and when it went beyond those bounds, neither the chief usher nor the National Park Service were of much help to the subcommittee.

Occasionally, it became evident that some members of the Appropriations Committees did not quite appreciate the place of the chief usher in the presidential staff system or, indeed, the position of the National Park Service outside it. During hearings in 1947, the then chairman of the House Appropriations Subcommittee on Independent Offices, Richard Wigglesworth, asked the associate director of the National Park Service if he could explain a very large increase in the White House Office budget request for 1948, which, of course, he could not answer.[59] The question not only indicated a serious lack of understanding on the part of the chairman about the organization of a unit of government for which his subcommittee had direct responsibility, but it also marked the limits to which the Appropriations Committees would go in questioning the annual budget for the presidential staff.

During the 1950s and 1960s, the director of the Bureau of the Budget was dispatched to testify on the presidential staff budget, but the presence of someone more senior than the chief usher or the representative from the National Park Service seems to have made little difference to the substance of the Appropriations Subcommittee hearings. Comity prevailed, and the unwritten rule that Congress should not interfere with presidential housekeeping matters was upheld without any difficulty. When the Appropriations Subcommittee on General Government Matters convened in 1959 to hear testimony on the president's compensation, the White House Office budget, and the Special Projects Fund, Chairman George Andrews opened the session with the words, "There are three items, gentlemen that require very little discussion."[60] In 1953 Bureau of the Budget Director Joseph Dodge began his testimony on the White House Office budget request by reminding the subcommittee members that "there has been, I believe, a tradition that the Bureau of the Budget and the president do not change the legislative requests and the legislative branch does not change the White House request."[61] On some occasions, the House Appropriations Subcommittee hearings contain no evidence of any discussion whatsoever on the White House staff budget request, and the requested amounts appear in tabular form only in the record.[62]

The tradition of comity was so effective in preventing any serious congressional examination of the presidential staff budget for so many years that perhaps it is not surprising that the Appropriations Committees in both the House and the Senate were so casual and ill-informed about the amount of money they regularly appropriated for the staffing of the presidential branch. Nothing better illustrates this than the history of the Special Projects Fund.

The Special Projects Fund was requested by President Eisenhower in 1955, at the behest of the Bureau of the Budget, and was first effected through a supplemental appropriation in fiscal year 1956. The original purpose of the Special Projects Fund was explained to the Appropriations Subcommittees by the then director of the Bureau of the Budget, Rowland Hughes. In his testimony in the Senate he said:

> The president has occasion, as you know, to do special jobs in connection with the coordination and planning of the Executive work which does not apply to any one particular department. In that connection, he has appointed some special assistants, and instead of carrying those special assistants in the regular budget of the White House, it seemed advisable to set up a separate item which would be better from two viewpoints.
>
> The cost of these activities is difficult to forecast, although they are not of an emergency nature. At the same time, they are not susceptible to assignment to the regular agencies of the Government because they cut across the functions of the established departments.
>
> Secondly, I believe that a separate new appropriation is the best method of financing such activities. It gives an opportunity to consolidate these special projects in one place so that budgetary control can be maintained and the Congress will have an opportunity to gain an easier understanding of the purposes for which the funds are used.[63]

Without much difficulty, the Eisenhower administration managed to extract from the Appropriations Committees a discretionary Special Projects Fund of $1.25 million for fiscal year 1956, a sum that amounted to two-thirds of the regular White House Office staff budget at the time. Not a great deal of attention was given to the Special Projects supplemental in 1955, and even less attention thereafter, when it came to be seen as a regular appropriation in addition to the White House Office budget and various other discretionary funds (principally the Emergency Fund and the Management Improvement Fund) used to pay for presidential staff support.[64]

The original pretext for a separate Special Projects appropriation—to finance a different kind of staff work from that of the White House Office—was quickly forgotten and discarded, even by administration spokesmen. In 1960, for example, the following exchange over the Special Projects Fund between Elmer Staats of the Bureau of the Budget and Appropriations Subcommittee Chairman George Andrews took place in the House:

Mr. Staats: Really it is an extension of the White House staff set up to coordinate various specific fields. Under a different president these fields might be different but President Eisenhower has felt that these four areas I have mentioned here were the ones he wanted a special staff in.

Mr. Andrews: Well, as a matter of fact, then, this is just an addition to the White House staff?

Mr. Staats: I think that would be a correct statement.[65]

In 1965 Staats told the same subcommittee that "it is important to look at the White House Office and the Special Projects requirements together, because they are used, to some degree, for the same general purposes."[66] In 1969 the Nixon administration had requested and received $2.5 million for the Special Projects Fund. In 1970 James Schlesinger told the Senate Appropriations Subcommittee that the Special Projects Fund had "also been used on occasion to augment the White House staff complement in new areas of activity,"[67] and the following year Caspar Weinberger announced to the House subcommittee that up to 20 percent of the Special Projects Fund could be made available to reimburse the White House Office, admitting that this was one method of reducing the "official" White House Office payroll.[68]

Administration testimony on the Special Projects Fund during the late 1950s and 1960s was remarkably repetitive. Year after year, the same basic information was provided to the Appropriations Subcommittees in response to the same, very basic, questions from committee members, and little of that information penetrated the institutional memory of the subcommittees. Almost a decade after the Special Projects Fund had been established, the chairman of the House Appropriations Subcommittee, J. Vaughan Gary, was asking Elmer Staats to explain the difference between the Special Projects Fund and the appropriations for the upkeep of the Executive Mansion,[69] a question that demonstrates a remarkable lack of basic knowledge on the part of the subcommittee's chairman.

Not until 1973 did the Appropriations Committees begin to question the Special Projects Fund with any serious intent, and that, of course, was prompted by the events of Watergate. As a result, a great deal of information was squeezed out of a weakened administration at a time when the long-standing tradition of comity had broken down temporarily. Legislators finally came to realize that, in the words of Senator Joseph Montoya, "the Special Projects account was just a facade for adding more people to the White House payroll."[70] They also realized that the abuse of the Special Projects Fund was a result of their own neglect. "It was a matter of comity, the Congress wasn't supposed to be interested in how the fund was spent," said Howard Robison, the ranking Republican on the House Appropriations Subcommittee.[71]

Not surprisingly, given the climate of the times, the Special Projects Fund was abandoned for fiscal year 1974 and thereafter, but it was abandoned in name only. The traditional desire on the part of the Appropriations Committees to give the president what he wanted for staffing quickly reasserted itself, and the amount of money lost by the termination of the Special Projects Fund was restored in a supplemental appropriation to the regular White House Office budget late in 1973.[72] Congress had merely eliminated the discretionary nature of the fund, not the funding itself.

The attitude of the Appropriations Committees toward the Special Projects Fund was illustrative of the approach to oversight of the presidential staff budget as a whole. Comity ruled, and even an event as traumatic as Watergate breached that tradition only in a very minor way. The Watergate years resulted in more intensive scrutiny by the Appropriations Subcommittees and the eventual termination of the discretionary nature of some parts of the presidential staff budget,[73] but very little else changed. The tradition of comity reasserted itself surprisingly quickly with respect to the fiscal oversight of the presidential staff.

Consider, for example, the attempt of Representative Clarence Miller of Ohio to reduce the fiscal year 1980 appropriation for the White House Office. Miller was the ranking Republican on the House Appropriations Subcommittee with jurisdiction over the White House staff budget. The House Appropriations Committee had granted the full budget request for the White House Office of $18,210,000, but, when the bill came to the floor of the House in July 1979, Miller moved to reduce the amount by $710,000. His proposed amendment elicited this response from Representative Tom Steed, the then chairman of the subcommittee:

> Mr. Chairman, I rise in opposition to the amendment. Mr. Chairman, this item has a very unusual and peculiar relationship to the House. This is the item where the President of the United States says, "I need these resources to do my own personal job." This is the president's personal staff. I do not see how anybody on Earth could vote to cut this item without their calling the President of the United States a man they do not believe because they are saying, "I know more about what it takes to be the President of the United States than he does." For the sake of the honor of this House, we ought not to meddle with this particular item.

He concluded by saying, "I cannot recall a time in the history of Congress that this item has ever been changed from what the president said he wanted."[74]

The amendment was easily defeated, and Representative Steed was almost correct in what he said about the refusal of Congress to tamper with White House Office budget requests. For example, in only three of the twelve fiscal years from 1971 to 1982 did the House of Representatives alter the original amount requested for the White House staff by the president (see table 5.1). In two cases, the total reductions by the Appropriations Committee amounted to less than 1 percent of the original request and in one case just over 1 percent. In only one instance during this period did the Senate Appropriations Committee, and the Senate as a whole, change the amount approved by the House, disregarding fiscal years 1977 and 1978 when a technicality prevented the White House Office appropriation from passing on the House floor. The refusal of the Appropriations Committees to tamper with the presidential staff budget is not just confined to the president's personal staff in the White House Office. A number of other EOP units have been treated in much the same way. For example, during the same period (fiscal years 1971–82), the original budget requests for the Council of Economic Advisers and for the National Security Council were altered only very marginally in four of the twelve years. In the other eight years, the original amount requested survived the appropriations process in both the House and the Senate without any reduction whatsoever.

The historic tradition of comity between the legislative and presidential branches of government has rendered the appropriations process impotent as a tool of fiscal oversight of the presidential branch. Such is the impact of comity that the House Appropriations Committee behaves quite uncharacteristically when it deals with the presidential branch budget request. It does not follow the strategic premise it applies to the executive branch, that budgets should be reduced. On the contrary, the committee does all it can to ensure that the president gets every cent he asks for. As for the norm of "intensive subcommittee specialization," it is worth noting what Fenno had to say on this point:

> [The] restricted scope of decision making helps members obtain the kind of intimate, detailed knowledge of an agency that facilitates budget cutting. Members believe that in order to uncover unnecessary expenditures, one must "dig, dig, dig, behind closed doors day after day" in "the salt mines of Congress." And they use their knowledge of "the facts" and their style of "hard work" to help sell the House on the necessity for budget reductions.[75]

In fact, very little digging has ever been done by the House subcommittee on Treasury, Postal Service and General Government Appropriations in regard to the presidential staff budget, making this a major exception to the norm. The record shows that the subcommittee has possessed very little specialized knowledge about the structure and funding of the presidential branch. Moreover, successive hearings have revealed some ignorance and a great deal of confusion among members of that subcommittee on a subject of

TABLE 5.1.

CONGRESSIONAL TREATMENT OF WHITE HOUSE OFFICE
APPROPRIATIONS REQUESTS FOR FISCAL YEARS
1971–82 (IN MILLIONS OF DOLLARS)

Fiscal Year	Budget Request	House Committee	House Floor	Senate Committee	Senate Floor	Final Appropriation
1971	8.550	8.550	8.550	8.550	8.550	8.550
1972	9.342	9.342	9.342	9.342	9.342	9.342
1973	9.767	9.767	9.767	9.767	9.767	9.767
1974	9.110	9.110	9.110	9.110	9.110	9.110
1975	16.510	16.367	16.367	16.367	16.367	16.367
1976	16.946	16.763	16.763	16.763	16.763	16.763
1977	16.530	16.530	0[a]	16.530	16.530	16.530
1978	17.580	17.580	0[a]	17.580	17.580	17.580
1979	16.907	16.907	16.907	16.907	16.711	16.711
1980	18.210	18.210	18.210	18.210	18.210	18.210
1981	20.373	20.373	20.373	20.373	[b]	20.373
1982	22.346	22.278	22.278	22.278	[b]	22.278

SOURCE: Data compiled by Louis Fisher of the Congressional Research Service from committee reports and appropriation bills. This table does not reflect adjustments by subsequent supplemental appropriations.

a. The total appropriation was stricken on the House floor on a point of order because no authorizing language had been enacted.

b. Bill not acted on by full Senate. Final appropriation provided by continuing resolution.

which they ought to be masters. The Senate Appropriations Committee has shown even less interest in the presidential staff and generally takes its cue from its counterpart in the House.

The practice of comity has been strongly defended in both the House and Senate and by Republicans and Democrats,[76] but it also has its critics. As Senator Walter Mondale once pointed out:

Comity between the branches of government, we were told, required that we not look at the authority for the White House staff positions or the budgets for those positions. Yet for too long, "comity" meant that the White House has been given whatever it wanted. And unless Congress uses its power to authorize programs and appropriate money, comity becomes "comedy"—a cruel joke slowly sapping the vitality of any possible system restraints on unaccountable presidential power.[77]

Mondale's message has, for the most part, fallen on deaf ears, and members of Congress who, like him, question the norm of comity, have found themselves in a minority on Capitol Hill. Even the events of Watergate failed to induce any substantial shift toward support for more intensive oversight of the presidential staff budget, and as those events have receded in the memories of legislators, the tradition of comity has reasserted itself and the appropriations process has returned to something like its pre-Watergate state.

It would, however, be inaccurate to say that Watergate has had no longer-term impact on the fiscal oversight of the presidential branch. Both the House and Senate Subcommittees on Treasury, Postal Service and General Government Appropriations are now much better informed about the Executive Office of the President than they were in the past, and they no longer demonstrate the confusion and ignorance that often characterized their hearings in the 1950s and 1960s. Questions about the activities and organization of the presidential staff are now asked at subcommittee hearings, even in regard to the White House Office appropriations, and no longer do major items get through the subcommittees without comment, as happened in the 1950s. In fact, some of the questioning in recent years has been unusually intensive, much of it prompted by controversies generated by the White House staff itself. For example, both subcommittees now routinely extract information about the number of detailees in the EOP as more evidence has come to light about White House detailing practices, particularly around election time. The abuse of White House perquisites, especially free travel, has also shaped the agenda of the subcommittees in the past few years and detailed questions have been put to White House representatives on the use of chauffeur-driven cars, government aircraft, White House dining facilities, fitness centers, and medical services. Most recently, President Clinton's pledge to reduce the presidential staff by 25 percent elicited some critical and heated questioning, which, at the least, added to the general skepticism in Congress and the media about the real extent of the proposed reductions, especially after the White House had requested a supplemental appropriation to fund an increase in staff for President Clinton's first year in office.[78]

Even the most casual observer would have to admit that there now exists a greater degree of fiscal oversight of the presidential staff than in the pre-Watergate period. But it is only relative, and it is accountability only in the sense of answerability. No significant changes in presidential staffing have resulted from the more intensive scrutiny of the presidential staff budget by the Appropriations Committees, nor has the House Appropriations Committee shown any greater desire to trim the EOP budget request than it showed before Watergate. That is precluded by comity, and the tradition of comity is still defended as strongly as it ever was.

Take, for example, a challenge on the House floor to the EOP appropriations bill in 1993. John Boehner, a second-term Republican Congressman representing the Eighth District of Ohio, moved an amendment to the Treasury, Postal Service and General Government Appropriations Bill to cut the sum of $1.2 million from various funds appropriated for the vice president. Boehner was objecting to the expenditure of a similar sum of money on renovations to the vice president's official residence, funded from the budget of the Navy rather than the vice president's office. The Congressman believed that the vice president was using taxpayer funds that were never meant to be used for such purposes and that his amendment was a way of reclaiming that money for the taxpayer.[79] It was also a way of scoring a partisan political point, but Steny Hoyer, the Democratic chairman of the Subcommittee on Treasury, Postal Service, and General Government Appropriations chose to respond to Boehner's maneuver first by reminding his colleagues about the principle of comity and then responding to the partisan nature of Boehner's amendment. "There is an important principle involved here," Hoyer told the House. "That is a principle of comity between two coequal branches.... We ought not to start playing politics simply because the administrations have changed.... I am going to show how consistently Democrats on this side of the aisle supported Presidents Reagan and Bush in their request, unchanged, untouched, unaltered. Let us not depart from that excellent and sound principle of comity between the executive and legislative branches now for purely partisan reasons."[80] Boehner's amendment was defeated quite easily.

Oversight through Legislation

One telling comment on the casual manner in which Congress had handled appropriations for the presidential staff was the revelation in 1973 that there was no legislative authorization for most of the personnel employed in the White House Office. In fact, since 1948, Congress had routinely appropriated funds for additional White House Office staff without altering Sections 105 and 106 of Title 3 of the *United States Code,* which permitted the president to appoint only six administrative assistants and eight other secretaries to the White House Office. By 1973, those 14 authorized White House aides had been supplemented by some 500 additional personnel whose unauthorized salaries were being paid regularly from the public purse, notwithstanding Rule XXI.2 of the rules of the House of Representatives, which specifically states that no appropriation shall be reported in any general appropriation bill for any expenditure not previously authorized by law.

The practice of approving unauthorized appropriations for the presidential staff was first challenged by Representative John Dingell (D-Mich.) when a supplemental White House Office appropriation came before the Committee of the Whole House in August 1973. In accordance with Rule XXI, Dingell raised a point of order objecting to the language containing the unauthorized appropriation, which the chair was obliged to sustain. Consequently, most of the White House Office supplemental appropriation for fiscal year 1974 was removed from the bill when it was formally reported to the House. Even then, comity prevailed, and the appropriation was eventually restored by a House-Senate conference committee at the insistence of the Senate. Dingell's protest was not without effect, however, for it marked the beginning of a five-year effort to provide proper legislative authority for the White House staff culminating in the passage of the White House Personnel Authorization-Employment Act of 1978. That legislation is also significant because it stands as the only serious attempt by Congress to oversee the activities of the presidential branch in the aftermath of Watergate.

As a result of the embarrassment to the House Appropriations Committee caused by the Dingell point of order, the committee requested that the Nixon administration submit draft legislation to restore proper authorization for the number of staff in the White House Office. The bill (H.R. 14715) was prepared by the Office of Management and Budget and introduced in April 1974 by Representative Thaddeus Dulski (D-N.Y.), then chairman of the House Post Office and Civil Service Committee, the committee to which the legislation was referred.[81] Needless to say, the draft bill reflected the interests of the Nixon administration rather more than the concerns of the Post Office and Civil Service Committee. For example, it proposed that Congress authorize thirty-five White House Office positions at Executive Level II, despite the fact that this would have allowed the president to increase the number of senior staff by two and a half times the existing level and that the Post Office and Civil Service Committee, in its report on presidential staffing published two years earlier, had been extremely critical of the increasing number of highly paid staff in the Executive Office of the President.[82] The Nixon administration bill also proposed that an unlimited number of staff on the General Schedule salary scale be authorized for the White House Office. This, of course, included what were then the supergrade GS16–GS18 positions. After changes had been made in committee, the bill passed the House and a similar version passed the Senate in 1974, but the House failed to approve the conference version because of an outstanding problem over a minor provision in the bill. Similar legislation (H.R. 6706) was introduced in 1975 with some sense of urgency as the White House Office appropriation was again subjected to points of order in the House, but the legislation died in the Senate.

A third attempt, or rather a series of attempts, to provide the necessary authorization was launched during the 95th Congress in 1977 and 1978, when H.R. 11003 eventually cleared the House and the Senate and was signed by President Carter on 2 November 1978. This final effort represented a more aggressive approach on the part of members of the House Post Office and Civil Service Committee, particularly Representatives Herbert Harris (D-Va.), Patricia Schroeder (D-Colo.), and Morris Udall (D-Ariz.) who cosponsored the legislation. As well as terminating the practice of appropriating unauthorized funds, the legislation was also designed to curb the growth of the presidential staff and make it more accountable to Congress. The initial Harris-Schroeder-Udall bill in the 95th Congress (H.R. 6326) contained a number of controversial measures, including a ceiling on the total number of White House Office staff at 401, and a limit on the number of senior aides employed on the Executive Level scale (not more than 44) and at the then GS16–GS18 grades (not more than 21). The legislation also proposed that the president be required to submit an annual report to Congress containing very specific information about the White House Office staff. This was to include the names of all employees, their salaries, titles, job descriptions, and the amount of reimbursement made by the White House Office to departments and agencies from whom staff had been detailed.

Those proposals represented a major challenge to the tradition of comity, a challenge that was all the more surprising because it came from Democrats in Congress at the same time that a Democrat had arrived in the White House. The proposals were not welcomed by the Carter administration. At first, it managed to stall the legislation in 1977 by persuading the Post Office and Civil Service Committee to await the completion of a Carter-initiated study of the organization of the EOP and, later, by urging a delay until the House had considered the president's ensuing Reorganization Plan No. 1.[83] Thereafter, the main concern of the administration was to get the overall limit on White House Office personnel removed from the bill and to modify the reporting requirement.

The Carter administration's argument against the major provisions of the Harris-Schroeder-Udall bill was summed up conveniently by James McIntyre, then deputy director of OMB, at the first of four House hearings on the legislation:

> We urge that the committee give due recognition to the fact that—the staff is the personal staff of the president—that the practice of comity and requirements of the Office necessitate that the president have maximum flexibility in staffing his office.[84]

But traditional appeals to comity and flexibility held little attraction for the bill's floor manager, Herbert Harris. He responded at the same hearing:

> Let me plead that this subcommittee is not in the business of making sure that what's been going on in the past is what's continuing. We want to see a revolution of new ideas and new approaches here, some new concepts, as far as the way things are run. You know, I really hope that we will look at these issues not as the way they have been done in the past, but as the way they should be done in the future.[85]

And, later, on the floor of the House, Harris said:

> The fundamental point here is to make sure power is in the hands of accountable people: the Cabinet. Executive advisers and special assistants to the president have their proper advisory role. But our form of government does not vest in them unlimited powers. They are unelected and sometimes inaccessible. Quite simply, our Government should not be run by, and our president should not depend on, a "palace guard." Centralized power in the hands of a few anonymous individuals is contrary to a democracy. This bill is a very fundamental policy measure reaching to the heart of our Government.[86]

The administration's delaying tactics allowed it time to temper the enthusiasm of Herbert Harris. A new bill (H.R. 10657) was introduced in the House of Representatives in January 1978. The Post Office and Civil Service Committee reported a clean bill in March (H.R. 11003), and the legislation eventually cleared the House on 13 April, after being defeated on a procedural matter the previous week. Gone from the 1977 version was the limit on the total size of the White House Office. The new legislation limited only the number of executive-level and supergrade-level staff. The bill also provided authorization for, and limited the number of senior appointments on, the staff of the Executive Residence, the vice president's staff, the Domestic Policy Staff, and the newly created Office of Administration. It also required that the president report to Congress on the number of detailees employed in each of the units covered by the bill.[87] The reporting requirement was subsequently extended to cover all full-time employees in those units. The amended House bill passed the Senate on 14 July and both chambers agreed to the conference version in early October.

According to Herbert Harris, Vice President Walter Mondale was instrumental in persuading sponsors of the bill to remove the overall limit on the White House staff. The administration's view was that Congress was making Carter pay for Nixon's mistakes.[88] The vice president was less successful in getting the House to modify the reporting provision that required the president to provide the name, title, general job description, and salary of every employee in the White House. The Senate, however, was persuaded and insisted on its version of the reporting requirement in the conference committee, where House managers conceded.[89] There was less pressure for such legislation in the Senate, and the Senate Post Office and Civil Service Subcommittee was more amenable to the concerns of the White House than its counterpart in the House, according to the subcommittee's staff director at the time.[90] It is also interesting to note that although Herbert Harris managed the bill on the House side and was an ardent advocate for the reporting requirement, he was not chosen to be one of the House members on the conference committee where the administration won its victory. "The leadership felt more comfortable without me," said Harris.[91]

The passage of the White House Personnel Authorization-Employment Act of 1978 marked the first time in thirty years that Congress had formally authorized an increase in the president's personal staff. It was also the first time since the EOP was established that Congress had attempted to make the president accountable for the number of staff he employed and to limit his ability to expand his staff at will.

The White House Personnel Authorization-Employment Act (Public Law 95-570) authorizes the president to appoint to the White House Office not more than twenty-five employees at Executive Level II, not more than twenty-five at Executive Level III, and not more than fifty at the GS18 level. Below GS16, the president has authorization to appoint as many employees as he determines, and there is no upper limit on the total size of the White House Office staff. The act also limits the number of senior appointments in the Executive Residence, the Office of the Vice President, the Domestic Policy Staff, and the Office of Administration. It grants authorization for the president to appoint as many temporary consultants and experts in the White House, as provided for in appropriations legislation, and it insists on public accountability for personnel borrowed or detailed by the White House from departments and agencies, and for the reimbursement of the detailing department after 180 calendar days in any fiscal year.

Section 113 of the act requires the president to submit a personnel report to Congress for each fiscal year. The report must show the number of staff employed in the White House Office, the Executive Residence of the White House, the Office of the Vice President, the Domestic Policy Staff, and the Office of Administration, broken down into three different salary categories (Executive Level V and above, GS16–GS18, and those below GS16). It also requires the president to report the number of individuals detailed to those offices for more than thirty days, show the number of days in excess of thirty for which each individual was detailed, and list the number of consultants employed in those offices, together with the total number of days they were employed.

Herbert Harris and his colleagues had hoped that the White House Personnel Authorization-Employment Act would strengthen congressional oversight of the presidential branch and correct some of the worst abuses of presidential staffing, but its impact has been slight since its passage, and it has now sunk into oblivion and obscurity as far as all but a handful of legislators are concerned.

The legislation did remedy one problem satisfactorily. It established the necessary authorization for existing presidential staff and thus ended the objections to White House Office appropriations under Rule XXI. John Dingell's efforts in 1973 to stop passage of a supplemental appropriation bill were emulated on several later occasions by Herbert Harris, who succeeded in defeating the regular White House Office appropriation for fiscal years 1977 and 1978 by invoking points of order against the use of authorization language in an appropriation bill. In both instances the Senate restored the funds after the House protest. These challenges to the legality of the White House Office appropriations did not bother the White House unduly. The tradition of comity was too entrenched for the White House Office to be denied its annual appropriation and, in any case, the Senate Appropriations Committee could always be relied upon "to act as a lenient appeals court," as Fenno has put it.[92] What the legislation did do was end an embarrassing intra-House of Representatives dispute between an authorizing committee and an appropriating committee, the result of which was that a low-prestige authorizing committee had reminded the powerful Appropriations Committee that it still existed and was not prepared to tolerate challenges to its authority with respect to the size of the presidential branch.

The act did not succeed in limiting the total size of the White House Office staff, despite widespread concern in the aftermath of Watergate about the swelling of the presidency. The ceiling of 401 personnel, written into the 1977 legislation, was dropped from the 1978 version after objections from the White House, and it was a provision that very few legislators were moved to protect. In any event, concern on Capitol Hill had been focused rather more intently on the increase in the number of highly paid aides in the White House Office than on the overall size of the presidential staff. In this respect, neither could it be said that the White House Personnel Authorization-Employment Act did much to curb the expansion in the number of senior White House aides because the new ceilings on Executive Level and supergrade positions (fifty of each) were considerably in excess of the numbers actually employed under those categories at the time. At the beginning of 1978, President Carter had fifty-two staff at these levels in the White House Office,[93] thus the legislation gave him an opportunity to double the number of his top aides as long as he could extract the additional appropriations to fund these positions. There does appear to have been a small increase in the number of senior White House Office staff immediately after the legislation was signed, although it is difficult to ascertain the precise figure because of the way in which staff numbers were reported to Congress by the Carter administration.[94] Table 5.2 shows the number of senior staff employed in the White House Office since the legislation came into force. The totals fluctuate from year to year, and if one takes the reported figures for 30 September, there have been some years when the number of senior staffers in the White House Office actually fell below the Carter 1978 level. On the other hand, there was a steady upward creep in the number of senior aides during the Bush years, especially the number appointed to Executive Level positions. What the figures also show is that no president has yet exploited the full scope of the staff authorization in the 1978 legislation, which permits up to 100 appointees at the executive and supergrade levels.[95]

TABLE 5.2.
EXECUTIVE-LEVEL AND SUPERGRADE STAFF IN THE
WHITE HOUSE OFFICE, 1979–93[a]

Fiscal Year	Executive Level	Supergrade	Total
1979	44	32	76
1980	48	30	78
1981	47	40	71
1982	41	1	42
1983	41	17	58
1984	39	22	61
1985	31	21	52
1986	27	16	43
1987	37	14	51
1988	42	15	57
1989	17	21	38
1990	21	21	42
1991	22	32	54
1992	36	31	67
1993	45	50	95

SOURCE: The White House Office, "Aggregate Reports on Personnel Pursuant to Title 3, U.S Code, Section 113," 1979—93.

a. Figures for 1979 and 1980 represent the cumulative total of all individuals who occupied poisitons in this category regardless of length of service during the fiscal year. Figures for 1981 onward show the number of staff employed in each category on 30 September in that fiscal year. The 30 September figure was not given in the reports for 1979 and 1980.

The act also tried to tackle the problem of detailing staff from the departments and agencies to work in the White House. It succeeded in introducing an element of accountability into this time-honored and hitherto informal practice, but it did not force presidents to curb the use of detailees, as some post-Watergate critics would have wished. Detailing of staff had long been regarded with suspicion because it enabled presidents to augment their White House staffs without admitting to the extra numbers and without paying for the services of the individuals concerned, who remained on the payrolls of the detailing departments or agencies.

The White House Personnel Authorization-Employment Act required that the detailing agency be reimbursed for staff borrowed by the White House for more than 180 days in any fiscal year and that the number of detailees working in excess of 30 days in any fiscal year be reported to Congress. To some extent, it might be argued that the the legislation could tempt presidents to increase, rather than decrease, the number of "borrowed" staff in the White House. It allows presidents to detail staff for up to 180 days without this being charged to any part of the EOP budget; it allows them to detail staff for up to 30 days without having to account for them; and it imposes no limit on the number of detailees that the president can have at any one time.

Two years after the act came into operation, President Carter showed what scope there still was for the use of detailees in the White House Office. The 1980 personnel report to Congress indicated that 205 detailees had been borrowed that year, a fourfold increase over the previous year's figure (see table 4.3 on page 119). Of those 205, almost a quarter had been used for more than six months. It was no coincidence that 1980 was an election year. A report in the *Washington Post* revealed that many of the detailees had been assigned to the "outreach" or "liaison" units within the White House Office, and that between September 1979 and February 1980, at least nineteen detailees were loaned to the White House without ever having worked in the departments or agencies from whose budgets their salaries were being drawn.[96] In 1990 a General Accounting Office inquiry revealed that the Bush administration had been doing much the same thing. While investigating another matter, the GAO discovered that the Department of Energy had improperly hired three Schedule C employees for detail to the White House, two of whom had never worked in the Department of Energy.[97]

It is difficult to compare the extent of detailing to the White House before and after the passage of the 1978 legislation because the pre-1978 data on detailees is so unreliable and there is no way of discovering how long each detailee served in the White House or the EOP agency to which he or she was assigned. Some recent data from the Congressional Research Service do show a steady increase in the use of detailees by the White House Office during the 1960s and then a dramatic fall after President Nixon's "honest budget" (see page 115) in 1971.[98] The data in the White House personnel reports since 1979 (see table 4.3 on page 119) show quite clearly that the 1978 act did not succeed in curbing the use of detailees. Although the number of detailees has fluctuated from year to year, as have the aggregate number of days worked by those detailees, there has been a noticeable increase during the fourteen years of reporting under the act. As one measure, the mean number of detailees in the White House Office during the Bush presidency was eighty-four, almost twice the level of the first figures reported by the Carter administration, and the utilization of detailees (i.e., total number of days worked per fiscal year) averaged 17,742 under Bush, compared with the 6294 reported by the Carter administration for fiscal year 1979.

The reporting requirement has been the least effective provision of the White House Personnel Authorization-Employment Act. Experience has shown that the information it yields is of little value to legislators charged with oversight of the presidential branch, and congressional attempts to strengthen this section of the legislation have been singularly unsuccessful.

The personnel reports have frustrated members of the House Post Office and Civil Service Committee on a number of fronts.

Legislators cannot derive from the reports the actual number of staff positions in the White House Office, and the other units covered by the act, because the president is required to report only the number of *individuals* employed during a fiscal year. To make sense of this cumulative total, one would need to know how many positions had been held by more than one individual during the period covered by the report, but the reports do not show the level of staff turnover. The Reagan administration began the practice of reporting the actual number of staff employed on the last day of the fiscal year, 30 September, along with the cumulative total for the fiscal year. This is a welcome improvement on the Carter reports, although there can be no certainty that the 30 September figure is a fair reflection of the size of the staff over the whole of the fiscal year.

Another problem is that the reporting format does not require a separate account of the numbers of staff in two of the categories in which a staff ceiling has been imposed. Although Section 105 fixes an upper limit of twenty-five staff at Executive Level II in the White House Office and twenty-five at Executive Level III, Section 113 merely requires a single figure to be reported for all Executive Level staff, so it becomes impossible to tell whether the limits on the number of very senior staff have been exceeded at any time during the fiscal year.

The reports also fail to give an accurate picture of the number of detailees on the president's staff because the legislation requires only the number of individuals detailed for more than thirty days to be given. Those working for less than thirty days go unreported. Furthermore, the accuracy of the reporting of detailees leaves a lot to be desired. A General Accounting Office audit of the level of detailing to the White House, conducted in 1986–87, discovered a significant level of underreporting of the number of detailees employed for more than thirty days during President Reagan's first term. For example, in 1985, the number of detailees in the White House Office for more than thirty days was, according to the GAO, almost two and a half times greater than the figure given to Congress in the personnel report for that year.[99]

The major weakness of the reporting requirement, however, is its scope. Most of the EOP units, including some of the largest, such as the Office of Management and Budget, the Office of the U.S. Trade Representative, and the National Security Council, are not covered by the White House Personnel Authorization-Employment Act, so their staff totals and use of detailees are not reported to Congress. Yet the same concerns (i.e., the number of senior staff and the use of detailees) are just as relevant to those units as they are to units included in the scope of the legislation. For example, when the Senate Appropriations Subcommittee raised questions about the detailing practices of the National Security Council in 1988, it found that there were considerably more detailees on the NSC staff that year than there were full-time staffers whose positions were funded from the regular NSC budget appropriation.[100]

Beyond these very specific defects, which are not significant enough to concern legislators other than those on the oversight committees, there is one major problem with the reporting requirement that does affect the oversight capacity of Congress. Nothing in the personnel reports gives any indication of who does what in the White House. No individuals are named and no functions are described, nor does the act require this information to be provided. At various times after the act came into operation, Representatives Herbert Harris, Patricia Schroeder, and Geraldine Ferraro (D-N.Y.), the successor to Harris as chair of the Post Office and Civil Service Subcommittee on Human Resources, tried to persuade the White House to develop a more acceptable reporting format to include this kind of information, but failed to do so. The Reagan administration was just as reluctant to provide details about the functions of individual White House staff as the Carter administration was determined to have the requirement removed from the final version of the legislation in 1978.

The White House Personnel Authorization-Employment Act has had little impact on the White House or on Congress, largely attributable to the fact that the teeth were removed from the legislation before it reached the president for signature and that the personnel reports submitted to Congress under Section 113 provide little stimulus to more effective oversight of the presidential staff. The authors of the legislation hoped that their efforts would impose an effective form of accountability on the president in regard to issues that had hitherto been hidden from public scrutiny by the cloak of comity, but their hopes have gone unfulfilled.

An attempt was made in 1992 to revise the White House Personnel Authorization-Employment Act, but the major defects of that legislation were not really at the center of the concerns of those who sponsored the effort to write a new law. What bothered some members of Congress on this occasion were the so-called hidden costs of running the White House, a relatively new problem that had come to light largely as a result of the travel abuses perpetrated by John Sununu, President Bush's chief of staff. Sununu's use of government cars and planes prompted the Subcommittee on Human Resources of the House Post Office and Civil Service to hold hearings on who actually paid for many of the services used by the White House. These included the costs of operating Air Force One, Marine Corps One (the president's helicopter), the White House Motor Pool, and the expenses associated with Camp David and the White House Mess. All these facilities are funded from the budgets of other departments and agencies and the Subcommittee on Human Resources estimated only approximately 30 percent of the true cost of running the Executive Office of the President is represented in the official budget for the EOP.[101] To this end, the chairman of the subcommittee,

Paul Kanjorski (D-Pa.), introduced a bill in the House on 10 September 1992 to consolidate these hidden costs into the EOP budget and to make the president publicly accountable for such expenditures, particularly the costs of travel for the president and the presidential staff. The bill did contain some amendments to the 1978 act, the most significant of which was the imposition of limits on the total number of staff that could be employed in those units of the EOP covered by the original legislation. The White House Office, for example, was to have a ceiling of 415 personnel. The bill also proposed to change the arrangements regarding reimbursement for detailees, so that the White House would have to cover the cost of detailees after 30 days instead of 180 days as provided for in the original authorization. But Kanjorski's bill did nothing to improve the reporting requirement, nor did it attempt to bring any additional EOP units within the scope of the legislation. The bill was reported out of the subcommittee in mid-September and passed the full committee the following week, but never reached the floor of the House before the end of the 1992 session, and thus the 1978 act remains unchanged. Representative Kanjorski indicated that he would try again the following year,[102] but that was said before it was known that a Democrat would be occupying the White House in 1993.

The White House Personnel Authorization-Employment Act of 1978 has turned out to be little more than a congressional housekeeping measure that temporarily restored the importance of a low-prestige authorizing committee. It has had negligible effect on the organization, management, and accountability of the presidential staff. The subject of presidential staffing no longer commands the attention or interest of legislators it did in the wake of Watergate, and the chances of the 1978 act being amended and strengthened are now very remote, and almost nil after the failure of the Kanjorski effort in 1992. Furthermore, some of the most vocal and determined supporters of more effective oversight of the presidential staff in the post-Watergate era have since left the arena. Herbert Harris, the most ardent enthusiast in the House, lost his seat in the 1980 election and failed to win it back in 1982. Geraldine Ferraro gave up her membership of the House Post Office and Civil Service Committee and her subcommittee chair when she gained a more prestigious assignment on the House Budget Committee in the 98th Congress, and eventually vacated her seat in the House in order to be Walter Mondale's running mate in the 1984 presidential election. Morris Udall retired from the House in May 1991 because of ill health. Patricia Schroeder is currently the ranking Democrat on the Post Office and Civil Service Committee, but also has considerable seniority on the Armed Services and Judiciary Committees, and that has meant less time for overseeing the presidential staff. Paul Kanjorski remains on the House Post Office and Civil Service Committee, but the Subcommittee on Human Resources, which he chaired in 1992 and used as his vehicle for pushing his legislation to reauthorize the White House staff, was abolished at the beginning of the 103d Congress in

1993. Without the impetus of another crisis like Watergate, there is little incentive for other legislators to pick up where these particular Post Office and Civil Service Committee members left off, and as Watergate recedes into history, concern in Congress about the weakness of Public Law 95-570 will itself fade away.

Informal Oversight: An Example

Whenever members of Congress choose to publicize their concerns about the activities of the presidential staff, oversight of a kind is being performed. Critical remarks from legislators usually have at least the minimal effect of focusing attention on the operations of the White House, if only fleetingly, and occasionally the consequences can be more far-reaching. There are plenty of opportunities for Senators and Representatives to make individual protests, and they do not necessarily require the forum of an oversight committee, an appropriations committee, or any other committee.

Informal oversight is used here to mean any congressional scrutiny of the presidential branch that occurs beyond the established framework of committees with jurisdiction in that area. It can have many guises, and by its very nature there is very little pattern or regularity to it. That makes it almost impossible to generalize about the consequences and effectiveness of informal oversight, so, rather than attempt to account for every instance of informal oversight of the presidential branch, it would be more useful and economical to focus on one example and draw lessons from that.

The activities of the White House Office of Congressional Relations provide a useful case study of informal oversight of the presidential branch. This is an area of presidential staff work that most members of Congress have encountered directly, it is an activity that has been the subject of complaints by legislators during several different administrations, and it is an area where significant constraints have limited the ability of Congress to take any substantial remedial action to curb the president's staff.

Although members of Congress derive important benefits from the services provided by the White House Office of Congressional Relations,[103] there has clearly been a less than wholehearted acceptance of presidential staff lobbying of Congress, and complaints about unacceptable lobbying have been leveled against most recent administrations. There have been several vehicles for such complaints. Journalists, for example, can quickly put a legislator's expressions of dissatisfaction into print. One committee chairman in the 87th Congress told *U.S. News and World Report:*

> People up here are coming to resent the horde of lobbyists the White House sends to the Capitol. A member of Congress thinks he has a responsibility to his district or state to decide for himself. But now he encounters the president's people everywhere, pursuing him, demanding, some threatening

—and all trying to tell him what he must do. Members talk about it much more and the resentment against such tactics is spreading.[104]

Similar complaints appeared in an article by Meg Greenfield in *The Reporter* a few months later:

The most widely shared and loudly voiced grievance that Congress has against administration practices concerns the unremitting attention it receives from those it describes simply and without affection as "the young men." ... Legislators who still cherish the notion that they themselves will decide how to vote appear to have been at various times amused, confused, and infuriated by the discombobulation of incoming messages they have received, not only (or even) from the appropriate White House office of Lawrence O'Brien but from other department and agency aides as well.[105]

Complaints about White House lobbying sometimes reach the floor of the House and Senate. In 1962, for example, Representatives Gerald Ford (R-Mich.), and John Byrnes (R-Wisc.) and Senator Kenneth Keating (R-N.Y.) all spoke out about the Kennedy administration's lobbying pressure on the debt-limit extension legislation.[106] They particularly resented the linkage between their votes and the continuation of defense contracts in their districts, and Keating later remarked that he hoped there would not be a repetition of this kind of lobbying when the debt-limit bill reached the Senate.[107] After a similar episode, when Gerald Ford himself was in the White House, there were vociferous complaints by three Republican members of the House and one Democrat about the behavior of White House lobbyists.[108] One of the complainants, Representative Larry Pressler (R-S.D.) publicized the threats of "political trouble" made by presidential aide Vernon C. Loen in the *Congressional Record*. He also wrote to President Ford saying that he did not respond to "this negative threatening type of lobbying" and announced his intention to introduce legislation to regulate administration lobbying.[109] Loen resigned his White House post the following month.

Legislators frequently hang their complaints about White House lobbying on an obscure piece of legislation, passed in 1919 and amended in 1948, known as the Lobbying with Appropriated Money Act (18 U.S.C. 1913). It prohibits the use of public funds "to pay for any personal service, advertisement, telegram, letter, printed or written matter, or any other device, intended or designed to influence in any manner a Member of Congress, to favor or oppose, by vote or otherwise, any legislation or appropriation by Congress." The maximum penalty for violation of the antilobbying law is a fine of $500 and a year's imprisonment. In addition to this blanket law, legislators have frequently attached antilobbying clauses to appropriation bills.[110] In 1973, Senators Edmund Muskie (D-Me.) and Hubert Humphrey

(D-Minn.) invoked the antilobbying laws to object to a public relations kit issued by the Nixon White House for use in a campaign against the "spend-thrift Democratic-controlled Congress" and asked the General Accounting Office to investigate the legality of the White House action. The GAO concluded that on this occasion the Nixon administration had violated an anti-lobbying provision in the Treasury, Post Office and General Government Appropriations Act of 1973, but insisted that the Department of Justice would have to determine whether 18 U.S.C. 1913 had been violated because of the possibility of fines and imprisonment.[111] The Justice Department is pivotal in this area of congressional oversight. The GAO can only investigate whether appropriated monies were used in the course of the action that legislators complain about. For Congress to go any further would require the Department of Justice to institute criminal proceedings against the administration of which it is a part. Needless to say, the Justice Department has been reluctant to do so.

When confronted with possible violations of 18 U.S.C. 1913, the Justice Department has tended toward a very liberal interpretation of the law, and it usually finds that no breach of the statute has occurred. For example, in 1962, Representative Glenard Lipscomb (R-Calif.) complained about an unsolicited letter he had received from Sargent Shriver requesting congressional support for further legislation relating to the Peace Corps. The fact that the communication was unsolicited is important because the antilobbying law allows the administration to communicate with legislators on issues before Congress if requested to do so. Lipscomb had first ascertained from the General Accounting Office that appropriated funds had been used by Shriver in the preparation and mailing of the letter and similar letters to other members of Congress. He then requested that the Department of Justice determine whether the law had been violated in the light of the GAO findings. The reply he received from Assistant Attorney General Herbert J. Miller explained why the department found that no breach of the statute had occurred. Miller's opinion rendered the Lobbying with Appropriated Money Act almost meaningless:

> Personal contact with Members of Congress by executive officers are [sic] both sanctioned and required by article II, section 3 of the Constitution, which provides in significant part that the president "shall from time to time ... recommend to their consideration such measures as he shall judge necessary and expedient." The power to recommend measures to Congress would appear clearly to comprehend and include the power to urge arguments upon individual Members of Congress in support of such measures. Necessarily the president must entrust part of this function to subordinate officers within the executive branch. Our Federal Government could not function efficiently if the president and his subordinates could not do so....

> In view of the foregoing, the Department is of the opinion that 18 U.S.C. 1913 cannot be construed to preclude the head of an executive agency from using its facilities to address an unsolicited letter to Members of Congress with respect to pending legislation.[112]

Informal oversight of the kind just described relies essentially on the power of publicity and the degree of embarrassment it can bring to an administration, rather than on any legal constraints imposed on the presidential staff. White House lobbying generally attracts more criticism than any other routine staff activity, yet there has been no serious attempt by Congress, even in the post-Watergate period, to put some teeth into a statute rendered almost totally meaningless by the Department of Justice. It might be suggested that the lack of willingness on Capitol Hill to tighten up a very weak law is, in part, because few lawmakers would want to bite the hand that feeds them and permanently deprive themselves of the benefits that the White House Office of Congressional Relations can provide. Those benefits can be significant, and this aspect of comity is discussed further in the next section. In any case, presidents sometimes respond to adverse criticism of the activities of their staff, and perhaps that is the most that members of Congress can hope for. The departure of Vernon Loen from the Ford White House after Representative Pressler's attack on him was more than coincidence, even though Loen denied that his leaving had anything to do with the incident.[113] The Kennedy administration also responded to the mounting criticism in 1962 of its lobbying techniques when the Special Counsel sent a memorandum to all department and agency heads drawing attention to the requirements of 18 U.S.C. 1913.[114]

THE PERVASIVENESS OF COMITY

Ever since the Executive Office of the President was established in 1939, Congress has shown a marked reluctance to enforce, let alone strengthen, its oversight of the presidential branch. Even the events of Watergate, which helped crystallize a great deal of criticism of the White House staff, did little to increase enthusiasm for improving congressional oversight in this area. Those efforts that were made came from a handful of legislators who were never able to convince the majority of their colleagues on Capitol Hill to share their concerns with the same intensity, and today the presidential branch remains relatively immune from congressional scrutiny of any kind.

That immunity is not necessarily because established techniques of oversight are ineffective, but rather because the presidential branch is treated, and has always been treated, as a special case. The post-Watergate response by Congress to the institutional problems of the presidential branch showed clearly enough that the underlying beliefs and values encapsulated in the notion of comity are a powerful obstacle to those who seek to apply to the president's staff the same standards of accountability to which departments and agencies are subjected. One therefore needs to ask why the belief in comity is so pervasive within Congress and why Congress was so reluctant to tackle the problems of presidential staffing when, at the same time, it could barely be restrained in its attack on presidential powers and prerogatives.

The notion of comity is a fairly simple one to grasp, but beyond dictionary definitions, there is something elusive about it. Members of Congress rarely discuss comity. It is quietly accepted by most of them and mentioned only when the "informal understanding" is being challenged, as it was during the 1970s. Neither have political scientists concerned themselves with the practice of comity, and there are no empirical studies one can draw on to help discover what sustains this arrangement between Congress and president and why it is so widely supported by legislators. So the following explanation is somewhat speculative and certainly lacks a basis in any quantifiable survey-research data. But no account of congressional oversight of the presidential branch would be complete without an attempt to come to terms with the pervasiveness of comity in the contemporary Congress.

Tradition is one important reason. The origins of comity go back to the debates in the very first Congress when James Madison and his colleagues discussed the question of presidential compensation (see pages 13–15) and, in doing so, showed due regard for the proprieties of the separation of powers. They refused to direct how the president should spend his expenses, in the belief that Congress had no right to do so. They even refused to distinguish between the president's salary and his expense allowance, and voted him one lump-sum compensation to be used as he saw fit. Today the belief that the president alone should determine what he needs to do his job is a widely shared one, and contemporary members of Congress think no differently on this matter from their counterparts of almost 200 years ago.

Tradition, however, does not explain everything, and members of Congress have occasionally shown a willingness to overturn traditions when it has been in their interests to do so. Moreover, although the tradition of comity between president and Congress is a very long-standing one, it is not an unbroken one. For example, little regard was paid to notions of comity in the post–Civil War period, and in one instance during that time, Congress went so far as to reduce the size of the president's staff and specify the nature of one of the positions it was funding (see page 18).

Given that the power of tradition has limitations as an explanatory factor, I would suggest that the practice of comity has been reinforced by two relatively recent developments in American government, one being the significant growth in the size of congressional staffs since the end of the 1960s, and the other, the role of the White House Office of Congressional Relations since the Kennedy administration.

Although the numbers of staff employed by individual members of Congress and by congressional committees have increased throughout the twentieth century, there has been a significant expansion since the end of the 1960s. In 1967, there were 5804 staff attached to the Capitol Hill offices of members of the House and Senate. Ten years later, that number had almost doubled to 10, 486. In 1991, there were 10,406 staff working in the offices of House members in Washington and their home districts—an average of 24 per member. In 1967, each member of the Senate employed an average of 17.5 staff. By 1991, they had an average of 57 each. Today, a new member of the House has the opportunity to hire at least the same number of staff that each Senator had twenty-five years ago. There has also been a corresponding explosion in the number of staff employed by House and Senate Committees—from 1337 in 1970 to 3231 in 1991—and if one includes the staffs of the congressional support agencies, like the Congressional Research Service, the Office of Technology Assessment, and the Congressional Budget Office, then the number of staff working on Capitol Hill in one capacity or another is in excess of 24,000.[115]

There are many reasons for the huge increase in congressional staffs over the past two decades,[116] but it was a development that attracted far less academic and media attention than the expansion of the presidential staff during roughly the same period. The growth of congressional staff has had some beneficial effects on Capitol Hill, but it has also created many problems and a little embarrassment. Some of the criticisms now being voiced about the consequences of the explosion of congressional staff, particularly the professional staff, are remarkably similar to those made about the swelling of the presidency in the early 1970s. The influence of congressional staff on policy and decision making has been questioned, so too has the capacity of the staff to increase the workloads on Capitol Hill and to isolate the members they work for. Michael Malbin, especially, has been highly critical of the way in which the expansion of professional staff in Congress has weakened the deliberative role of individual members and is helping to bury them under the weight of their own paperwork, "just as surely as if the staff never existed."[117]

It may just be that most members of Congress are reluctant to go too far in criticizing presidential staffing practices for fear of drawing attention to their own staff explosion and the problems that has brought with it. Although presidents have no power to reduce the appropriations for Congress, they do have plenty of scope to make an issue out of the size of the congressional staff, particularly its costs, if they so choose. As Ornstein, Mann, and Malbin note, "the costs of running Congress have grown along with the staff," and "today's Congress is now more than a $2 billion dollar enterprise."[118] In 1967 the appropriation for the legislative branch was almost $222 million. In 1992 it was $2.3 billion, an increase substantially in excess of the rise in the consumer price index for the same period.[119] In an era when big spending is electorally unpopular, when the budget deficit is the number-one policy problem, and when members of Congress are being drawn ever closer to their constituents, one can understand the reluctance of elected representatives to get involved in a dispute with the president over presidential staffing, with the consequent risk that congressional staffing practices might be exposed in the process. Comity thus becomes a matter of convenience for members of Congress—a way of protecting their important, but potentially embarrassing, staffing resources.

In recent years the tradition of comity has been threatened by the potential congressional response to particular presidential branch scandals, namely Watergate, the Iran-*contra* affair, and John Sununu's abuses of White House perks. In each instance, there was pressure from certain members of Congress to curb these excesses, and some of the proposed curbs would have breached comity. But, comity is a two-edged sword, and although the White House has been much more reserved than Congress in wanting to test its limits, the presidential branch does have the capacity and will to do so when pushed. Take, for example, one of the most recent instances of threats to comity—Congressman Kanjorski's 1992 effort to get Congress to pass a White House Personnel Reauthorization Act, which, among other things, set a ceiling on the total number of staff a president could have in the White House Office. At about the same time that Kanjorski's subcommittee started to press the Bush administration for information on the true cost of presidential travel and other "hidden" White House expenses, OMB Director Richard Darman retaliated. Using some complex, creative accounting, he reduced the legislative branch appropriations request for fiscal year 1993 by $172 million. Darman's action was a flagrant breach of the tradition of comity. It was also unlawful, as the budget request for Congress is statutorily exempted from OMB review. The chairman of the relevant House Appropriations Subcommittee, Vic Fazio (D-Calif.), called Darman's action a "significant incursion into the prerogatives of the legislative branch," and his counterpart in the Senate, Harry Reid (D-Nev.), said that his committee would simply ignore it because it was "an obvious violation of the principle of comity."[120] In the end, nothing came of Darman's ploy, and nothing came of Kanjorski's bill.

The practice of comity can also be seen in the context of the benefits that legislators derive from the services performed for them by the presidential staff, principally by the White House Office of Congressional Relations. It is now apparent that those services can be of significant help to legislators, and those who do benefit from them are less likely to participate in congressional efforts to place restrictions on, or reduce the size of, the presidential staff. It would simply not be in their interests to bite the hand that feeds them, and many members of the president's party in Congress are now accustomed to being fed rather well.

What members of Congress ask of the White House in the way of favors, what they get, and what price they pay are questions that few of those involved are willing to discuss beyond the merest generalities. But what is important for our present purposes is the fact that congressional demands for administration services, beyond straightforward routine requests, are now channeled through, and tightly controlled by, the White House staff, a legacy of the revolution in congressional liaison techniques introduced and practiced by Lawrence O'Brien during the Kennedy and Johnson years.[121]

Just after the 1960 election, Richard Neustadt prepared several memoranda for the president-elect on various aspects of White House and executive branch organization. One on the subject of congressional liaison contained a number of suggestions about the kind of role that Lawrence O'Brien was about to step into.[122] The memorandum finished with a short comment on possible extensions of O'Brien's job. Neustadt suggested that, in time, O'Brien could explore the practicalities of making departmental budgets, procurements, and contracts regularly serve the president's own purposes with Congress. He pointed out that, in recent years, there had never been a systematic effort in this field and added that although it would be hard to organize and harder to sustain, it would be well worth exploring.

O'Brien not only explored the possibilities of using government projects in the way that Neustadt had suggested but he also put into practice a system in which the White House Office of Congressional Relations served as the control point for all administration favors to members of Congress. Government contracts, government jobs, and a variety of political services were provided by the White House staff under O'Brien's direction. The O'Brien system constituted an important and highly controlled tool of congressional liaison. O'Brien subsequently made a point of denying that all this was done on a quid pro quo basis,[123] but his own papers, now available at the John F. Kennedy Library in Boston, show quite clearly that an exchange relationship existed between the White House and Congress, and although there is no evidence of specific favors being traded for specific votes, there was a clear expectation on the part of the White House that legislators for whom favors were done would reciprocate at some time in the future.[124]

The O'Brien papers also provide us with the clearest picture yet of the sorts of demands made by members of Congress. The Lawrence O'Brien Staff Files at the Kennedy Library consist of a separate folder for each legislator, in which are contained Office of Congressional Relations memos about the member of Congress and a record showing favors requested, favors granted, and miscellaneous information relating to the voting performance of each individual. For example, Representative George Huddleston's (D-Ala.) file shows three entries for April 1961. Under "Miscellaneous," it notes that Huddleston supported Kennedy on a key vote:

4/4: W [Henry Hall Wilson] says Member voted with us against Ayres substitute to minimum wage.[125]

Because most of his southern Democratic colleagues voted for the Ayres substitute and, thus, against Kennedy, Huddleston's vote was well received by the White House. The entry for 25 April states:

Member req. wire from Pres to Archbishop Thos. J. Toolen re his rec. Medal of Commandr. of the Order of Merit from Ital. govern.

The third entry notes simply:

4/27: Wire sent.

Huddleston's file shows that forty-six favors were granted to him during the 87th Congress (1961–62), ranging from constituent-related favors like the one just noted to a $2 million Air Force contract awarded to the Hayes International Corporation in his home district.[126]

Requests for government projects were quite common. A memo to O'Brien from one of his assistants, Charles Daly, for example, concerned Representative Ken Gray (D-Ill.) and notes:

Above all else, Ken Gray wants a hospital project in West Frankfort. I've told him you're pushing this very hard (you are). He understands it has about a 50-50 chance.[127]

Efforts were also made to award government contracts to the district of Representative Sidney Herlong (D-Fla.). A memorandum from Henry Hall Wilson, O'Brien's assistant handling the House of Representatives, dated 27 January 1962, reveals that Herlong had major political problems back home:

In the Florida redistricting Rep. Herlong received two new counties from the Republican district—Pasco County, the principal town of which is Dade City, and Hernando County, the principal town of which is Brooksville. He's extremely nervous about these counties, and even brought them up to me. As you know, Herlong could well be the key to our program this year. I suggest that it is worthwhile giving every contract-awarding agency notice to put the Herlong label on these counties for the purposes of our notices.[128]

Patronage was also in demand, as would be expected. Maryland Democratic Congressman Samuel Friedel needed a lot, according to a memo from Claude Desaultels of the OCR staff to Lawrence O'Brien:

Cong Friedel has been saying, for the past few weeks, that his problems would be solved if he could just get some more patronage. I have asked him for some young attorneys and the PR job at Labor, as per your recent memos. However, he is thinking in terms of something more substantial—particularly the managership of SBA in Baltimore, as well as the State Directorship of FHA.[129]

The memo goes on to note that, although this would upset other Democratic Congressmen from Maryland, the White House should do it nevertheless.

Most of the patronage requests were to get constituents into jobs. One, at least, was a request to get a constituent out. Henry Hall Wilson told O'Brien in April 1962:

You'll recall that Henry Gonzalez was much exercised about wanting to get a Republican GSA employee out of San Antonio. He is now out. Gonzalez is happy.[130]

One Congressman wanted patronage for himself. In February 1962, Claude Desaultels recorded that

Congressman John Dingell called to say that he would like to be appointed to some honorary commission or committee. It would be helpful to his stature. He said "he has been a good boy in the last year or so."[131]

Beyond the traditional demands for patronage and pork, a variety of requests were channeled through the Office of Congressional Relations. Several members asked for presidential support for their pet legislation. Clem Miller (D-Calif.) even asked OCR to intervene to overcome Bureau of the Budget objections to three of his bills.[132] Miller also urged Lawrence O'Brien to help him avoid an unfavorable outcome to the California redistricting due to take place in 1961. Miller felt he could be redistricted out of Congress, ending his usefulness to the administration. There were even instances of Republican Congressmen asking for help over redistricting.[133] Other members requested similar help with constituency difficulties. One example from the file on Representative Julia Hansen (D-Wash.) will suffice to illustrate the kinds of political services that the White House was called on to provide. On 23 May 1962 Charles Daly wrote to Lawrence O'Brien:

Julia Hansen is getting some real heat from lumber interests regarding that industry's many problems. She would like Secretary Hodges to ease her difficulties by calling representatives of the lumber people to Washington for a conference. I am asking him to do that.... The Congresswoman would very much like to get on the Public Works Committee. She asked for your help. I told her you were most reluctant to inject the White House into Committee selections, but that I felt sure you would drop a word if the opportunity arose.[134]

There were also requests for personal favors, but they were recorded along with all the others. Representative Joe Evins (D-Tenn.) wanted to get his father-in-law into a presidential press conference. Representative Peter Frelinghuysen (R-N.J.) wanted two sheets of Project Mercury stamps autographed by John Glenn for his son. Senator Ellender (D-La.) wanted seven pens used for signing the 1962 farm bill to give his grandchildren.

Members of Congress lean heavily on the services provided by the White House staff, and the O'Brien model has been adopted, with some variations, by successive administrations. As Eric Davis has noted, "The decisions O'Brien made regarding the organization and functioning of the White House Congressional Relations Office established the framework within which the liaison effort was conducted not only in the Kennedy White House, but also under Presidents Johnson, Nixon, and Ford. Indeed, the continuity in the organization and functioning of the liaison staffs across the transition from a Democratic to a Republican administration in 1969 is noteworthy."[135] Support for the practice of comity would not be at all inconsistent with ensuring the continuation of the services provided by the presidential staff.

THE CONSEQUENCES OF COMITY

The temptation to breach the tradition of comity is undoubtedly greater during a period of divided government when the party in control of Congress can make political capital from an attack on a presidential branch managed by the opposing party. In the post-Watergate era, much of which has, to date, been an era of divided government, the tradition of comity has been tested on a number of occasions, by a variety of means, and the events of Watergate may have had a significant, long-term impact on the attitudes of legislators toward this unwritten and cozy arrangement between the presidential branch and Congress. But although the tradition of comity has been tested, it has not been successfully challenged by either side and remains strong enough to resist the kind of attempts described in this chapter by one branch to interfere with the so-called housekeeping arrangements of the other, even after such palpably bad "housekeeping" as Watergate, the Iran-*contra* affair, and the antics of John Sununu.

Comity, by definition, weakens the potential of Congress to oversee the organization and functions of the presidential branch in any effective way, and it would seem that if congressional oversight is to be strengthened, then comity must be weakened. Surprisingly though, outside Congress, little attention has been given to the desirability and possibility of improving congressional scrutiny and presidential branch accountability. There has been a flood of reformist literature on the presidency over the last two decades, much of it specifically related to the presidential staff, but as we see in the next chapter, very few of the reform proposals focus on strengthening congressional oversight. Post-Watergate perspectives on the presidential branch have been directed toward other ends.

6. POST-WATERGATE PERSPECTIVES ON THE PRESIDENTIAL STAFF

The wake of the Vietnam war and the events of Watergate brought a flood of literature on how to right the wrongs of the American presidency. Presidential staffing was an important component of that literature. Among scholars, politicians, journalists, and former presidential aides who contributed to this post-Watergate publication boom, there was widespread agreement that the president's staff was a significant institutional and structural problem, not just a problem about the particular individuals who worked for Richard Nixon and whose penchant for illegal activities landed them in jail. There was no school of thought arguing that the prison sentences imposed on H.R. Haldeman, John Ehrlichman, Charles Colson, John Dean, and others were in any way a solution to the problems of presidential staffing, nor even an effective deterrent to any further abuse of power and position in the White House. The bulk of the reformist literature focused on how to make the presidential staff system more democratically and politically acceptable, rather than on how to prevent future White House aides from breaking the law. Indeed, there was an implicit assumption, at least in the scholarly literature, that the illegal activities of Nixon's aides were consequent upon the broader organizational and functional framework in which the president's personal staff operated, an assumption that has since been articulated explicitly and explained by one writer as a phenomenon, not just of presidential staffs, but of personal staffs in any organization.[1]

Consensus among the post-Watergate critics of the presidential branch extended far beyond the fundamental premise on which they based their reform proposals. Not only did they assert that the problem was an institutional one, but there was also remarkable unanimity in the literature about the specific defects of the staff system. The size of the presidential staff, its power, its politicization, and its behavioral problems were issues at the core of the reform debate in the 1970s. The differences among the major contributors to the debate were more likely to be found in the remedies they proposed than in the diagnosis.

There was also considerable similarity in the broad picture being painted of the presidential staff. Few of the post-Watergate critics were so acerbic and condemning as George Reedy,[2] but equally few had anything good to say about the staff system. In fact, Bradley Patterson's highly sympathetic account of the role and function of the White House staff stands out as a lone attempt in the 1970s to redress what he believed was a less than honest representation of how those around the president operated. He concluded his short article with a message to the post-Watergate presidential aide. "Don't be bashful," he said. "You will continue to be unloved and misunderstood and most of you will work in anonymity—but you do the nation's work well, in an ennobling place."[3] That was very much a minority view at the time.

As was pointed out at the beginning of this book, the post-Watergate criticism of the presidential staff was part of a broader attack on the growth and abuse of presidential power, culminating in the Johnson and Nixon years. Most commentators agreed with Arthur Schlesinger, Jr., that the presidency had gotten out of control and badly needed new definition and restraint,[4] but there were differing opinions on how presidential power ought to be restrained. Philippa Strum, for example, summed up the view of those who called for a reduction in presidential power when she wrote that it is "far more desirable to have a president limited in his capacity to achieve acceptable goals, than it is to have an unlimited president who could easily achieve unacceptable goals."[5] Others saw it differently. Theodore Sorensen warned that "we cannot endlessly add to the powers of the presidency with a Lincoln in mind without increasing a Nixon's opportunity to do harm. But we cannot unduly weaken the office with a Nixon in mind without hampering a law-abiding president's power to do good."[6] Similarly, Schlesinger feared that "the revulsion against inordinate theories of presidential power may produce an inordinate swing against the presidency and thereby do essential damage to our national capacity to handle the problems of the future."[7]

What Schlesinger feared ultimately came to pass. Gerald Ford, the president without an electoral mandate, seemed to be stumbling politically, as well as physically, from the moment he pardoned Richard Nixon; and Jimmy Carter, the candidate who ran against the imperial presidency and the Washington establishment, was never able to make Washington work for him. The second half of the 1970s was perceived to be a period of dangerously weak presidential leadership and the major crisis of the Carter administration, the seizure of the hostages in Teheran, not only symbolized the impotence of the United States on the world stage but also dramatically highlighted the diminished authority and effectiveness of the presidency.

The Ford and Carter years spawned another wave of "crisis-of-the-presidency" literature, reflecting the dilemma in which many commentators found themselves. Although ever mindful of the Johnson-Nixon years and the need for greater presidential accountability, by the end of the 1970s writers were trying to grapple with what seemed to be major and damaging constraints on presidential leadership imposed as part of the post-Watergate reaction to the excesses of earlier times. Scholars were now concentrating on what Thomas Cronin called the "imperiled" presidency.[8]

That concern resulted in a new dimension to the discussions of presidential staffing. Emphasis shifted from accountability to efficiency in the presidential branch, and even before the Carter administration had come to an end, the thrust of the reform literature was being directed toward ways in which the staff system could operate more effectively, instead of emphasizing proposals to limit the activities of presidential aides. When it comes to matters of presidential staffing, concerns about accountability and efficiency are not mutually exclusive, but they do not blend very easily, and in evaluating post-Watergate perspectives on the presidential branch, one must be conscious that the literature incorporates reactions to two different sets of problems encountered in the 1970s and 1980s. The direction of any particular set of reform proposals will be determined, to a large extent, by whether the reformers were reacting to the Johnson-Nixon era or to the Ford and Carter experience, although it is true to say that some concerns are shared by both groups of reformers. And it would be going too far to separate completely the reform agenda of the early 1970s from the proposals developed at the end of the decade and the beginning of the 1980s.

SIZE AS A PROBLEM

One of the issues on which there was a broad consensus between the two wings of the post-Watergate reform movement was the size of the presidential branch. There has been almost universal agreement since the 1960s that the president's staff, particularly the White House Office staff, is too large and that its numbers ought to be reduced. "A strong presidency needs a strong and competent staff," wrote Thomas Cronin, "but a strong and able leader in the White House would keep the executive office staff to a minimum."[9] Similarly, Stephen Hess noted that "beyond a certain number, White House aides become counterproductive,"[10] and Theodore Sorensen claimed that "too large a staff is not in the public interest."[11] Cronin, Hess, and Sorensen published shortly after Nixon's departure from the White House. Some years later, a prestigious panel, convened by the National Academy of Public Administration under the joint chairmanship of Don K. Price and Rocco Siciliano, reviewed the needs of the presidency for the 1980s in the light of the Ford and Carter experience. Its very first recommendation was this:

> The trend toward enlargement of the immediate White House staff should be reversed. Rigorous efforts should be made to keep this staff small. It should be structured to serve the immediate functional and personal needs of the president, not to reflect various special interests.[12]

The authors of the report went on to explain that "the desire for a trim White House staff is not intended to constrain, but rather to enhance the president's ability to function effectively."[13]

The dysfunctional consequences of a large presidential staff, as perceived by post-Watergate critics, have already been discussed. What we now need to examine are the remedies put forward to correct the dysfunction, and certainly the almost universal desire to reduce the number of presidential aides warrants closer scrutiny.

It is interesting to note that none of the authors just cited were very specific about what size the presidential staff ought to be. Cronin simply said that it ought to be kept "to a minimum." Hess talked about staff size "beyond a certain number." Sorensen objected to "too large a staff," and the Price-Siciliano report spoke of the need "to keep this staff small." Yet it might be argued that if the sheer size of the staff is itself a problem, then reform proposals ought to specify either an optimum number of presidential assistants or identify those staff functions within the EOP that either were unnecessary or else could be performed by an executive branch department or agency.

Optimum numbers presented difficulties. No critics suggested a return to the 6 administrative assistants that Brownlow had proposed in 1937, and none were happy with the 500 to 600 White House aides employed by President Nixon, but an acceptable number between 6 and 600 seemed to be elusive to almost everyone. The Price-Siciliano panel took the view that "the optimum size of a staff cannot be determined by formulas and quotas,"[14] and most reformers shared that position. One or two, however, mentioned hard numbers. In writing a report of a conference on the institutionalized presidency held in the spring of 1974, Ernest S. Griffith suggested that twenty-five "active, responsible assistants would appear to be desirable in the White House Office."[15] He was effectively recommending a reduction of about 75 percent in the senior ranks of the presidential staff. Two former assistant secretaries in the Carter administration went even further. They believed that if a president could start from scratch and completely rebuild the EOP, he could operate with a total Executive Office (not just White House Office) staff of thirty to forty professionals. They also admitted that this proposal was a fantasy because of the radical reorganization that would be necessary.[16]

Most critics were much less specific and preferred to see the issue in terms of staff functions rather than optimum numbers. Stephen Hess, for example, thought that presidents could increase their effectiveness by reducing the number of White House aides "to those who can be kept reasonably apprised of their intentions."[17] A similar formula was adopted by Richard Neustadt, who noted that Franklin Roosevelt's personal staff "meant only those who helped him do what was required of him day to day, manning his schedule, drafting his speeches, guarding his signature, nursing the press corps, or, during the war, dealing with Stalin and Churchill.... All other aides were 'institutional.'"[18]

Thomas Cronin also adopted a functional approach. He suggested that a reduction in the number of presidential staff could be attained by the consolidation of Cabinet departments into superdepartments along the lines of President Nixon's ill-fated reorganization plan of 1971. Cronin believed that fewer, but larger, departments would reduce the interdepartmental jurisdictional disputes, and therefore "less need would exist for many of the interest group brokers and special councils that now constitute so much of the excess baggage in the overstaffed executive office."[19] Walter Mondale came to a similar conclusion. "If the Cabinet departments were properly reorganized along modern lines, much of the coordinating role which the White House offices supposedly perform could be eliminated."[20]

Others stressed the distinction between advisory and operating staff. Those with operating responsibilities had no business being in the White House in the first place and ought to be removed.[21] The Price-Siciliano report said much the same, but even more obtusely. It made no attempt to specify which particular staff functions should be dropped and merely said that "the Executive Office of the President should be reduced to encompass only those functions that are vital to the president in the performance of his government duties."[22] Given that the concern about the sheer size of the presidential staff was so central to the post-Watergate reaction, it is perhaps surprising that the proposals to reduce the numbers were so lacking in specificity and direction. There was confusion right from the start, with some reformers targeting just the White House Office and others seeing the need for staff reductions across the whole of the EOP.

Those writers who simply urged a cut in the number of White House staff, without indicating where the reductions were to be made, found a sympathetic listener in Jimmy Carter, who subsequently demonstrated just how meaningless numbers could be on their own. In the early days of his presidency, Carter pledged to reduce the size of the White House staff by one-third,[23] and later he claimed to have cut the staff from 485 to 351, but most of his reduction was, in fact, a transfer of staff from the White House Office to new units in the EOP, particularly the Office of Administration. As Dom Bonafede noted, "the alleged reductions are largely the result of bookkeeping gimmicks ... what is labeled a 'reduction' is simply a rejiggling of organizational boxes."[24] What Carter had done was to show how presidents could reduce the size of the staff without making the slightest bit of difference to the way the White House Office functioned. Many of those Carter transferred were administrative support staff, not the highly paid senior operatives who were, allegedly, the cause of the problems of the presidential branch. Quite often, the post-Watergate demand for a smaller presidential staff ignored this distinction. Mail-room personnel, telephone switchboard operators, and presidential photographers are included in the numbers making up the White House Office, just as are the president's national security adviser, congressional relations aide, and chief of staff. The point is that numbers of staff alone reveal nothing about the functional problems of the presidential branch, particularly the problems of the White House Office.[25]

There was another weakness in the arguments of those who simply asserted that a smaller White House staff would be better. They tended to ignore lessons from the past, from the time when the president's staff was very small. So much of the post-Watergate literature was based on the assumption that the president's staff began with Brownlow, but presidential staffs existed before Brownlow, and although they were smaller in size, many of the adverse behavioral characteristics of the post-Brownlow staffs had their antecedents in the presidential staffs of the nineteenth and the early twentieth centuries.[26]

John F. Kennedy, for example, was not the first president to recruit senior presidential staff from the ranks of his election campaign team. That was how Daniel Lamont got his White House job under Cleveland, as did John Addison Porter, McKinley's first secretary, and Joseph Tumulty and George Christian, who served Woodrow Wilson and Warren Harding respectively. Richard Nixon was not the first president to be surrounded by "a palace guard." Herbert Hoover also had that experience, and so did President Taft when Charles Dyer Norton was his senior aide. Even Nicolay and Hay were accused of restricting access to President Lincoln in the mid-nineteenth century. Scandal and corruption were also not unknown before Brownlow, and modern presidential staffs would have to go a long way to emulate the level of corruption associated with President Grant's military aides, Orville Babcock and Horace Porter. Hamilton Jordan, President Carter's chief of staff, was often accused of lacking judgment, humility, and discipline, and of displaying excessive arrogance in his White House post, but the very same criticisms were made of John Addison Porter at the beginning of the McKinley administration. H.R. Haldeman may have broken every one of Brownlow's guidelines about how presidential staff should behave, but they had been broken long before Brownlow wrote them by a succession of politically powerful aides serving nineteenth- and early twentieth-century presidents. One could go on drawing parallels, but the point has been made. What many post-Watergate reformers seemed not to notice was that the dysfunctions they identified in a bloated presidential staff system had also occurred in previous presidential administrations where the number of staff had been small.

One also needs to ask how far the prescriptions for staff reductions were consistent with the analysis the reformers themselves had made of the causes of presidential staff expansion. As noted in chapter 3, initial explanations for the growth of staff were cast in terms of broad and very significant developments within the American political system. Stephen Hess, for example, identified a number of causes of staff growth that were clearly societal, not presidential, in origin (see page 47). To Hess, the expansion of the presidential staff reflected some of the most profound political changes in twentieth-century America, and, of those he singled out, not one can be fairly attributed in origin to any one president. If this is the case, would it therefore be wrong to think that any substantial reduction in the size of the presidential staff would depend on a reversal of those complex developments that caused the expansion in the first place? In Hess's terms, this would mean, among other things, reducing American commitments on the world stage; shifting power, responsibility, and resources back to state and local governments; instituting a major reduction in the role of government; returning to a Taftian concept of the scope of presidential power; and so on. To say that this would constitute a difficult agenda for any president, or for the president and Congress combined, would be a gross understatement, and thus one might easily conclude that the presidential staff is not readily susceptible to a reduction in size. Not so, according to Hess. "Trimming the White House staff," he claims, "is a relatively simple matter for presidents, if there is the will. The political risks are modest. The authority exists."[27] That claim sits uneasily with the analysis on which it is based.

There were also some difficulties with the arguments of those who advocated a functional approach to reducing the size of the presidential staff. Although reformers had a clear general view of what functions ought not to be located in the Executive Office of the President, the principles they enunciated did not translate easily into guidelines for staff reductions. The target for many of the critics was presidential staff involvement in operational aspects of policy making, a function they believed rightfully belonged in the departments and agencies. The principal culprits were seen to be the expanding policy staffs in the presidential branch (the Domestic Policy Staff and the NSC staff), and it was believed that if operations were divorced from advisory and coordinating functions, less staff would be needed in the EOP. In practice, such recommendations present problems because of the hazy, almost indefinable line between the "acceptable" textbook role of senior presidential aides—policy advice, policy coordination, and what writers now like to call process management—and the "unacceptable" role of interfering with the work of departments and agencies. Analytical dichotomies, such as staff and line, policy making and policy implementation, and politics and administration, defy application at the highest levels of the presidential staff. Presidential staff do not follow organizational theories, models, or ideal types. They respond to the needs of the president they serve and recent presidents have encouraged their senior aides to get involved in "unacceptable" work in addition to their traditional functions. Staff can, and do, take on operational responsibilities as well as providing advice and coordination, and this makes it difficult to relate staff reductions to functions in any specific way.

It was even more difficult for reformers like Cronin and Mondale to be specific about where staffing reductions could be made. Their proposals were consequent on prior and major changes in the structure and functioning of the executive branch. They could not anticipate the numbers of presidential aides that might be dispensed with if such a transformation of the Cabinet departments took place. All they could do was make the logical point that if there were fewer departments, there would likely be less of a coordination problem for the presidential staff and therefore less need of staff.

The functional approach to the issue of presidential staff size also led a number of critics beyond the question of what presidents and their staffs ought not to be doing and into discussions about what they should be doing and how well equipped they are to do it. This emphasis on function and efficiency, particularly after the Ford-Carter years, revealed some serious worries about the capacity of the presidency to perform the tasks it ought to be performing. Being essentially prescriptive in nature, the literature contained many recommendations for reform and change, and a number of those recommendations centered on the establishment of new presidential staffs, even though their authors were simultaneously advocating reductions in the size of the presidential branch. The Price-Siciliano report was typical. "Much of the more vocal criticism of the Executive Office of the President," it proclaimed, "has been directed at its sheer size. There is no question that this is an area where smaller would be better."[28] Yet the same report contained proposals for a new economic affairs staff, a policy research and analysis staff, a program evaluation staff, and a Federal Assistance Administration staff.

Such seemingly contradictory proposals might be explained away. The creation of new staff units designed to enhance efficiency in the presidential branch was not necessarily incompatible with reductions in the overall size of the staff, and as most critics were not very specific about the total size of the presidential staff or the number of personnel needed for the new staff units, it would be unfair to accuse the reformers of wanting it both ways. Moreover, some of the leading critics, including the Price-Siciliano committee, were keener to reduce the size of the president's personal staff in the White House Office than to limit the functioning of what they saw as an institutional staff in the EOP. Nevertheless, the call for new presidential staff units when, at the same time, extolling the virtues of smallness, was far from unambiguous and inevitably raised doubts about just how central size itself was to the problems of the presidential staff.

The fact that size became so central to the post-Watergate critique of the presidential staff owes a lot to the work of political scientist Thomas Cronin. He may not have been the first to discover that the president's staff was getting larger, and certainly not the first to draw attention to the implications of this in print (the House Post Office and Civil Service Committee can probably claim that honor), but it was Cronin, more than anyone else, who publicized the discovery, and it was his writings that served as a reference point for so many others in the post-Watergate period. Cronin coined the phrase "the swelling of the presidency." It was he who penned the oft-quoted line, "Today, the President needs help merely to manage his help," and it was in his widely read text, *The State of the Presidency* (1975), that readers encountered the bare statistics, in graphic form, detailing the expansion of the presidential staff from Franklin D. Roosevelt to Gerald Ford.

Many took their cue from Cronin. The size factor was seen to offer an attractive and plausible explanation of the state of the presidential staff after Nixon, and the available quantitative data—a rarity in the study of the American presidency[29]—were eagerly employed to confirm staff size as a critical variable. But Cronin's own caution and qualification about the importance of staff size in explaining the dysfunctions of the institutionalized presidency were overlooked by many of those who followed in his footsteps. "Perhaps it is not so much a matter of how big the presidential staffs are as it is a matter of for what purposes they are used," he suggested at the end of his "bigger has not been better" paragraph. He also pointed to the possibility that large staffs were not necessarily a bad thing. "A large executive entourage," Cronin wrote, "may indeed furnish a president with the kind of help that will make him an able manager and a responsive democratic leader ... the executive office, properly staffed, could be a very valuable presidential and national resource, almost regardless of size."[30]

Cronin's own reservations raised some doubts about the significance of numbers to the problems of presidential staffing, but the post-Watergate reform literature has ignored them. By and large, it has treated the statistics on presidential staff size purely quantitatively, failing to examine the qualitative dimensions of the measure, and has made no attempt to come to terms with the basic difficulty of how to calculate the size of the staff. Critics have also tended to assert that certain dysfunctions flow from large staffs without establishing that these dysfunctions are absent in small staffs. The history of the presidential staff suggests that they are not. The president's ability to control his own staff depends not so much on the numbers of personnel working for him, but rather on what those people are directed to do and on the president's style and method of management. It should be remembered that it only took a handful of President Nixon's senior staff to arrange the various projects that ultimately led to the Watergate break-in. Most of the 500 to 600 staff accredited to the White House Office at the time were uninvolved and unaware of what was going on. Similarly, in the Reagan years, even fewer senior presidential staff initiated and carried out the Iran-*contra* affair. Large staffs are certainly no precondition for presidential disasters.

One reform proposal has resulted from the focus on size, and that is that the number of presidential staff needs to be reduced. Moreover, the ease with which that proposal has been advanced, yet so often isolated from the complex and varied reasons that led to the increase in the size of the presidential staff in the first place, has obscured the immense practical difficulty of implementing the proposal. Reducing the size of the presidential staff eventually became not just a reform proposal from the political science profession but political orthodoxy when, in the 1992 election campaign, all three presidential candidates committed themselves to cutting staff numbers, and, unlike the political scientists, the politicians were prepared to say by how much. President Bush appeared as the boldest, advocating a reduction in the "operating budget" of the EOP by one-third,[31] Ross Perot thought that the White House and Congress could reduce their staffs by 30 percent, and Governor Clinton settled on a 25 percent target.[32]

What really matters so far as presidential staffing is concerned is not the total number of presidential staff, but the extent of the senior staff who have policy-making and decision-taking responsibilities. Then the problem is how to control them and make them accountable. Reducing their numbers does not necessarily improve control and accountability. All it ensures is that unless the responsibilities heaped on the president of the United States are diminished substantially, the remaining senior staff will carry an even heavier workload than they have done in the past, something that President Clinton quickly discovered when he tried to implement his campaign promise during his first year in the White House.[33]

CHECKING STAFF POWER

It goes without saying among post-Watergate reformers that the growth of presidential staff power was an unwelcome and undesirable development in American government. Almost all of the leading critics objected to the unaccountability of these new decision makers in Washington and the consequent displacement of the more traditional sources of authority in the executive branch, namely the members of the president's Cabinet. There was also broad agreement on how to remedy the situation. In essence, the thrust of post-Watergate reform proposals involved redefining the role of the presidential staff to limit its policy-making power and restoring what was seen to be the rightful and proper place of Cabinet members in the policy-making process.

Any effort to redefine the role of the presidential staff with the aim of curtailing its power inevitably brings us back to Brownlow. As has been stressed throughout this book, Brownlow maintained a sharp distinction between an administrative support staff for the president and a powerful political staff serving the president in a policy-making capacity. Explicit in the Brownlow report and Executive Order 8248 are the precise requirements and conditions necessary for non-political staff assistance to the president, and implicit is the warning that organizational and structural constraints are not sufficient to prevent presidential aides from moving beyond an administrative role into a more highly charged political one. Brownlow's emphasis was on self-constraint. The attitudes, character, and perception of the staff were the crucial variables, and in the absence of the right personal qualities, there would be little to prevent those inside the White House from assuming the political prominence that has characterized the presidential staff for the last two decades.

In this respect, it might be argued that the Brownlow report addressed the problem of controlling the presidential staff more acutely than many contemporary commentators have done. Brownlow may have been unrealistic about the possibility of confining the staff to the role that he envisaged and perhaps too eager to emulate what he saw in the British Cabinet Office, but he was certainly well aware of the potential that a president's personal staff would have to upset established power relationships and patterns of authority within the executive branch. In Brownlow's vision there could be no halfway house. A president has the choice of either a purely administrative staff or a political one.

Post-Watergate reformers have thought differently. They have rejected the notion that the role of the presidential staff has to be defined rigidly and checked by their own self-constraint. They have been unwilling to accept Brownlow's notion that administration at the presidential level can be divorced from politics or that the presidential staff can be relied on to curb its own excesses. Instead, critics have constructed a framework that recognizes that White House aides are political animals and will perform political functions, but attempts to limit their power by a combination of role redefinition and external constraints.

This halfway house discovered by the post-Watergate reformers is built around the idea of what Heclo and Salamon have called "process management."[34] Presidential staff should be concerned with how things get done, rather than what gets decided, and the questions of how things get done and how they ought to get done, at the highest level of American government, were addressed more critically and more seriously during the 1970s and 1980s than ever before. What one sees in that literature is an attempt to extend Brownlow's notion of administrative management, although the language of administration has now given way almost entirely to the language of management. That has taken discussion on the subject far beyond the bounds of the public administration discipline that Brownlow knew and into the worlds of cognitive psychology, organizational behavior, decision-making theory, and so on.[35]

There has been much debate about the most desirable structures and organizational principles around which process management in the presidential branch ought to be built, but, on a general level, there has been broad agreement in the literature about the role that presidential staff ought to play. Heclo and Salamon say they should be "process managers." The

Price-Siciliano panel said they ought to be "facilitators" and "honest brokers."[36] Alexander George, in his important work on multiple advocacy in presidential decision making, has used the terms "custodian" and "custodian-manager" to describe the role of senior presidential aides in safeguarding the process by which policy is made.[37] Insofar as checking staff power is concerned, the essence is the same. They have all proposed that presidential staff roles be redefined in terms of a more collegial approach to the management of policy making in the presidential branch.

One of the lesser-known examples of post-Watergate reformist thinking broadly encapsulates these ideas quite conveniently. The report of the Panel on the Electoral and Democratic Process, which formed part of President Carter's Commission for a National Agenda for the Eighties, contained a recommendation that three policy coordination staffs be created, each to be headed by an assistant to the president. It described the functions of these senior White House aides as follows:

> These new presidential advisers and their staffs could help the president manage the flow of information and decisions. Advisers' roles should be kept flexible, allowing them to act as troubleshooters for the president and as critics of the departmental programs and functions, to provide analysis independent of affected agencies, and to inform the president of problems in the implementation of policy. Such advisers could also serve as a link between the president and the executive agencies, communicating presidential priorities and ensuring the implementation of presidential decisions. Finally, these advisers could be used as brokers among agencies to ensure that presidential priorities are followed, particularly in cases of overlapping jurisdictions.[38]

In the reform literature, job descriptions like the one above have been designed to prevent the presidential staff from usurping the policy-making role of the Cabinet. The paragraph just cited is immediately preceded in the report of President Carter's panel by the claim that "the proposal reaffirms the policy-making role of the President and his Cabinet, but also ensures that Presidential advisers are used to facilitate policy making, but not to make policy."

Role definitions such as that imply that there is a distinct boundary between facilitating, brokering, coordinating, and process management, on the one hand, and policy making on the other, but that is where some uncertainty begins to creep in. Heclo and Salamon, for example, admit that "there can be no neat separation between process management and policy management ... the difference is one of degree rather than of kind."[39] Similarly, the Price-Siciliano panel urges a policy advocacy role for the presidential staff, while confessing that this is not entirely compatible with the report's overall concern to limit the power of the staff in the policy-making process. The authors of the report define the policy functions of the presidential staff as follows:

> First the staff must be, and must be seen to be, facilitators who manage a deliberative process that gives a fair hearing to all sides. Second, they must be presidential representatives, ensuring that consultation and interdepartmental work bring forth proposals with a government wide—rather than simply departmental—perspective. Third, they must be sufficiently knowledgeable to offer substantive advice to the president when this seems necessary.[40]

They then hint at, and understate, the extent of the problem with such a mixture of roles.

> No person or staff unit can perform all these services in perfect combination. The president, however, must expect the personnel of the Executive Office to try to do so. He must insist that their honest brokerage function does not passively produce the lowest common denominator of departmental agreement. Hearing their substantive advice, he must be sure that their privileged access has not denied a fair hearing to others. The president must be "unreasonable" enough to demand that they represent his interests, but not entangle him in and commit to the outcome of interdepartmental or other consultation except when he so chooses.[41]

If any one reason can be singled out to explain the growing power of the presidential staff during the last three decades, it must be the way senior aides have asserted a policy advocacy role within the White House, because policy advocacy from that vantage point has been tantamount to policy making. To limit staff power, the opportunities for the staff to become policy advocates would have to be restricted. Brownlow tried to do this by drawing precise boundaries to the range of staff functions, at least insofar as the White House staff was concerned. The post-Watergate reformers, by contrast, have drawn such broad and indistinct demarcation lines in the guise of process-management terminology that it is difficult to see what there is in these new role definitions that would prevent presidential staff from behaving in the future exactly as they have done in the past. If Brownlow's executive assistants could make the leap to policy makers, what is there to stop the process managers of the 1980s and 1990s from doing the same? The reformers have given them a role that is much closer to the policy-making process than Brownlow intended, and the gap that process managers would have to bridge to become policy makers is much narrower than the one Brownlow designed.

The attempt to redefine presidential roles has had a dual purpose, particular after the Ford-Carter years. Although reformers wanted to regulate the policy-making power of senior White House aides because that power did not accord with notions of democracy and accountability, they were just as much concerned with the rationality and efficiency of the presidential policy-making process and were just as keen to propose reforms in this area. That also involved redefining what presidential staff assistants ought to be doing, and the attempt to do so, in the context of efficiency rather than accountability, is considered further on in this chapter.

The second element of constraint on presidential staff power in the post-Watergate literature envisages a return to what is often labeled "collegial leadership." This can take many forms, but, in essence, most proposals involve restoring some measure of authority to heads of departments individually and to the Cabinet collectively. Stephen Hess, the best-known proponent of this view, believes that, because "Cabinet officers ... collectively define what is doable in the executive branch" and "have major responsibility for the implementation of presidential policy,"[42] they should be the principal advisers to the president and the primary spokesmen for the administration, and the Cabinet should be the focal point of the White House staff system.[43]

Similarly, Bradley Nash concluded in a postscript to his thirty-five-year-old study of presidential staffing: "It now appears more clear than ever that a determined use of the Cabinet system, essentially augmented by well developed staff organization, presents the best approach to effective and responsive administration."[44] From the perspective of Capitol Hill, Walter Mondale concurred. "The more complete the sphere of authority of the Cabinet officers in dealing with major policy problems," he wrote, "the more likely future presidents will be able to deal with them rather than a staff member in the White House. And the more relevant and helpful these Cabinet officers are to future presidents, the better the executive branch will be able to relate to the Congress."[45] Graham Allison has promoted the idea of an executive committee of the Cabinet (he calls it "ExCab") as the chief forum for decisions on all major policy issues.[46] The multiple-advocacy theorists also emphasize that their new advisory system must operate at the Cabinet level,[47] and, although the Price-Siciliano report avoids the notion of the Cabinet as a collective decision-making body, it too advocates a much closer and more confidential relationship between the president and the heads of executive departments.[48]

Watergate was not the first political crisis to generate demands for a revival of the Cabinet, even for some form of Cabinet government, but never before had the presidential staff been the context within which the reform proposals were set. This produced a set of arguments in support of resuscitating the Cabinet and a vision of the role of Cabinet members in the presidential policy-making process that reflected the problems of the day. These proposals were thus quite distinct from attempts to promote the idea of Cabinet government, or variations of it, at earlier times in American history. But along with new arguments in favor of making the Cabinet and collegiality the keys to reform, there were also new arguments against doing so.

Richard Fenno's classic study, written at the end of the 1950s, expresses the conventional wisdom on the political weakness of the Cabinet,[49] and that work alone is enough to cast doubt on the ability of the Cabinet and its members to constrain the power of the presidential staff. But, since the Eisenhower presidency, which was the last administration covered by Fenno, the condition of the Cabinet has deteriorated even further in status, prestige, and power, and that decline cannot be reversed, or even arrested, simply by asserting that Cabinet revitalization would be a good thing for responsible government in the United States.

It would take a good deal more than that to repair the long-term institutional damage done to the Cabinet during the Nixon years, although many of those who advocate a shift toward a more collegial form of government do not appear to regard the long-term consequences of Nixon's actions as a barrier to the implementation of reform. They seem to think that, providing the United States gets a president with the will to use the Cabinet as his principal source of advice and the ability to attract talented individuals to head the executive branch departments, the Cabinet could be restored to its textbook role. They envisage a Cabinet under new management that would not be burdened by any of the baggage it acquired with former owners and that would be able to assume a positive role in policy making because the president wants it that way. But, after what Richard Nixon did, one might justly question whether it would be that simple.

Nixon's predecessors may well have ignored their Cabinets in practice, but they were usually prepared to maintain a pretense of Cabinet importance and did make use of the individual talents of the members of the Cabinet, even though they discarded the collectivity. Nixon did neither. He did not pretend, and the fiction was destroyed during his administration by a very public exposure of the fundamental weakness of the Cabinet in American government. It was well summed up in John Ehrlichman's infamous statement on the role of the Cabinet. "It should be like a corporation," he said, "where the executive vice presidents (the cabinet officers) are tied closely to the chief executive, or to put it in extreme terms, when he says jump, they should only ask how high."[50]

It is difficult to quantify the extent of the institutional damage done to the Cabinet by President Nixon, but one may begin to get some idea of how the status and authority of the Cabinet and its members were affected by considering what remained of the traditional roles and functions of Cabinet officials at the beginning of Nixon's second term of office. The short answer is very little. The Cabinet rarely met as a collective body. Its members were not the principal advisers to the president, either collectively or individually, and most of them were not even advisers of any kind. Neither were they any longer the principal spokesmen for the administration. That role had been usurped by the presidential staff. They were also beginning to lose their function as the link between the administration and key interest groups as the White House Office itself became the focus of interest-group representation. Cabinet members no longer had a privileged relationship with the president, and as Secretary of Interior Walter Hickel found out, some of them had no relationship at all with Richard Nixon. By Nixon's second term, as Nelson Polsby has remarked, few Cabinet members had any public standing or constituencies of their own (see page 138) and after the White House reorganization of January 1973, most of them were effectively demoted by being required to work under the direction of the White House staff. Even their functions as managers of their departments were being undermined by increasing White House intervention in that area. Who in Washington, after all this, would not have had doubts about Jimmy Carter's emphatic preinaugural statements promising "Cabinet government" in his administration? And Carter's failure to deliver on this promise was, in part, a measure of the longer-term impact of Richard Nixon.[51]

The post-Watergate reformers who advocate a restoration of the power of Cabinet officials also tend to ignore the widening gulf between president and Cabinet as a result of the post-1968 changes to the presidential nomination and election process. It is not just that the new nomination rules and campaign finance laws have affected the function and purpose of the White House staff (as discussed in chapter 4) but also that they have changed the relationship between the president and his Cabinet officials, largely as a result of the reduced dependency of the presidential candidate on the party. Traditionally, recruitment to the Cabinet was based on rewards to important power brokers within the president's political party, but the party no longer determines its nominee nor delivers the vote to its presidential candidate. There are no party power brokers in the presidential elections of today. Stephen Hess believes that this development offers presidents a previously unthinkable freedom in the selection of Cabinet officers, giving them the opportunity to make high-caliber appointments.[52] So it does, but it also weakens whatever political base the Cabinet used to have and makes it even less likely that presidents will feel inclined to make Cabinet members partners in the policy-making process.

A second consequence of party reform has been to promote the importance of electoral considerations in the work of the president and his staff, at least as far as first-term presidents are concerned. Newly elected presidents are well advised to hold on to their campaign organization during the first term in office, given that the reformed nomination system provides so many incentives for others to challenge an incumbent seeking renomination. Presidents do this by giving campaign staff White House jobs, and it is hardly surprising that the holders of those jobs tend to view their functions in electoral terms. When the electoral connection becomes so central to White House staff work (witness the quick exit of Baker, Meese, Deaver, and Edward Rollins from the Reagan White House once Reagan had been reelected and there were no more elections to fight), the role of the already weakened Cabinet becomes even less relevant and more remote from what goes on at the center of power. The only way to close the gap between president and Cabinet would be for the president to fill Cabinet positions, as well as White House jobs, with election campaign staff, but, then, that is not quite the sort of Cabinet that post-Watergate reformers have been looking for.

Ultimately, however, the major weakness of the post-Watergate desire to reinvigorate the Cabinet has been its inability to come to terms with the fact that the White House staff has grown in power at the expense of the Cabinet because presidents themselves have wanted it that way. Whatever the defects of the presidential staff system and however mistaken presidents might be in their thinking about the presidential staff, most postwar presidents have signified that it has served their purposes better than the Cabinet system. Even Jimmy Carter, the president most committed to the Cabinet since Eisenhower, eventually came to reject his earlier way of thinking. Those who have seen hope in the revival of the Cabinet have been fully aware that only the president can make that hope a reality. In Cabinet reform, says Cronin, structural change is "minimal relative to the attitudinal changes that must take place on the part of a president, his staff and cabinet members."[53] "Above all, the president must want the Cabinet to be an effective instrument of advice," says Stephen Hess.[54] But why should presidents want to change their attitudes, and why should they want the Cabinet to be an effective instrument of advice? From the outside looking in, there are a hundred and one good reasons for believing that "presidential leadership will be more effective when it is rooted in shared responsibility," to quote Hess again,[55] but presidents are on the inside looking out, and their on-the-job experience has driven most of them in the opposite direction. Reformers have never adequately explained why the textbook virtues of Cabinet government and collegial leadership have had so little appeal to the one person who really counts.

THE POLITICIZATION OF THE PRESIDENTIAL STAFF

Just as post-Watergate commentators objected to the size and power of the presidential staff, so, too, they criticized the increasing politicization of what was once intended to be an institutional staff for the presidency. The expanding size and growing power of the presidential staff was, for the most part, seen as a problem concerning the White House Office in particular. Politicization, or what some writers have referred to as "deinstitutionalization," was a problem for the whole of the Executive Office of the President. There was a widely shared view in the post-Watergate literature that the practice of placing loyal presidential appointees in those key EOP posts originally intended to be occupied by career professionals ran counter to the best interests of the presidency. The growing politicization of the institutional arm of the presidential staff could, it was claimed, cost presidents the benefits of expertise, professionalism, objectivity, and continuity. Indeed, it was a development that conflicted with what Herbert Kaufman identified as one of the three "core values" of American public administration—"the quest for neutral competence."[56]

The notion that career professionals could and should provide objective advice to elected political leaders predates the Brownlow report, but Brownlow made it the basis of his whole approach to presidential staffing in 1937. He had even suggested that some of the presidential staff in the White House Office should be drawn from the career civil service to do a tour of duty with the president, after which they would be restored to their former positions, a suggestion no president has followed. The commitment to neutral competence has remained very strong in the world of public administration, but it is a commitment that has never been shared by post-Brownlow presidents.

Starting with Eisenhower, presidents have tried to balance neutral competence in the EOP with a capacity to respond to the needs of political leadership in the White House. As noted previously, it was Eisenhower who first brought in a noncareer official to head the Bureau of the Budget, and it was Eisenhower who began the politicization of the National Security Council staff by creating the post of national security adviser in the White House Office and giving the appointee charge of the NSC staff, notwithstanding the existence of an executive secretary of the NSC. Eisenhower pointed the way to what eventually became a major assault on the doctrine of neutral competence by President Nixon and his successors.[57] That annoyed post-Watergate critics, who believed Nixon had established an undesirable imbalance between neutral competence and what Terry Moe has called "responsive competence"[58]—the imbalance being in favor of the latter.

Defenders of neutral competence have not denied that political responsiveness is a legitimate concern of the president, but they have argued that neutral competence has legitimate claims as well, and that these need to be protected when presidents decide to increase the number of political appointees to critical institutional positions in the EOP.[59] The reason is twofold. First, politicization has enormous costs when objective, professional advice may be submerged by the overriding pressures of personal loyalty to the president on the part of political appointees who are likely to be highly suspicious of career civil servants. Second, politicization poses risks to the longer-term interests of the presidency. Implicit in many post-Watergate critiques is the distinction between the president of the day and the presidency as a continuing institution of government. On the one hand, critics recognize that any incoming president has the right to organize his staff as he wishes, but, on the other hand, they argue that this freedom should not jeopardize the continuity of an office that has been temporarily inherited and that will be passed on to someone else in four or eight years' time.

Both of these concerns were highlighted in the report of the Price-Siciliano panel. At the beginning of the report, the panel asserted that the president needed a reliable base of nonpartisan, unbiased advice in order to exercise political management, and they strongly recommended that

> [t]he institutional staffs reporting to the president should have a highly professional ability to supply objective and factual information. This need is particularly stringent for those staffs responsible for policy development, administrative management and coordination, and budgeting.[60]

The report went on to note, with respect to the development of the EOP, that

> [t]here has been a pronounced shift away from the Brownlow Committee's recommendations that the Executive Office should be staffed heavily by career personnel. The Executive Office is thus deprived of people who are skilled in staff roles, experienced in government management and suited to lend continuity and consistency.[61]

The idea of a president being free to shape the EOP to his own design, yet at the same time being constrained by the longer-term interests of the presidency might appear to be internally contradictory. The post-Watergate critics did not resolve the contradiction; instead they tended to stress the long-term perspective. The Price-Siciliano panel stressed it heavily. In a section headed "A Strategy for Reform," the report said:

> Proposals for change in the Executive Office must recognize that the presidency is occupied by an individual with personal preferences, needs, interests and methods of operating. Formal designs for the Executive Office which go against the grain of this fundamental reality are useless.

Then, in what might easily be seen as an attempt to go against the grain of reality, the report continued:

> However, this country can no longer afford the luxury of a de novo educational process every time a new president assumes office. Whatever a president's personality, the Executive Office must be adjusted to the needs of constitutional government in the modern era. The internal arrangement and

staff resources of the Office must be able to serve a succession of presidents and to cope with continuing national problems.[62]

The reason presidents have not shared this commitment to the values of neutral competence is because, as Terry Moe has argued in an important contribution challenging the very assumptions of the neutral competence school, these long-standing beliefs about how presidents should behave are "entirely inconsistent with the way presidents have viewed their own incentives, resources, constraints."[63] Those incentives, according to Moe, are structured by the dynamics of political leadership and thus by political support and opposition, political strategy, and political tradeoffs.[64] Moe criticizes the reform literature for trying to resolve fundamentally political problems with fundamentally nonpolitical solutions, and for ignoring the potential positive contributions of politicization to the various components of presidential leadership.[65]

The gap between the political framework within which presidents operate and the rational-organization framework reformers would like to see imposed on the presidency is enormous. Reformers would close that gap by trying to persuade presidents to see the merits and virtues of an institutional perspective on the office they inherit. They have been trying to convince future occupants of the White House that management of the process of government must be their first priority, and, like Brownlow, many post-Watergate reformers have adopted a view of politics as management.

The management perspective is very evident in the Price-Siciliano report. Discussing the broad task ahead of it, the panel states that "we can begin to strengthen the forces of cohesion and integration in our political system by strengthening the capacity of the presidency for leadership. It is to this need that our report is addressed."[66] A few pages further on it claims that the presidency has now "acquired its own internal problems of governability."[67] Five pages later, in a statement about the nature of presidential power, the panel argues that

> of equal importance to the structure of the presidency are the skills which a given president brings to that office. These skills are inherently political ones, resting on such tangibles as "prestige," "leadership," and "influence" which can compensate for the weaknesses and accentuate the strengths of the president's statutory and constitutional powers. In short, the president is a political manager, as well as "chief executive" or "general manager." What counts in the long run is how well he manages the processes of politics.[68]

Thus, in a short space, terms like *leadership, governability,* and *influence* become by-products of *management,* and the nearest the panel comes to a definition of management is also a bold assertion of the primacy of management in politics.

> It is possible for a president to excel in weighing the pros and cons of each policy option, and yet have little continuing influence on the larger processes and working relationships of government. Most of the president's acts of decision are probably of far less importance than the way in which he works through others to meet the nation's needs. That, after all, is the real meaning of presidential management.[69]

Post-Watergate reformers have reacted to the growing politicization of the presidential branch by trying to persuade presidents to "think institutionally," urging them, in the words of Hugh Heclo, "to be sensitive to the idea that there is an organized life and value that is larger than the preferences of any individual or policies of the passing moment."[70] Had presidents themselves joined in the debate, this is a view they might well have been inclined to challenge. They would probably have pointed out that "organizational life and value" does not stir voters, nor does it show up in the opinion polls as an issue of pressing concern at election time, however much it ought to, nor is it what gets first-term presidents reelected. They might have reminded reformers that the three presidents who have done the most in this century to upset organizational life and values—Franklin Roosevelt, Richard Nixon, and Ronald Reagan—were all reelected in landslide victories. Presidents might also have emphasized that they operate within a political system that, from their perspective, is one of multiple centers of opposition to presidential power and that the constraints imposed by other political forces do not allow them the freedom to indulge in the kind of policy-making processes reformers have urged on them. Had presidents gotten involved in the debate over the post-Watergate presidency, they may have wondered why they were being criticized for not thinking institutionally when, from their perspective, the reformers were at fault by neglecting to think politically.

Had they engaged with the post-Watergate critics, presidents might also have challenged two underlying assumptions that the critics of politicization have made in their arguments. Experience would prompt them to question the notion that objective, expert advice from professionals is somehow superior to what they might receive from presidential appointees who are sensitive to the political needs of the president. Given the constraints they face, presidents would surely measure the advice given to them in terms of its utility, rather than its objective correctness, and such utility would depend on its political realism. Ultimately, advice is translated into presidential choices and decisions that are intensely political, and that is why responsive competence becomes more relevant to presidential needs than neutral competence as far as presidents themselves are concerned.

Presidents might also have been tempted to question the distinction reformers make between the president and the presidency, a distinction that is
vital to the arguments used against politicization and deinstitutionalization.
On one level, the distinction is perfectly intelligible because no individual
holds the office of president forever, and a fairly regular succession of presidents since 1789 gives meaning to the notion of the presidency. On any
other level, unless one is prepared to see the office of president as nothing
more than a clerkship, then the presidency is really a historical concept, tangible only in the sense of being the sum total of the leadership exercised by
present and former presidents. In other words, the presidency is what presidents have made of it, and therefore it is difficult to see how presidents
could make a meaningful distinction between how they structure their office
to serve their interests as president and how they structure their office to
serve the interests of the presidency. From the perspective of the president in
power, they are one and the same thing. What presidents choose to do as
president, they also do for the presidency because of what the presidency is.

Politicization of the institutional presidency has been a cause of concern
to post-Watergate reformers because it runs counter to so many of the classic textbook virtues of neutral competence. To a succession of presidents,
however, these virtues are found only in textbooks. In practice, neutral competence has not been what presidents have sought. Responsive competence,
achieved through politicization or deinstitutionalization, has, from their perspective, served them much better. Indeed, the gulf between the textbook
approach to staffing the presidency and the approach adopted by most postwar presidents is so great that one may be tempted to ask whether the institutionalized presidency, originally advocated by Brownlow fifty years ago,
has not just been a figment of the imagination of political scientists and public administrators. If it ever did exist, presidents have shown by their actions
that they have not been enamored of it and, more recently, have been inclined to bury it.

IMPROVING EFFICIENCY AND EFFECTIVENESS

The recent emphasis in the post-Watergate literature on enhancing the efficiency and effectiveness of the presidential branch is part of a more wide-
ranging concern about presidential leadership generated by the experience of
the Ford and Carter administrations. It is so wide-ranging, in fact, that some
critics talk of a crisis of the American presidency that can be resolved only
by radical reforms of the whole political system. James MacGregor Burns,
for example, has pleaded for "transforming leadership" to initiate party renewal and "moderate" constitutional change to meet "human needs and
wants," although the constitutional changes he advocates are anything but
moderate.[71] Theodore Sorensen is another radical reformer who has called

for a period of coalition government to break the political gridlock in the United States, a coalition Cabinet, president and vice president from different parties, a renunciation of partisanship from both parties, and a depoliticized president who would refuse to run for a second term.[72]

The Price-Siciliano report also speaks in the language of crisis. The panel shared with Burns and Sorensen major doubts about the capacity of the United States to govern itself in the 1980s. It, too, sees problems with the major features of the political system and it also thinks that reform must begin with the presidency.[73] But, unlike the agendas of Burns and Sorensen, the reform agenda of the Price-Siciliano panel is confined to what could be achieved by presidents themselves within the framework of the Executive Office of the President. In comparison with the kinds of changes that Burns and Sorensen demand, such reforms as those proposed by the Price-Siciliano panel may appear to be merely organizational, perhaps even trivial. They are, however, more typical of the post-Watergate approach to reform, more realizable than the grand designs put forward by Burns and Sorensen, and they focus attention on the problems of presidential staffing that tend to get shunted aside by the more radical reformers. For the moment then the Burns and Sorensen approaches must be put aside.

The effort to improve the efficiency and effectiveness of the presidential branch has two major strands running through it. First, it offers a set of proposals to refashion existing presidential staff units and establish new ones, and, second, it suggests redefining the role of the staff. Role definition has already been discussed in this chapter in the context of limiting staff power, but it is also a vital ingredient of the efficiency and effectiveness reforms and must be considered in that light as well.

There are numerous proposals for reforming the organization of the presidential branch to make it a more efficient and effective staff unit, and this, too, is an area where some broad measure of agreement exists among reformers about what needs to be done. The Price-Siciliano report provides a useful starting point, not only because it encapsulates the range of proposals canvased by post-Watergate reformers but also because it provides, as a preamble to its reform agenda, a concise statement of what it sees as the major inadequacies of the Executive Office of the President. The panel identifies eleven shortcomings, which can be summarized as follows:

1. The Executive Office is better attuned to the president's short-term political needs and crisis management than it is to longer-range policy and administrative considerations.
2. The shift away from Brownlow's recommendation that the EOP be staffed heavily by career civil servants has been detrimental from the point of view of consistency and continuity.
3. EOP staff have assumed decision-making powers that properly belong with the executive branch departments and agencies.

4. There is confusion in organization and responsibilities within the EOP and between the EOP and line agencies.
5. There are no reliable means for integrating the perspectives of EOP staff and those of the departments and agencies.
6. The division of the key EOP staff into the domestic policy staff and the National Security Council staff is ineffective.
7. Certain economic issues receive inadequate attention.
8. Policy and program coordination lack coherence and consistency.
9. Too many financial commitments are made independent of the budget process.
10. The managerial side of the work of OMB has been neglected.
11. The EOP has no provision for a staff concerned with long-range developments and planning.[74]

This list of defects in the EOP emphasizes efficiency and management problems more than questions of staff accountability and control. Only the third of the eleven faults identified focuses on the latter. What follows from this diagnosis is primarily a management-efficiency reform agenda built on to the earlier post-Watergate concerns about reducing the power of the presidential staff and bringing Cabinet officials back into the policy-making process. In this, the Price-Siciliano report has much in common with other prescriptions for reforming the presidential branch.

The absence of a long-range planning unit has been high on the list of weaknesses to be corrected. Presidents need help in setting priorities and overseeing the quality of planning and evaluation throughout the government, argues Cronin. He suggested that an Office of Planning and Program Evaluation be attached to what was, at the time of his writing, the Domestic Council and saw it as a "center for experimentation," a body that could test policies before they were implemented on a national scale.[75] Heineman and Hessler place more emphasis on long-term planning than on policy evaluation. They argue for a planning office to be located in OMB, staffed by professionals from the EOP and the departments. Their focus would be five to fifteen years ahead and they should be able to develop an agenda of longer-term policy priorities.[76] President Carter's Commission for a National Agenda for the Eighties thought similarly. It urged that the long-range policy analysis staff should be small, sufficiently close to the president to enhance its use, "but adequately removed to prevent its focus from becoming highly political." It suggested that the unit might emphasize "broad-gauged studies of the economy, energy problems and trends in the supply of natural resources" and should publish its studies in a manner that would attract wide readership.[77]

The approach adopted by the Price-Siciliano panel differed slightly. The panel hesitated to use the term *planning* because of the "exaggerated fears and misunderstandings" associated with the word. It proposed the establishment of a new office of policy research and analysis within the EOP and a separate program-evaluation staff to be located within the Office of Management and Budget.[78] A large part of the panel's discussion of long-term policy research was taken up countering an important objection to this proposal. The product of the future-oriented studies produced by this staff unit would not be plans for future policy, but reports on long-range trends in key policy areas. This, the panel argues, would dispel the fear presidents might have that policy goals and the policy agenda would be fixed by a "planning agency" inside the EOP, thus involving them in matters they would rather not be involved in. "We clearly intend this function to have no such effects," says the panel,[79] but whether or not intentions are enough of a guarantee to prevent what presidents fear could happen is an arguable point.

The possible objections to a long-term policy analysis unit go beyond the one that the Price-Siciliano panel has tried to head off. Neither the Price-Siciliano panel nor other reformers advocating a long-term policy analysis–planning unit have faced up to the question of incentives. If presidents naturally get locked into short-term policy considerations and crisis management, as many commentators have claimed, then one must ask what incentive exists for presidents to commit staff resources to projects geared to a time span beyond the end of their term of office. The existence of a long-term policy analysis staff cannot itself take the president out of the short-term perspective within which he operates, and long-term planning cannot anticipate the short-term pressures affecting decision making at the point at which the long term has been reached.

One response to such criticism might be that long-term policy analysts can offer valuable perspectives on immediate problems facing the president and that their labors would not be entirely for the benefit of the president's successors. Yet, if that is so, then it is difficult to imagine how the policy analysis staff could be confined to the role the Price-Siciliano panel has in mind. As soon as presidents open the door to long-range policy analysts, then that staff unit would have an interest in immediate policy decisions, and, presumably like any other staff unit in the EOP, it will fight to have its interest heard. When that happens, the results of long-range policy research inevitably become the policy goals of at least that section of the presidential staff. One can easily understand the dilemma facing any president seriously considering such a proposal. From his perspective, this is a case of what may be good for the presidency is not necessarily good for the president, and it is interesting to note that the Price-Siciliano recommendation for a policy research and analysis staff begins with the words, "The Executive Office of the President needs institutionalized arrangements for longer term policy research and analysis."[80] It does not say "the president needs...."

The publication of the Price-Siciliano report, with its strong support for a long-term policy analysis staff in the EOP, coincided with the beginning of the Reagan administration, which was not only unimpressed and unpersuaded by such proposals but was committed to taking the presidential branch in the opposite direction. Reagan established what a former policy analyst in the EOP, Walter Williams, has labeled an "anti-analytic presidency," marked by a deleterious decline in institutional analytic capacity throughout the executive branch, especially within the EOP where ideological commitment and rigidity had replaced rigorous policy analysis.[81] Moreover, Williams argues that faulty policy analysis during the Reagan years led directly to policy failures, of which the ballooning budget deficit, the Iran-*contra* affair, and the savings-and-loan scandal were just three examples. Ten years after the publication of Price-Siciliano, Williams was pleading even more strongly for a major institutional fix for the EOP in which a greatly enhanced policy-analysis capacity was one of the organizing principles of his approach to reform.[82]

Until the advent of the Clinton administration, many post-Watergate reformers drew attention to the absence from the EOP of an economic affairs staff to coordinate the economic policy process and recommended that such a staff should be established, headed by a White House assistant or economic policy coordinator. Almost all the proposals stressed that this new staff ought to be a secretariat concerned only with process management and not another group of substantive economists duplicating the work of the Council of Economic Advisers, the Office of Management and Budget, and the Treasury.[83] The model many of the reformers have in mind is President Ford's Economic Policy Board.

The argument in favor of a new economic affairs staff is expressed in terms of bringing coherence to an incoherent policy-making system. That incoherence, critics believed, derived from what was observed to be the uncoordinated input of a large number of economic policy advisers around the president and their inability to integrate the economic aspects of domestic and foreign economic policy.[84]

Because the proposed economic affairs staff was to be a coordinating body and not an advisory body, it was not seen by post-Watergate reformers as a threat to the Council of Economic Advisers (CEA). Some writers even suggested that the existence of an economic affairs secretariat could actually enhance the work of the CEA by reducing its involvement in matters that are not central to its purposes. The Price-Siciliano panel identifies these as "including microeconomic and sectoral issues and the specific economic implications of agency policies and programs."[85] It should be noted, however, that some of the reformers think the CEA ought not to be located in the Executive Office at all. Heineman and Hessler have claimed that the council's "narrow base in academia" is no longer sufficiently sturdy to support a lead role in presidential economic policy making, and although they recognize that it will not be moved to the Treasury, that is where they think the council ought to be located.[86] Bradley Nash also suggests that the Treasury, if not a new Department of Economic Affairs, should be the home of the CEA on the grounds that its present location makes it hard to avoid the suspicion that the council's prognostications and recommendations "may sometimes be related to the President's political needs or programs."[87] Presumably, Nash believes that the CEA's objectivity is compromised by its proximity to the president, but one wonders how far its usefulness would be compromised if much more of its work were unrelated to the president's needs.

The success of a new economic affairs staff, as proposed by the post-Watergate reformers, would depend, in part, on the prior removal of two obstacles inherent in the presidential policy-making process. First, the attainment of greater coherence in economic policy making would require that the president's foreign policy advisers treat international economic policy issues as matters of *economic* rather than *foreign* policy and be willing to let international economic policy problems be resolved through the economic policy channel rather than the foreign policy–national security channel. What likelihood is there of this happening? The interrelatedness of domestic and foreign economic policy became a fact of life in the late 1970s and the 1980s, and by the end of that decade, the collapse of the Soviet Union, the end of the Cold War, and the attempt to define "a new world order" have strengthened that connection even further. Yet the specialized division of labor in the White House is incongruent with the changing nature of economic policy. As long as foreign policy advice comes from foreign policy specialists with an international perspective on political problems, one can see little possibility that they would look at foreign economic policy as economic policy first and foreign policy second. This, of course, does not mean that major problems with both domestic and foreign policy implications could not be resolved within the presidential branch, but it does mean that the creation of a new economic policy coordinating staff could be guaranteed to alter the perspectives through which senior advisers come at economic policy issues.

The second question that would have to be resolved before an economic policy staff could begin to operate successfully is: Where does one draw the dividing line between domestic policy and economic policy? When the Domestic Policy Staff has been prominent in White House policy deliberations, as it was during the Carter years under Stuart Eizenstat, it has had a major voice in economic policy. If economic policy is handed over to an economic affairs staff, what then is left for the domestic affairs staff? Can domestic policy be considered in any meaningful way by one group when economic policy is handled by another? The answer will not be found in the reform literature because reformers do not explore the nexus adequately. One senses that many reformers think in terms of the primacy of economic policy and a downgrading of the domestic affairs staff, which might offer one solution. Otherwise, the artificial distinction between economic and domestic policy, a distinction to be cemented in two separate presidential staff units, remains a problematic one, especially in view of the politically competitive environment within which presidential staff operate. Although there is a possibility that greater coherence in policy making might result from the establishment of an economic affairs staff, it is also conceivable that new sets of interests and perspectives may become attached to this additional bureaucratic layer in the EOP, interests contrary to, and in competition with, other staff units. That, in turn, lessens the prospects for coherence.

The new economic affairs staff, as it emerges from the post-Watergate reform literature, is meant to stand alongside the domestic affairs staff and foreign affairs staff to form the major policy coordinating units in a restructured EOP. The reformers have little to say about the domestic affairs staff, more or less accepting the way this unit has evolved since President Nixon created the Domestic Council in 1970. Heineman and Hessler suggest that the assistant for domestic affairs and his small support staff confine their attention to about thirty-five major domestic policy initiatives and not try to manage the whole range of interagency domestic policy problems.[88] The reformers also express the hope that a more institutional domestic affairs unit might emerge, staffed with some career professionals who would be able to transcend changes of administration,[89] but little else is to be altered. The NSC staff, on the other hand, ought to be replaced by a new international affairs staff, according to the Price-Siciliano panel and President Carter's National Agenda Commission. Both groups saw the new name as a useful way of emphasizing that the international affairs staff ought not to be the policy advocate and policy maker that the NSC staff has been in the past. The Price-Siciliano panel goes further, arguing that the new name will point to a broader frame of reference for the international affairs staff, broader than the predominantly political and military concerns of the NSC staff. The proposed new international affairs staff would focus on economic, social, and cultural matters as well.[90]

The idea of a new economic policy staff surfaced again most recently in a series of recommendations for reorganizing U.S. government put together jointly by the Carnegie Endowment for International Peace and the Institute for International Economics and presented in the form of a memorandum of advice to President-elect Clinton (see pages 64–65). Whether the arguments from these two prominent Washington think tanks persuaded the new president, or whether its recommendations merely coincided with his own thinking on the structure of policy advice, is not known, but President Clinton did move swiftly to establish precisely the kind of economic policy staff that the Carnegie-IIE report, along with many other post-Watergate reformers, had suggested. Clinton's National Economic Council was intended to be a coordinating body that would integrate domestic and economic policy advice and link domestic economic policy with foreign economic policy in the White House (see pages 66–67). If the new structure works as intended, it will vindicate at least one part of the post-Watergate reform effort and stand as one of the few instances where the reformers and the president have been on the same wavelength. It is, however, too early to assess the impact of Clinton's National Economic Council and make a judgment on whether it has fulfilled the hopes of those who have pondered the problem of coherence in the economic policy-making process. At the time of writing, too little is known about how the National Economic Council staff works with other EOP units, especially the National Security Council and the Domestic Council staffs, primarily because the fluidity and flexibility of staff organization in the Clinton White House make it extraordinarily difficult to isolate the impact of one particular staff unit designed specifically to integrate its work with other staff units, and vice versa.

Reformers have also suggested a new staff unit to assist the president in the area of intergovernmental affairs. They have in mind something more than the present White House intergovernmental affairs staff who liaise with state and local government leaders. What the reformers would like to see is a presidential staff to oversee and coordinate federal government programs at the state and local levels, given the inability of the executive branch departments and agencies to do this successfully themselves. The boldest proposal comes from James MacGregor Burns, who recommends the establishment of presidential agencies "in several hundred regions throughout the country," working directly under the supervision of the president "to integrate all government policies, federal, state, and local, that relate to priority areas."[91]

Thomas Cronin has noted some objections to this proposal, principally related to the ease with which a regionalized or localized presidential staff could be politicized to accommodate powerful state and local leaders, but he believes, nonetheless, that some innovation along these lines is warranted and that presidents ought to give substantial attention to this matter.[92]

The Price-Siciliano panel recommends a new "federal assistance administration staff," located in OMB and built on OMB's existing but inadequate intergovernmental affairs staff, which at present "lacks the necessary mandate and resources" to deal with the management of federal assistance programs. Like Cronin, the panel recognizes the political difficulties inherent in this area. "The federal assistance structure has become the new form of political patronage," it claims, asserting that any significant improvement in the management of federal aid to the states would require "a firm commitment from the president and Congress."[93]

Even if the president and Congress gave that commitment, there could be no assurance that the new staff unit would succeed where other attempts have failed. The problem of managing federalism today is enormous, and discussion of it is beyond the scope of this book, but even the most casual observer of federal-state relations would hesitate to predict the success of any particular institutional response to a very complex political problem. To some extent, the proposal has also been overtaken by events. Both the Reagan and Bush administrations chose to tackle the problems of federalism by loosening federal control over the states and localities, and the proposal to create a new federal assistance staff was directly at odds with that policy. It is also at odds with the President Clinton's attitude to federal-state relationships,[94] and his commitment to reduce the size of the presidential staff by 25 percent. One might also question the consistency of this particular proposal with other aspects of the post-Watergate reform agenda because no other suggested reform would have a greater capacity than this one to take the presidential staff into the business of policy implementation and into the areas that departments and agencies see as their responsibility. Rather than help reduce tensions between the departments and agencies and the presidential staff, the proposal for a federal assistance administration staff would be guaranteed to exacerbate the situation.

The reason that the Price-Siciliano panel wanted to locate its proposed new federal assistance administration staff in the Office of Management and Budget is because it saw the unit as part of a coherent package of reforms designed to improve the management functions of the presidential branch, with OMB as the natural home. The Price-Siciliano panel gives greater attention to reform of OMB than most other post-Watergate reformers. It makes specific recommendations to improve OMB's budgetary process, administrative management capability, program evaluation, and regulatory decision making, in addition to improving the administration of intergovernmental assistance.[95] Perhaps the panel's particular emphasis on OMB can partly be explained by the management background of twenty-three of its twenty-six members, nine of them having served in the Bureau of the Budget.

One final area in which reformers are agreed on the need for change is at the very core of the White House Office itself. They call for a new White House secretariat to manage the routines of the president and the EOP. The Price-Siciliano panel emphasizes that this secretariat would not be engaged in substantive decision making, "but would be entirely process-oriented." The staff would be small, about fifteen members, and of the highest caliber. It would be professional, discreet, self-effacing, impartial yet politically sensitive, and committed to an effective presidency.[96] In short, it is the same recommendation that Brownlow made forty years earlier when he proposed that six executive assistants be added to the president's personal staff. Stephen Hess differs slightly from the mainstream in this regard. Because he believes that the Cabinet must be the focal point of the presidential staff system, he sees the secretariat as a Cabinet secretariat, linking the president and his Cabinet, instead of dividing them, as existing senior White House aides tend to do.[97] For the most part, however, the reformers are concerned with efficiency, more so than accountability, when they promote a new White House secretariat, and they see in that proposal some hope of maintaining continuity and institutional memory when the presidency changes hands from one president to another.

Organizational reforms such as those considered here, are complemented in the literature by behavioral reform proposals that aim to redefine the role of the presidential staff. Previously, these proposals were discussed in the context of reducing staff power vis-à-vis members of the president's Cabinet, but they now also need to be considered as a vital element in the debate on improving the efficiency and rationality of the presidential decision-making process. The essence of the argument is that presidents need a member or members of their staff to manage the diversity of views on any given matter so that all views, including unpopular ones, get a fair hearing. The advisory process needs to be supervised by a neutral, objective, nonpartisan assistant whose job is to ensure that the president does not receive an unbalanced view of policy issues. The staff assistant performing this function has variously been described, as noted before, as a "facilitator," "honest broker," "process manager," or, what Alexander George has called the "custodian-manager."

George has offered the most sophisticated and systematic statement on the need for a custodian in the policy-making process.[98] The custodial role is a vital part of his multiple-advocacy model of presidential policy making. Multiple advocacy is a prescriptive theory that, among other things, requires a manager "to create the basis for structured, balanced debate among policy advocates drawn from different parts of the organization," so that diverse views can be harnessed "in the interests of rational policy making."[99]

The custodian is specifically charged with a number of tasks necessary to achieve a structured and balanced presentation of views to the president. The custodian needs to ensure that there is no major maldistribution of resources among the various actors in the policy-making process so that the power, influence, and competence, or the analytical, bargaining, or persuasive skills, of any one advocate will not distort the substance of issues. The point here is that the most effectively presented policy option might not necessarily be the best policy option.[100] Where there exists maldistribution of resources among those advocating policy options, it is the job of the custodian to try to strengthen the resources of the weaker advocates. The custodian must also make sure that unpopular options are presented to the president, that the president is never dependent on a single channel of advice, that arguments presented to the president are independently evaluated, and, finally, that the operation of the policy-making process is monitored constantly so that possible malfunctions can be identified and corrected.[101] Some dangerous malfunctions of the advisory process relating to postwar national security decision making are discussed at length by George.[102]

To perform the custodian-manager role, the presidential assistant appointed to the job must avoid potential role conflicts. The custodian cannot be a policy adviser, policy advocate, or spokesperson for the administration on behalf of existing policy. Those roles would compromise the integrity of the custodial role. Neither can the custodian be what George calls a watchdog concerned with the president's personal power stakes. Enhancing the president's political influence and safeguarding the multiple-advocacy process also do not mix. Nor do responsibility for implementing policy decisions and managing multiple advocacy combine satisfactorily.[103]

Alexander George sees the custodian role as critical to the effective performance of presidential policy making. In his multiple-advocacy model, not all presidential staff would be custodians. Presidents would still need advisers and advocates, spokespersons, implementers, and political managers on their staffs, but they would also need a custodian to carry out a vital staff function that is currently not being performed. George originally developed the multiple-advocacy prescription in the context of foreign policy making. It was subsequently extended by Roger Porter to fit the economic policy arena as well,[104] and there is no obvious reason why it should not be equally relevant to any other major area of presidential decision making. Not all post-Watergate reformers have taken up George's multiple-advocacy system in its entirety, and there have been doubts expressed about it, but popular post-Watergate notions of presidential staffers as facilitators, honest brokers, or process managers, are derivative of, and variations on, George's multiple-advocacy custodian.

I.M. Destler is one who has had reservations about Alexander George's notion of the custodian. Destler argues that any prescriptive theory that concentrates on role definition but neglects to show how the key actor (in this case, the custodian) can develop the leverage needed to play the role effectively will be incomplete. In this respect, Destler sees problems with George's custodian because presidential staffers who have acquired power and leverage have done so by playing precisely those roles George claims are incompatible with that of the custodian. According to Destler, the custodian would still need considerable leverage to carry out his functions successfully, but the purity of his role deprives him of the very means by which powerful presidential aides have acquired leverage in the past. Given this dilemma, Destler sees a real danger that the custodian "would rapidly be reduced to an isolated spokesman for rationality."[105]

Whether or not one accepts Destler's reservations, and Alexander George certainly does not,[106] Destler has raised important questions about the relationships between any redefinition of presidential staff roles and the internal political behavior of the presidential branch. Such questions have implications for all variants of the custodian function espoused in the post-Watergate reform literature, not just George's version. Custodians, honest brokers, facilitators, or process managers, however their role is defined, will need leverage and strong backing from the president to overcome the built-in competitiveness and conflict between presidential advocates and the possibility that those who have leverage will use it to bypass what in effect will be a new regulatory mechanism at the highest level of government.

The post-Watergate variants of George's custodian are diluted versions of the one general approach. They are less specific in defining the task of the manager and less ambitious in what they hope it might achieve, but they all see the need for senior staff to manage the process of policy advice to ensure that the president is presented with balanced and carefully examined policy options. But, then, of course, Brownlow's staff system was designed with much the same purpose in mind some fifty years ago.

REFORM, REFORMERS, AND PRESIDENTS

The organization of the presidential branch is by no means the only aspect of the presidency to have occupied the minds of political scientists during the post-Watergate period. In fact, the political science of the American presidency has made greater advances during the past two decades than at any other time in the twentieth century. It has now broken the bounds of its traditional institutional prescriptive preoccupations and has been enriched by interdisciplinary insights, such as those provided by Barber and Buchanan,[107] by an expanding number of empirical studies of presidential decision making,[108] by the application of quantitative techniques of analysis,[109] by the utilization of comparative perspectives,[110] and by increasing concern about the future direction of this subfield of American government.[111] There has never been as much variety in the study of the presidency as there is today.

Notwithstanding these developments, the institutional prescriptive approach still dominates the field, and there always seems to be a market for new proposals to reform the American presidency. Watergate was just one of the many events of this century that have stimulated prescriptive writing, and neither is it the most recent. The bicentennial of the U.S. Constitution provided the excuse for unleashing yet another batch of reform proposals.[112] From the 1940s onward, the institution of the presidency has had little respite from political scientists with a persistent urge to change it.

Prescriptions for change come in three sizes. The first is the grand design, necessitating substantial changes in the way American politics is conducted and, often, major constitutional revision. Under this heading, one would include the Burns and Sorensen proposals mentioned earlier, Theodore Lowi's pleas for a multiparty system "to give the presidency more of a party base than it has had in the modern era,"[113] and the variants of the Westminster model espoused by Charles M. Hardin and Lloyd Cutler as alternatives to the separation of powers.[114] Such schemes are bold, radical, sometimes ingenious, and often very effective ways of highlighting weaknesses in the existing state of the presidency, but only the most optimistic of optimists would have much hope that these proposals could ever become reality. They are destined to remain on the drawing board forever.

A second category offers less sweeping proposals for change, but ones that would require, at the least, cooperation and agreement between president and Congress to initiate them and, in most instances, a constitutional amendment to put them into effect. Here one would include the item veto, the nonrenewable six-year presidential term of office, a presidential-congressional team ticket, and the inclusion of members of Congress in the Cabinet. All of these would operate within the existing constitutional separation-of-powers structure, although the last one is inconsistent with the separation-of-powers doctrine, and none could be classed as a radical change to the Constitution, even though some would necessitate amending it. These proposals are also destined to remain on the drawing board. Advocates of such changes have yet to gain any degree of popular backing for their ideas and have even been unable to forge a consensus of elite opinion behind their plans. For every supporter of the single six-year presidential term, for example, there seems to be another advocating the repeal of the Twenty-Second Amendment's two-term limitation. Opinion is also divided over the item veto, even though that particular constitutional reform is now linked with the very real political and economic problems of the appalling budget deficit in the United States.[115] The proposal to seat legislators in the president's Cabinet, and the related plan to put Cabinet members in Congress, have been around in various forms for most of this century. Lack of consensus and popular support for these proposals would be only the first hurdle on the road to implementation. The process of amending the Constitution itself is a major obstacle. The Founding Fathers made it so easy to defeat a proposed constitutional amendment and so difficult to get one passed.

The third group of reforms are those that an incumbent president could initiate without reference to the other branches of government or to the constitutional amending process, and most of the reforms considered in this chapter would fall into this category. It would not need the approval of Congress for the president to operate a multiple-advocacy advisory system, nor would it take a constitutional amendment for the president to establish a long-range policy planning staff. All that is needed is presidential will. These are microchanges compared with the macroreforms proposed by Burns, Sorensen, Lowi, and Hardin, and it is no wonder that the reformers who operate at this level must see much more hope of achieving their goals. All they need to do is to persuade the president of the need for change.

There is no doubt that some of the reformers who operate at this level are in the business of trying to persuade presidents and are not merely writing to stimulate debate among university students and faculty on the structures of American government. Ben Heineman and Curtis Hessler's 400-page reform proposal was written in the style of its title, *Memorandum for the President*. The reader of the book becomes a privileged intruder on the private advice that these two former officials were offering to President Carter's successor.

The Price-Siciliano report was also no mere academic exercise. The National Academy of Public Administration's announcement of the project in April 1980 made clear that this was to be a report to the president and Congress, and it promised that preliminary findings would be made available to the presidential candidates after the party conventions in August.[116] Furthermore, the academy's press release tacitly implied that the report would stand alongside the Brownlow, Hoover, Heineman, and Ash reports as a major document on the organization of the presidency, although, of course, it is distinguished from its illustrious predecessors by virtue of the fact that it originated as a private undertaking by an impartial body and was not initiated at the behest of the president or Congress. The National Academy gained the endorsements of Presidents Ford and Carter for the project, received financial backing from several large corporations and foundations, and put together a panel and research staff that constituted the most distinguished group to have considered the problems of presidential management since the team that Roosevelt put together under Brownlow. The effort made by the National Academy to boost the status of the report prior to its completion was perhaps a necessary act to elevate the document above the mass of reform-oriented literature published since Watergate and make the president of the United States sit up and listen.

Making presidents listen to reform proposals is difficult at the best of times, but because there is an oversupply of prescriptive literature, those who want to influence the future shape of the presidency now seem to require entrepreneurial skills to sell their wares in the marketplace. Reformers now have to organize to promote and broker reform proposals. In 1982, a Committee for a Single Six-Year Presidential Term was established with financial backing to press for the adoption of this particular proposal by the bicentennial year of 1987.[117] A broader range of reforms was also being promoted by the Committee on the Constitutional System, cochaired by Lloyd Cutler, Douglas Dillon, and Senator Nancy Kassebaum, and supported by the Dillon Fund and other foundations. Although many of the proposals advanced by these groups have been around for a long time, the difference in the post-Watergate era is that reformers are now attempting to turn those proposals into issues and have them placed on the political agenda. Reforming the presidency is no longer just a matter of diagnosing ills and discovering remedies, but seems to have become a political activity requiring organization, financial backing, group pressure, and the obligatory Washington names behind it all.

What, then, of presidential responses to post-Watergate ideas about the role and function of the presidential staff? How successful were the promoters of these microreforms in persuading presidents to do what they alone had the capacity to do without requiring the prior endorsement of the Congress or the American people? The short answer is that they were not very successful at all. Post-Watergate presidents have turned a deaf ear to the reformers, even to the Price-Siciliano panel, which made such an effort to promote its product and so well encapsulated the post-Watergate perspective on the presidential branch. None of the major themes or recommended reforms that have emerged from the numerous reviews of the operation of the presidential staff system were adopted by Presidents Carter, Reagan, or Bush. In fact, all three presidents steered the presidential branch in the opposite direction. To date, President Clinton has not shown a great deal of interest in the structures of the presidency either, and with one exception—the creation of the National Economic Council—has ignored what the post-Watergate reformers have been pleading with post-Watergate presidents to do.

In the years since Watergate, presidents have shown little desire to reverse the centralization of power in the White House; neither have they made any effort to depoliticize the presidential branch. Ideas about neutral competence, institutional continuity, and objective professional advice seem to have had little impact on Carter, Reagan, or Bush despite the fact that a powerful and politicized White House staff got each of them into trouble. Moreover, the trend toward assuring responsive competence in the presidential branch has now been extended to the executive branch. President Carter laid the groundwork with the Civil Service Reform Act of 1978, which established the Senior Executive Service, and that in turn gave President Reagan the opportunity to open up the highest levels of the bureaucracy to a significantly greater number of political appointees. When this was combined, as it was, with the overriding requirement of loyalty to Reagan's policies and values as a precondition of appointment to an executive position, it enabled President Reagan to exert greater influence over the bureaucracy than most of his immediate predecessors were able to do.[118]

Proposals for rational and more efficient decision-making structures have not fared any better. The principal developments in the organization of the presidential staff since Nixon's departure have been related to the outreach and promotional functions, rather than to policy making. For the most part, and with the exception of President Clinton's economic policy staff, it is in the public relations area that new staffs have been created, not in areas where post-Watergate critics identified structural weaknesses. As for multiple advocacy, that remains firmly in the realm of abstract theory. It is interesting to contrast the vision of the multiple-advocacy theorists with the reality of the advisory process in the Reagan White House as described by David Stockman in his controversial memoir. Stockman relates how he and Murray Weidenbaum, then chairman of the Council of Economic Advisers, produced a critical forecast of economic growth and inflation at the beginning of 1981 after a seemingly irreconcilable difference between the two. Stockman writes that, on 7 February, "we made the worst possible bargain. If he'd agree to keep the real growth rate 'reasonably high,' I would go along with whatever inflation figure he thought he could live with as a professional economist." Stockman then says that this compromise added an extra $700 billion to the forecast gross national product over five years and an extra $200 billion in "phantom revenues."[119] So much for rational economic policy making in the White House!

As more becomes known about the Bush administration, that might provide the best example of the problems of implementing multiple advocacy in the White House. Roger Porter, who had written extensively about multiple advocacy and the need for an honest broker on the president's staff, had the rare opportunity to translate academic theories into reality when he was appointed as President Bush's assistant for economic and domestic policy. By most accounts, Porter did just this during his four years in charge of the Office of Policy Development. But, in some of the most recent accounts, written by frustrated, conservative policy activists in the Bush White House, Roger Porter has emerged as a major target for criticism, at the core of which is Porter's conception of his role as an honest broker in the policy-making process. In a brutal and severe account of Porter's performance, his deputy in the Office of Policy Development, Charles Kolb, has written:

> Porter evidently saw his role in the Bush Administration as that of managing the process, not advocating any particular approach, outcome, or direction. His Reagan Administration predecessors, on the other hand, had been *zealous* partisans in developing policies that reflected Ronald Reagan's governing principles. Since Bush himself lacked a concrete domestic vision, Porter was left with virtually nothing to manage except the discrete assignments his superiors asked him to undertake.... Porter was ... an apparatchik whose passion was process. Some members of his staff joked occasionally about printing lapel buttons saying "Born to Process" and then wearing them around the White House and Old Executive Office Building corridors. When it came to substance, on the other hand, he was so reticent as to be literally a nonplayer.

Kolb, himself a policy activist with obviously little patience for multiple-advocacy theories, concluded that "Porter's honest-broker mentality left him wholly at the mercy of more ambitious and aggressive players like OMB's Darman (and Darman's chief aides) or William Reilly, the Administrator of the Environmental Protection Agency."[120] John Podhoretz, who came from the same stable as Kolb, similarly blames Porter in his recent account of the Bush presidency. "The position of domestic policy adviser," he writes, "was one of almost limitless possibility. Unfortunately, Porter proved a man of almost infinite limits. At a time when the Republican party was in a wild ferment of new ideas and policies in fields from education to welfare, Porter proved singularly uninterested in the ideas and instead obsessed over detail—not what to do, but how to do it."[121]

These two accounts are written from a passionate and one-sided perspective and neither attempts to explain things from Porter's viewpoint; that was not their intention. Yet, although neither author analyses Porter's role as an academic political scientist might have done, both have provided a useful illustration of just how inhospitable a highly politicized White House can be toward the concept and practice of multiple advocacy. I.M. Destler's fears that a custodian or honest broker might "rapidly be reduced to an isolated spokesman for rationality" (see page 226), may well have found some empirical foundation in the experiences of Roger Porter during the Bush presidency.

The only concession made by Carter and Reagan to post-Watergate reformers was a small reduction in the total size of the presidential staff, but some of the Carter reductions were achieved by sleight of hand (e.g., by transferring the White House Office administrative staff to a new Office of Administration), and none of the reductions could be called significant in regard to their effect on the role and function of the presidential branch. In any case, the proposal to reduce the size of the staff was the weakest part of the post-Watergate critique, and as has been suggested throughout this book, staff size itself is not such a critical element of the problems of the presidential branch. Unfortunately, as the 1992 presidential election demonstrated, pledging to reduce the size of the presidential staff has now become a popular, convenient, and uncontroversial ingredient of campaign rhetoric to persuade voters that presidents, or presidents-to-be, will deal seriously with the complex problems of how an expanding presidential branch fits into the framework of American government.

Why, then, have post-Watergate presidents and their advisers been so unresponsive to suggestions for reforming the presidential branch, and why have they been so determined to take it in a direction contrary to the one reformers have advocated? Could it be that they have been unaware of all the discussion during the past decade over the role and function of the presidential staff? Hardly likely, given the professional efforts made to promote reform blueprints in recent years. Could it be disdain for the whole notion of institutional reform because it serves to distract from issues of policy and politics? Again, an implausible explanation given the positive response of past presidents to reform proposals. Franklin Roosevelt adopted the Brownlow report without hesitation. Lyndon Johnson attempted to implement the recommendations of the Heineman Commission, and President Nixon used the Ash Commission report as the basis of his administrative strategy.[122] President Carter's reform panel, the President's Commission for a National Agenda for the Eighties, reported too late in his term for the one-term president to act on its recommendations. So presidents have responded to reform proposals before, but they were responding to reform proposals from bodies they themselves had established, which does suggest that there is an important difference between internally initiated reform efforts and those being generated beyond the gates of the White House.

The more likely explanation for the unresponsiveness of post-Watergate presidents to the post-Watergate reform agenda is simply that those proposals were of little use to them. Presidents and reformers are fundamentally at odds with one another over the very basis on which the reformers have argued their case. There is obviously something about being president that makes one see virtues in politicizing the EOP and centralizing power in the White House. Equally, Cabinet government and rational decision-making processes have little appeal to the one person who counts. The way in which a succession of post-Brownlow presidents have behaved in office shows that they remain unconvinced by the arguments of reformers such as those who have been prominent since Watergate. The way reformers continue to advocate remedies that are contrary to clear and continuing trends in the development of the presidential branch shows that they have yet to come to terms with the reality of the presidential perspective on the presidency.

7. THE PRESIDENTIAL BRANCH AND THE FRAMEWORK OF AMERICAN GOVERNMENT

The development of the presidential branch has been remarkably rapid and consequent on profound changes in the wider political environment. Undoubtedly it has been one of the most significant innovations within the framework of American government over the past fifty years. The presidential branch is now a structurally complex, functionally sophisticated, and politically powerful unit operating at the very heart of the governmental process and has clearly expanded the president's capacity for leadership. In three critical areas—management of the executive branch, political outreach, and policy formulation—the presidential branch has enabled presidents to do things they would otherwise be unable to do on their own, and without such assistance, the modern presidency would be a perilously weak institution. For that very reason, few would want to deny that the presidential branch has a necessary function and legitimate role in the structure of American government.

There has never been much dispute about the necessity for an Executive Office of the President. It was a constant theme in many of the early writings on the post-Brownlow staff system,[1] and no one has seriously argued since then that the president would be better off without such help. But political scientists have been rather more uncertain about the legitimacy of the presidential staff in the structure of government, and doubts on this score predate Watergate.[2] From the early days of the EOP, there has been a lurking suspicion in the minds of political scientists that the presidential staff could become an awkward and potentially dangerous body. By the time of Watergate, those suspicions were no longer lurking but were being articulated publicly by political scientists and by many outside the profession.

The presidential staff occupies an ambivalent position within the framework of American government. Constitutionally, it can only be regarded as an extension of the president, having no separate identity of its own. It does the president's bidding as though the president were doing it himself, and, unlike some other divisions of the executive branch, the presidential staff has no statutory or constitutional obligations to any other branch of government beyond those specifically laid on the president. Ultimately, the president himself is answerable for the activities of his staff. The staff are "the president's 'arms' and 'fingers' " to aid in performing his constitutional duty to see "that the laws are faithfully executed," claimed Chief Justice Warren Burger in his dissenting opinion in *Harlow v. Fitzgerald*.[3]

This literal view of the place of the presidential staff within the constitutional framework of American government finds its clearest expression in the doctrine of executive privilege, a practical manifestation of the immunity that shields the president's immediate staff from the usual application of congressional oversight, and a vindication in Watergate, where President Nixon's resignation had a lot to do with what staff assistants did in his name and on his behalf.

On the other hand, the presidential staff also has a life of its own. Its senior members become well-known public figures. They are perceived to be influential and powerful operators at the center of decision making. They are seen to be instrumental in setting the tone and direction of presidential policy, not simply automatons responding to every presidential direction without question. Senior presidential staffers may sometimes disregard presidential instructions when their judgments of what is in the best interests of the president conflict with his, and they certainly exercise a degree of discretion in the way they execute their functions. Many of the more recent criticisms of the presidential staff reflect the notion of the staff having a separate identity. For example, the staff is often accused of bringing problems into the White House that do not properly belong there, an indication of the independent initiative residing with the staff, and of isolating the president from the outside world, a testimony to the control and gatekeeping powers of the staff. The separate identity of the presidential staff is also apparent when presidents are sometimes forced to repudiate what staffers have said publicly in the name of the president and, on the odd occasion, when staffers have actually repudiated their own president. For example, just one month before the 1992 presidential election, Richard Darman, director of the Office of Management and Budget, was quoted in the *Washington Post* contradicting President Bush's recanting of his decision to raise taxes as part of the 1990 budget deal with Congress. Darman called Bush's recantation "sheer idiocy" that could not be justified "intellectually and morally."[4] There have also been occasions when the presidential staff, rather than the president, is held responsible when things go wrong at the highest level of American government. President Reagan's controversial decision to visit the German military cemetery at Bitburg, which contained the graves of forty-nine members of Hitler's storm troopers, was one example of blame being laid on the staff, irrespective of the fact that the president approved of, and later defended, the decision.[5] Finally, it must also be emphasized that, notwithstanding their vantage point and proximity to the president, presidential aides must compete for the attention of the president along with other influential elites in Washington.

The Supreme Court has also recognized the separate identity of the presidential staff, although that recognition was not entirely free of the ambivalence associated with attempts to locate the staff in the constitutional scheme of things. In 1982 the Court reversed the findings of the Court of Appeals for the District of Columbia in two related cases regarding the dismissal of an employee of the Department of the Air Force and his subsequent legal action against President Nixon and two of Nixon's White House staff members. Ernest Fitzgerald had lost his job shortly after testifying before the Joint Economic Committee of Congress about cost overruns on the C5A transport plane. After lengthy litigation, his appeal against the dismissal was successful and he subsequently filed an action for damages against former President Nixon and against Bryce Harlow and Alexander Butterfield, two Nixon aides, who, Fitzgerald claimed, participated in a conspiracy to violate his constitutional and statutory rights. In *Nixon v. Fitzgerald*,[6] the Court held that the president was entitled to absolute immunity from damages liability for acts committed during his tenure in office, but in *Harlow v. Fitzgerald* the Court ruled that White House aides were not to be treated like the president and were not entitled to blanket protection of immunity from damages.[7]

There can be no question about the legitimacy of the existence of a presidential staff. There is no way that the mere existence of a staff is contrary to the spirit of the Constitution and, of course, the Executive Office of the President was established under the authority of statute law and is regularly sanctioned by Congress through the appropriations process. The question of legitimacy arises over what the presidential staff does, not over its right to exist. Implicit in much of the post-Watergate critique is the notion that staff involvement in presidential decision making beyond a certain point is illegitimate; that point being where the staff begins to usurp the authority of the heads of departments and reduce the capacity of Congress to hold decision makers accountable.

Such doubts about the proper role of the presidential branch also arise in part because the presidential branch is not anchored in the Constitution as firmly as the legislative and judicial branches, or even the executive branch. But to reiterate a point made at the beginning of this book, its political prominence derives from a vacuum in the Constitution relating to how and from whom presidents seek advice and assistance. By not writing into the Constitution any provision for a presidential advisory mechanism, the Founding Fathers ensured that presidents would be free to determine who they consult and who they use to help them exercise executive power. In a sense, therefore, the constitutional weakness of the presidential branch has also been a source of its political strength and its power within the American system of government.

That does not mean that the presidential branch is invulnerable. By not being firmly anchored in the Constitution, it lacks the protection that the Constitution provides to the other branches of government. It has, for example, no powers to protect itself from a congressional attack should Congress ever decide that it has had enough of a powerful presidential staff. It also lacks any powers to protect itself from future presidents who may choose to organize their presidency in a very different way and dispense with a large, specialized, and powerful staff system. In that respect, the presidential branch might be compared to the constitutional status of the Cabinet, and it could be replaced by some other form of advice and assistance if future presidents chose to do so, in just the same way as presidents have dispensed with the Cabinet over the past thirty years or so.

While Congress has not shown any willingness to challenge the power of the presidential branch in any significant way, in spite of two clear invitations to do so in the form of Watergate and the Iran-*contra* affair, it has nevertheless interfered a great deal with the structure and organization of the Executive Office of the President and presidents have had to tolerate a certain amount of congressional intervention in what is, constitutionally speaking, a presidential prerogative. In fact, Congress has done as much to determine what constitutes the presidential branch as presidents have done, and there is a growing list of staff structures and functions within the presidential branch that have been placed there by Congress, often serving the purposes of Congress rather than the genuine staffing and advisory needs of the president. Furthermore, it is not always easy for presidents to get rid of these unwanted bodies, as President Clinton discovered after his unsuccessful effort to abolish the Council on Environmental Quality in 1993. But presidents must be thankful that Congress has not interfered more than it has done. If it did decide to curtail the power of the presidential branch in a significant way, there would be few constitutional provisions to protect the presidential branch from that challenge.

The constitutional vulnerability of the presidential branch is, however, just an academic question for the foreseeable future. No president since Franklin Roosevelt has even hinted at replacing the new branch of government that FDR created, and none of the experts who write about the presidential staff has conceived of any radically different method of operating the presidency that did not require the kind of staff system that has evolved since FDR's years in the White House. Neither is Congress likely to mount any real threat to the power of the presidential branch. During the past fifty years, a modus vivendi has been reached between the president and Congress over the role and development of the presidential branch. Presidents tolerate congressional interference with its structure and functions, and Congress tolerates an increasingly powerful, and sometimes excessively powerful, body at the very center of the decision-making process because it has neither the will nor the interest nor the incentive to reverse a half century of significant institutional development in American government. Congress has the capacity to exercise more rigorous oversight of the presidential branch, and the fact that it does not do so effectively points to a weakness of the legislative branch in carrying out its constitutional responsibilities. The exemption of the presidential branch from the exercise of congressional oversight is not the fault of the presidential branch.

The presidential branch draws considerable institutional strength from the attitude adopted by Congress because that allows it to operate beyond the confines of effective accountability and responsibility, at least on a day-to-day basis. Moreover, when accountability and responsibility do come into play, they have affected the presidential branch at the individual, rather than the institutional, level. In those two well-known instances of abuse of presidential branch power, Watergate and the Iran-*contra* affair, individuals were blamed for misdeeds; some were indicted, some even served prison sentences, and, of course, one president was forced to resign as a consequence of what his staff did in his name. But the institution remained intact. Nothing that was done by Congress in the wake of Watergate or Iran-*contra* substantially weakened or checked the institutional base and power of the presidential branch.

In general, there is nothing illegitimate about the presidential staff assuming the power that it has assumed in recent years except where its exercise of power has transgressed the law and the Constitution. The Constitution allows the president remarkable latitude in organizing his advice and assistance. If presidents wish to use White House aides as their principal advisers and delegate to them a central role in policy making, then that is their prerogative. The trend toward centralization of power in the White House may well be undesirable, but there is a difference between what is undesirable and what is illegitimate within the structure of American government. In any event, a succession of presidents have given their imprimatur to the development of the staff system and have demonstrated their preference for governing through a presidential branch instead of relying on the executive branch to respond to presidential direction. For presidents, at least, the evolution of the presidential staff into its present form has been a far from undesirable development.

The presidential branch fits uneasily into the structure of American government. The literal view of its place within the constitutional framework, as a body that operates as an extension of the president himself—Chief Justice Burger's "arms and fingers" interpretation—understates its real role and function and consequently its power and authority. Although it might be constitutionally correct to describe the presidential branch in this way, such a view subscribes to the staff a misleadingly passive part in the operation of government. The presidential branch fits uneasily into the structure of government primarily because it is not firmly rooted in the Constitution, yet it challenges the power of the executive and legislative branches, and the extent of that challenge may not yet be fully realized or understood.

The existence of the presidential branch has certainly upset the traditional relationship between the executive branch and the president, essentially because the presidential staff has behaved precisely as Brownlow urged it not to do. The interposition of senior staff between the president and his top political executives in the departments and agencies has fundamentally altered the pattern of decision making in government and has reduced the status and authority of members of the Cabinet. The Executive Office of the President controls and coordinates in the name of the president, and the object of its control and coordination is the executive branch. The tendency toward the politicization of the EOP further alienates the executive branch from the presidential branch and makes that relationship appear more and more an adversarial one.

The presidential branch also frustrates the legislative branch by thwarting congressional attempts to intervene in and control the policy-making process. The existence of a well-organized and functionally specialized presidential staff reduces the president's dependency on the executive branch for advice and information, and so makes the legislature's ties with departments and agencies less potent than they once were. The staff also enables the president to organize public support for his policies that can constrain the ability of Congress to reshape those policies to its own desires. The involvement of the staff in presidential policy making has also had the effect of placing a significant amount of policy making beyond the scope of congressional oversight, as long as Congress maintains its traditional regard for the practice of comity and its unwillingness to challenge the assertion of executive privilege. In short, the presidential branch is a relatively new obstacle to the exercise of power by the executive and legislative branches, an obstacle that did not exist fifty-five years ago.

A separate presidential branch has evolved within the structure of American government from presidential staffing practices begun in 1789 and developed through the nineteenth and early twentieth centuries. The implementation of the Brownlow recommendations in 1939 allowed presidents to change the scale of staff operations and turn their staffs into the instruments of government they have become today. Although some commentators have provided useful insights into the variety of different ways that post-Brownlow presidents have organized and used their staffs,[8] it should be emphasized that from Franklin D. Roosevelt onward, all presidents have contributed to, or sanctioned, the development of the staff into its present form, and none has seriously attempted to change or reverse its general developmental direction.

An active, prominent, and powerful presidential staff is now a fact of life in American government. The many and complex causes that account for the development of the staff into its present state are unlikely to be reversed in the foreseeable future, and it is highly improbable that President Clinton's successors will want to dismantle what Roosevelt, Truman, Eisenhower, Kennedy, Johnson, Nixon, Ford, Carter, Reagan, and Bush all found to be such a desirable asset. Yet there is more ambivalence here, for although the presidential branch is a powerful player within the framework of American government, many of the sources of its political strength are, at the same time, sources of serious institutional weakness.

Much of the power that can be wielded by senior presidential aides, for example, derives from their close personal relationship, loyalty, and working proximity to the president, and often that stems from prior service to the president either as part of the election campaign team or as staffers to the president in a former political office. Presidents tend to staff the presidential branch with the people they know best and feel most comfortable with, and generally, that means those who accompanied the president on the long and often difficult road to the White House. The number of Georgians at the senior level of President Carter's staff was conspicuous, as was the number of Californians on President Reagan's staff and Arkansans on President Clinton's staff. In their election campaigns, each of these three presidents exploited their status as Washington outsiders, and as presidents, they staffed their principal institutional support with outsiders. But by doing so, they ran the risk of depriving themselves of the skills, knowledge, and expertise that even adroit politicians need when they take over the reins of power. This institutional danger was well illustrated in the tragedy that marred the early days of the Clinton administration when, in July 1993, Deputy Counsel to the President Vincent Foster committed suicide, apparently as a result of the pressure of work in the White House. Foster left a suicide note, the first line of which spoke volumes about the institutional weakness of the presidential branch. His confession that he "made mistakes from ignorance, inexperience and overwork"[9] could equally be the epitaph of so many who get to work in the White House. The presidential branch is an institution where newcomers have to learn on the job, and where every four or eight years, almost all its personnel are newcomers.

Because the presidential branch is usually cleared out when a new president takes office, it is an institution that lacks institutional continuity. Neither the executive branch nor the legislative branch nor the judicial branch suffers in the same way. When newcomers join those bodies, they are joining institutions with experienced personnel already in place. Not so the presidential branch, particularly its engine, the White House Office. Vice President Al Gore was quite correct to say, as he did in his "reinventing government" report, that the White House Office is "regularly reinvented with each change of administration."[10] But that can be a crucial institutional weakness as well as a strength. The presidential branch is dynamic within broad parameters, but sometimes that dynamism can mean that presidential staffs can spend a lot of time reinventing the wheel and making mistakes in the process because of the lack of institutional knowledge and expertise that even the most dynamic institutions require. President Clinton managed to recover from a catalogue of errors early on in his administration—the Zoe

Baird and Kimba Wood appointments, the White House Travel Office episode, the Lani Guinier nomination, a war with the Washington press corps, the defeat of his economic stimulus package in Congress, and the embarrassing compromise over the gays-in-the-military issue—all of which were, in large measure, a product of staff inexperience and poor judgment; but these incidents served to underline just how vulnerable the presidential branch can be at the beginning of a new administration when those vital institutional characteristics are missing.

Where, then, does that leave the conventional post-Watergate prescription for reforming the presidential staff system? Insofar as a large part of the prescription advocates turning back the clock and restoring a presidential advisory system that has long ceased to exist, it is unlikely to get much of a response from those in power. Post-Watergate reformers want to constrain the role and function of the presidential staff. Presidents in office have shown that they have no desire to constrain it. In discussing the problem of reforming the presidency, Richard Fenno said that "it is difficult to see how [the president] can be forced to be assisted in any particular way by the general will of political scientists if he does not so wish. . . . The most elaborate scheme is no stronger than the base of presidential acquiescence on which it must rest."[11] Similarly, Aaron Wildavsky warned that compelling the president "to use staff as we would like him to is a means of forcing our preferences on him. We ought not to be surprised if he resists this kind of help."[12] Experience has shown that there is no base of presidential acquiescence toward the bulk of the post-Watergate reform agenda; instead we see a great deal of presidential resistance to it.

The Executive Office of the President was designed as an administrative entity, but it has become a political entity competing for power in the pluralistic and fragmented structure of American government. As such, its activities and power are more likely to be constrained by the political forces competing against it and by the interplay of the other branches of government with the presidential branch than by the largely futile attempt to persuade presidents to adopt a contrived set of changes that run counter to the basic purposes for which the staff system now exists.

The interplay of the presidential branch with the executive and legislative branches is still an uncharted area of American government. Of course, much was written about the cataclysmic events of the Nixon years, but what happened then has not fundamentally altered the development of the presidential branch. What needs to be looked at now is how the presidential branch relates to the other branches of government in normal times, in a period when the legislative and executive branches may be beginning to come to terms with the existence of this new institution and assessing their responses accordingly.

DIVISIONS OF THE EXECUTIVE OFFICE OF THE PRESIDENT, 1939–94

Division	Date and Method of Establishment	Date and Method of Termination
WHITE HOUSE OFFICE*	1939 Executive Order	
Bureau of the Budget*	1939 Reorganization Plan	1970 Reorganization Plan
National Resources Planning Board	1939 Reorganization Plan	1943 Public Law
Office of Government Reports	1939 Reorganization Plan	1948 Public Law
Liaison Office for Personnel Management	1939 Reorganization Plan	1953 Executive Order
Office of Emergency Management	1940 Executive Order	1953 Executive Order
Office of War Mobilization	1943 Executive Order	1944 Executive Order
Office of War Mobilization and Reconversion	1944 Public Law	1946 Executive Order
COUNCIL OF ECONOMIC ADVISERS*	1946 Public Law	
NATIONAL SECURITY COUNCIL*	1949 Reorganization Plan	
National Security Resources Board	1949 Reorganization Plan	1953 Reorganization Plan
Office of Defense Mobilization	1950 Executive Order	1958 Reorganization Plan
Office of the Director for Mutual Security	1951 Public Law	1953 Reorganization Plan
Telecommunications Adviser to the President	1951 Executive Order	1953 Executive Order
President's Advisory Committee on Government Organization	1953 Executive Order	1961 Executive Order
National Aeronautics and Space Administration	1958 Public Law	1973 Reorganization Plan
Office of Defense and Civilian Mobilization (redesignated as Office of Civil and Defense Mobilization one month after establishment)	1958 Reorganization Plan	1961 Public Law
Office of Science and Technology	1962 Reorganization Plan	1973 Reorganizion Plan
Office of Special Representative for Trade Negotiations**	1963 Executive Order	1975 Public Law

Organization	Established	Terminated/Changed
Office of Economic Opportunity	1964 Public Law	1975 Public Law
National Council on Marine Resources and Engineering	1966 Public Law	1971 Funding discontinued
Office of Emergency Preparedness	1968 Public Law	1973 Reorganization Plan
Council for Urban Affairs	1969 Executive Order	1970 Executive Order
President's Foreign Intelligence Advisory Board	1969 Executive Order	1977 Executive Order
COUNCIL ON ENVIRONMENTAL QUALITY	1969 Public Law	
Office of Telecommunications Policy	1970 Reorganization Plan	1978 Reorganization Plan
OFFICE OF MANAGEMENT AND BUDGET	1970 Reorganization Plan	
Domestic Council	1970 Reorganization Plan	1977 Reorganization Plan
Council on International Economic Policy	1971 Presidential Memorandum/ Public Law	1977 Expiration of authority
Office of Consumer Affairs	1971 Executive Order	1973 Executive Order
Special Action Office for Drug Abuse Prevention	1971 Executive Order	1975 Public Law
Federal Property Council	1973 Executive Order	1977 Executive Order
Energy Policy Office	1973 Executive Order	1974 Executive Order
Council on Wage and Price Stability	1974 Public Law	1981 Public Law
Presidential Clemency Board	1974 Executive Order	1975 Executive Order
Energy Resources Council	1974 Public Law	1977 Public Law
OFFICE OF THE SPECIAL REPRESENTATIVE FOR TRADE NEGOTIATIONS (renamed OFFICE OF THE U.S. TRADE REPRESENTATIVE in 1979)**	1975 Public Law	
Office of Drug Abuse Policy	1976 Public Law	1978 Reorganization Plan
OFFICE OF SCIENCE AND TECHNOLOGY POLICY	1976 Public Law	
Domestic Policy Staff (name changed to Office of Policy Development in 1981)	1977 Reorganization Plan	1993 Replaced by Domestic Policy Council
OFFICE OF ADMINISTRATION	1977 Reorganization Plan	
National Critical Materials Council	1984 Public Law	1993 Funding discontinued

Division	Date and Method of Establishment	Date and Method of Termination
National Space Council	1988 Public Law	1993 Funding discontinued
OFFICE OF NATIONAL DRUG CONTROL POLICY	1988 Public Law	
NATIONAL ECONOMIC COUNCIL	1993 Executive Order	
DOMESTIC POLICY COUNCIL	1993 Executive Order	

NOTE: Existing divisions of the EOP are shown in capitals. The above list contains only the units formally established within the EOP as separate entities. It does not list offices established within another EOP division (e.g., the Office of Federal Procurement Policy established within OMB in 1974 or the now defunct Council for Rural Affairs that President Nixon created as part of the White House Office). Neither does the list include the presidential agencies formally classified as an independent agency within the executive branch. (President Ford's Economic Policy Board is one example: it is frequently listed in texts as being part of the EOP, but it never was.)

* Division created prior to its establishment within the Executive Office of the President.

** The position of Special Representative for Trade Negotiations was established as part of the Trade Expansion Act of 1962 but was not formally designated within the EOP. That was done at the beginning of the following year when the Office of the Special Representative was established within the EOP under an executive order signed by President Kennedy. The termination of the office in 1975 was merely a legal formality so that it could be reestablished under statute law. In effect, what is now the Office of the U.S. Trade Representative has been in continuous existence since 1962. The change of name to the Office of the U.S. Trade Representative was implemented by President Carter's Reorganization Plan No. 3 of 1979.

NOTES

1. The Presidential Branch: An Introduction

1. Bradley H. Patterson, Jr., *The Ring of Power: The White House Staff and Its Expanding Role in Government* (New York: Basic Books, 1988), 5.
2. The positions of the three candidates on the White House staff are conveniently summarized in "Blueprints for Cutting the U.S. Work Force," *Washington Post*, 26 October 1992, A19.
3. See Jeffrey H. Birnbaum, "Clinton Bends under Pressure from Congress," *Wall Street Journal*, 17 November 1992, A20.
4. President's Committee on Administrative Management, *Administrative Management in the Government of the United States* (Washington, D.C.: Government Printing Office, 1937), p. 3.
5. Franklin D. Roosevelt, *The Public Papers and Addresses of Franklin D. Roosevelt* (New York: Random House, 1938), 5:670.
6. President's Committee on Administrative Management, *Administrative Management in the Government of the United States*, 2.
7. Ibid., 5.
8. Clinton Rossiter, "The Constitutional Significance of the Executive Office of the President," *American Political Science Review* 43, no. 6 (1949): 1214.
9. Nelson W. Polsby, "Some Landmarks in Modern Presidential-Congressional Relations," in *Both Ends of the Avenue*, ed. Anthony King (Washington, D.C.: American Enterprise Institute, 1983), 20.
10. See Howard E. McCurdy, "Crowding and Behavior in the White House," *Psychology Today* 15, no. 4 (1981): 22.
11. Rossiter, "The Constitutional Significance of the Executive Office," 1217.
12. Ibid., 1214.
13. George A. Graham, "The Presidency and the Executive Office of the President," *Journal of Politics* 12, no. 4 (1950): 600.
14. Stephen K. Bailey, "The President and His Political Executives," *Annals of the American Academy of Political and Social Science* 307 (1956): 31–32.
15. Thomas E. Cronin, *The State of the Presidency* (Boston: Little, Brown, 1975), 118.
16. George Reedy, *The Twilight of the Presidency* (New York: New American Library, 1970), xiv.
17. John Dean, *Blind Ambition: The White House Years* (New York: Simon and Schuster, 1976).
18. See John Hart, "Presidential Power Revisited," *Political Studies* 25, no. 1 (1977).
19. Cronin, *The State of the Presidency*, 25.
20. See, for example, Charles M. Hardin, *Presidential Power and Accountability* (Chicago: University of Chicago Press, 1974).
21. See, for example, Arthur M. Schlesinger, Jr., *The Imperial Presidency* (Boston: Houghton Mifflin, 1973), x.

22. National Academy of Public Administration, *A Presidency for the 1980s* (Washington, D.C.: National Academy of Public Administration, 1980).

23. President's Special Review Board, *Report of the President's Special Review Board,* 26 February 1987 (Washington, D.C.: Government Printing Office, 1987), IV-10–IV-12.

24. U.S. House of Representatives Select Committee to Investigate Covert Arms Transactions with Iran and U.S. Senate Select Committee on Secret Military Assistance to Iran and the Nicaraguan Opposition, 100th Cong., 1st sess., House Rept. No. 100-433, Senate Rept. No. 100-216, *Report of the Congressional Committees Investigating the Iran-Contra Affair* (Washington, D.C.: Government Printing Office, 1987), 11–22.

25. Allan R. Gould, "Sununu Is Called Smart, Decisive and Impatient," *New York Times,* 20 November 1988, 28.

26. Burt Solomon, "No-Nonsense Sununu," *National Journal,* 16 September 1989, 2249.

27. See Colin Campbell, "The White House and the Presidency under the 'Let's Deal' President," in *The Bush Presidency: First Appraisals,* ed. Colin Campbell and Bert A. Rockman (Chatham, N.J.: Chatham House, 1991), 210–16.

28. Ibid., 199–202.

29. It was revealed, among other things, that Sununu had used military planes to visit his dentist in New Hampshire and to take him to a ski vacation in Colorado, a government limousine to attend a stamp auction in Manhattan, and had solicited the use of corporate jets to attend party political functions. See R.W. Apple, Jr., "Sununu's Power Wanes in Furor Over His Travel," *New York Times,* 24 June 1991, A1; Maureen Dowd, "Indispensability of Sununu Is Creating Hard Questions," *New York Times,* 26 June 1991, A1.

2. The Presidential Staff: 1789–1939

1. See Leonard D. White, *The Federalists: A Study in Administrative History* (New York: Macmillan, 1948), 496.

2. Ibid., 32.

3. Leonard D. White, *The Jeffersonians: A Study in Administrative History, 1801–1829* (New York: Macmillan, 1951), 71–72.

4. Charles F. Adams, ed., *Memoirs of John Quincy Adams* (Freeport, N.Y.: Books for Libraries Press, 1968), 6:374.

5. See, for example, Thomas E. Cronin, *The State of the Presidency* (Boston: Little, Brown, 1975), 118; Edward H. Hobbs, *Behind the President: A Study of Executive Office Agencies* (Washington, D.C.: Public Affairs Press, 1954), 86; Michael Medved, *The Shadow Presidents* (New York: Times Books, 1979), 11; William C. Spragens, "White House Staffs 1789–1974," in Bradley D. Nash et al., *Organizing and Staffing the Presidency* (New York: Center for the Study of the Presidency, 1980), 17. I think this error can be traced back to the work of Leonard White, who is somewhat inconsistent about what Congress did, or did not do, with respect to funding staff assistance for the President. In the first of his four-volume administrative history of the presidency White said, "Congress, however, made no appropriation for an official secretary to the Chief Executive." See *The Federalists,* 495. In the second volume he claimed that "Congress allowed a private secretary and no more." See *The Jeffersonians,* 74. In the

third volume, White returned to his original position: "The official life of Presidents was made much more burdensome because Congress allowed them no funds for private secretaries or administrative assistants." See *The Jacksonians: A Study in Administrative History 1829–1861* (New York: Macmillan, 1954), 82.

6. This section draws heavily on Louis Fisher's contribution to the House of Representatives 1978 report on presidential staffing. See U.S. House of Representatives, Committee on Post Office and Civil Service, 95th Cong., 2d sess., *Presidential Staffing: A Brief Overview,* Committee Print 95-17 (Washington, D.C.: Government Printing Office, 1978), 4–6. For the text of the debate, see U.S. Congress, *Annals of the Congress of the United States,* 1632–37 and 644–45.

7. Noble E. Cunningham, *The Process of Government Under Jefferson* (Princeton: Princeton University Press, 1978), 44.

8. White, *The Federalists,* 494.

9. Ibid.

10. Michael Medved, *The Shadow Presidents* (New York: Times Books, 1979), 11; White, *The Jacksonians,* 82.

11. White, *The Federalists,* 496.

12. Cunningham, *The Process of Government Under Jefferson,* 37.

13. White, *The Federalists,* 37.

14. Albert E. Berg, ed., *The Writings of Thomas Jefferson* (Washington, D.C.: Thomas Jefferson Memorial Association, 1907), 11:137.

15. White, *The Jacksonians,* 84.

16. White, *The Jeffersonians,* 119–25.

17. U.S. House of Representatives, 18th Cong., 2d sess., *House Report No. 79,* 18 January 1825, 23–25.

18. White, *The Jacksonians,* 83.

19. 4 Stat. 663, chap. XCI.

20. 11 Stat. 228, chap. 108.

21. George Ticknor Curtis, *The Life of James Buchanan* (New York: Harper & Brothers, 1883), 2:236.

22. Ibid.

23. W.W. Price, "Secretaries to the President," *The Cosmopolitan* 30, no. 5 (1901): 488.

24. Curtis, *The Life of James Buchanan,* 237.

25. 14 Stat. 444, chap. 166.

26. 16 Stat. 236, chap. 251.

27. 21 Stat. 216, chap. 225.

28. 31 Stat. 972, chap. 830.

29. Leonard D. White, *The Republican Era 1869–1901: A Study in Administrative History* (New York: Macmillan, 1958), 102–3.

30. Medved, *The Shadow Presidents,* 13.

31. Ibid., 32–38.

32. Ibid., 37.

33. Ibid., 39–52.

34. Ibid., 53.

35. See Harry Barnard, *Rutherford B. Hayes and His America* (New York: Bobbs-Merrill, 1954), 405.

36. Kenneth E. Davison, *The Presidency of Rutherford B. Hayes* (Westport, Conn.: Greenwood Press, 1972), 92–93.

37. Ibid., 93.
38. See White, *The Republican Era,* 103.
39. See Medved, *The Shadow Presidents,* 79–80.
40. Margaret Leech, *In the Days of McKinley* (New York: Harper, 1959), 127.
41. Ibid., 128.
42. Ibid., 127.
43. 42 Stat. 636, chap. 218.
44. 42 Stat. 1227, chap. 72.
45. 45 Stat. 1230, chap. 270.
46. Arthur S. Link, *Wilson: The New Freedom* (Princeton: Princeton University Press, 1956), 141.
47. See Medved, *The Shadow Presidents,* 177–78.
48. William Allen White, *A Puritan in Babylon: The Story of Calvin Coolidge* (New York: Macmillan, 1938), 260–61.
49. Link, *Wilson: The New Freedom,* 20.
50. See Guy B. Hathorn, "C. Bascom Slemp: Virginia Republican Boss, 1907–1932," *Journal of Politics* 17, no. 2 (1955): 259–60.
51. Medved, *The Shadow Presidents,* 126.
52. Ibid., 169.
53. Ibid., 191.
54. Link, *Wilson: The New Freedom,* 143–44.
55. Medved, *The Shadow Presidents,* 188–89.
56. See Richard Polenberg, *Reorganizing Roosevelt's Government 1936–1939* (Cambridge, Mass.: Harvard University Press, 1966), 6.
57. Clinton L. Rossiter, "The Constitutional Significance of the Executive Office of the President," *American Political Science Review* 43, no. 6 (1949): 1207.
58. Polenberg, *Reorganizing Roosevelt's Government,* 20.
59. President's Committee on Administrative Management, *Administrative Management in the Government of the United States* (Washington, D.C.: Government Printing Office, 1937), 2.
60. Ibid., 3.
61. Ibid.
62. Herbert Emmerich, *Essays on Federal Reorganization* (Tuscaloosa: University of Alabama Press, 1950), 90.
63. Edward S. Corwin, *The President: Office and Powers,* 4th ed. (New York: New York University Press, 1957), 96.
64. Louis Brownlow, *The President and the Presidency* (Chicago: Public Administration Service, 1949), 106.
65. See, for example, B.B. Schaffer, "Brownlow or Brookings: Approaches to the Improvement of the Machinery of Government," *New Zealand Journal of Public Administration* 24, no. 2 (1962).
66. See Polenberg, *Reorganizing Roosevelt's Government,* chap. 10.
67. See James Roosevelt, "Staffing My Father's Presidency: A Personal Reminiscence," *Presidential Studies Quarterly* 12, no. 1 (1982): 48.
68. All quotations in this section are from President's Committee on Administrative Management, *Administrative Management in the Government of the United States,* 5.
69. See Louis Brownlow, *A Passion for Anonymity* (Chicago: University of Chicago Press, 1958), 381.
70. Ibid., 397.

71. See Polenberg, *Reorganizing Roosevelt's Government,* 222.
72. See Brownlow, *The President and the Presidency,* 105; and *A Passion for Anonymity,* 357.
73. Brownlow, *The President and the Presidency,* 106; and Polenberg, *Reorganizing Roosevelt's Government,* 20.
74. See Harold Wilson, *The Governance of Britain* (London: Weidenfeld & Nicholson and Michael Joseph, 1976), 94.
75. A useful source for the texts of the Brownlow report, the Reorganization Act of 1939, and Executive Order 8248 is Frederick C. Mosher, ed., *Basic Documents of American Public Administration 1776–1950* (New York: Holmes and Meier, 1976), 110–49.
76. Henry F. Graff, "White House Secretaries," *Encyclopedia of the American Presidency* (New York: Simon and Schuster, 1994), 4:639.
77. See Edward H. Hobbs, *Behind the President: A Study of Executive Office Agencies* (Washington, D.C.: Public Affairs Press, 1954), 32–33.
78. Ibid., 34.
79. See President's Committee on Administrative Management, *Administrative Management in the Government of the United States,* 16.
80. The vision of some budget directors was extremely limited. See Larry Berman, *The Office of Management and Budget and the Presidency, 1921–1979* (Princeton: Princeton University Press, 1979), 7–9.
81. Richard E. Neustadt, "Presidency and Legislation: The Growth of Central Clearance," *American Political Science Review* 57, no. 4 (1954): 642.
82. Berman, *The Office of Management and Budget and the Presidency,* 14.
83. See ibid., 12–15.
84. Hobbs, *Behind the President,* 35.
85. Under Section 5 of the Reorganization Act of 1939 reorganization plans submitted by the President would become law if Congress did not pass a concurrent resolution opposing the plan.
86. For a fuller account of the short life of the National Resources Planning Board see Hobbs, *Behind the President,* chap. 3; and for a description of its operations, see Charles E. Merriam, "The National Resources Planning Board," *Public Administration Review* 6, no. 2 (1941).
87. See Polenberg, *Reorganizing Roosevelt's Government,* 33–84 and 93–94.
88. The work of the Liaison Office for Personnel Management is described by its first head in William H. McReynolds, "The Liaison Office for Personnel Management," *Public Administration Review* 6, no. 2 (1941).

3. The Development of the Executive Office of the President

1. A list of all the divisions of the Executive Office of the President since 1939 is contained in the appendix.
2. See Edward S. Flash, *Economic Advice and Presidential Leadership* (New York: Columbia University Press, 1965), 16.
3. See Anna Kasten Nelson, "National Security I: Inventing a Process (1945–1960)," in *The Illusion of Presidential Government,* ed. Hugh Heclo and Lester M. Salamon (Boulder, Colo.: Westview Press, 1981), 230.
4. For a more detailed account of the different conditions imposed on presidential

reorganization authority since 1932 see Louis Fisher, *Constitutional Conflicts between Congress and the President,* 3d ed. (Lawrence: University Press of Kansas, 1991), 136–38.

5. *Immigration and Naturalization Service v. Chadha,* 103 S. Ct. 715 (1983).
6. See Fisher, *Constitutional Conflicts between Congress and the President,* pp. 106–10.
7. President Clinton established the National Economic Council by Executive Order No. 12835 on 25 January 1993 and the Domestic Policy Council by Executive Order No. 12859 on 16 August 1993, although the latter was, in effect, a change of name for the staff of the Office of Policy Development. For fiscal year 1994, the Clinton administration sought no funding for the National Space Council and the National Critical Material Councils, thus effectively abolishing those units. Congress refused to terminate the Council on Environmental Quality as President Clinton had requested.
8. U.S. House of Representatives, Committee on Post Office and Civil Service, 92d Cong., 2d sess., Committee Print 19, *A Report on the Growth of the Executive Office of the President 1955–1973* (Washington, D.C.: Government Printing Office, 1972), 2–3.
9. Ibid., 5. Statistics on the size of the White House Office need to be treated cautiously. See the discussion in the next chapter.
10. Thomas E. Cronin, *The State of the Presidency* (Boston: Little, Brown, 1975), p. 118; Stephen Hess, *Organizing the Presidency* (Washington, D.C.: Brookings Institution, 1976), 9.
11. These were the Emergency Fund for the President (established in 1940), the Special Projects Fund (established in 1955), and the Management Improvement Fund (established in 1954). The most important of these was the Special Projects Fund, discussed in chapter 5.
12. U.S. Congress, 92d Cong., 2d sess., *Congressional Record* 118 (20 June 1972): 21512.
13. U.S. House of Representatives, Committee on Post Office and Civil Service, 95th Cong., 2d sess., Committee Print 95-17, *Presidential Staffing: A Brief Overview* (Washington, D.C.: Government Printing Office, 1978), 57.
14. John Helmer, "The Presidential Office: Velvet Fist in an Iron Glove," in *The Illusion of Presidential Government,* ed. Hugh Heclo and Lester M. Salamon, 61.
15. Ibid., 61–63.
16. See Cronin, *The State of the Presidency,* 121–24.
17. Hess, *Organizing the Presidency,* 150–51.
18. See Ann Devroy, "Clinton Announces Cut in White House Staff," *Washington Post,* 10 February 1993, A1.
19. Helmer, "The Presidential Office: Velvet Fist in an Iron Glove," 60–62.
20. Hugh Heclo, "One Executive Branch or Many?" in *Both Ends of the Avenue,* ed. Anthony King (Washington, D.C.: American Enterprise Institute, 1983), 38.
21. Hess, *Organizing the Presidency,* 76.
22. John Hart, "Staffing the Presidency: Kennedy and the Office of Congressional Relations," *Presidential Studies Quarterly* 13, no. 1 (1981).
23. See Roger B. Porter, "Economic Advice to the President: From Eisenhower to Reagan," *Political Science Quarterly,* 98, no. 3 (1983).
24. Quoted in Bertram Gross and John P. Lewis, "The President's Economic Staff during the Truman Administration," *American Political Science Review* 68, no. 1 (1954): 114.

25. On the origins of the Council of Economic Advisers, see Nelson W. Polsby, *Political Innovation in America* (New Haven: Yale University Press, 1984), 100–112.

26. See David Naveh, "The Political Role of Academic Advisers: The Case of the U.S. President's Council of Economic Advisers 1946–1976," *Presidential Studies Quarterly* 11, no. 4 (1981): 494–95. Of the four members who did not join the council from university posts, three came from prestigious think tanks, two of them from Brookings and one from the American Enterprise Institute.

27. Edwin G. Nourse, *Economics in the Public Service* (New York: Harcourt, Brace, 1953), 107.

28. Walter Heller, *New Dimensions of Political Economy* (Cambridge, Mass.: Harvard University Press, 1966), 15.

29. Edward S. Flash, *Economic Advice and Presidential Leadership* (New York: Columbia University Press, 1965), 305.

30. Heller, *New Dimensions of Political Economy*, 53.

31. See Flash, *Economic Advice and Presidential Leadership*, 26; and Edward H. Hobbs, *Behind the President: A Study of Executive Office Agencies* (Washington, D.C.: Public Affairs Press, 1954), 99–102.

32. Nourse, *Economics in the Public Service*, 373–78; Francis H. Heller, ed., *The Truman White House: The Administration of the Presidency, 1945–1953* (Lawrence: Regents Press of Kansas, 1980), 179–95.

33. See Flash, *Economic Advice and Presidential Leadership*, chaps. 2 and 3.

34. Gross and Lewis, "The President's Economic Staff during the Truman Administration," 119–20.

35. Commission on Organization of the Executive Branch of Government, *The Hoover Commission Report on the Organization of the Executive Branch of Government* (New York: McGraw-Hill, 1950), 13–14.

36. See Flash, *Economic Advice and Presidential Leadership*, 99; Naveh, "The Political Role of Academic Advisers," 496.

37. See Sherman Adams, *Firsthand Report: The Story of the Eisenhower Administration* (New York: Harper & Brothers, 1961), 155–56.

38. *Public Papers of the Presidents: Dwight D. Eisenhower 1953* (Washington, D.C.: Government Printing Office, 1960), 355–59.

39. Ibid., 358.

40. See Flash, *Economic Advice and Presidential Leadership*, 169.

41. See Porter, "Economic Advice to the President," 415–16.

42. See Saul Engelbourg, "The Council of Economic Advisers and the Recession of 1953–1954," *Business History Review* 54, no. 2 (1980).

43. Flash, *Economic Advice and Presidential Leadership*, 162–72.

44. Ibid., 271.

45. Ibid., 175–76. It is interesting to note that when Walter Heller was offered the position of chairman of the CEA by Kennedy, Heller sought a specific assurance from the president-elect that there would be no White House economic policy assistant such as Eisenhower had had. See Irving Bernstein, *Promises Kept: John F. Kennedy's New Frontier* (New York: Oxford University Press, 1991), 124.

46. The best definition of "the new economics" is Heller's own in *New Dimensions of Political Economy*, chap. 2.

47. Flash, *Economic Advice and Presidential Leadership*, 272–74.

48. See Porter, "Economic Advice to the President," 410.

49. Interview with the author, 29 August 1972.

50. E. Magnuson, "Shake-Up at the White House," *Time*, 21 January 1985, 22.
51. See Colin Campbell, *Governments Under Stress* (Toronto: University of Toronto Press, 1983), 108–9; Dom Bonafede, "Stuart Eizenstat—Carter's Right-Hand Man," *National Journal*, 9 May 1979, 946.
52. President Eisenhower had operated a Council on Foreign Economic Policy from December 1954, but it was not formally part of the EOP, nor did the presidential staff constitute 50 percent of its membership, as was the case with Nixon's Council.
53. Henry Kissinger asserts that the reason why the Council on International Economic Policy failed was that Peter Peterson, the assistant to the president for international economic affairs, was undermined by Secretary of the Treasury John Connally, who refused to send memoranda through Peterson or receive instructions from him. "He had reduced Peterson to the role of a spectator even before Nixon ended Peterson's agony by appointing him Secretary of Commerce." Henry Kissinger, *The White House Years* (Boston: Little, Brown, 1979), 951–52.
54. See Richard P. Nathan, *The Administrative Presidency* (New York: Wiley, 1983), 51–53.
55. Richard M. Nixon, *RN: The Memoirs of Richard Nixon* (New York: Grosset & Dunlap, 1978), 909.
56. The establishment of the Economic Policy Board is described in detail in Roger B. Porter, *Presidential Decision Making: The Economic Policy Board* (Cambridge, England: Cambridge University Press, 1980), 39–45.
57. Ibid., 42.
58. Ibid., 45.
59. Ibid., 40.
60. See ibid., 174–252.
61. Ibid., 212.
62. According to the U.S. Office of Personnel Management's Federal Civilian Workforce Statistics, there were over 220 staff attached to the Council in September of 1979.
63. See Campbell, *Governments Under Stress*, 108.
64. See ibid., 122; and I.M. Destler, *Making Foreign Economic Policy* (Washington, D.C.: Brookings Institution, 1980), 222–24.
65. For a critique of Carter's economic management by two members of his administration see Ben W. Heineman and Curtis A. Hessler, *Memorandum for the President: A Strategic Approach to Domestic Affairs in the 1980s* (New York: Random House, 1980), 252–66.
66. Porter, "Economic Advice to the President," 413.
67. David Hoffman, "Two-Track White House Decision Process Can Go Off the Track," *Washington Post*, 5 December 1982, A18.
68. Peter T. Kilborn, "Reagan Disowns Feldstein Report, Tells Senators to Throw It Away," *New York Times*, 4 February 1984, 1. See also Dick Kirschten, "Inner Circle Speaks with Many Voices, But Maybe That's How Reagan Wants It," *National Journal*, 25 May 1983, 1102.
69. Robert D. Hershey, Jr., "Happy Days for Economic Advisers," *New York Times*, 5 September 1989, A16.
70. See ibid., see also Michael Duffy and Dan Goodgame, *Marching in Place: The Status Quo Presidency of George Bush* (New York: Simon and Schuster, 1992), 245–46.

71. Peter T. Kilborn, "Tight White House Control Marks Bush Economic Policy," *New York Times*, 26 March 1989, 1.

72. Bob Woodward, "The President's Key Men: Splintered Trio, Splintered Policy," *Washington Post*, 7 October 1992, A1.

73. See Richard L. Berke, "Bush Asks for Resignations of Top Aides After Election," *New York Times*, 13 October 1992, A17.

74. John P. Burke, *The Institutional Presidency* (Baltimore: Johns Hopkins University Press, 1992), 26.

75. One particular personality, that of Richard Darman, was critical in the making of economic policy in the Bush administration. For a useful description, from one very disaffected White House staff member, of how Darman's personality overpowered the structure, see Charles Kolb, *White House Daze: The Unmaking of Domestic Policy in the Bush Years* (New York: Free Press, 1994), chaps. 3 and 4.

76. President Reagan's second Chairman of the CEA, Martin Feldstein, resigned in June 1984 and was not replaced until early 1985. In the interval, a second member of the council, William Poole, had left, and a third, William Niskanen, had announced his intention to leave.

77. National Academy of Public Administration, *A Presidency for the 1980s* (Washington, D.C.: National Academy of Public Administration, 1980), 17; President's Commission for a National Agenda for the Eighties, *The Electoral and Democratic Process in the Eighties* (Washington, D.C.: Government Printing Office, 1980), 70.

78. Carnegie Endowment and Institute for International Economics, "Special Report: Policymaking for a New Era," *Foreign Affairs* 72, no. 5 (1992–93): 180–81.

79. See Destler, *Making Foreign Economic Policy*, 221.

80. Ibid.

81. The concept of issue networks is explained in Hugh Heclo, "Issue Networks and the Executive Establishment," in *The New American Political System*, ed. Anthony King (Washington, D.C.: American Enterprise Institute, 1978).

82. Executive Order 12835—Establishment of the National Economic Council, January 25, 1993, *Weekly Compilation of Presidential Documents* 29, no. 4 (1 February 1993): 95.

83. Ibid., 94.

84. Leslie Wayne and Saul Hansell, "Clinton Economic Point Man Is Quiet—But Determined," *New York Times*, 18 January 1993, D1; Brett D. Fromson, "Clinton Turns to a Wizard of Wall Street," *Washington Post*, 24 January 1993, H1.

85. For an early assessment of Rubin's performance see John B. Judis, "Old Master: Robert Rubin's Artful Role," *New Republic*, 13 December 1993, 21–28.

86. The Central Intelligence Agency, although statutorily responsible to the National Security Council, is generally regarded as an independent agency and is not usually counted as part of the Executive Office of the President.

87. See Alfred D. Sander, "Truman and the National Security Council 1945–1947," *Journal of American History* 59, no. 2 (1972).

88. Ibid., 369; I.M. Destler, "National Security Advice to U.S. Presidents: Some Lessons from Thirty Years," *World Politics* 29, no. 2 (1977): 147.

89. As Clark Clifford notes in his memoirs, "Given the way the American government was organized, President Truman liked to say, the U.S. was lucky—damn

lucky—to have won World War II. 'We must never fight another war the way we fought the last two,' he told me more than once." Clark Clifford, *Counsel to the President: A Memoir* (New York: Random House, 1991), 146.

90. See Sander, "Truman and the National Security Council 1945–1947," 370–73, and Nelson, "National Security I: Inventing a Process (1945–1960)," 231–32.

91. Nelson, "National Security I: Inventing a Process," 231. The internal politics of the Truman administration over national security reform is graphically described in Clifford, *Counsel to the President,* chap. 9.

92. Paul Y. Hammond, "The National Security Council as a Device for Interdepartmental Coordination: An Interpretation and Appraisal," *American Political Science Review* 54, no. 4 (1960): 900.

93. Destler, "National Security Advice to U.S. Presidents," 147.

94. See Sander, "Truman and the National Security Council," 378–79.

95. Hammond, "The National Security Council as a Device for Interdepartmental Coordination," 901.

96. Harry S. Truman, *Years of Trial and Hope 1946–1952* (New York: Doubleday, 1956), 59. Truman also made his view of the council's role explicit in a letter to members of the Council in July 1948. See John Prados, *Keepers of the Keys: A History of the National Security Council from Truman to Bush* (New York: Morrow, 1991), 30.

97. Nelson, "National Security I: Inventing a Process," 236–37.

98. Sander, "Truman and the National Security Council," 387.

99. Destler, "National Security Advice to U.S. Presidents," 146.

100. Stanley L. Falk, "The National Security Council Under Truman, Eisenhower and Kennedy," *Political Science Quarterly* 79, no. 3 (1964): 412–17.

101. For a fuller description of the Eisenhower NSC system, see Robert Cutler's testimony to the Jackson subcommittee reprinted in Henry M. Jackson, ed., *The National Security Council: Jackson Subcommittee Papers on Policy Making at the Presidential Level* (New York: Praeger, 1965), 111–39; Robert Cutler, "The Development of the National Security Council," *Foreign Affairs* 34, no. 3 (1956); Phillip G. Henderson, *Managing the Presidency: The Eisenhower Legacy—From Kennedy to Reagan* (Boulder, Colo.: Westview Press, 1988), chaps. 4 and 5.

102. See Destler, "National Security Advice to U.S. Presidents," p. 148; Falk, "The National Security Council under Truman, Eisenhower and Kennedy," 423–26; Nelson, "National Security I: Inventing a Process," 252–57.

103. Phillip G. Henderson, "Advice and Decision: The Eisenhower National Security Council Reappraised," in *The Presidency and National Security,* ed. R. Gordon Hoxie (New York: Center for the Study of the Presidency, 1984), 153–86.

104. Nelson, "National Security I: Inventing a Process," 249.

105. John P. Burke and Fred I. Greenstein, *How Presidents Test Reality: Decisions on Vietnam, 1954 and 1965* (New York: Russell Sage Foundation, 1989), 57 and 59.

106. U.S. Senate, Committee on Government Operations, Subcommittee on National Policy Machinery, 86th Cong., 2d sess., *Organizational History of the National Security Council* (Washington, D.C.: Government Printing Office, 1960), 32.

107. Jackson, *The National Security Council,* 39.

108. Theodore C. Sorensen, *Kennedy* (New York: Harper & Row, 1965), 285.

109. They managed to distinguish between being in charge of the NSC and being in charge of national security policy, and so did Eisenhower. See Nelson, "Na-

tional Security I: Inventing a Process," 250, and Fred I. Greenstein, *The Hidden-Hand Presidency: Eisenhower as Leader* (New York: Basic Books, 1982), 106–7.

110. See, for example, Destler, "National Security Advice to U.S. Presidents," 171, and Alexander L. George, *Presidential Decision Making in Foreign Policy: The Effective Use of Information and Advice* (Boulder, Colo.: Westview Press, 1980), 196–206.

111. Destler, "National Security Advice to U.S. Presidents," 158.

112. Kissinger, *The White House Years*, 30.

113. On Kissinger's operating style and his empire-building activities, see Walter Isaacson, *Kissinger: A Biography* (New York: Simon and Schuster, 1992), esp. chap. 10.

114. Kissinger, *The White House Years*, 47.

115. See Cyrus Vance, *Hard Choices: Critical Years in America's Foreign Policy* (New York: Simon and Schuster, 1983), 114–15; also I.M. Destler, "National Security Management: What Presidents Have Wrought," *Political Science Quarterly* 95, no. 4 (1980–1981): 581–83.

116. Zbigniew Brzezinski, *Power and Principle: Memoirs of the National Security Adviser 1977–1981* (New York: Farrar, Straus and Giroux, 1983), 17.

117. Edwin Meese III, *With Reagan: The Inside Story* (Washington, D.C.: Regnery Gateway, 1992), 110. There was, of course, much more to the explanation for Allen's lack of status in the Reagan White House. He was the subject of an FBI investigation over a large amount of cash found in his White House office safe, was generally unpopular with the Washington establishment, especially the media, and was also very unpopular with some senior White House staffers who, allegedly, engineered his subsequent resignation. See Suzanne Garment, *Scandal: The Culture of Mistrust in American Politics* (New York: Random House, 1991), 60–74.

118. For a detailed account of the operation of the NSC machinery under Reagan, see John Prados, *Keepers of the Keys: A History of the National Security Council from Truman to Bush* (New York: Morrow, 1991), 447–547.

119. Harold Hongju Koh, *The National Security Constitution: Sharing Power After the Iran-Contra Affair* (New Haven: Yale University Press, 1990), 2.

120. "A Working National Security Team," *New York Times*, 10 July 1988, E30.

121. See Larry Berman and Bruce Jentleson, "Bush and the Post-Cold War World: New Challenges for American Leadership," in *The Bush Presidency: First Appraisals*, ed. Colin Campbell and Bert A. Rockman (Chatham, N.J. Chatham House, 1991), 102; Andrew Rosenthal, "National Security Adviser Redefines Role, Drawing Barrage of Criticism," *New York Times*, 3 November 1989, A16.

122. Christopher Madison, "No Sharp Elbows," *National Journal*, 26 May 1990, 1277.

123. Quoted in Rosenthal, "National Security Adviser Redefines Role," A16.

124. At the time of writing NSD-1 is still a classified document. The following is based on an unclassified summary of NSD-1 entitled "National Security Council Organization," dated 17 April 1989.

125. U.S. House of Representatives, Committee on Appropriations, 102d Cong., 2d sess., *Treasury, Postal Service and General Government Appropriations for Fiscal Year 1993, Part 3* (Washington, D.C.: Government Printing Office, 1992), 291.

126. Berman and Jentleson, "Bush and the Post-Cold War World," 103.

127. Terry Eastland, *Energy in the Executive: The Case for a Strong Presidency* (New York: Free Press, 1992), 197–98.

128. Don Oberdorfer, "New NSC Framework Established," *Washington Post*, 22 January 1993, A15.

129. Jim Hoagland, "Flaws and Fissures in Foreign Policy," *Washington Post*, 31 October 1993, C7.

130. Kissinger, *The White House Years*, 30.

131. Ibid.

132. Vance, *Hard Choices*, 35–36.

133. Philip A. Odeen, "Organizing for National Security," *International Security* 5, no. 1 (1980).

134. Destler, "National Security Management: What Presidents Have Wrought," 583.

135. In his memoirs Kissinger says, "Though I did not think so at the time, I have become convinced that a President should make the Secretary of State his principal adviser and use the national security adviser primarily as a senior administrator and co-ordinator to make certain that each significant point of view is heard." *The White House Years*, 30.

136. See Larry Berman, *The Office of Management and Budget and the Presidency, 1921–1979* (Princeton: Princeton University Press, 1979), chap. 2.

137. See David C. Mowrey, Mark S. Kamlet, and John P. Crecine, "Presidential Management of Budgetary and Fiscal Policy Making," *Political Science Quarterly* 95, no. 3 (1980): 396–401.

138. Allen Schick, "The Problem of Presidential Budgeting," in Heclo and Salamon, *The Illusion of Presidential Government*.

139. Ibid., pp. 91–94.

140. See James E. Anderson, "Presidential Management of the Bureaucracy and the Johnson Presidency," *Congress and the Presidency* 2, no. 2 (1984): 145–46; Allen Schick, "A Death in the Bureaucracy: The Demise of Federal PPB," *Public Administration Review* 33, no. 2 (1973).

141. See Paul E. Peterson and Mark Rom, "Lower Taxes, More Spending, and Budget Deficits," in *The Reagan Legacy: Promise and Performance*, ed. Charles O. Jones (Chatham, N.J.: Chatham House, 1988).

142. Peter M. Benda and Charles H. Levine, "Reagan and the Bureaucracy: The Bequest, the Promise, and the Legacy," in Jones, *The Reagan Legacy*, 113.

143. William Greider, "The Education of David Stockman," *Atlantic Monthly* 248, no. 6 (1981): 32 and 38.

144. Steven Mufson, "Remaking a Culture at the OMB," *Washington Post*, 14 February 1993, H1.

145. See Peter M. Benda and Charles H. Levine, "OMB's Management Role: Issues of Structure and Strategy," in U.S. Senate, Committee on Governmental Affairs, 99th Cong, 2d sess., *Office of Management and Budget Evolving Roles and Future Issues*, Committee Print 99-134 (Washington, D.C.: Government Printing Office, 1986), 73–145.

146. See Allen Schick, "The Budget Bureau That Was: Thoughts on the Rise, Decline and Future of a Presidential Agency," *Law and Contemporary Problems* 35, no. 3 (1970): 529–30.

147. Quoted in Stephen Wayne, *The Legislative Presidency* (New York: Harper & Row, 1978), 187.

148. Louis Fisher, *Presidential Spending Power* (Princeton: Princeton University

Press, 1975), 56–57.

149. *Public Papers of the Presidents: Richard M. Nixon 1970* (Washington, D.C.: Government Printing Office, 1971), 259.

150. Berman, *The Office of Management and Budget and the Presidency,* 113–15.

151. See, for example, National Academy of Public Administration, *A Presidency for the 1980s,* chap. 4.

152. Hugh Heclo, "OMB and the Presidency: The Problem of 'Neutral Competence,'" *Public Interest,* no. 38 (1975): 81.

153. See Christopher C. DeMuth and Douglas H. Ginsburg, "White House Review of Agency Rule Making," *Harvard Law Review* 99 (1986): 1075–76; Benda and Levine, "Reagan and the Bureaucracy," 114–20.

154. Benda and Levine note that there was a perceptible slowdown in regulatory activity during Reagan's first term. The total number of regulations issued by government agencies declined appreciably after the issue of Executive Order 12291. See "Reagan and the Bureaucracy," 118.

155. The council was established on 31 March 1989, seemingly under the authority of Reagan's Executive Order 12291. The council, though not formally designated as part of the Executive Office of the President, was staffed from the Vice President's Office and the Office of Information and Regulatory Affairs.

156. See, for example, Jeffrey H. Birnbaum, "White House Competitiveness Council Provokes Sharp Anger Among Democrats in Congress," *Wall Street Journal,* 8 July 1991, A8; Dana Priest, "Competitiveness Council under Scrutiny," *Washington Post,* 26 November 1991, A19; Christine Triano and Nancy Watzman, "Quayle's Hush-Hush Council," *New York Times,* 20 November 1991, A27.

157. Richard E. Neustadt, "The White House Staff: Later Period," in *The Truman White House: The Administration of the Presidency 1945–1953,* ed. Francis H. Heller (Lawrence: Regents Press of Kansas, 1980), 100.

158. See Wayne, *The Legislative Presidency,* 37.

159. John H. Kessel, *The Domestic Presidency: Decision Making in the White House* (North Scituate, Mass.: Duxbury Press, 1975), 13–15.

160. *Public Papers of the Presidents: Richard M. Nixon 1970,* 259.

161. Hess, *Organizing the Presidency,* 131.

162. John D. Ehrlichman, *Witness to Power: The Nixon Years* (New York: Simon and Schuster, 1982), 243.

163. Kessel, *The Domestic Presidency,* 14; Committee on Post Office and Civil Service, *A Report on the Growth of the Executive Office of the President 1955–1973,* 5.

164. Kessel, *The Domestic Presidency,* 108.

165. See Wayne, *The Legislative Presidency,* 120.

166. See Berman, *The Office of Management and Budget and the Presidency,* 116.

167. See Wayne, *The Legislative Presidency,* 122–28.

168. See Dom Bonafede, "Stuart Eizenstat: Carter's Right Hand Man," *National Journal,* 9 June 1979, 944–48.

169. See Larry Light, "White House Domestic Policy Staff Plays an Important Role in Formulating Legislation," *Congressional Quarterly Weekly Report,* 6 October 1979, 2199–2204.

170. The "issue clusters" were agriculture, transportation and labor, government reorganization, energy and natural resources, arts and humanities, economics and tax, housing and finance, human resources (health), human resources (employment), and civil rights and justice.

171. Quoted in Light, "White House Domestic Policy Staff Plays an Important Role in Formulating Legislation," 2200.

172. See Bonafede, "Stuart Eizenstat: Carter's Right Hand Man," 944.

173. For an assessment of Reagan's Office of Policy Development see Margaret Jane Wyszomirski, "The Roles of a Presidential Office for Domestic Policy: Three Models and Four Cases," in *The Presidency and Public Policy Making*, ed. George C. Edwards, Steven A. Shull, and Norman C. Thomas (Pittsburgh: University of Pittsburgh Press, 1986).

174. Maureen Dowd, "Bush's Adviser on Domestic Policy: The Perfect Man to Process Details," *New York Times*, 29 March 1990, A18.

175. See Burt Solomon, "In Bush's Image," *National Journal*, 7 July 1990, 1647; Kolb, *White House Daze*, chap. 2.

176. See Ann Devroy, "Yeutter Offered Top Bush Policy Post as White House Retools for Campaign," *Washington Post*, 25 January 1992, A10.

177. The functions of the three arms of the Clinton Office of Policy Development are described in White House testimony to the House Appropriations subcommittee. See U.S. House of Representatives, Committee on Appropriations, 103d Cong., 1st sess., *Treasury, Postal Service and General Government Appropriations for Fiscal Year 1994, Part 3* (Washington, D.C.: Government Printing Office, 1993), 494.

178. See Gwen Ifill, "Off-the-Books Advisers Giving Clinton a Big Lift," *New York Times*, 1 April 1993, A16; Michael K. Frisby, "At the White House, Titles Offer Few Clues about Real Influence," *Wall Street Journal*, 26 March 1993, A1.

179. Committee on Appropriations, *Treasury, Postal Service and General Government Appropriations for Fiscal Year 1994, Part 3*, 378.

180. "Remarks Announcing a New Environmental Policy," 8 February 1993, *Weekly Compilation of Presidential Documents* 29, no. 6 (15 February 1993). See also Ann Devroy, "Clinton Announces Plan to Replace Environmental Council," *Washington Post*, 9 February 1993, A6.

181. Tim Kenworthy, "Clinton Plan on CEQ Sparks Tiff with Environmentalists," *Washington Post*, 25 March 1993, A22.

182. Gary Lee, "Bipartisan House Bill Backs Efforts to Elevate EPA to Cabinet Status," *Washington Post*, 4 November 1993, A10.

183. See the 1992 testimony of President Bush's Director of ONDC, Bob Martinez, before the House Appropriations Subcommittee in U.S. House of Representatives, Committee on Appropriations, 102d Cong., 2d sess., *Treasury, Postal Service and General Government Appropriations for Fiscal Year 1993, Part 3* (Washington, D.C.: Government Printing Office, 1992), 324–442.

184. See Michael Isikoff, "Under Clinton, Drug Policy Office's Hot Streak Melts Down," *Washington Post*, 10 February 1993, A14.

185. The White House, Office of the Press Secretary, "Press Briefing by Chief of Staff Thomas McLarty," 9 February 1993, 2 and 7.

186. See Richard E. Neustadt, "Presidency and Legislation: The Growth of Central Clearance," *American Political Science Review* 48, no. 3 (1954).

187. See Wayne, *The Legislative Presidency*, chap. 4.

188. James R. Killian, *Sputnik, Scientists and Eisenhower* (Cambridge, Mass.: MIT Press, 1977), 66.

189. *Public Papers of the Presidents: Dwight D. Eisenhower 1957* (Washington, D.C.: Government Printing Office, 1958), 767.

190. Killian, *Sputnik, Scientists and Eisenhower*, 29.

191. Ibid., 205.
192. *Public Papers of the Presidents: John F. Kennedy 1962* (Washington, D.C.: Government Printing Office, 1963), 281.
193. Ibid., 280–82.
194. See Edward J. Burger, Jr., *Science at the White House: A Political Liability* (Baltimore: Johns Hopkins University Press, 1980), 9.
195. David Z. Beckler, "The Precarious Life of Science in the White House," *Daedalus* 103, no. 3 (1974): 118.
196. See ibid.
197. See Burger, *Science at the White House: A Political Liability,* 9.
198. Beckler, "The Precarious Life of Science in the White House," 120.
199. For a fuller account of the weaknesses of the science advisory mechanism in the Nixon administration see Bruce L.R. Smith, *The Advisers: Scientists in the Policy Process* (Washington, D.C.: Brookings Institution, 1992), 169–79.
200. See Beckler, "The Precarious Life of Science in the White House," 127–29.
201. See Killian, *Sputnik, Scientists and Eisenhower,* 254–59.
202. See William J. Lanouette, "Carter's Science Adviser: Doing Part of His Job Well," *National Journal,* 6 January 1979, 14–19; Philip M. Boffey, "Science Adviser Moves Beyond Rocky First Year," *New York Times,* 20 October 1982, B8. Keyworth provides a useful account of his work as President Reagan's first science adviser in his "Science Advice during the Reagan Years," in *Science and Technology Advice to the President, Congress and Judiciary,* ed. William T. Golden (New York: Pergamon Press, 1988), 182–203.
203. Figures from the U.S. Office of Personnel Management's Federal Civilian Workforce Statistics series show that OSTP was functioning with less than a dozen staff in 1988, but President Bush expanded its number to near fifty during his term of office. This number does not include detailees attached to OSTP.
204. See Maureen Dowd, "Bush Appoints 13 to Science Panel," *New York Times,* 3 February 1990, 12.
205. Graeme Browning, "Unwanted Advice?" *National Journal,* 18 May 1991, 176.
206. Smith, *The Advisers: Scientists in the Policy Process,* 181–82.
207. See Daniel Southerland, "Gibbons Confirmed as President's Science Adviser," *Washington Post,* 29 January 1993, A21.
208. Beckler, "The Precarious Life of Science in the White House," 115.
209. I.M. Destler, *American Trade Politics,* 2d ed. (Washington, D.C.: Institute for International Economics, 1992), 20.
210. See Anne H. Rightor-Thornton, "An Analysis of the Office of the Special Representative for Trade Negotiations: The Evolving Role, 1962–1974," in *Commission on the Organization of the Government for the Conduct of Foreign Policy* (Washington, D.C.: Government Printing Office, 1975), 391.
211. Both the Department of Commerce and the Department of the Treasury had been considered as an alternative to State for trade negotiation responsibility. Farm groups and labor interests reacted strongly against a role for Commerce on the grounds that its behavior would be even worse than State. Treasury was seen as an unsatisfactory alternative because of the fear that it would let its own concerns with monetary policy dominate trade negotiations. See Rightor-Thornton, "An Analysis of the Office of the Special Representative for Trade Negotiations," 91. Wilbur Mills also objected to Commerce on the grounds that it was incompetent and insufficiently responsive to agricultural interests. See Destler, *American Trade Politics,* 19.

212. Rightor-Thornton, "An Analysis of the Office of the Special Representative for Trade Negotiations," 92.

213. Destler, *American Trade Politics,* 20.

214. Rightor-Thornton, "An Analysis of the Office of the Special Representative for Trade Negotiations," 93.

215. Destler, *American Trade Politics,* 108.

216. Rightor-Thornton, "An Analysis of the Office of the Special Representative for Trade Negotiations," 95.

217. Ibid., 96.

218. Destler, *American Trade Politics,* 108.

219. For a useful, brief account of Strauss's skills in handling the 1979 legislation see Robert A. Pastor, "The Cry-and-Sigh Syndrome: Congress and Trade Policy," in *Making Economic Policy in Congress,* ed. Allen Schick (Washington, D.C.: American Enterprise Institute, 1983), 174–80.

220. "Message to Congress Transmitting Reorganization Plan No. 3 of 1979, 25 September 1979," *Public Papers of the Presidents: Jimmy Carter 1979* (Washington, D.C.: Government Printing Office, 1980), 1729–31.

221. See Destler, *American Trade Politics,* 113–16, for an account of the circumstances that gave rise to the Carter reorganization proposal.

222. Between September 1979 and September 1980, the staff of USTR increased from 43 to 127 full-time equivalent employees. Figures taken from U.S. Office of Personnel Management, Federal Civilian Workforce Statistics, *Monthly Release,* September 1979 and September 1980.

223. *Public Papers of the Presidents: Jimmy Carter 1979,* 1729.

224. Destler, *American Trade Politics,* 117.

225. Ibid., 118–20.

226. Clyde H. Farnsworth, "On the Front Lines in Trade Wars," *New York Times,* 15 August 1986, A10.

227. Destler, *American Trade Politics,* 125.

228. James M. Lindsay, "Congress and Foreign Policy: Why the Hill Matters," *Political Science Quarterly* 107, no. 4 (1992–1993): 621.

229. See Pietro S. Nivola, "Trade Policy: Refereeing the Playing Field," in *A Question of Balance: The President, Congress and Foreign Policy,* ed. Thomas E. Mann (Washington, D.C.: Brookings Institution, 1990), 238.

230. See Destler, *American Trade Politics,* 131–37.

231. Ibid., 136.

232. See Peter Behr, "Fight Over New Trade Representative Stays Hot," *Washington Post,* 19 December 1992, C1; Asra Q. Nomani and Bob Davis, "Trade-Post Fight Rates High on Meanness Meter," *Wall Street Journal,* 1 December 1992, A18.

233. For the arguments in favor of abolishing USTR and creating a new Department of Trade, see Bruce Stokes, "Organizing to Trade," *Foreign Policy,* no. 89 (1992–93). The case against is put by Destler in *American Trade Politics,* 248–51.

234. See Dom Bonafede, "The Mystery of the Executive Office Budget," *National Journal,* 16 June 1979, 1006; Bradley H. Patterson, Jr., *The Ring of Power: The White House Staff and Its Expanding Role in Government* (New York: Basic Books, 1988), 321.

235. For example, Theodore J. Lowi, *The Personal President* (Ithaca: Cornell University Press, 1985), 5.

236. For a description of the work of these units, see Patterson, *The Ring of Power*, 309–35.

237. Author's interview with William Hopkins, 9 May 1984.

4. The White House Staff

1. Robert Ferrell, *Off the Record: The Private Papers of Harry S. Truman* (New York: Harper & Row, 1980), 40.

2. See above, page 37.

3. U.S. House of Representatives, Committee on Post Office and Civil Service, 92d Cong., 2d sess., Committee Print 19, *A Report on the Growth of the Executive Office of the President 1955–1973* (Washington, D.C.: Government Printing Office, 1972).

4. Thomas E. Cronin, *The State of the Presidency* (Boston: Little, Brown, 1975).

5. The "full-time equivalent employment" figure is provided in the budget from fiscal year 1951 onward. Prior to 1951, staff size was shown in terms of "man-years" and, from 1939 to 1941, as "budgeted positions."

6. Cronin, *The State of the Presidency*, 119.

7. U.S. House of Representatives, Hearings Before a Subcommittee of the Committee on Appropriations, 86th Cong., 1st sess., *General Government Matters Appropriations for 1960* (Washington, D.C.: Government Printing Office, 1959), 127.

8. U.S. Senate, Hearings Before the Subcommittees of the Committee on Appropriations, 93d Cong., 1st sess., *Supplemental Appropriations for Fiscal Year 1974, Part 1* (Washington, D.C.: Government Printing Office, 1973), 340.

9. U.S. House of Representatives, Hearings Before a Subcommittee of the Committee on Appropriations, 91st Cong., 2d sess., *Departments of Treasury, Post Office and Executive Office Appropriations for 1971, Part 3* (Washington, D.C.: Government Printing Office, 1970), 4–9.

10. U.S. House of Representatives, Committee on Post Office and Civil Service, 95th Cong., 2d sess., *Presidential Staffing: A Brief Overview*, Print 95-17 (Washington, D.C.: Government Printing Office, 1978), 57.

11. Ibid., 58.

12. For example, the "actual manpower" figure for 1970 given by Fisher-Relyea is 491, but the authors also state in their report that there were 273 detailees on the White House staff in 1970 and, when that figure is added to the official White House Office staff and the Special Projects Fund staff, the grand total becomes 576. This means either that not all the detailees have been included in the figure of 576 or that the Federal Civilian Workforce Statistics did include some of them in its totals.

13. Stephen J. Wayne, *The Legislative Presidency* (New York: Harper & Row, 1978), 220–21.

14. This is always a difficult task because detailees spend different lengths of time in the White House during any one year, which makes the task of calculating an aggregate total of the number of detailees almost impossible.

15. Gary King and Lyn Ragsdale, *The Elusive Executive: Discovering Statistical Patterns in the Presidency* (Washington, D.C.: CQ Press, 1988), 206–9.

16. I have explored the issue of White House staff growth during the Eisenhower years in some detail. See John Hart, "Eisenhower and the Swelling of the Presi-

dency," *Polity* 24, no. 4 (1992): 673–91.

17. The act (Public Law 95-570) also requires the President to report on staff numbers in the Office of Vice President, the Domestic Policy Staff (known as the Domestic Policy Council in the Clinton administration), the Office of Administration, and the Executive Residence at the White House. The reporting requirement of the act is discussed more fully in chapter 5.

18. It is appropriate to note here that an audit of the Executive Office of the President carried out by the General Accounting Office in 1987 found that the data submitted under the terms of the White House Personnel Authorization-Employment Act consistently underreported the number of detailees who fell within the scope of the reporting requirement. See U.S. General Accounting Office, *Personnel Practices: Detailing of Federal Employees to the White House,* GAO/GGD-87-102BR, July 1987, 3.

19. The distinction between "detailees" and "assignees" was first made in a written White House response to questions from Senator Domenici arising from the Senate Appropriations Subcommittee hearing on the Executive Office budget request for fiscal year 1989. Assignees were defined as those employees placed in EOP agencies who "are representing, or doing the work of, their 'home' or assigning agencies. These employees can serve in a liaison role ... reporting to their assigning agency on any policy decisions or actions which may have an impact on the assigning agency; or they can perform the work of their parent agency, although physically located in EOP facilities." See U.S. Senate, Hearings Before a Subcommittee of the Committee on Appropriations, 100th Cong., 2d sess., *Treasury, Postal Service and General Government Appropriations for Fiscal Year 1989, Part 3* (Washington, D.C.: Government Printing Office, 1988), 1158.

20. U.S. House of Representatives, Hearings Before a Subcommittee of the Committee on Appropriations, 103d Cong., 1st sess., *Treasury, Post Office and General Government Appropriations for Fiscal Year 1994, Part 3* (Washington, D.C.: U.S. Government Printing Office, 1993), 480–81.

21. U.S. Office of Personnel Management, *Federal Civilian Workforce Statistics, Employment and Trends as of November 1992* (Washington, D.C.: Government Printing Office, 1992), 16.

22. Ever since the first report in 1979, there has been a discrepancy between the staff totals reported by the White House as at 30 September and those reported by the Office of Personnel Management in the Federal Civilian Workforce Statistics for the same month, with the latter being higher. This may be due to the fact that the OPM figures include non-permanent part-time staff (or what the White House calls "intermittent" staff), counting them just the same as the permanent staff. The "intermittent" staff are reported separately in the White House reports, but not in a way that they can be included in the aggregate total.

23. The commitment was "We will reduce the White House staff by 25 percent and challenge Congress to do the same." See Governor Bill Clinton and Senator Al Gore, *Putting People First: How We Can All Change America* (New York: Times Books, 1992), 25.

24. "Remarks on Reduction and Reorganization of the White House Staff," 9 February 1993, *Weekly Compilation of Presidential Documents* 29, no. 6 (15 February 1993): 162–63.

25. Ann Devroy, "Adding Up Clinton's Cuts," *Washington Post,* 30 September 1993, A1.

26. Bradley H. Patterson, Jr., *The Ring of Power: The White House Staff and Its Expanding Role in Government* (New York: Basic Books, 1988), 339.

27. This was triggered more by John Sununu's abuses of White House perquisites (see above, p. 11) than Patterson's book. In 1992 the House of Representatives Post Office and Civil Service Committee estimated that 70 percent of the real costs of the EOP are hidden in the budgets of other federal departments and agencies. See U.S. House of Representatives, Committee on Post Office and Civil Service, 102d Cong., 2d sess., *White House Personnel Reauthorization Act of 1992*, Report 102-985, 3 October 1992, 3. The proposed legislation progressed no further than the floor of the House.

28. John Osborne, *The White House Watch: The Ford Years* (Washington, D.C.: New Republic Books, 1977), 445.

29. Richard E. Neustadt, "Staffing the Presidency: Premature Notes on the New Administration," *Political Science Quarterly* 93, no. 1 (1978): 7.

30. Emmette S. Redford and Richard T. McCulley, *White House Operations: The Johnson Presidency* (Austin: University of Texas Press, 1986), 33.

31. U.S. House of Representatives, Hearings Before a Subcommittee of the Committee on Appropriations, 93d Cong., 1st sess., *Treasury, Post Office and General Government Appropriations for Fiscal Year 1974, Part 3* (Washington, D.C.: Government Printing Office, 1973), 603–9.

32. U.S. House of Representatives, Hearings Before a Subcommittee of the Committee on Appropriations, 97th Cong., 1st sess., *Treasury, Post Office and General Government Appropriations for Fiscal Year 1982, Part 3* (Washington, D.C.: Government Printing Office, 1981), 154.

33. Greg Schneiders, "Goodbye to All That," *Newsweek*, 24 September 1979, 23.

34. President's Committee on Administrative Management, *Administrative Management in the Government of the United States* (Washington, D.C.: Government Printing Office, 1937), 5.

35. John R. Steelman and Dewayne H. Kreager, "The Executive Office as an Administrative Co-ordinator," *Law and Contemporary Problems* 21, no. 4 (1956): 699.

36. Richard F. Fenno, Jr., *The President's Cabinet* (Cambridge, Mass.: Harvard University Press, 1959), 142.

37. Cronin, *The State of the Presidency*, 122.

38. Jeffrey L. Pressman and Aaron Wildavsky, *Implementation: How Great Expectations in Washington Are Dashed in Oakland* (Berkeley: University of California Press, 1984), 133–34.

39. Richard E. Neustadt, "Presidential Management," in *Improving the Accountability and Performance of Government*, ed. Bruce Smith and Richard D. Carroll (Washington, D.C.: Brookings Institution, 1982), 93.

40. Dom Bonafede, "Powell and the Press: A New Mood in the White House," *National Journal*, 25 June 1977, 985.

41. Stephen Hess, "All the President's Reporters: A New Survey of the White House Press Corps," *Presidential Studies Quarterly* 22, no. 2 (1992): 312.

42. See John Anthony Maltese, *Spin Control: The White House Office of Communications and the Management of Presidential News* (Chapel Hill: University of North Carolina Press, 1992).

43. The role of the congressional liaison staff is discussed more fully in Wayne, *The Legislative Presidency*, chap. 5.

44. See Eric L. Davis, "Legislative Liaison in the Carter Administration," *Political*

Science Quarterly 95, no. 3 (1979); Charles O. Jones, *The Trusteeship Presidency: Jimmy Carter and the United States Congress* (Baton Rouge: Louisiana State University Press, 1988), chap. 5.

45. See Elizabeth Wehr, "Public Liaison Chief Dole Reaches to Outside Groups to Sell Reagan's Programs," *Congressional Quarterly Weekly Report*, 6 June 1981, 975–78; Mark A. Peterson, "The Presidency and Organized Interests: White House Patterns of Interest Group Liaison," *American Political Science Review* 86, no. 3 (1992): 612–25.

46. Nelson W. Polsby, *Consequences of Party Reform* (New York: Oxford University Press, 1983), 129.

47. See Louis W. Koenig, *The Chief Executive* (New York: Harcourt, Brace and World, 1968), 315.

48. See, for example, Norman Ornstein, "The Open Congress Meets the President," in *Both Ends of the Avenue*, ed. Anthony King (Washington, D.C.: American Enterprise Institute, 1983).

49. John Dean, *Blind Ambition* (New York: Simon and Schuster, 1976), 30.

50. Jeb Stuart Magruder, *An American Life: One Man's Road to Watergate* (New York: Atheneum, 1974), 71.

51. Ibid., p. 101.

52. Zbigniew Brzezinski, *Power and Principle: Memoirs of the National Security Adviser 1977–1981* (New York: Farrar, Straus and Giroux, 1983), 76–77.

53. Lewis A. Dexter, "Court Politics: Presidential Staff Relations as a Special Case of a General Phenomenon," *Administration and Society* 9, no. 3 (1977).

54. Dean, *Blind Ambition*, 38.

55. Ibid., 38–40.

56. Rowe, quoted in Robert L. Lester, "Developments in Presidential-Congressional Relations: FDR–JFK," Ph.D. dissertation, University of Virginia, 1969, 44.

57. Neustadt, quoted in John Hart, "Staffing the Presidency: Kennedy and the Office of Congressional Relations," *Presidential Studies Quarterly* 13, no. 1 (1983): 105.

58. Dick Kirschten, "New Intergovernmental Affairs Chief Charts Less Abrasive Course," *National Journal*, 8 October 1983, 2064.

59. There are even significant differences among seemingly similar operating styles. See the comparison of Franklin D. Roosevelt and John F. Kennedy in Richard E. Neustadt, "Approaches to Staffing the Presidency: Notes on FDR and JFK," *American Political Science Review* 57, no. 4 (1963).

60. Michael Grossman and Martha J. Kumar, *Portraying the President* (Baltimore: Johns Hopkins University Press, 1981), 89.

61. Hart, "Staffing the Presidency," 102–5.

62. See Edward S. Corwin, *The President: Office and Powers*, 4th ed. (New York: New York University Press, 1957), 490–91.

63. Richard F. Fenno, Jr., *The President's Cabinet* (Cambridge, Mass.: Harvard University Press, 1959), 41.

64. Corwin, *The President: Office and Powers*, 301.

65. Fred I. Greenstein, *The Hidden-Hand Presidency* (New York: Basic Books, 1982), 113.

66. See Cronin, *The State of the Presidency*, 177.

67. Arthur M. Schlesinger, Jr., *A Thousand Days: John F. Kennedy in the White House* (London: Andre Deutsch, 1965), 596; Theodore C. Sorensen, *Kennedy* (New York: Harper & Row, 1965), 283.

68. Quoted in Cronin, *The State of the Presidency*, 168.

69. See John D. Ehrlichman, *Witness to Power: The Nixon Years* (New York: Simon and Schuster, 1982), 110–11.

70. *Public Papers of the Presidents: Richard M. Nixon 1973* (Washington, D.C.: Government Printing Office, 1974), 5.

71. Nelson W. Polsby, "Presidential Cabinet Making: Lessons for the Political System," *Political Science Quarterly* 93, no. 1 (1978): 16.

72. Ehrlichman, *Witness to Power*, 106.

73. See Edwin Meese, "The Institutional Presidency: A View from the White House," *Presidential Studies Quarterly* 13, no. 2 (1983).

74. Chester A. Newland, "Executive Office Policy Apparatus: Enforcing the Reagan Agenda," in *The Reagan Presidency and the Governing of America*, ed. Lester M. Salamon and Michael S. Lund (Washington, D.C.: Urban Institute Press, 1984), 153–61.

75. See John Hart, "Executive Reorganization in the USA and the Growth of Presidential Power," *Public Administration* 52 (1974).

76. R. Gordon Hoxie, "Staffing the Ford and Carter Presidencies," in *Organizing and Staffing the Presidency*, ed. Bradley D. Nash, Milton S. Eisenhower, R. Gordon Hoxie, and William C. Spragens (New York: Center for the Study of the Presidency, 1980), 50.

77. Gerald R. Ford, *A Time to Heal* (New York: Harper and Row, 1979), 131.

78. Quoted in Dom Bonafede, "Carter White House Staff Is Heavy on Functions, Light on Frills," *National Journal*, 12 February 1977, 234.

79. Joseph A. Califano, *Governing America* (New York: Simon and Schuster, 1981), 402–48.

80. Quoted in Austin Ranney, "The Carter Administration," in Austin Ranney, ed., *The American Elections of 1980* (Washington, D.C.: American Enterprise Institute, 1981), 32.

81. See Bob Woodward, "The President's Key Men: Splintered Trio, Splintered Policy," *Washington Post*, 7 October 1992, A1.

82. For a sense of the animosities that existed between senior Reagan White House staff, see, for example, Peggy Noonan, *What I Saw at the Revolution: A Political Life in the Reagan Era* (New York: Random House, 1990), 168–69; Edwin Meese III, *With Reagan: The Inside Story* (Washington, D.C.: Regnery Gateway, 1992), chap. 8; Lyn Nofziger, *Nofziger* (Washington, D.C.: Regnery Gateway, 1992), chap. 9.

83. Corwin, *The President: Office and Powers*, 82; Henry Jones Ford, *The Rise and Growth of American Politics* (New York: Macmillan, 1898), 78; Henry B. Learned, *The President's Cabinet* (New York: Burt and Franklin, 1912), 85.

84. Woodrow Wilson, *Constitutional Government in the United States* (New York: Columbia University Press, 1908), 138.

85. Ford, *The Rise and Growth of American Politics*, 77–78.

86. Corwin, *The President: Office and Powers*, 209.

87. But see Louis Fisher's qualification in his *The Politics of Shared Power: Congress and the Executive* (Washington, D.C.: CQ Press, 1981), 8. Senate Rule 36 still makes provision for the president to meet with the Senate for the consideration of executive business.

88. Richard E. Neustadt, *Presidential Power: The Politics of Leadership* (New York: Wiley, 1960), 39–40.

89. Ibid., 41.

90. See Margaret Jane Wyszomirski, "The De-institutionalization of Presidential Staff Agencies," *Public Administration Review* 42, no. 3 (1982).

91. Richard Rose, "Governments Against Sub-governments: A European Perspective on Washington," in *Presidents and Prime Ministers,* ed. Richard Rose and Ezra Suleiman (Washington, D.C.: American Enterprise Institute, 1980), 338.

92. Terry Moe, "The Politicized Presidency," in *The New Direction in American Politics,* ed. John E. Chubb and Paul E. Peterson (Washington, D.C.: Brookings Institution, 1985), 239.

93. See Dan Rather and Gary Paul Gates, *The Palace Guard* (New York: Harper & Row, 1974). The praetorian guard label came from Robert L. Hartmann, *Palace Politics: An Inside Account of the Ford Years* (New York: McGraw-Hill, 1980).

94. Charles Kolb, *White House Daze: The Unmaking of Domestic Policy in the Bush Years* (New York: Free Press, 1994), 183.

95. George Reedy, *The Twilight of the Presidency* (New York: New American Library, 1970), 94.

96. Cronin, *The State of the Presidency,* 139; Stephen Hess, *Organizing the Presidency* (Washington, D.C.: Brookings Institution, 1976), 153.

97. Reedy, *The Twilight of the Presidency,* 88–89.

98. Califano, *Governing America,* 411.

99. Abraham Holtzman, *Legislative Liaison: Executive Leadership in Congress* (Chicago: Rand McNally, 1970), 67.

100. Cronin, *The State of the Presidency,* 163.

101. See Colin Seymour-Ure, *The American President: Power and Communication* (London: Macmillan, 1982), 78.

102. Reedy, *The Twilight of the Presidency,* xv.

103. Ibid., xiii.

104. See Michael Medved, *The Shadow Presidents* (New York: Times Books, 1979), 111.

105. See Patrick Anderson, *The President's Men* (New York: Doubleday, 1968), 13.

106. In "The Federalist No. 51." Benjamin Fletcher Wright, ed., *The Federalist* (Cambridge, Mass.: Harvard University Press, 1966), 356.

5. *Congress, Comity, and the Presidential Branch*

1. Arthur M. Schlesinger, Jr., *The Imperial Presidency* (Boston: Houghton Mifflin, 1973).

2. See James L. Sundquist, *The Decline and Resurgence of Congress* (Washington, D.C.: Brookings Institution, 1981).

3. For a useful survey of the literature see Joel D. Aberbach, *Keeping a Watchful Eye: The Politics of Congressional Oversight* (Washington, D.C.: Brookings Institution, 1990), chap. 2.

4. See Roger H. Davidson and Walter J. Oleszek, *Congress Against Itself* (Bloomington: Indiana University Press, 1977), 96–100.

5. Morris S. Ogul, *Congress Oversees the Bureaucracy* (Pittsburgh: University of Pittsburgh Press, 1976), 181.

6. Morris P. Fiorina, "Congressional Control of the Bureaucracy: A Mismatch of Incentives and Capabilities," in *Congress Reconsidered,* ed. Lawrence C. Dodd and Bruce I. Oppenheimer (Washington, D.C.: CQ Press, 1981), 341.

7. Sundquist, *The Decline and Resurgence of Congress,* 327.

8. See, for example, Ogul, *Congress Oversees the Bureaucracy,* 21.

9. See Louis Fisher, *The Politics of Shared Power: Congress and the Executive* (Washington, D.C.: CQ Press, 1981), chap. 3; Sundquist, *The Decline and Resurgence of Congress,* 335–40; David S. Broder and Stephen Barr, "Hill's Micromanagement of Cabinet Blurs Separation of Powers," *Washington Post,* 25 July 1993, A1.

10. Aberbach, *Keeping a Watchful Eye,* 19.

11. See Lawrence C. Dodd and Richard L. Schott, *Congress and the Administrative State* (New York: Wiley, 1979), 165–68.

12. Three EOP units are under the jurisdiction of other appropriations subcommittees. The Subcommittee on Commerce, Justice, State, the Judiciary and Related Agencies has jurisdiction over the Office of the U. S. Trade Representative. The Subcommittee on Veterans Affairs, HUD, and Independent Agencies has jurisdiction over the Council on Environmental Quality and the Office of Science and Technology Policy.

13. Richard F. Fenno, Jr., *Congressmen in Committees* (Boston: Little, Brown, 1973), 111, 255.

14. Ogul, *Congress Oversees the Bureaucracy,* 57.

15. Ibid., 82.

16. Fenno, *Congressmen in Committees,* 5.

17. Ibid., 67.

18. Ogul, *Congress Oversees the Bureaucracy,* 39.

19. Fenno, *Congressmen in Committees,* 110–11.

20. Ibid., 283; Ogul, *Congress Oversees the Bureaucracy,* 39.

21. U.S. House of Representatives, Committee on Post Office and Civil Service, 92d Cong., 2d sess., Committee Print 19, *A Report on the Growth of the Executive Office of the President 1955–1973* (Washington, D.C.: Government Printing Office, 1972), 11.

22. Fenno, *Congressmen in Committees,* 94–97.

23. Ibid., 48.

24. Ibid., 194–95.

25. Ibid., 199.

26. Stephen Horn, *Unused Power: The Work of the Senate Committee on Appropriations* (Washington, D.C.: Brookings Institution, 1970), 163.

27. Ogul, *Congress Oversees the Bureaucracy,* 153.

28. Walter J. Oleszek, *Congressional Procedures and the Policy Process,* 2d ed. (Washington, D.C.: CQ Press, 1984), 232.

29. Ibid.

30. Dodd and Schott, *Congress and the Administrative State,* 242.

31. "Continuous watchfulness" is the terminology used in the Legislative Reorganization Act of 1946, which formalized the oversight function. The Legislative Reorganization Act of 1970 used the term "legislative review" to describe congressional oversight.

32. G. Calvin Mackenzie, *The Politics of Presidential Appointments* (New York: Free Press, 1981), 175.

33. Ibid., 187; Arthur Maass, *Congress and the Common Good* (New York: Basic Books, 1983), 182.

34. See Fisher, *The Politics of Shared Power,* 144.

35. See Ronald C. Moe, "Senate Confirmation of Executive Appointments: The

Nixon Era," *Proceedings of the Academy of Political Science* 32, no. 1 (1975): 145.

36. See the testimony of Richard E. Neustadt, I.M. Destler, and Thomas Franck in U.S. Senate, Committee on Foreign Relations, 96th Cong., 2d sess., *The National Security Adviser: Role and Accountability* (Washington, D.C.: Government Printing Office, 1980), 29–45.

37. In 1985, Congress came close to breaching the tradition when it mandated the appointment of a Special Assistant to the President for Agricultural Trade and Food Aid to assist and advise the President on food assistance programs and agricultural trade (Public Law 99-198, Sec. 1113). The title of Special Assistant is usually associated with an appointment in the White House Office, but this legislation specified only that "the Special Assistant shall serve in the Executive Office of the President." In both the Reagan and Bush administrations, the Special Assistant was located in the White House Office. This position has not been filled in the Clinton administration.

38. Sundquist, *The Decline and Resurgence of Congress,* 318–19.

39. See Bruce Adams and Kathryn Kavanagh-Baran, *Promise and Performance: Carter Builds a New Administration* (Lexington, Mass.: D.C. Heath, 1979), 159–60; Suzanne Garment, *Scandal: The Culture of Mistrust in American Politics* (New York: Times Books, 1991), 43–47.

40. Sundquist, *The Decline and Resurgence of Congress,* 319.

41. In 1977 the Senate Environment and Public Works Committee rejected President Carter's nomination of Marion Edey to be a member of the Council on Environmental Quality. See Adams and Kavanagh-Baran, *Promise and Performance,* 161.

42. U.S. Senate, *The National Security Adviser: Role and Accountability,* 2.

43. Louis Fisher, *Constitutional Conflicts between Congress and the President* (Princeton: Princeton University Press, 1985), 204.

44. See, for example, U.S. Senate, Committee on Government Operations, 94th Cong., 1st sess., Hearings Before the Subcommittee on Intergovernmental Relations, *Executive Privilege—Secrecy in Government* (Washington, D.C.: Government Printing Office, 1976).

45. Raoul Berger, *Executive Privilege: A Constitutional Myth* (Cambridge, Mass.: Harvard University Press, 1974), 1.

46. Congress has been more willing to challenge the claim of executive privilege with respect to executive branch officials. There have been several instances during the past decade when the threat of contempt proceedings against executive branch officials has eventually induced cooperation with Congress and forced the release of information demanded by congressional committees. See Fisher, *Constitutional Conflicts between Congress and the President,* 209–12.

47. See U.S. House of Representatives, Committee on Appropriations, 97th Cong., 1st sess., Rept. No. 97-171, *Treasury, Postal Service and General Government Appropriation Bill 1982* (Washington, D.C.: Government Printing Office, 1981), 30, 61–63.

48. See U.S. House of Representatives, Committee on Appropriations, 97th Cong., 1st sess., Hearings Before a Subcommittee of the Committee on Appropriations, *Treasury, Postal Service and General Government Appropriations for Fiscal Year 1982, Part 3* (Washington, D.C.: Government Printing Office, 1981), 388–90.

49. See Aberbach, *Keeping a Watchful Eye,* chap. 2.

50. U.S. Senate, 93d Cong., 1st sess., Hearings Before the Subcommittee on Inter-governmental Relations of the Committee on Government Operations and the Subcommittees on Separation of Powers and Administrative Practice and Procedure of the Committee on the Judiciary, *Executive Privilege, Secrecy in Government and Freedom of Information* (Washington, D.C.: Government Printing Office, 1973).

51. The sequence of events in the uncovering of Iran-*contra* is described in detail in U.S. House of Representatives Select Committee to Investigate Covert Arms Transactions with Iran and U.S. Senate Select Committee on Secret Military Assistance to Iran and the Nicaraguan Opposition, 100th Cong., 1st sess., House Rept. No. 100-433, Senate Rept. No. 100-216, *Report of the Congressional Committees Investigating the Iran-Contra Affair* (Washington, D.C.: Government Printing Office, 1987), 285–324.

52. Ibid, xv.

53. Ibid., 423.

54. The recommendations of the Iran-*contra* investigating committee are to be found in ibid., 423–27.

55. Harold Hongju Koh, *The National Security Constitution* (New Haven: Yale University Press, 1990), 16, 20.

56. Ibid., 16–22.

57. Ibid., 18.

58. Ibid., 157.

59. U.S. House of Representatives, Committee on Appropriations, 80th Cong., 1st sess., Hearings Before a Subcommittee of the Committee on Appropriations, *Independent Offices Appropriations Bill for 1948* (Washington, D.C.: Government Printing Office, 1947), 15.

60. U.S. House of Representatives, Committee on Appropriations, 86th Cong., 1st sess., Hearings Before a Subcommittee of the Committee on Appropriations, *General Government Matters Appropriations for 1960* (Washington, D.C.: Government Printing Office, 1959), 123.

61. In fact, neither the president nor the Office of Management and Budget has the power to alter the budget request submitted by Congress. It is exempt by law from executive branch review. For Dodge's statement see U.S. House of Representatives, Committee on Appropriations, 83d Cong., 1st sess., Hearings Before a Subcommittee of the Committee on Appropriations, *Independent Offices Appropriations for 1954* (Washington, D.C.: Government Printing Office, 1953), 626.

62. See, for example, U.S. House of Representatives, Committee on Appropriations, 84th Cong., 2d sess., Hearings Before a Subcommittee of the Committee on Appropriations, *General Government Matters Appropriations for 1957* (Washington, D.C.: Government Printing Office, 1956), 27–28; and U.S. House of Representatives, Committee on Appropriations, 85th Cong., 2d sess., Hearings Before a Subcommittee of the Committee on Appropriations, *General Government Matters Appropriations for 1959* (Washington, D.C.: Government Printing Office, 1958), 89–90.

63. U.S. Senate, Committee on Appropriations, 84th Cong., 1st sess., Hearings Before a Subcommittee of the Committee on Appropriations, *General Government Matters Appropriations for 1956* (Washington, D.C.: Government Printing Office, 1955), 4.

64. On discretionary funding see Louis Fisher, "Confidential Spending and Govern-

ment Accountability," *George Washington Law Review* 47, no. 2 (1979).

65. U.S. House of Representatives, Committee on Appropriations, 86th Cong., 2d sess., Hearings Before a Subcommittee of the Committee on Appropriations, *General Government Matters Appropriations for 1961* (Washington, D.C.: Government Printing Office, 1960), 85.

66. U.S. House of Representatives, Committee on Appropriations, 89th Cong., 1st sess., Hearings Before a Subcommittee of the Committee on Appropriations, *Treasury-Post Office and Executive Office Appropriations for 1966* (Washington, D.C.: Government Printing Office, 1965), 885.

67. U.S. Senate, Committee on Appropriations, 91st Cong., 2d sess., Hearings Before a Subcommittee of the Committee on Appropriations, *Treasury, Post Office and Executive Office Appropriations for Fiscal Year 1971* (Washington, D.C.: Government Printing Office, 1970), 1230.

68. U.S. House of Representatives, Committee on Appropriations, 92d Cong., 1st sess., Hearings Before a Subcommittee of the Committee on Appropriations, *Treasury, Post Office and Executive Office Appropriations for 1972, Part 4* (Washington, D.C.: Government Printing Office, 1971), 260–61.

69. U.S. House of Representatives, Committee on Appropriations, 88th Cong., 2d sess., Hearings Before a Subcommittee of the Committee on Appropriations, *Treasury-Post Office Departments and Executive Office Appropriations for 1965* (Washington, D.C.: Government Printing Office, 1964), 872.

70. U.S. Senate, Committee on Appropriations, 93d Cong., 1st sess., Hearings Before the Subcommittees of the Committee on Appropriations, *Supplemental Appropriations for Fiscal Year 1974, Part 1* (Washington, D.C.: Government Printing Office, 1970), 338.

71. U.S. House of Representatives, Committee on Appropriations, 93d Cong., 1st sess., Hearings Before a Subcommittee of the Committee on Appropriations, *Treasury, Post Office and General Government Appropriations for Fiscal Year 1973, Part 3* (Washington, D.C.: Government Printing Office, 1973), 623–24.

72. See Dean L. Yarwood, "Oversight of Presidential Funds by the Appropriations Committees: Learning from the Watergate Crisis," *Administration and Society* 13, no. 3 (1981): 308–9.

73. The Emergency Fund for the President was also terminated as of fiscal year 1974. It was replaced by the Unanticipated Needs Fund, for which the President must account to Congress.

74. U.S. Congress, 96th Cong., 1st sess., *Congressional Record* 125 (16 July 1979): H5967.

75. Fenno, *Congressmen in Committees,* 97.

76. For examples, see Yarwood, "Oversight of Presidential Funds by the Appropriations Committees," 329–31.

77. Walter F. Mondale, *The Accountability of Power: Toward a Responsible Presidency* (New York: McKay, 1975), 92.

78. U.S. House of Representatives, Committee on Appropriations, 103d Cong., 1st sess., Hearings Before a Subcommittee of the Committee on Appropriations, *Treasury, Post Office and General Government Appropriations for Fiscal Year 1994, Part 3* (Washington, D.C.: Government Printing Office, 1993), 821–68.

79. U.S. Congress, 103d Cong., 1st sess., *Congressional Record* 139 (18 June 1993): H3801.

80. Ibid.

81. For the background to this legislation see U.S. House of Representatives, Com-

mittee on Post Office and Civil Service, 93d Cong., 2d sess., *Authorization for Staff Support in the White House Office and for the Executive Duties of the Vice President* (Washington, D.C.: Government Printing Office, 1974).

82. U.S. House of Representatives, *A Report on the Growth of the Executive Office of the President 1955–1973*, 10.

83. U.S. Congress, 95th Cong., 2d sess., *Congressional Record* 124 (4 April 1978): 8633.

84. U.S. House of Representatives, Committee on Post Office and Civil Service, 93d Cong., 2d sess., Hearing Before the Subcommittee on Employee Ethics and Utilization, *Authorization for the White House Staff* (Washington, D.C.: Government Printing Office, 1977), 3.

85. Ibid., 22.

86. U.S. Congress, 95th Cong., 2d sess., *Congressional Record* 124 (4 April 1978): 8633–34.

87. U.S. House of Representatives, Committee on Post Office and Civil Service, 95th Cong., 2d sess., Rept. No. 95-979, *White House Personnel Authorization* (Washington, D.C.: Government Printing Office, 1978).

88. Author's interview with Herbert E. Harris, 3 December 1982.

89. U.S. House of Representatives, Committee on Post Office and Civil Service, 95th Cong., 2d sess., Conference Report to Accompany H.R. 11003, Rept. No. 95-1639, *White House Personnel Authorization* (Washington, D.C.: Government Printing Office, 1978), 3.

90. Author's interview with Knox Walkup, 23 November 1982.

91. Harris interview.

92. Fenno, *Congressmen in Committees*, 199.

93. U.S. Congress, 95th Cong., 2d sess., *Congressional Record* 124 (4 April 1978): 8635.

94. The personnel reports submitted by President Carter under Section 113 of the act show only the "cumulative number" of individuals employed during the fiscal year and not the actual number of staff positions or the number of staff at a particular time of the year.

95. On 11 October 1983, Representative Patricia Schroeder did issue a press release accusing the Reagan administration of exceeding the authorized ceilings established in the 1978 act—"Reagan Appointed 107 to High-Paid White House Staff Positions in First Two Years, Compared to 38 Appointed by President Carter"—but this was strongly denied by the Reagan administration. Implicit in the Schroeder criticism, however, was that one key member of Congress was not prepared to accept the data reported by the White House under the terms of the act. She claimed to have used a different set of figures supplied by the President's Assistant for Management and Administration.

96. Walter Shapiro, "White House Taps Departments for 'Borrowed' Staff," *Washington Post*, 23 February 1980, 1.

97. U.S. General Accounting Office, *Personnel Practices: The Department of Energy's Use of Schedule C Appointment Authority*, GAO/GGD-90-61, March 1990, 5–6.

98. "Detailed or Otherwise Assigned Personnel in Offices Within the Executive Office of the President," Congressional Research Service, 13 April 1992.

99. U.S. General Accounting Office, *Personnel Practices: Detailing of Federal Employees to the White House*, GAO/GGD-87-102BR, July 1987, 3.

100. U.S. Senate, Committee on Appropriations, 100th Cong., 2d sess., Hearings Be-

fore the Subcommittees of the Committee on Appropriations, *Treasury, Postal Service and General Government Appropriations for Fiscal Year 1989, Part 3* (Washington, D.C.: Government Printing Office, 1988), 1140–41.

101. U.S. House of Representatives, Committee on Post Office and Civil Service, 102d Cong., 2d sess., Rept. No. 102-985, *White House Personnel Reauthorization Act of 1992* (Washington, D.C.: Government Printing Office, 1992), 3. See also Charles R. Babcock, "The Hidden Costs of the White House," *Washington Post*, 3 December 1992, A19.

102. Quoted in Charles R. Babcock, "Hard to Pin Down What Taxpayers Give at the Top Office," *Washington Post*, 19 October 1992, A19.

103. See John Hart, "Congressional Reactions to White House Lobbying," *Presidential Studies Quarterly* 11, no. 1 (1981): 84–86.

104. "What They Say About JFK: Congressmen Tell What's on Their Minds," *U.S. News and World Report*, 30 July 1962, 32.

105. Meg Greenfield, "Why Are You Calling Me, Son?" *The Reporter*, 16 August 1962, 30.

106. See Donald Smith, "Turning Screws: Winning Votes in Congress," *Congressional Quarterly Weekly Report* 34, no. 17 (1976): 950.

107. U.S. Congress, 87th Cong., 2d sess., *Congressional Record* 108 (18 June 1962): 10762.

108. Smith, "Turning Screws: Winning Votes in Congress," 954.

109. See ibid; see also Louis Fisher, Congressional Research Service Rept. No. 78-147 Gov., *White House-Congress Relationships: Information Exchange and Lobbying* (Washington, D.C.: Congressional Research Service, 1978), 74.

110. See Fisher, *White House-Congress Relationships*, 51–53.

111. Ibid., 66–67.

112. U.S. Congress, 87th Cong., 2d sess., *Congressional Record* 108 (15 May 1962): 8449–51.

113. Smith, "Turning Screws: Winning Votes in Congress," 947.

114. Hart, "Congressional Reactions to White House Lobbying," 90.

115. See Norman J. Ornstein, Thomas E. Mann and Michael J. Malbin, *Vital Statistics on Congress, 1993–1994* (Washington, D.C.: CQ Press., 1994), 126–40.

116. See Ibid., pp. 121–25; Harrison W. Fox, Jr., and Susan Webb Hammond, *Congressional Staffs: The Invisible Force in American Lawmaking* (New York: Free Press, 1977), chap. 2.

117. Michael J. Malbin, *Unelected Representatives: Congressional Staff and the Future of Representative Government* (New York: Basic Books, 1980), 6–7.

118. Ornstein, Mann and Malbin, *Vital Statistics on Congress*, 124.

119. Ibid., pp. 138–39.

120. See Dana Priest, "Stealing Congress's Thunder: Darman 'Adjusts' Budget Downward," *Washington Post*, 10 February 1992, A9.

121. See Eric L. Davis, "Congressional Liaison: The People and the Institutions," in *Both Ends of the Avenue*, ed. Anthony King (Washington, D.C.: American Enterprise Institute, 1983); Abraham Holtzman, *Legislative Liaison: Executive Leadership in Congress* (Chicago: Rand McNally, 1970), chap. 9; John F. Manley, "Presidential Power and White House Lobbying," *Political Science Quarterly* 93, no. 2 (1978); Stephen J. Wayne, *The Legislative Presidency* (New York: Harper & Row, 1978), chap. 5.

122. See John Hart, "Staffing the Presidency: Kennedy and the Office of Congressional Relations," *Presidential Studies Quarterly* 13, no. 1 (1983).

123. Lawrence F. O'Brien, *No Final Victories: A Life in Politics from John F. Kennedy to Watergate* (New York: Doubleday, 1974), 119.
124. Hart, "Congressional Reactions to White House Lobbying," 84.
125. The Kitchin-Ayres substitute to the Kennedy minimum-wage bill was a measure, sponsored by the conservative coalition in the House, that proposed a lower minimum wage and a more restricted coverage than the administration wanted.
126. O'Brien Staff Files, JFK Library, Box 7.
127. Ibid., Box 6.
128. Ibid., Box 7.
129. Ibid., Box 6.
130. Ibid.
131. Ibid., Box 4.
132. See Hart, "Congressional Reactions to White House Lobbying," 84.
133. See ibid., 85.
134. O'Brien Staff Files, Box 7.
135. Davis, "Congressional Liaison: The People and the Institutions," 62.

6. Post-Watergate Perspectives on the Presidential Staff

1. See Nicole Woosley Biggart, "Scandals in the White House: An Organizational Explanation," *Sociological Inquiry* 55, no. 2 (1985).
2. See George Reedy, *Twilight of the Presidency* (New York: New American Library, 1970).
3. Bradley H. Patterson, Jr., "The Bashful Bureaucracy," *The Bureaucrat* 7, no. 1 (1978): 84.
4. Arthur M. Schlesinger, Jr., *The Imperial Presidency* (Boston: Houghton Mifflin, 1973), x.
5. Philippa Strum, *Presidential Power and American Democracy* (Pacific Palisades, Calif.: Goodyear, 1972), 86.
6. Theodore C. Sorensen, *Watchmen in the Night: Presidential Accountability After Watergate* (Cambridge, Mass.: MIT Press, 1975), 76.
7. Schlesinger, *The Imperial Presidency*, x.
8. Thomas E. Cronin, "An Imperiled Presidency," in *The Post-Imperial Presidency*, ed. Vincent Davis (New Brunswick, N.J.: Transaction Books, 1980).
9. Thomas E. Cronin, *The State of the Presidency* (Boston: Little, Brown, 1975), 119–20.
10. Stephen Hess, *Organizing the Presidency* (Washington, D.C.: Brookings Institution, 1976), 159.
11. Sorensen, *Watchmen in the Night*, 99.
12. National Academy of Public Administration, *A Presidency for the 1980s* (Washington, D.C.: National Academy of Public Administration, 1980), 17.
13. Ibid., p. 17.
14. Ibid.
15. Ernest S. Griffith, *The American Presidency* (New York: New York University Press, 1976), 216.
16. Ben W. Heineman, Jr., and Curtis A. Hessler, *Memorandum for the President: A*

Strategic Approach to Domestic Affairs in the 1980s (New York: Random House, 1980), 203–4.

17. Hess, *Organizing the Presidency*, 160.

18. Richard E. Neustadt, "The Constraining of the President: The Presidency After Watergate," *British Journal of Political Science* 4, no. 4 (1974): 391–92.

19. Cronin, *The State of the Presidency*, 270.

20. Walter F. Mondale, *The Accountability of Power: Toward a Responsible Presidency* (New York: McKay, 1975), 102.

21. See, for example, Sorensen, *Watchmen in the Night*, 98, and William F. Mullen, *Presidential Power and Politics* (New York: St. Martin's Press, 1976), 232.

22. National Academy of Public Administration, *A Presidency for the 1980s*, 16.

23. See Dom Bonafede, "Meeting the President's Payroll," *National Journal*, 14 May 1977, 760.

24. Dom Bonafede, "The Mystery of the Executive Office Budget," *National Journal*, 16 June 1979, 1006.

25. In many respects, President Clinton's campaign pledge to reduce the White House staff by 25 percent turned out to be a variant on the Carter model of how to prune the presidential staff. In the Clinton version, the term "White House staff" and "Executive Office staff" were used interchangeably and confusingly, and, although the 25 percent reduction applied to the EOP, not just the White House Office, two of the largest units within the EOP, the Office of Management and Budget and the Office of the U.S. Trade Representative, were excluded from the count, thus making the actual reduction much less than 25 percent of all the presidential staff posts. Moreover, many of the the posts that were lost in the Clinton cuts consisted of nonpolitical support staff and posts held by detailees, which were not official EOP budgeted positions. The real Clinton staff reductions came from three EOP units; the Office of Administration, the Council on Environmental Quality, which he proposed to abolish, and the Office of National Drug Control Policy, which was drastically reduced in size. But by trying to portray these cuts as White House staff reductions, the President managed to generate a great deal of skepticism in the media and encouraged reporters to focus on the cuts that were not made rather than those that were. See, for example, Ann Devroy, "Clinton Releases Worker Bees," *Washington Post*, 7 February 1993, A18; Thomas L. Friedman, "Clinton Trimming Lower-Level Aides," *New York Times*, 10 February 1993, A1; Ann Devroy, "President Defends Claim of 25% Staff Reduction," *Washington Post*, 1 October 1993, A23.

26. See chap. 2.

27. Hess, *Organizing the Presidency*, 154.

28. National Academy of Public Administration, *A Presidency for the 1980s*, 12.

29. See Emmet J. Hughes, *The Living Presidency* (New York: Coward, McCann & Geoghegan, 1972), 20; George C. Edwards, "Quantitative Analysis" in *Studying the Presidency*, ed. George C. Edwards and Stephen J. Wayne (Knoxville: University of Tennessee Press, 1983).

30. Cronin, *The State of the Presidency*, 118–19.

31. President Bush's campaign commitment was somewhat artful. It was dependent on Congress also cutting its staff by one-third, and, moreover, Bush did not specifically promise to cut staff numbers, but rather to cut the "operating budget" of the EOP. There is a significant difference between reducing the "operating budget" of the EOP and cutting staff. Staff salaries amount to less than half of

the total budget for the Executive Office of the President. It is conceivable, therefore, that the "operating budget" of the EOP could be reduced by one-third without effecting any significant staff cuts at all.

32. The candidates' proposals for reducing the White House staff are reproduced in "Blueprints for Cutting the U.S. Work Force," *Washington Post,* 26 October 1992, A19.

33. Responding at a press conference at the end of September 1993 to a question about how genuine his White House staff cuts were, President Clinton told journalists, "Well, we have cut it [the White House staff]. I can guarantee people around here have been complaining about it because we're handling more mail, doing more work, and carrying a bigger load than this White House has carried in more than a dozen years, and we're doing it with fewer people." See *Weekly Compilation of Presidential Documents* 29, no. 39 (4 October 1993): 1924.

34. Hugh Heclo and Lester M. Salamon, eds., *The Illusion of Presidential Government* (Boulder, Colo.: Westview Press, 1981), 83.

35. See, for example, Alexander L. George, *Presidential Decision Making in Foreign Policy: The Effective Use of Information and Advice* (Boulder, Colo.: Westview Press, 1980).

36. National Academy of Public Administration, *A Presidency for the 1980s,* 16.

37. Alexander L. George, "The Case for Multiple Advocacy in Making Foreign Policy," *American Political Science Review* 66, no. 3 (1972): 761, and *Presidential Decision Making in Foreign Policy,* 195.

38. President's Commission for a National Agenda for the Eighties, Report of the Panel on the Electoral and Democratic Process, *The Electoral and Democratic Process in the Eighties* (Washington, D.C.: Government Printing Office, 1980), 69.

39. Heclo and Salamon, *The Illusion of Presidential Government,* 83.

40. National Academy of Public Administration, *A Presidency for the 1980s,* 38.

41. Ibid.

42. Hess, *Organizing the Presidency,* 207.

43. Ibid., p. 214.

44. Bradley D. Nash, "Staffing the Presidency: A 1980 View," in *Organizing and Staffing the Presidency,* ed. Bradley D. Nash, Milton S. Eisenhower, R. Gordon Hoxie, and William C. Spragens (New York: Center for the Study of the Presidency, 1980), 155.

45. Mondale, *The Accountability of Power,* 100.

46. Graham Allison, "The Advantages of a Presidential Executive Cabinet," in *The Post-Imperial Presidency,* ed. Vincent Davis, 120.

47. See, for example, Roger B. Porter, *Presidential Decision Making: The Economic Policy Board* (Cambridge, England: Cambridge University Press, 1981), 215.

48. National Academy of Public Administration, *A Presidency for the 1980s,* 37.

49. Richard F. Fenno, Jr., *The President's Cabinet* (Cambridge, Mass.: Harvard University Press, 1959).

50. Quoted in Cronin, *The State of the Presidency,* 153.

51. See Dom Bonafede, "Carter Sounds Retreat from 'Cabinet Government,'" *National Journal,* 18 November 1978, 1852–57.

52. Hess, *Organizing the Presidency,* 179.

53. Thomas E. Cronin, *The State of the Presidency,* 2d ed. (Boston: Little, Brown, 1980), 293.

54. Hess, *Organizing the Presidency*, 216.
55. Ibid., 218.
56. Herbert Kaufman, "Emerging Conflicts in the Doctrines of Public Administration," *American Political Science Review* 50, no. 4 (1956).
57. See John Hart, "Eisenhower and the Swelling of the Presidency," *Polity* 24, no. 4 (1992).
58. Terry Moe, "The Politicized Presidency," in *The New Direction in American Politics*, ed. John E. Chubb and Paul Peterson (Washington, D.C.: Brookings Institution, 1985).
59. See, for example, Hugh Heclo, "OMB and the Presidency: The Problem of 'Neutral Competence,' " *Public Interest*, no. 38 (1975): 91.
60. National Academy of Public Administration, *A Presidency for the 1980s*, 4.
61. Ibid., 12.
62. Ibid., 15.
63. Moe, "The Politicized Presidency," 266.
64. Ibid., 239.
65. Ibid., 266–68.
66. National Academy of Public Administration, *A Presidency for the 1980s*, 3.
67. Ibid., 5.
68. Ibid., 10.
69. Ibid., 39.
70. Hugh Heclo, "One Executive Branch or Many?" in *Both Ends of the Avenue*, ed. Anthony King (Washington, D.C.: American Enterprise Institute, 1983), 49.
71. James MacGregor Burns, *The Power to Lead: The Crisis of the American Presidency* (New York: Simon and Schuster, 1984), 234–38.
72. Theodore C. Sorensen, *A Different Kind of Presidency* (New York: Harper & Row, 1984).
73. National Academy of Public Administration, *A Presidency for the 1980s*, 3.
74. Ibid., 12–14.
75. Cronin, *The State of the Presidency*, 1st ed., 273–79.
76. Heineman and Hessler, *Memorandum for the President*, 247–48.
77. President's Commission for a National Agenda for the Eighties, *The Electoral and Democratic Process in the Eighties*, 72–73.
78. National Academy of Public Administration, *A Presidency for the 1980s*, 19–20, 26.
79. Ibid., 19.
80. Ibid.
81. Walter Williams, *Mismanaging America: The Rise of the Anti-Analytic Presidency* (Lawrence: University Press of Kansas, 1990), 13–14.
82. Ibid., chaps. 7 and 8.
83. See, for example, Heineman and Hessler, *Memorandum for the President*, 223; Roger B. Porter, "The President and Economic Policy: Problems, Patterns, and Alternatives," in Heclo and Salamon, *The Illusion of Presidential Government*, 226; President's Commission for a National Agenda for the Eighties, *The Electoral and Democratic Process in the Eighties*, 70.
84. See Heineman and Hessler, *Memorandum for the President*, 221; National Academy of Public Administration, *A Presidency for the 1980s*, 17.
85. National Academy of Public Administration, *A Presidency for the 1980s*, 18. See also Porter, "The President and Economic Policy," 225.
86. See Heineman and Hessler, *Memorandum for the President*, 211 and 222.

87. Nash, "Staffing the Presidency: A 1980 View," 165.
88. Heineman and Hessler, *Memorandum for the President*, 207–8.
89. See, for example, National Academy of Public Administration, *A Presidency for the 1980s*, 18.
90. Ibid., 19.
91. James MacGregor Burns, *Uncommon Sense* (New York: Harper & Row, 1972), 132.
92. Cronin, *The State of the Presidency*, 1st ed., 279–83.
93. National Academy of Public Administration, *A Presidency for the 1980s*, 27.
94. Clinton sees federal-state relations in the context of his "reinventing government" program and has stated his desire to deregulate the relationship, giving states and localities more responsibility for the implementation and management of programs. He sees the role of the federal government not to manage programs, but to evaluate their effectiveness after they have been given a chance to work. See his remarks to the National Conference of State Legislatures on 27 July 1993, in *Weekly Compilation of Presidential Documents* 29, no. 30 (2 August 1993): 1474–78.
95. National Academy of Public Administration, *A Presidency for the 1980s*, 23–29.
96. Ibid., 20–23.
97. Hess, *Organizing the Presidency*, 213.
98. Alexander L. George, *Presidential Decision Making in Foreign Policy: The Effective Use of Information and Advice* (Boulder, Colo.: Westview Press, 1980). See also his "The Case for Multiple Advocacy in Making Foreign Policy," *American Political Science Review* 66, no. 3 (1972).
99. George, "The Case for Multiple Advocacy in Making Foreign Policy," 751.
100. See ibid., 759.
101. George, *Presidential Decision Making in Foreign Policy*, 195–96.
102. See ibid., chap. 6; "The Case for Multiple Advocacy in Making Foreign Policy," 769–81.
103. See George, "The Case for Multiple Advocacy in Making Foreign Policy," 781–83.
104. Porter, *Presidential Decision Making: The Economic Policy Board*.
105. See I.M. Destler, "Comment; Multiple Advocacy: Some 'Limits and Costs,'" *American Political Science Review* 66, no. 3 (1972): 787.
106. See Alexander L. George, "Rejoinder to 'Comment' by I.M. Destler," *American Political Science Review* 66, no. 3 (1972).
107. James David Barber, *The Presidential Character: Predicting Performance in the White House* (Englewood Cliffs, N.J.: Prentice Hall, 1972); Bruce Buchanan, *The Presidential Experience: What the Office Does to the Man* (Englewood Cliffs, N.J.: Prentice Hall, 1978).
108. See, for example, John P. Burke and Fred I. Greenstein, *How Presidents Test Reality* (New York: Russell Sage Foundation, 1989); Jeff Fishel, *Presidents and Promises* (Washington, D.C.: CQ Press, 1985); John H. Kessel, *The Domestic Presidency: Decision Making in the White House* (North Scituate, Mass.: Duxbury Press, 1975); Paul Light, *The President's Agenda: Domestic Policy Choice from Kennedy to Carter* (Baltimore: Johns Hopkins University Press, 1982); Roger B. Porter, *Presidential Decision Making: The Economic Policy Board* (Cambridge, England: Cambridge University Press, 1981).
109. See, for example, Steven J. Brams, *The Presidential Election Game* (New Ha-

ven: Yale University Press, 1978); Richard A. Brody, *Assessing the President: The Media, Elite Opinion and Public Support* (Stanford: Stanford University Press, 1991); George C. Edwards, *The Public Presidency* (New York: St. Martin's Press, 1983); Matthew Robert Kerbel, *Beyond Persuasion: Organizational Efficiency and Presidential Power* (Albany: SUNY Press, 1991).

110. See, for example, Richard Rose and Ezra N. Suleiman, eds., *Presidents and Prime Ministers* (Washington, D.C.: American Enterprise Institute, 1980); Colin Campbell and Margaret Jane Wyszomirski, eds., *Executive Leadership in Anglo-American Systems* (Pittsburgh: University of Pittsburgh Press, 1991).

111. See, for example, George C. Edwards and Stephen Wayne, eds., *Studying the Presidency* (Knoxville: University of Tennessee Press, 1983); George C. Edwards, John H. Kessel, and Bert Rockman, eds., *Researching the Presidency: Vital Questions, New Approaches* (Pittsburgh: University of Pittsburgh Press, 1993).

112. See, for example, Donald L. Robinson, *Reforming American Government: The Bicentennial Papers of the Committee on the Constitutional System* (Boulder, Colo.: Westview Press, 1985); James L. Sundquist, *Constitutional Reform and Effective Government*, Revised Edition (Washington, D.C.: Brookings Institution, 1992).

113. Theodore J. Lowi, *The Personal President* (Ithaca: Cornell University Press, 1985), 207.

114. Charles M. Hardin, *Presidential Power and Accountability* (Chicago: University of Chicago Press, 1974); Lloyd N. Cutler, "To Form a Government," *Foreign Affairs* 59, no. 1 (1980).

115. See Sundquist, *Constitutional Reform and Effective Government*, 281–94.

116. See Thomas E. Cronin, "News Notes," *Presidential Studies Quarterly* 10, no. 3 (1980): 519–20.

117. See Ben J. Wattenberg, "Six Years in the White House?" *Washington Post*, 26 December 1982, D7.

118. See Edie Goldenberg, "The Permanent Government in an Era of Retrenchment and Redirection," and Laurence E. Lynn, "The Reagan Administration and the Renitent Bureaucracy," in *The Reagan Presidency and the Governing of America*, ed. Lester M. Salamon and Michael S. Lund (Washington, D.C.: Urban Institute Press, 1984).

119. David Stockman, *The Triumph of Politics* (New York: Harper & Row, 1986), 96–97.

120. Charles Kolb, *White House Daze: The Unmaking of Domestic Policy in the Bush Years* (New York: Free Press, 1994), 34–36.

121. John Podhoretz, *Hell of a Ride: Backstage at the White House Follies 1989–1993* (New York: Simon and Schuster, 1993), 84.

122. See Richard P. Nathan, *The Administrative Presidency* (New York: Wiley, 1983).

7. The Presidential Branch and the Framework of American Government

1. See, for example, George A. Graham, "The Presidency and the Executive Office of the President," *Journal of Politics* 12, no. 4 (1950); Fritz Morstein Marx, *The President and His Staff Services* (Chicago: Public Administration Service,

1947); Don K. Price, "Staffing the Presidency," *American Political Science Review* 40, no. 6 (1946); Clinton L. Rossiter, "The Constitutional Significance of the Executive Office of the President," *American Political Science Review* 43, no. 6 (1949).

2. See Stephen K. Bailey, "The President and His Political Executives," *Annals of the American Academy of Political and Social Science* 307 (1956).

3. 451 U.S. 825 (1982).

4. Quoted in Bob Woodward, "Primary Heat Turned Deal into a 'Mistake,'" *Washington Post*, 6 October 1992, A1.

5. Gerald M. Boyd, "Blame Falling on White House Staff for Uproar over Visit to Cemetery," *New York Times*, 1 May 1985, 9.

6. 457 U.S. 731 (1982).

7. The majority opinion of the Court, however, also left open the possibility that White House aides could claim the same immunity as the President, depending on the circumstances and on the nature of the functions they were discharging.

8. See, for example, Stephen Hess, *Organizing the Presidency* (Washington, D.C.: Brookings Institution, 1976); Richard T. Johnson, *Managing the White House* (New York: Harper & Row, 1974); Samuel Kernell and Samuel L. Popkin, eds., *Chief of Staff: Twenty-Five Years of Managing the Presidency* (Berkeley: University of California Press, 1986).

9. See Michael Isikoff and Dan Balz, "Foster Note Reveals an Anguished Aide," *Washington Post*, 11 August 1993, A1.

10. Report of the National Performance Review, *From Red Tape to Results: Creating a Government That Works Better and Costs Less* (Washington, D.C.: Government Printing Office, 1993), 139.

11. Richard F. Fenno, Jr., *The President's Cabinet* (Cambridge, Mass.: Harvard University Press, 1959), 268.

12. Aaron Wildavsky, "Salvation by Staff: Reform of the Presidential Office," in Aaron Wildavsky, ed., *The Presidency* (Boston: Little, Brown, 1969), 700.

INDEX